Mission Mystique

7:30 — 4:00pm

Belief Systems
in Public
Agencies

Charles T. Goodsell
Virginia Tech

CQ PRESS

A Division of SAGE
Washington, D.C.

CQ Press
2300 N Street, NW, Suite 800
Washington, DC 20037

Phone: 202-729-1900; toll-free, 1-866-4CQ-PRESS (1-866-427-7737)

Web: www.cqpress.com

Cover design: Auburn Associates
Composition: C&M Digitals (P) Ltd.

Photo Credits:
Courtesy of the Peace Corps: 236, 237
Courtesy of Charles T. Goodsell: 27, 46, 55, 65, 83, 103, 104, 106, 110, 140, 145, 147, 157, 177, 194, 201

⊗ The paper used in this publication exceeds the requirements of the American National Standard for Information Sciences—Permanence of Paper for Printed Library Materials, ANSI Z39.48-1992.

Printed and bound in the United States of America

14   13   12   11   10   1   2   3   4   5

Library of Congress Cataloging-in-Publication Data

Goodsell, Charles T.
    Mission mystique: belief systems in public agencies / Charles T. Goodsell.
        p. cm. (Public affairs and policy administration series)
    Includes bibliographical references and index.
    ISBN 978-1-933116-75-4 (pbk. : alk. paper) 1. Organizational effectiveness—United States—Psychological aspects. 2. Mission statements—United States. 3. Administrative agencies—United States—Management. I. Title.

    JK421.G65 2011
    352.3'40973—dc22

                                                                    2010032791

Dedicated to My Intellectual Mentors

*Wen Chao Chen, who encouraged me to go for
broke in my life and career*

*John Merriam Gaus, who opened my eyes to the
moral imperatives of administration*

*Arthur Aaron Maass, who showed me how to
pursue the academic life with gusto*

*Rexford Guy Tugwell, who inspired me to
think boldly and independently*

Contents

Figures, Tables, and Boxes

Preface

The initial seed for this book was planted on October 27, 2003, when a former doctoral student, James Ortiz, led me on a tour of the Department of the Interior in Washington, D.C. As we passed by the offices of the several bureaus in that department, I asked Jim and other high officials which one had the best reputation. The immediate and unanimous answer was the National Park Service, with the Fish and Wildlife Service a close second.

This response caused me to wonder why. What exactly is it about the Park Service that makes it stand out? What attitudes and behaviors are behind its eminence? Might we learn something from this agency that could have broader application?

This book, completed seven years later, is the end result of those musings. In it, I in effect set forth a fresh meaning for "good" or "best" public administration. It draws upon not only the Park Service, but three other highly reputed federal agencies: the National Weather Service, Centers for Disease Control and Prevention, and Peace Corps. Ideas were sought also from a set of premier agencies at the state and local levels, the Virginia State Police and the Department of Social Services for Mecklenburg County, N.C. Interviews were conducted with approximately 100 members of these organizations and other informed individuals.

Two major concepts frame the book. One, "mission mystique," is the notion that truly exceptional public agencies possess a radiating aura of special importance and excitement that derives from the substantive nature of the work they do and how they do it. The second is a kind of Weberian ideal type (in the normative sense) that consists of nine general attributes organized in matrix form as a template. Individual manifestations of the template are referred to as agency "belief systems," in that their properties are interrelated and embody powerful flows of emotional affect.

The following propositions preview the primary ways the book redefines superior-quality public administration:

- The most apt image for good public administration is not an economic model of efficient production, but a social model of institutional vitality.
- The most relevant normative context for the daily work of administration is not codes of ethics or constitutions, but mission and program values.
- The most consequential mission sense stems not from written statements or a unified goal, but competing aims that stimulate internal debate.
- Administrative "reform" is often best accomplished not by adopting the latest management fad, but by paying closer attention to mission expression, intrinsic motivation, cultural strength, agency history, internal dissent and habits of ongoing renewal.
- When dealing with complex public problems administrative effectiveness lies not in checking whether planned performance is achieved, but in delegating wide latitude to high-capacity agencies.
- The core institutions of public administration are not policy networks involving private parties, but public agencies that bring legal accountability and democratic values to dispersed public action.
- Except at founding moments, optimal administrative leadership is attained not by installing heroic innovators, but by balancing the steering actions of able leaders and the stabilizing influences of a robust culture.
- The responsibility of public agencies never to flout the law or trample on democratic principles must be accompanied by an equivalent responsibility to foster public trust in government and recruit talented employees with the promise of exciting work.

It is my hope that the detailed cases in this volume will themselves capture the imagination of readers, and that the theoretical and normative points advanced will stimulate wide scholarly discussion.

ACKNOWLEDGMENTS

I wish to thank my faculty colleagues at Virginia Tech's Center for Public Administration and Policy for hearing out my ideas as they developed, especially when their less than enthusiastic reactions led me to think further and deeper. I also appreciate the assistance of James Ortiz and of Jason M. Sonnenfelt for his date manipulation work. The book could not have been written without the time and contributions offered by the many persons I consulted and interviewed for an understanding of the agencies studied (names given at the book's end). The staff of the Virginia Tech library was of inestimable help, especially at the interlibrary loan department.

Several scholars took the time to review the initial book proposal for CQ Press and provide valuable feedback: Robert Denhart, Arizona State University; Michael McGuire, School of Public and Environmental Affairs, Indiana University; James Pfiffner, George Mason University; Richard Stillman, University of Colorado–Denver; and Frank Thompson, Rutgers University. Robert Denhart also reviewed early chapters, as did Shelly Arsneault, Fullerton University; Lori Glasgow, School of Planning and Public Policy, University of South Carolina; Thomas Main, Baruch College, City University of New York; and Paul Posner, George Mason University. I greatly appreciate their time and gained much from their critiques.

The several personnel I interacted with at CQ Press were immensely helpful in various ways. Editorial director Charisse Kiino actively encouraged me from the start and guided me away from unpromising directions. Development editor Nancy Matuszak had a marvelously gentle way of insisting that weak spots in the manuscript be strengthened. Production editor Belinda Josey kept me on track as the book was physically put together, and arranged it so that I could personally compile the index. Copy editor Talia Greenberg caught innumerable departures from good form and patiently endured my propensity to keep rewriting. All this fine help does not mean, of course, that I am not fully responsible for everything said in the book.

Finally, I would like to mention two special people. My dear wife, Liz, life mate for over half a century, listened to me try out my ideas, kept up my morale when it sagged and brought her uncanny spelling knowledge to bear when neither spell check nor dictionary served. John Daniel ("J. D.") Stahl, my close friend for many years, was always inquiring about the progress of the project and often shared with me his own intellectual adventures in his chosen scholarly field of children's literature. The day before I wrote these words, he lost a valiant battle with leukemia in the prime of life.

Mission Mystique and a Belief System Template

MANY SEE THE FIELD OF PUBLIC ADMINISTRATION AS IN
DECLINE. I do not share this view. At the same time, I have no interest in resurrecting the field's traditions formed during the Progressive Era, New Deal or World War II. I do, however, contend that strong administrative agencies within government are critical in our current times. Without them we could not confront the millennium's great problems such as a degrading environment, a fragile global economy and outbreaks of radical religious fundamentalism around the world. Although collaboration and networks are certainly needed to deal with these problems, competent and dedicated government organizations are essential as well. For purposes of lawful and democratic governance, these organizations should lead the collaborations and form the nodes of the networks. In light of this, the point is not to dwell on public administration's supposed decline, but to consider how its highest possible potential can be reached.

I argue in this book that in addition to insisting that bureaucracies be honest, lawful, efficient, responsible, ably led and adequately financed, we must take the next step by going beyond correcting what is wrong to capitalizing on what is right. My working assumption is that if we look at government agencies around us that stand out as "best," we will find they consist of cohesive groups of women and men who are "turned on" by something. But by what? Not their paychecks, nor the latest reform gimmicks, but by *the very work they are doing:* stopping child abuse, fighting forest fires, battling epidemics. Less dramatic activities have consequences deep into the future too, such as building safe highways, helping children learn and allowing the aged to live out their days in dignity. People doing these things find their working lives important precisely because the work they are doing is important. Public administration's highest level of attainment is

1

reached when the energy generated by serious engagement in important public tasks finds its way into all aspects of agency life. The question asked in this book is, how do we conceive of and move toward that state?

THE IDEA AND STUDY OF MISSION MYSTIQUE

My answer is embodied in a notion called *mission mystique*. This is a quality of public agencies that can serve as a reference point for promotion of animated and reflective administration. It lays the basis for conscious development of strong institutional *belief systems* for agencies that center on a compelling *public mission.*

In the mission mystique organization, employees labor not merely to implement laws faithfully or to run programs efficiently, as critical as these requirements are. The act of carrying out the mission itself kindles passion. Men and women work hard and creatively because they want to make the most emphatic mark possible on the community and world with respect to their mission. This sense of dedication and diligence is then noticed by attentive publics and confers on the institution an aura of special pride and commitment. The institution in effect becomes endowed with a kind of magnetism or institution-level charisma. The analogy in the armed forces is the "crack" military units of which all those in uniform are in awe.

The choice of language is deliberate. My Random House dictionary's first meaning for the word *mystique* is "a framework of doctrines, ideas, beliefs or the like, constructed around a person or object, endowing him or it with enhanced value or profound meaning." An illustration of applying the concept to an institution is Morehouse College in Atlanta, Ga. The president of this small, male, historically African-American college, Dr. Robert Franklin, drums into the heads of the students that they are at Morehouse to acquire the "five wells": well-read, well-spoken, well-traveled, well-dressed and well-balanced. The title of one of his recent commencement speeches was "The Soul of Morehouse and the Future of the Mystique."[1]

My dictionary's second meaning for the word is "an aura of mystery or mystical power." This definition is less helpful to us but not entirely out of place, for the emotive nature of the first definition cannot always be put into words. Indeed, this may be one of the attractions of mystique. Still, if we want to do something practical with mission mystique we need to spell out its elements, as was done by President Franklin at Morehouse.

A New Normative Model

I begin along this line by noting the significance of the modifier *mission.* Use of this term derives from the truism that conviction is tied to purpose. The aura that surrounds highly respected agencies centers on the organization's reason for being. Hence my terminology is *mission* mystique. It is the construct's underlying foundation in that it permeates the institution's culture, animates its workforce and inspires a desire to improve.

A full set of the concept's elements, which I offer as the template for a new normative model for the field, was developed during the course of studying in extensive detail six outstanding public organizations that from outward appearances are premier in their respective policy realms. The personal experience of "entering into" these entities was the source of most of my ideas. The template's components formed over five years of concerted research and were not complete until the end of the journey. Yet, interestingly enough, even though the six agencies collectively "authored" the model, none of them fully measured up to it. As in the Weberian ideal type, the particular diverges from the ideal, but in multiple examples of its class is represented in the ideal's essence. Such individuation is itself helpful in emphasizing that all institutions are unique and must be accepted as such. While I hope that practitioners will benefit from this undertaking by being encouraged to experiment with some of my ideas, they will not find universal "one size fits all" nostrums in this book. Indeed, because of the underlying premise that coherence derives from the particular mission, each application of the template must be unique.

Belief System

Clarification is also needed for the phrase "belief system." On first blush such language seems out of place in our practical, skeptical field. We are, of course, familiar with systems of all kinds in public administration, but they are tangible management or information systems, not intangible belief systems. Furthermore, the word *belief* denotes acting on faith rather than fact, something more suited to the ecclesiastic, not bureaucratic, realm. Worse, associating subjective conviction with the comprehensive notion of *system* implies a unified dogma, which is even more alienating.

Let me hasten to say that by emphasizing belief I am not leading us down a road to absolutist, doctrinal public administration. First, the word *belief* does not mean an absence of reason or of empirical experience. In fact, convincing beliefs must reflect both. Second, belief systems need not claim possession of absolute truth; that is the task of sacred beliefs—and agency beliefs are decidedly secular, with the only "truth" being true to one's principles. This means that multiple, and conflicting, beliefs will inevitably hold sway in the pluralistic bureaucracy that democracy spawns. Third, the belief systems to which I refer are not at the level of universal abstractions. Arthur Denzau and Douglass North would call them "shared mental models" by which individuals make sense of complex problems not amenable to rational choice, doing so through perception-shaping cultures and ideas. To Louis Howe they would be "weak ontologies," or commitments to an administrative perspective that allows "enchantment" while eschewing authoritarian dogmatism.[2]

Whether we recognize it or not, many belief systems are already enshrined in the field of public administration. Examples are faith in the rule of law, the primacy of the chief executive and the values of economy and efficiency. Policy analysis, incentive-based entrepreneurship, public-private partnerships and stakeholder analysis also embody worldviews that involve systemic beliefs. None of these ideas is irrefutably "right" in the sense of being objectively true; rather, each is a social construction that is subjectively accepted by many and hence creates its own "reality" in practice. Mission mystique is the same, and I hope it can occupy one corner of the field's enacted meaning.

Bureaucracy and Mission Mystique

As all students of public administration know, much of our literature (and society) views bureaucracies in a decidedly negative light. Worthless or dangerous government departments are also social constructions, although widely shared ones. Many see public bureaucracy, as a general proposition, replete with turf fixation, silo isolation, rule obsession and tendencies toward aggrandizement. The point this specter makes for us is that mission mystique must not be allowed to degenerate into a Frankenstein's monster. In-group tightness and isolation, along with true believer attitudes, could easily allow that to happen.

Again, permit me three clarifications in this regard. First, I lay down as preconditions to mission mystique acceptance of the Constitution and laws of the land, as well as responsiveness to legal enactments of the two political branches of government and to the judicial interpretations of the third branch. Thus if mission mystique morphs into a monster it is, by definition, no longer mission mystique. Second, whereas the template incorporates what I call qualified—i.e., limited—policy autonomy, this independence must be within reason and confined to realms where political superiors have not spoken or to the practice of advocacy and not outright disobedience or sabotage. That is to say, when top executive officials or legislative bodies countermand exercise of such autonomy, the agency must yield. Third, I would point out that empirical research on bureaucratic behavior offers ample evidence that agency officials are aware of their responsibilities to elected officials and tend to support a new administration in power even when the changes are contrary to personal views.[3]

Agencies of Study

A word or two on the research itself. The initial idea for this book came from a visit I paid to the U.S. Department of the Interior in 2003. On that occasion I talked with several career department officials and asked, among other things, whether any of the bureaus in their "Department of Everything," as they call themselves, stood out. Their response was, unhesitatingly, that the National Park Service (NPS) is No. 1. Reflecting on this consensus, two conceptual questions I had not thought of previously came to mind: Could the features of this highly touted bureau be distilled out to form a model of excellence? Could other highly successful agencies in American government be found to have similar characteristics? My ultimate answer to both questions was yes, but over the subsequent years I was surprised by how much unfolding this idea involved.

The organizations studied included the NPS and three other federal agencies: the Centers for Disease Control and Prevention, the National Weather Service and the Peace Corps. Other levels of government were represented by the Virginia State Police and the Department of Social Services of Mecklenburg County, N.C. (Charlotte). They were picked because of their range of missions represented and standout reputations, with convenience of location a secondary factor. In each study, I began by absorbing website postings and published literature. Then I visited the headquarters of each organization and conducted open-ended interviews with top executives and several managers. I also traveled to field installations to talk to persons down the hierarchy, along with informed outsiders like retirees, elected officials, clients, critics and bureaucrats from elsewhere. The 105 persons interviewed or consulted for the book are named in a list at the end. Supplementing these sources were internal reports, government documents, newspaper articles, Internet blogs and direct observation. For the reader's convenience, an appendix provides summary data on each of the six institutions.

In writing each agency study I try figuratively to bring the reader into that organization's unique world. Sufficient detail is provided to allow readers to consider implications of their own and to evaluate my conclusions. I do not use a uniform format of presentation but allow each story to be told on its own terms. In different ways and to different degrees I address history, legal grounding, organization, leadership, programs, culture, policy, politics and conduct. Every study begins, however, with a critical incident that "brings to life" that agency's world, and ends with an overall assessment of fit with the mission mystique template.

LITERATURE PERTINENT TO MISSION MYSTIQUE

I turn now to the literature that influenced most fully the theoretical positions taken in this book. After beginning with lines of inquiry that are instructive for their contrast to my approach, I discuss sources that were important for developing the mission mystique concept from the standpoints of purpose, motivation and culture.

This book is not a public sector replay of *In Search of Excellence* and similar studies. Thomas Peters and Robert Waterman's 1982 business classic also builds a model of organizational quality from examples of outstanding cases, but success for these authors is measured by quantitative corporate criteria like market share and return rates. By contrast, success in my study is defined as possessing an intensity of purpose, energized culture and capacity to change. Also, whereas the "lessons" drawn by Peters and Waterman are strategies for CEOs to follow, mine consist of broad institutional attributes intended for public administrators generally to adopt if appropriate.[4]

Second, this book is not on the topic of *branding,* even though in recent years that term has migrated to government from the business world. While for the marketplace of commerce the concept of branding makes sense, mission mystique is not appealing to buyer desires but to meeting societal needs. It is noteworthy, however, that theorists of branding are split into two camps. One uses market surveys and electronic data collection to target precisely individual wants. The other school of thought is dedicated to implanting "passionbrands" or "superbrands" in the public's mind that attract loyal patrons over time, sometimes drawing on archetypes to that end. The latter is a slightly closer analogy to our subject.[5]

A third line of contrasting research is on the high-reliability organization. Todd La Porte, originator of this work, points out how aircraft carriers, nuclear power plants, air traffic control systems and blood supply networks must be absolutely failure-free to the greatest extent possible. Hence the institutional quality of uppermost significance in these systems is constancy. It is achieved by precise goals, standard operating procedures, feedback information systems and redundant controls. While La Porte's work possesses a normative thrust similar to the tone of this book, mission mystique calls for a capacity to change, not just dependability or predictability.[6]

Organization and Institution

We turn now to works that contribute directly to development of the book's theoretical positions. The single most important source in this regard is Philip Selznick's *Leadership in Administration: A Sociological Interpretation,* first published in 1957.[7] One of Selznick's most important ideas for us is his analytical distinction between the organization and the institution. The first is a formal system of objectives and rules expressly designed to achieve the coordination and discipline needed for complex work. It is a creature of human rationalism set up (or modified) at a given moment in time to achieve a current purpose. An institution is an organization upon which a mantle of informal relationships and shared values has settled. Not deliberately designed, it is a natural product of social needs and pressures that emerge organically over time. As a man-made organism, it evolves, adapts, responds and prizes the founding heritage from which it came.

Thus while the organization is a rational instrument to achieve other purposes, the institution and its work possess inherent worth. The organization becomes institutionalized when it is infused with values beyond the technical requirements at hand. The leader's task is to build on the existing social base to form a core of members who immerse themselves in the institution's culture as they attend to their daily tasks. The organism reflects its own evolving values while adapting continuously to the external environment. Behavior in support of the institution's own purposes is spontaneously motivated rather than contrived.

Selznick says that the totality of the institution's rational and normative attributes forms a "distinctive competence," or character, that sets it apart as unique. The essential ingredients of this competence are possession of a clearly defined mission and an embodiment of the mission's values within the normative fabric of the institution. The result is that its members are personally bathed in these values as they execute and elaborate policy. Meanwhile, the institution's leadership must be prepared to defend the integrity of the institution's values against undesired encroachment. Other responsibilities are to mediate internal conflict and maintain a spirit of voluntary coordination when possible.

One of my former students, Larry Terry, wrote a book titled *Leadership of Public Bureaucracies* that was partly inspired by Selznick's work.[8] In it he presented a concept of "administrative conservatorship" that builds on Selznick's notion of distinctive competence. Terry argues that leaders of public organizations should see themselves not as heroic agents of change but as conservers of the "wholeness" or integrity of their institution's distinctive competence. This includes interpreting the mission appropriately, which means not merely referring mechanically to the text of an organic act but drawing from its spirit a proper reading for the current times. Thus administration extends beyond mere enforcement of the law, or even delegated authority, to a creative preservation of distinctive competence as circumstances change over time.

distinctive competence – character

Leadership

The writings of Selznick and his followers stress the importance of the leader, and properly so. Someone must launch the institution, i.e., take a freshly minted organization with a statutory purpose and turn it into a value-laden institution with distinctive competence. Also insightful and compelling personalities are needed when radical new directions are necessary. Yet Arjen Boin and Tom Christensen, in an essay on the development of public institutions, argue that the forward movement of bureaucracies is characterized by advancing complex goals in an exposed political environment.[9] This means agency leadership must embrace subtleties that a purely "great man" theory of progress could overlook.

Boin and Christensen go on to say that public administration founders must overcome the liability of newness, develop effective practice, lay the basis for a belief system, mobilize external support and survive a fragile honeymoon. Thus their best bet may be to initiate norm-creation processes, experiment with ideas for symbol and action, and nudge rather than require members to participate in a process of acculturation. They summarize the leader's preferred role as facilitator of the development process, not imposer of direction or style.

Another pertinent concept regarding leaders and institutions is that of alignment between the two. Barry Dym and Harry Hutson develop this idea, illustrating it negatively by asking an MBA graduate to head a counterculture commune. Attaining good alignment involves picking leaders whose character and style match the type of organization, making sure the leader's values are consonant with the organization's culture, selecting someone whose skill set would be in harmony with the resources available to work with, and ascertaining whether the leader's personal objectives are in keeping with the mission and strategy of the organization.[10]

This view contrasts with the domineering entrepreneur for whom *In Search of Excellence* was written. Also, it is very different from active leadership roles favored by most public management theory. A contrary view would be that once the founding is complete and distinctive competence is intact, the time should come when leadership is not so much pulling the organization along but being a part of it. When this occurs, the institution may best be thought of as possessing its own trajectory; in effect, it shares a kind of leadership role.

Such an image is in keeping with another line of literature, that of the new institutionalism in political science. It is called "new" because its exponents, such as James March and Johan Olsen, wish to segregate themselves from traditional political science that emphasized the wording of laws and the details of formal organization. The new approach seeks to identify general, underlying patterns and processes in institutional development and behavior. Intellectual abstractions are favored such as the concepts of "appropriateness" (when an act complies with accepted norms) and "isomorphism" (the power consequences of a dominant paradigm).

For us, the most useful insight offered by this school is that institutions stand out in the political firmament as special because they persist over long periods of time despite changes in membership and leadership. Once set in motion, the elaborated rules, roles and symbols enable them to acquire a collective character and identity that is carried forward to successive generations. Equipped with an accumulation of knowledge and experience, the value of institutions lies in that, unlike single cooperating individuals, they have the potential to adapt to absorb imperatives of their environment and produce consistent, desirable outcomes. Neo-institutionalists refer to this feature as "historical efficiency."[11]

The Three Pillars of Institution

Moving to the field of organization theory, W. Richard Scott has introduced to the literature a three-part framework that has become influential: the three pillars of institutions.[12] Although Scott's objective is to use the pillars as means of contrasting different paradigms in the study of institutions, he admits that each pillar is found in any given organization. The first, called the regulative pillar, is a system of rules and accompanying rewards and punishments designed to ensure conformity to those rules. This pillar has an objective, coercive quality and operates by the mechanism of member self-interest. The second, called the normative pillar, consists of a set of values as to what is important and a set of norms on how things should be done. Accordingly, it defines goals and prescribes means to attain them. Members act not out of self-interest but because they personally agree with the values and norms. The third pillar is called cognitive. It frames meaning and thereby manipulates it. A culture of signs, symbols and rituals enunciates, reinforces and transfers shared values; even though subjectively formed, they take on the guise of undeniable truths. Together, the three pillars achieve the institution's legitimacy in the eyes of its members and observers.

The institution's culture, found in Scott's second and third pillars, is the prime mechanism for holding the institution's social pieces together and sustaining its ethos over time. Despite its obvious relevance to the public sector, academic interest in organizational culture originated in the business world. Early authors on the subject saw it as a site of manipulation by management in order to shake up the stultified attitudes of poor-performing corporations. Later the focus was broadened to cover organizational change in general, with the object being to increase worker motivation and augment managerial control. The underlying purpose of these culture studies is to foster "congruency" between the desires of workers and managers, i.e., to bring everyone over to management's side.

When the topic of organizational culture migrated to public administration, the aim shifted away from manipulation and in the direction of a better understanding of the phenomenon by the academy. J. Steven Ott has proposed four categories of cultural manifestation, a typology that expands the work of Edgar Schein.[13] The most overt elements are *artifacts.* These include architecture, office arrangements, graphic symbols and equipment. Also in this category are linguistic jargon, anecdotes, stories, myths and accounts of founding heroes. Somewhat less apparent are *behavior patterns,* i.e., attitudes, customs, habits, manners, shared expectations, styles of interaction, generic management practices, informal rules and ritual performances. A third category of cultural mechanism is *beliefs and values.* These include beliefs as to what is true, commitments as to what is desirable, philosophies and ideologies, concepts of identity, codes of ethics, tacit understandings, justifications for behavior, realms of knowledge, purposes of action and accepted visions of the future. The final category is *basic assumptions* below the surface of conscious thought—for example, the importance of law, the meaning of democracy, and definitions of corruption and fairness.

A number of public administration scholars have explored this topic. In his research on prisons, John Dilulio compared several correctional institutions, concluding that their successful management depends on building and maintaining a strong organizational culture. To do this, leaders should focus on results, infuse the organization with an ethic, manage by walking around, form alliances with outsiders, innovate incrementally, and stay in place at least eight years in order to absorb and influence the culture.[14]

My colleague Anne Khademian has published a book on organization culture that links the issues of leadership, mission and culture. Called *Working with Culture,* its central point is the importance of concentrating on the success of public programs.[15] She endorses agency cultures that help integrate program fragments and provide a navigational tool for actors in the political environment. In her view, the best ones (1) possess a robustness based on long history, (2) incorporate the value of program excellence at the team as well as individual level, and (3) strive for openness to change, learning, diversity and systemic thinking.

Khademian also warns that the organization's culture is not amenable to unilateral control or reengineering by managers. Instead, leaders must "work with the culture" as it evolves organically from its roots. She identifies these roots as (1) the organizational task or mission, (2) the resources provided to accomplish that task, and (3) the political environment's legacies, expectations and constraints. In doing such culture work the manager should identify the exact nature of program commitments, understand their connections to the roots of culture, think about what changes in the culture are needed, consult with fellow members of the organization on these changes, negotiate adjustments with the external environment's stakeholders and power-holders, and relentlessly practice and demonstrate the needed cultural innovations.

Sense of Mission

Another book that integrates strategy, mission and culture is *A Sense of Mission: Defining Direction for the Large Corporation,* by Andrew Campbell and Laura Nash.[16] These authors write from the perspective of business management and, after studying several British companies, have developed a model for maximizing motivation and output by means of such integration. To them the "sense of mission" has little to do with a written statement, but consists of a coherent set of authentically felt norms that possess genuine meaning for all employees. They propose a model made up of four components: (1) purpose—the fundamental, agreed-upon reason for the company's existence; (2) strategy—the commercial logic for the organization's competitive market posture; (3) policies—the action guidelines and behavioral patterns that are realized in practice; and (4) values—the beliefs and moral principles that are embedded in the company culture. In a diagram these components are placed at the four corners of a diamond, with purpose at the apex, strategy at the left corner, values at the right and policies at the bottom. The four points are connected by lines to show how fundamental purpose is translated into action by the mediation through two different lenses:

the left corner's rational strategy in meeting market competition and the right's noneconomic values and beliefs that additionally affect the organization, i.e., corporate standards and moral principles.

A second book from business management in the U.K. is *The Purpose-Driven Organization: Unleashing the Power of Direction and Commitment*, by Perry Pascarella and Mark Frohman.[17] In the context of the corporation, the authors contend that the direction and commitment of the organization as an entirety is best unleashed not by a single, masterful intervention, but by means of continuous, gradual change at all hierarchical levels and all work sites. The authors propose that a "purpose statement" be developed that combines three devices of socialization: the formal mission statement, a credo or code of ethics, and the current vision for the future. A synthesis of these becomes, ideally, a convincing conveyance of the institution's overall reason for being. Worked out over time and with extensive employee participation, this formulation, when produced and projected effectively, is said to generate a source of energy and commitment not obtained by compensation or promotion. The workforce's total extent of empowerment is defined as the aggregate force of every member's determination to achieve the agreed-upon end.

don't need compensation or promotion

Pascarella and Frohman contend that the purpose statement can be said to look to both past and future. On the one hand, it incorporates knowledge of the organization's history and a readiness to retain what already works well. On the other, it imagines a future state whose attainment requires flexible innovation in order to keep up with a fast-changing world. By looking in both temporal directions this way, stated purpose becomes like the keel in a boat that affords forward motion at maximum speed, along with adept maneuverability.

The Nature and Importance of Mission

A number of other writers have elaborated on the nature of mission as manifest in the public sector. James Q. Wilson speaks of "sense of mission," the same phrase used by Campbell and Nash. He, too, means not a statement of goals but a widely shared and warmly endorsed culture that is difficult to create but confers a feeling of special worth on members, aids in recruitment and socialization, and allows managers to economize on material incentives. Wilson likens it to Selznick's notion of distinctive competence.[18]

T. Zane Reeves, in a book on Vista and the Peace Corps, postulates that these two organizations have what he calls a "commitment culture," in contrast to the more common "process culture" found in American bureaucracy. Such agencies possess a "secularized missionary identity" that embraces the attributes of a clear sense of purpose, a shared set of values, a proclivity to take action, high employee morale, an abundance of creativity, the absence of a counterculture, and vigorous interaction with clients and citizens. Reeves expresses the opinion that the phenomenon is kept from forming at the federal level because of the periodic change of presidential administrations, and is perhaps more common at the state or local level of government.[19]

The literature on nonprofit organizations also recognizes the importance of mission, which is not surprising because such institutions depend on serving a cause to survive. E. B. Knauft, Renee A. Berger and Sandra T. Gray researched a "search for excellence"–type book on nonprofits and found that the outstanding ones have a clearly articulated mission, a leader who can set in motion a culture that motivates fulfillment of the mission, and a board that can bring in funds and provide a bridge to the community. The mission for such entities is constantly on the tongues of leaders and staff as they deal with board members and citizens. But while the organization is single-minded in pursuing the mission, it must also be prepared to adapt it to changing times.[20]

Psychologist Janet Weiss theorizes on the inner processes by which a mission frames and motivates the members of an organization, which she says happens in three ways. First, structures of knowledge stemming from the mission process incoming information. Categorizations are made and paths of causation assumed. Even though this framing has a stabilizing effect on information processing, conversations over mission within the organization can lead to new knowledge structures. Second, the mission motivates individuals by identifying a clear collective interest of the society, thus making possible intrinsic motivation from the work itself. Third, existence of the mission assists in the making of decisions by offering reference points for weighing what actions are desirable in the future, as well as justifying past actions.[21]

Commitment, Culture and Effectiveness

Yoash Wiener, an authority on behavioral approaches to management, develops a theory of normative commitment in the organization that is based not on instrumental logic but on internalized moral beliefs as to what should be done.[22] He proposes a model of causation that shows personal biological factors and home socialization as leading to personality needs, which in turn affect—within the organization—operant beliefs, motivations and commitments, intentions and behaviors. By pre-screening recruits, socializing new members and selecting dedicated leaders, the organization augments employee contributions beyond the logic of rational self-interest. Wiener measures organizational commitment by three variables: personal sacrifice to the organization, heightened persistence and long tenure, and mental preoccupation with the work.

My colleague Gary Wamsley has introduced to the organizational literature the notion of an institution's *constitution*.[23] By this he means the relatively stable "rules of the game" that permeate its normative order. Whether or not these rules are openly discussed or unspoken, their function is to lay out common expectations of what actions are acceptable and what are not. Rule content relates to such matters as the distribution of power among department heads, dominant policy coalitions and/or operational cadres, procedures for the succession and transfer of power, and tolerable versus intolerable methods of conflict and dissent.

Are mission-oriented agencies with a strong culture more effective than those without these characteristics? Hal Rainey and Paula Steinbauer undertook to build theory on the subject by canvassing the conclusions of several scholars on the interrelationship of mission orientation, leadership characteristics and task design.[24] This "search for excellence" asks what makes certain outstanding public organizations end up being "galloping elephants" among lesser animals. Their conclusion is that several factors seem causal, such as when authorities who oversee the organization are themselves supportive of its mission; supportive interest groups embrace the agency but are diverse enough not to "capture" it; the public generally is supportive, as are organizational allies and partners; relatively generous operating autonomy exists to allow creativity; and the organizational culture is strong, especially if linked to mission accomplishment, responsiveness and adaptability. Politically skillful leaders that serve for long tenures are also helpful, as well as professional groups that augment commitment and enhance autonomy. Finally, highly motivated employees are necessary, animated by three possible forces: public service motivation, or general dedication to concepts of public good; task motivation, or being drawn to a particular activity because of personal interest; and mission motivation, or belief in the inherent importance of the work being done. The authors refer to this last characteristic in terms of mission valence, i.e., whether one is personally negative or positive toward the mission. If the valence is positive and sufficiently so, an individual may self-select into the organization by applying for employment.

Considerable empirical work of a quantitative nature has been done to seek correlations between existence of a clear mission culture and effectiveness. Much of it is of little value because of inadequate measures of the variables, and overviews of studies in the business literature are inconclusive. John Kotter and James Heskett reported on the results of four studies of U.S. firms; their conclusion was that corporate culture seems to have a significant impact on long-term performance if the culture does not freeze stability.[25] Swedish scholar Mats Alvesson surveyed international research on the subject and found the verdict to be mixed, with the direction of causality sometimes running from performance to culture rather than in the opposite way.[26] Occasionally, research on government-employee motivation is more encouraging; for example, in a survey of employees of a New York state agency, Bradley Wright found that personnel are motivated to put their best efforts forward when they view their agency's work as significant and their own contribution to it as important. This is especially the case when they regard the job as hard, believe they are good at it, and clearly know its impact.[27]

A MISSION MYSTIQUE TEMPLATE

What, then, does mission mystique in action look like? Thinking of the passion-kindling nature of the mission as the central source of electric power in the turned-on public agency, what does the social circuitry within the institution look like that draws on that energy to operate an animated organization over time?

I call it a belief system—or belief system*s*, since all institutions by definition possess their individual characteristics. Still, I contend, a commonality exists among effective mission mystique belief systems to the extent that a set of key attributes is present. The word *system* suggests, these characteristics—nine in number—are interconnected. They form the foundation of the book's analysis, and for convenience I present them in abbreviated matrix form. The resulting construct is called a template rather than a model or blueprint, in that the cells present general guidance, not explicit instruction (see Figure 1.1).

A summary of the template's contents may be made by row. Each row of the matrix can be thought of as making, by virtue of the combined effect of its cells, a distinct contribution to mission mystique. Starting with the top row, its three cells collectively bestow an aura of being *endowed with a sense of purpose*—the agency is charged with an important public mission, achieving it responds to urgent needs, and past achievements are known. The middle row's trio of cells indicates the *presence of passion and commitment*—the organization's personnel are highly motivated, its culture is institutionalized and supportive, and its history is identified and celebrated. The bottom row's attributes *sustain the*

Figure 1.1 The Mission Mystique Belief System: A Template

System Requirements	Prime Qualities	Essential Elaborations	Temporal Aspects
A Purposive Aura	**1** A central mission purpose permeates the agency	**2** The societal need met by the mission is seen as urgent	**3** Has a distinctive reputation based on achievement
Internal Commitment	**4** Agency personnel are intrinsically motivated	**5** Agency culture institutionalizes the belief system	**6** Agency history is known and celebrated
Sustaining Features	**7** Beliefs are open to contestation and opposition	**8** Qualified policy autonomy to permit appropriate change	**9** Agency renewal and learning are ongoing

Source: Compiled by the author.

institution over time—internal dissent is voiced, room for creative policy action exists, and habits of organizational learning and renewal are ingrained. In sum, the institution possesses the following characteristics, enumerated as in the figure: (1) direction, (2) importance and (3) confidence; (4) dedication, (5) community and (6) identity; and (7) dissent, (8) policy space and (9) renewal.

The reader will note that I have not shown in the template features commonly thought of as present in any acceptable government agency, such as compliance to the Constitution and laws, observance of standard ethical practices, and at least minimally adequate resources. They are assumed to exist in the mission mystique agency, and an absence thereof results in ineligibility for the status. Another precondition, as mentioned earlier, is able leadership. This is obviously a critical factor, yet what "able" means in the context of mission mystique varies—a topic that is best addressed in the book's concluding chapter.

Mission Purpose

An emphatic definition of central institutional purpose, covered in cell 1, is a kind of "first among equals" in the array of mission mystique attributes. It gives the agency political direction, captures its importance, establishes its reason for being and forms the basis of its mystique. More than any other quality, a strong sense of mission is indispensable to morale, image and success. Without it, the organization is perceived as one more bureaucratic piece of furniture in the house of government—largely unnoticed, probably worn out, a likely boring place to work, and certainly possessing no distinction.

Organizations, private and public, have different ways of expressing their missions. The missions of corporations, crafted by management, center on achieving management's goals, with perhaps altruistic-sounding references to citizen needs and serving the community included. Mission statements in government, drafted with a political ear to the ground, often make the mistake of trying to incorporate every activity in the organization, and in the process of becoming so comprehensive they are utterly bland and instantly forgettable. Nonetheless, such statements are reverently framed and hung on office walls. Campbell and Nash are right in saying that a true sense of mission may have little to do with written documents; yet Pascarella and Frohman point out that the very act of having employees participate in the process of preparing a mission statement, credo or vision statement may generate energy and commitment.

In government we find two distinct types of mission articulation. One occurs when a new major goal is set by the legislative body, the implementation of which creates an agency. In these instances, what is called the organic act typically contains a clause that states the mission. This statement, a legal and symbolic act of conferral of delegated authority, becomes a powerful tool of acculturation inside the agency and of political persuasion outside it. If succinct enough to be easily remembered, the wording can become something of an agency mantra, repeated over and over in policy debates and legislative testimony. In this book I refer to such enunciated missions as "specified."

The second type of mission found in the public sector arises when legislative bodies, instead of embarking self-consciously on new initiatives, simply put in place the structures needed to carry out traditional, accepted functions of government. Examples are schools or universities in the case of public education and police or fire departments in the public safety function. In effect, the mere creation of the organization establishes its mission. In this book I call such missions "acknowledged." This does not mean these unstated purposes cannot be fashioned into culturally stirring or politically appealing rhetorical devices, however. For example, in this book we encounter instances where insistence on achieving the highest possible superiority in performing the traditional function becomes a mission rallying cry.

The literature on mission's contribution to organizational effectiveness makes much of the notion that a mission should be unitary. The assumption here is that having a single, clear goal concentrates the force of the mission and thus has the greatest impact on behavior. Wilson and others who tie mission to culture expand this logic to how a single mission strengthens the institution's entire thrust.

It would be a mistake, however, to jump to conclusions. Certainly, if the entity being discussed incorporates many missions because it is a composite department with many bureaus, the mission sense is weakened, perhaps to the point of disappearing. The Defense, Interior and Commerce Departments come to mind in this respect. In these instances, mission mystique is applicable only at the bureau or subdivision level, where a focused identity might exist.

Yet even at the bureau or small agency level, mission multiplicity may occur. The consequences of that will depend on various factors. If different facets of one central purpose can be identified, coherence is possible—for example, fighting crime versus preventing it. Also, competing but allied purposes may require separate identification, such as punishing tax cheaters while trying to get them to settle up. Still another possibility is projecting a meaningful yet vaguely defined mission so as to hold it open to further elaboration, such as expanding a campaign against domestic child abuse to patrolling the Internet for predators.

The bottom line is that to contribute to mystique the mission should have two characteristics. One is a compelling "bite," achieved by a crisp phrasing that captures the imagination by aiming for the high ground or even conveying élan. For example, a public works department would not say it fills potholes or collects garbage, but that it keeps the community clean and repaired. An airport authority would not describe its mission as operating an aviation terminal, but as providing the gateway to the city.

The second essential quality for the mission message is to constitute a concept that is sufficiently simple that it can be absorbed and remembered. It should not be a lengthy statement; in fact, the expression may not be reducible to a single exact text at all, but embody a single powerful idea. Illustrations would be reducing the community's carbon imprint (a recycling program) or enriching citizens nonmonetarily (a museum or arts center). The very imprecision of such concepts allows for future interpretation and may even evoke a bit of "mystery" mystique. The object is not clear expression but emotional voltage.

Urgent Need

When the agency mission addresses an urgent societal need, the importance of that mission is verified—the point of cell 2. Indeed, it is on this point that the organization's legitimacy is ultimately at stake. It goes without saying that all societal "needs" are constructed subjectively. Yet some are sufficiently agreed upon to take on the appearance of objective meaning. Examples are recessions, hurricanes and epidemics; when these catastrophes occur, regulators of the economy, emergency management agencies and public health departments receive public support—provided they are perceived as doing a good job.

Hopefully, many needs that government addresses are quite "real" in this sense. But citizens always disagree, of course, because policy problems bother people differentially. Thus agencies operate in an environment of political conflict and divided media attention. When treading this unsteady ground, the mission mystique agency must proceed carefully. If it is perceived as artificially inflating societal need by scare tactics, propaganda or loaded "needs assessments," long-run credibility is threatened. The better course is to track problems over time, report trends soberly, make recommendations justified by them and take full advantage of support offered by political allies and stakeholder groups. This measured approach is particularly essential if problems are "wicked," i.e., multifaceted and insoluble, like poverty, drugs, crime or obesity. Steady political pressure, an ability to capitalize on problem-illustrating news events when they occur, and a readiness to shift ground toward new and better ways to meet the need are the best way to maintain mission mystique when it is most essential: that is, when the need is unrelenting and probably getting worse.

Reputation and Record

Cell 3 in Figure 1.1 calls for two separate but related attributes: a distinctive reputation and a solid record of achievement. This is a tall order. Relatively new agencies are automatically excluded, in that they have not had time to obtain either. Many older ones will fall short of the standard too; by no means can the status of mission mystique be attained by all agencies.

As for reputation, there are few bureaucratic "passionbrands" like Ben and Jerry's ice cream. The popular view of government agencies is that collectively all of them are unreliable or worse. Yet surveys show that when citizens are questioned about services they commonly receive, a majority express approval of the results. Over several years the American Customer Satisfaction Index compiled by the University of Michigan Business School computed scores (on a range of 0–100) in the mid-80s for Social Security retirement benefits, high 70s for Veterans Affairs outpatient services, mid-70s for Medicare coverage and low 60s for Internal Revenue Service filings.[28]

The mission mystique agency need not be the winner of a popularity contest, however—only the possessor of a *distinctive* reputation. The organization ought to be known as good at what it does by those who matter, such as appropriation committees, political allies, important clients and program collaborators. Such fame is not tautological to mystique, by the way, as the latter involves many additional attributes, as the template shows.

The best route to a good agency reputation is an existing record of achievement in its distinct area. In the long run, the two assets of reputation and record are coupled anyway, as those familiar with the organization's domain will be well informed of when fame has outlived accomplishment. With respect to compiling a performance record, American public administration is unusual by world standards in how extensively it is assessed by independent sources: financial audits, program evaluations, performance measures, citizen surveys, inspector general reports, legislative oversight, judicial scrutiny, media investigations and whistle-blower publicity. An agency that survives all this review looking reasonably good cannot be too bad.

Speaking of competence, the concept of mission mystique does not reject the principle of being held externally accountable for proven effectiveness. What it adds is a supplemental paradigm of capacity assessment—one that moves beyond the notion of the agency as an instrumental tool whose accomplishments must be checked upon. Premier administrative institutions engaged in battling wicked societal problems should be accorded a status something like that of the qualified oncologist who is fighting to prolong your life as a cancer patient. Checking out the doctor's background and qualifications is prudent, and getting a second or third opinion is smart. In the end, however, you must trust that person's judgment that the doctor is doing everything conceivable on your behalf. In order to have this level of confidence, you must know that she or he is a trained and motivated specialist who is board-certified and a member of the medical profession in good standing; that as a human being the physician cares about your well-being and is investing all possible energy in allowing you to survive and have more good years; and that she or he does not rely on past laurels but takes short courses and keeps up with the field.

Similarly, the mission mystique agency possesses comparable attributes of reputation, record, focus, dedication and continuous updating. Just as with one's oncologist, the time comes to let go and trust; the best institutional effort available is at work. Thus in a constitutive instead of instrumental sense, the agency that embodies mission mystique represents *potential* effectiveness in that domain, time and place, perhaps the best conceivable.

Intrinsic Motivation

We move now to the middle row of the mission mystique template, which deals with motivation, organization culture and sense of identity. Behavioral scientists refer to "intrinsic" motivation as being moved by inner commitment to a cause. This contrasts with "extrinsic" motivation, which is activation by external rewards like pay and status. This is the subject of cell 4.

In our review of pertinent scholarship, we noted that Pascarella and Frohman anticipate that an alignment of shared purpose within the organization makes possible the creation of a normatively united workforce that generates an aggregate amount of energy that is impossible to mobilize any other way. Reeves states that occasionally we come across agencies made up of "secular missionaries" who are focused, enthusiastic and proactive. In his analysis of pillars, Scott argues that institutional motivation can be derived from rational self-interest, norms they share with the organization, and cultural frames imposed by it.

Just what is inside the black box of intrinsic motivation? Wiener theorizes that it starts with biological and family factors that then influence personality needs. These in turn lead to workplace beliefs and commitments. Resultant behavioral manifestations are self-sacrifice, preoccupation with the work, and lengthy tenure. Weiss speculates that the factor of mission enters into the picture by structuring and processing information, identifying a clear interest of society to pursue, and furnishing a basis for decisions. Rainey and Steinbauer speculate that the intensity of their galloping elephants is driven by three factors: general dedication to the public good, personal interest in the work and belief in the importance of the work (called mission motivation). These factors can encourage self-selection into the organization. And, if Wright is correct, belief in the importance of the mission and in one's ability to contribute to it strengthens motivation.

As we study the six agencies of this book, then, we should check for the following: the importance of mission versus pay as a motivator; the degree to which personnel seem united behind a cause; levels of morale and proactive conduct; whether personnel are preoccupied with their work; and whether family experiences, personal interests and belief in the work's importance influence seeking initial employment.

A Mission Mystique Culture

The agency's organizational culture, like the mission concept itself, affects all cells of the matrix. Whereas cell 1 accounts for what inspires the enterprise, cell 5 relates to the shared feelings that energize it. Both factors perform key integrating functions, and their adequate fulfillment is indispensable to mission mystique.

To Selznick, what sets an institution apart from a formal organization is the presence of shared values and relationships that evolve organically over time. An institutional community is formed that, along with technical capabilities, creates a distinctive competence. To Terry, the central concern is that leaders conserve the essence and integrity of this distinctive competence, even as details of agency life and work change. A theme of March and Olsen's neo-institutionalism is the institution's persistence over time and the "historical efficiency" that accumulates; this, in large part, is enabled by organizational culture. Campbell and Nash see the culture's values as mediating between the organization's purpose and policies, along with conscious leadership strategies based on economic considerations. Boin and Christensen urge that leaders should facilitate the development of an institutional belief system by initiating norm-creation processes, experimenting with symbolic meanings and nudging members to participate in the building of a culture.

Khademian makes the point that public administration cultures help integrate program fragments and also provide signposts for navigating the organization's political environment. She urges managers to work with culture by recognizing its relevance to program excellence. Meanwhile, they should also be thinking about how to nudge—but not impose—cultural innovations. Her approach to organizational change is a far cry from the view often found in the corporate world, which is to demolish traditional cultures and replace them with dynamic new ones that produce congruence with management's aims. Unless destruction of the agency's cultural integrity is intended (as sometimes happens when component organizations are consolidated), discarding rather than reshaping a usable organizational culture can be wasteful and destroy morale.

The ideal mission mystique culture does several things: it induces enthusiasm for the mission purpose, reinforces individual employee motivation, conveys a sense of work importance and the agency's competence in doing it, and supports a willingness to recognize agency shortcomings and experiment with change. Scott would argue that such a mission becomes embedded in the culture by his two last pillars, personally accepted norms and a constructed frame of meaning. Ott depicts this frame as including physical symbols like banners, verbal practices like stories, behavioral patterns such as rituals, and a variety of beliefs and commitments. For most public managers and government employees, it is probably this immediate cultural environment that is most salient for influencing their ongoing work lives, surpassing in daily impact background influences such as constitutional and democratic principles.

The mission mystique ideal anticipates substantial cultural coherence around a certain type of program activity, geographical place or utilized technology. Within the central cultural field, however, various subcultures are likely to exist. Optimally such cultural pluralism creates healthy tensions. Sometimes complicating the picture is the presence of one or more public service professions—that is, bodies of personnel that stand apart because of their special training, skills and standards of conduct. Rainey and Steinbauer note that such professions can enhance agency commitment and autonomy; yet it is also true they can be a source of internal independence, which may or may not be a bad thing. We will be on the lookout for these possibilities in the chapters to come.

An Honored Past

The importance of honoring the institution's past, covered in cell 6, is often forgotten in considerations of organizational mission and culture. I once heard a national authority on the public service, speaking in an open forum, dismiss agency history as useful as a recruiting tool but of no inherent importance. Writers on public administration generally urge that more attention be paid to the field's history, but they are usually referring to the discipline's own history, not that of its practicing institutions. Yet recording the institution's past, as any military historian will tell you, is extremely important.

Selznick's overall stance could be reduced to an aphorism: an institution is an organization wrapped in values. If that is so, it is also wrapped in memories. Recollections of the past are essential to the living organizational entity because they possess meanings that amplify what it stands for. These meanings connect what is pressing now to what happened before, converting contemporary events into the latest episode of an institutional saga. The contents of the saga will differ depending on who relates it. For retired old hands, the memories may extend back to the organization's founding. For those who were not present but experienced many of the crises and triumphs that happened since, the recollected past sets apart markers of change. For institutional outsiders who wish to understand the agency beyond the superficiality of statutes and tables of organization, delving into its origins and history is indispensable. This we do in the agency chapters to come.

The organization's history can also be seen as a process of forming an identity—i.e., compiling "who we are." It is like what we mention when strangers at a party ask us to tell them about ourselves: we say what state we are from, what our parents do or did and where we were educated. Similarly, the "who we are" institutionally is told by the circumstances of initial establishment, the founders and their concerns, and the events that shaped later development. Obtaining such insight is an essential part of socializing new employees, and hence a section on agency history is often incorporated in orientation sessions or initial training. The story is also periodically retold in other forms, such as anniversary celebrations, the dedication of plaques or buildings, and visits to agency museums.

In all of this activity, we must keep in mind, transferring historical insights to the next generation is not done by a methodical recital of facts. The narratives are colored by a point of view. Naturally, the agency wishes to preserve and present the good memories, not the bad. Also, culture's dominant values will bias the stories. The true aim of writing agency history, however, is not sound scholarship but building a storehouse of mythic meaning. For mission mystique agencies, the storehouse should be full.

Contested Beliefs

Discussion of cell 7 takes us to the template's bottom row of cells, where the projection of mission purpose (top row) and pursuit of that purpose (middle row) are made sustainable over time—by allowing dissent to surface, giving policymakers room to innovate, and insisting on continuous improvement and self-renewal.

Opportunities for contestation and opposition are particularly essential for the mission mystique agency because of the intense nature of convictions within it. These feelings can easily lead to arrogance, unchecked groupthink, and insistence that its mission is the only one that matters. Contesting this assumed monopoly over truth and right may be done at the level of blocking misguided individuals or challenging high policy; it can derive from internal features of the organization or depend on external sources of counter influence—but, somehow, it must be there.

Help in thinking through this problem comes from two scholars. One is political theorist Stephen White, originator of the phrase "weak ontology" that was mentioned earlier in the book. In his book *Sustaining Affirmation: The Strengths of Weak Ontology in Political Thinking,* White seeks ways to acquire firm beliefs without becoming trapped by absolutist thinking.[29] He addresses this issue in the realm of moral philosophy, where he is concerned that rejection by postmodernists and pragmatists of fixed ontological foundations, along with the doctrinal rigidities of communitarianism, feminism and sectarian fundamentalism, leaves little room for defensible affirmative beliefs that are based on convincing but debatable conviction. With the problem of conceiving the moral self as his impetus, White searches the ideas of several philosophers to determine whether a *contestable* yet *strong* belief system is possible. Simplifying his argument, and applying it in a way he does not visualize, White concludes that a belief system can avoid both nihilism and absolutism if it has planted within it a capacity for self-questioning. This way, even though certitude is never possible, certain "figurations" of universals can command tentative agreement; when applying them in practice, however, reflection and argumentation can follow that may mobilize a different view.

The second author is Rosemary O'Leary, author of *The Ethics of Dissent: Managing Guerrilla Government.*[30] This term refers to dissenters who try—using under-the-table means—to sabotage the policies adopted by government agencies. Although O'Leary admits some guerilla tactics are clearly unacceptable, she withholds blanket condemnation of them. Her larger message is that because of its centered authority and hierarchical organization, all administration is subject to becoming blind to needed criticism. Thus it is important that constructive ways be found to permit dissent. She endorses several ideas to this end, such as fostering a culture that welcomes dissent, creating multiple channels of communication, and training supervisors to treat dissent as discussion. She also points out that some dissenters dissent just to be heard, and thus boundaries must be set as to when it is tolerated.

Qualified Autonomy

On the topic of cell 8, *The Forging of Bureaucratic Autonomy: Reputations, Networks and Policy Innovation in Executive Agencies, 1862–1928,* by Daniel Carpenter, analyzes the emergence of a small number of competent, innovative and influential federal bureaus in the late nineteenth and early twentieth centuries.[31] Examples are Gifford Pinchot's Forest Service; Harvey Wiley's Chemistry Bureau; and Post Office programs of rural free delivery, parcel post and postal savings. Carpenter's view is that, because of savvy political leadership, strong cultures, networks of support, and the legitimacy-building effect of their work, these bureaus could carve out areas of political autonomy. This space for action was used to enlarge agency agendas within accepted zones of congressional deference and eventually win over public support. Carpenter concludes that, in these cases, bureaucratic autonomy was forged not at the expense of democratic principles, but in a symbiotic relationship with them.

Whether or not we should classify these early bureaus as instances of mission mystique, the autonomy Carpenter discusses might well serve as a standard for mystique agencies today. First, its scope is appropriate: sufficient so as to afford room to build and develop, yet not so great as to compromise representative government. Second, its use is appropriate: taking on new activities and creating new programs within a general conferral of authority, and using the leverage thereby attained to mobilize more support for an enhanced mission.

Now, a century later, conditions in the American polity have obviously changed. Autonomy must now be qualified in different ways. The enormous upgrading of the American presidency, and to some extent gubernatorial office as well, means negotiating policy space is more complicated than achieving a degree of legislative deference. Executive administrations today claim they control all of bureaucracy, even though its range has multiplied several times since the 19th century and only a small part of the terrain can be centrally tended at one time. Within that ample space agencies can, if they do not attract attention as being "out of line," innovate proactively.

An added factor is the mammoth growth of executive staff agencies and political appointees. This imposes a layer of supervision that must also be taken into account. Hopefully it can be penetrated by a network of personal contacts or coalition of political allies. Also to be considered is the proliferation of detached organizations that play a part in policy implementation, i.e., partners, contractors, grant recipients and other collaborators. Finally, the chronic revenue shortfalls that plague contemporary government add to the importance of any help autonomy provides in acquiring sufficient resources to sustain the mission.

A classic issue of public administration is whether the powerful bureaucratic forces of the modern state endanger democracy. Put in terms of this book, the question posed is: Will the strength of mission mystique lead to bypassing electoral processes and elected policymakers? This would lead to autonomy that is not "qualified." My short answer is that it can, but in most instances will not. The danger is greatest in sensitive areas where administration is prone to secrecy and where coercive power is a factor, such as the police, intelligence and national security functions. The FBI under J. Edgar Hoover and the CIA in the Bush II administration are notorious examples. But in most of the bureaucracy, I would argue, sufficient openness, transparency and independent reviewing power exist to bring bureaucratic abuses into the open so they can be dealt with by elected officials, the media and the courts. America is not, after all, a dictatorship where administration is the instrument of suppression; to the contrary, it is a populist republic where bureaucracy generally is scorned, checked, investigated and cut back, and a measure of mission mystique can be a counterbalance to such tendencies.

Agency Renewal

Over time, the mission mystique agency must be relentless in engaging in renewal processes by which continuous improvement is sought (cell 9). This is true not only to avoid the pitfalls of sloth or abuse, but to keep aims and practices up with ever-changing times.

To do so requires thoughtful strategies and habits of mind. The agency must remain dependable but incorporate a dynamic beyond the constancy of La Porte's high-reliability organization. At the same time, it should be innovative but not make a fetish out of change for its own sake. As urged by Terry, the integrity of the institution's distinctive competence must be preserved even as its applications alter. As warned by Wamsley, care must be taken not to throw out the agency's "constitutional" rules of the game and thereby cause havoc that inhibits sound change. Khademian advises that the agency should maintain connection with its cultural roots yet always be ready to "rework" the culture when necessary. Pascarella/Frohman ask metaphorically that the organization's purpose be seen as a keel that allows careful negotiation across the water from past knowledge to future state. Like Knauft's premier nonprofit organization, leaders and members must keep the timeless cause firmly in mind as they talk to the community about its changing needs.

Given this guidance, what should "renewal" in the mission mystique context mean? Substantial literature exists on organizational learning, a concept that seems quite compatible with what we are after.[32] Three types of organizational learning are often postulated. One is called single-loop learning, which is the ability of the organization to identify a problem and then "loop" around it to find a solution. An illustration of this is post-hoc analysis of mistakes that have been made or misguided conduct that has been uncovered. A second type of organizational learning is double-loop. Here, the organization not only addresses the immediate problem but loops around again and changes its norms so as not to have to continue facing the problem. Examples would be retraining sessions for employees or trying out new program ideas or installing new technologies.

The third learning type is triple-loop. It is the more drastic and lasting step of heightening generally the organization's capacity to change. Efforts are undertaken to reshape the agency's ethos so that it becomes culturally habituated to dealing with change as an ever-present possibility. This is not planning for expected future developments, but always being prepared to deal with any and all change that comes along regardless of its nature. Being "future-ready" in this way could cover policies, programs, structures and the workforce.

This completes the preliminaries for studying mission mystique. In the next chapter we begin entering the worlds of individual public agencies to explore their institutional belief systems in detail in order to learn if and how they embody passion, pride and charisma.

2

U.S. National Park Service

Caretaker of America's Best Idea

MILLIONS OF AMERICANS HAVE SEEN THE 2009 KEN BURNS TELEVISION DOCUMENTARY, "The National Parks: America's Best Idea." Burns' reverential treatment of the parks as the means by which a democratic nation finds it soul goes overboard on sentimentality, but nonetheless acknowledges appropriately the mystique of our great Western parks. This chapter examines the degree to which this aura rubs off onto the agency that administers them, the National Park Service (NPS). Its own mystique—a mission mystique—derives from the institution's mandate to take care of the nation's parks. While Wallace Stegner's famous phrase "The national parks are America's best idea" does not mean the NPS is America's best bureaucracy, the attitude conveyed by these words permeates this organization's belief system.

YOSEMITE, CRADLE OF THE NATIONAL PARK IDEA

The story begins in the Yosemite Valley, located in California some 200 miles into the Sierra Nevada mountains from San Francisco. Visitors enter this valley by a park road that winds upstream along the banks of the Merced River through a narrow gorge filled with azalea and pine. Suddenly, the canyon opens up onto a wide, flat meadowland of grasses, flowers and groves of black oak that is several miles long but seems only a few hundred yards wide, with the Merced meandering along its floor. On both sides and in the distance ahead enormous granite cliffs rise almost straight up to a height of 3,000 feet or more, creating an enclosed Garden of Eden sculpted by nature. In periods of sufficient rainfall the valley is rimmed by nine waterfalls that drop 300 to 2,000 feet.

    It was this paradise that spawned the national park idea around the time of the Civil War. A series of historic figures who all appeared within a short span of

Yosemite Valley, Yosemite National Park, Calif. The natural appeal of this place inspired the national park idea. Several of those who experienced it, including Frederick Law Olmsted, John Muir and Theodore Roosevelt, became key early figures in the national park movement.

Source: Photo by the author.

years served as midwives to the park's birth, making possible a unique convergence of efforts and influence. It is not inappropriate that Yosemite National Park is sometimes called "the mother church" of the system.

To the State of California

The first of these figures was Frederick Law Olmsted, the designer of Central Park in Manhattan and the father of landscape architecture. In 1863, after leaving behind his Central Park work, Olmsted moved to California to manage a goldmining estate in the southern Sierra Nevada. Looking for sources of water for processing ore one day, he followed the Merced upstream and entered the Yosemite Valley. Olmsted was entranced with this magnificent natural example of landscape beauty. He learned that President Abraham Lincoln had signed into law a federal land grant that transferred Yosemite Valley and the nearby Mariposa Grove of giant sequoia trees to the state of California to protect them from commercial exploitation. Olmsted, ready for a new career anyway, successfully got himself appointed chair of the newly formed Yosemite Commission, charged with administering the lands for the state.

Ever the visionary yet systematic planner, Olmsted wrote a detailed report describing the valley and grove. He also set forth a philosophy for their administration. Olmsted praised the capacity of undisturbed, majestic nature to invigorate the human mind, an opportunity he said was enjoyed by the European elite but not experienced by America's democratic masses. "Yosemite should be held, guarded and managed for the free use of the whole body of the people forever," he wrote, stating the essence of the national park idea. Although the report was not accepted by his fellow pro–private enterprise commissioners, excerpts were circulated among West Coast conservationists and its ideas were covered by the California press.[1] Half a century later Olmsted's son, Frederick Law Jr., drew key ideas from this legacy of his father when helping to draft the statute that created the National Park Service.

A second notable figure to be involved was John Muir, the famous naturalist, conservation philosopher and park advocate. After walking for several months throughout North America, Muir ran across the Yosemite Valley in 1868. He was so struck by what he saw that he obtained a job as a hotel handyman there; this gave him time to study the valley's flora and fauna, fostering an intense fascination with nature that stayed with him throughout his life.[2]

Over the next several years Muir published a number of articles on his naturalist observations in California. In 1889 he took up park advocacy following a camping trip to Yosemite in 1889 with Robert Underwood Johnson, editor of *The Century* magazine. Together the two commiserated over how concessionaires in Yosemite were allowing overdevelopment and ruination of the landscape. Muir wrote two well-timed articles on the subject for Johnson's magazine, and these helped greatly to fuel a movement to have Yosemite and Mariposa Grove removed from state control by California and be administered by the national government. It was primarily because of Muir and Johnson's efforts that Congress, in 1890, set aside some 1,500 square miles of "reserved forest lands" surrounding the Yosemite Valley, which today form the bulk of Yosemite and Sequoia National Parks.[3]

Yet the jewel-like enclaves of Yosemite Valley and Mariposa Grove were still in the hands of the state of California, and signs of reckless camping and uncontrolled development were becoming worse. Trees had been cut for firewood and lumber; grasses and flowers had been ravaged by grazing horses and sheep; meadows had been fenced for hayfields; and shack-like cabins, barns, chicken coops and a pigpen occupied the valley floor. Increasingly, Muir, Johnson and several professors and administrators of the University of California concluded that an "alpine club" should be formed as a "defense association" against such damage. To that end, the Sierra Club was founded on June 4, 1892, in San Francisco, with Muir as first president. While the Club's administrative center remained in the city, in 1898 a former woodworking shop at Yosemite was turned into its field headquarters.[4]

Seeking Federal Protection

What the national park idea needed now to fulfill its destiny was national political backing. The first step in this regard was taken in 1903 when Muir learned that President Theodore Roosevelt wished to go camping in Yosemite. Although TR had for years relished hunting in the West, he had not yet moved beyond the hunting and exploitation mentality that accompanied westward movement of the American frontier. Johnson recommended Muir as Roosevelt's guide, and Muir used the opportunity to promote the proposition that essential parts of the Western wilderness be preserved for future generations. This included the Yosemite enclaves, which he insisted must be taken back from California and protected by the federal government itself.

The two men, along with a pair of rangers, escaped from the presidential entourage and camped alone in the open for a night at Mariposa Grove. They woke up in the morning covered with snow, and proceeded by horseback north to Yosemite Valley, camping at Glacier Point and Bridalveil Meadow as they progressed (a marker designates the Bridalveil site).

The president was delighted with the experience, and he and Muir became fast friends. This relationship, which lasted until Muir's death in 1914, had enormous impact on the history of the national parks. Roosevelt supported the 1905 federal takeover of Yosemite Valley and Mariposa Grove, and for the rest of his presidency incorporated the national park cause into his Progressive Era agenda. By the time he left office he had signed bills creating five new national parks to add to the first one, Yellowstone, which had been established in 1872. Scores of other grand Western sites were acquired as well, including 18 national monuments; these were seized under an exceedingly broad interpretation of the Antiquities Act, signed by Roosevelt in 1906 to protect cultural sights like Mesa Verde. TR's last great "antiquities" acquisition was the Grand Canyon, which in 1919 became—along with Yellowstone—the most famous manifestation of the national park idea.

A Park System for the Public

One last step was needed to realize the dream of a "democratic" national park system. This was to bring the masses of America westward to visit their newly created treasures. The trip was costly, and attracting only the rich would reestablish the unwanted European tradition of associating unspoiled lands with the privileged. Two individuals were particularly important in this regard.

Carleton E. Watkins, who began his career as a daguerreotype portrait photographer in San Francisco, learned the new technology of wet-plate photography and took it to Yosemite. Beginning in 1861, two years before Olmsted moved to California, Watkins started exploring the area. Using a team of 12 mules to carry his 18-by-22-inch box camera, a portable darkroom and tanks to carry the wet plates, he photographed mountain peaks, waterfalls, boulder formations, giant sequoia and the valley floor itself. His mammoth exposures, timed up to an hour, required stillness of wind and hence were taken at dawn or in the early evening. He developed a style—a stark, meditative portrayal of nature that seemed to intensify human vision.[5]

Watkins' fame spread rapidly and he became well known in Europe as well as in the United States. Making numerous trips to the region over the years, he built a large corpus of Yosemite photos that became collectors' items. More than 1,000 of his stereoscopic views found their way into Victorian parlors. In 1864 an album of his prints helped convince Congress to grant Yosemite to California for preservation. When Olmsted took over the Yosemite Commission, he asked Watkins to be its photographer. It was Watkins' camera eye more than any other factor that initially attracted the world's attention to the valley.[6]

Another early visual artist to take Yosemite to the outside world was Albert Bierstadt, a German-born painter from New Bedford, Mass. After training in Europe, Bierstadt came across a collection of Watkins' photographs of Yosemite Valley in New York. This caused him to turn to Western vistas. Unlike Watkins, he pointedly departed from sober realism and painted his panoramic scenes with dramatic flourishes like brewing storms and glowing sunsets. Between 1864 and 1872 Bierstadt produced 15 large oil paintings of Yosemite scenes. Together with the work of Thomas Moran, famous for his paintings of Yellowstone, Bierstadt's paintings did much to bring adventurous tourists for the first time to the new railroad hotels and park lodges springing up in the mountains of the West.[7]

THE NATIONAL PARK SERVICE: A CAPSULE HISTORY

While the national park *idea* germinated in the late 19th century, the national park *institution* came into being in the twentieth. At this writing that organization, the National Park Service, has nearly reached its hundredth birthday. Except for the National Weather Service, it is this book's oldest administrative institution (see appendix).

The 19th century inheritance made the 20th century institution possible. Olmsted's concept for Yosemite provided the framework, Muir's preservation advocacy the doctrine, Roosevelt's Progressive policies the precedents, and Watkins and Bierstadt's images the fame. By the time World War I broke out in Europe in 1914 a well-organized parks lobby had been formed in Washington, D.C., with influential backers located throughout the country, including the Sierra Club and other groups. Prominent figures at the University of California at Berkeley were particularly influential.

By this time 37 national parks existed, although nothing like a park *system* existed. Nominally under the Department of the Interior, the parks were run autonomously by local superintendents or commanders of resident Army detachments; their internal management was haphazard, with an eye to profits for concessionaires.

Meanwhile, an existing bureaucratic entity in Washington was anxious to take the parks over: the Department of Agriculture's Forest Service. Like Muir, energetic founding chief of the Forest Service Gifford Pinchot had also won the support of TR, and served in both the Roosevelt and Taft administrations. He was a skilled administrative entrepreneur with a progressive vision of his own: the creation of a system of national forests that would be managed for timber, grazing, minerals, hydroelectric power and recreation. Pinchot worked hard to bring the national parks under his jurisdiction together with the national forests.

National Interest in a Park System

Lobbyists for the parks were aware of Pinchot's aspirations and saw his vision as a dire threat to the national park ideal. To head him off they sought to create a bureau of their own in the Department of the Interior, which would consolidate existing park units and then lay the basis for a permanent, integrated, pro-preservation national park system. During the three years of 1914–1916—in the midst of the First World War but just before the United States entered it—they succeeded, primarily because of the joint efforts of two men: Stephen T. Mather, a hard-driving business executive from Chicago, and Horace M. Albright, an aspiring Berkeley law student 23 years his junior.

Formation of this partnership was made possible by common connections to the University of California. Mather had gone to college at Berkeley in the 1880s, where one of his student friends was Franklin Lane, destined to become Woodrow Wilson's secretary of the Interior. Lane asked the chair of economics at Berkeley to come to Washington to be point man for creating a National Park Service, and he brought with him a young law graduate who had been helping run the economics department, Horace Albright. Although Albright plunged into the task of making contacts for the new agency on Capitol Hill, his boss was sidetracked to create the new Federal Reserve System and a new parks advocate was needed. This became Lane's college pal Stephen Mather, who by this time was head of Twenty Mule Team Borax in Chicago and a member of the Sierra Club. After a long conversation in Lane's office in December 1914, Mather persuaded Albright to remain in Washington rather than return to Berkeley so the two could join forces and establish a national parks agency.[8]

Passage of the Statute for a National Park Service

Mather's first step in the direction of creating a new agency was to organize a nationwide publicity campaign. For this he obtained the services of Robert Sterling Yard, successor to Robert Johnson as editor of *The Century*. Yard proceeded to generate scores of newspaper and magazine articles around the country that expanded national consciousness on the issue.

Mather then undertook a campaign to enlist the allegiance of the existing park managers in the project. With Albright's assistance, Mather dazzled a conference of park superintendents and concessionaires held at the Berkeley campus in his articulation of a vision for the parks. The founding duo then pitched the national parks message to newspaper editors and magazine publishers, including those at *The New York Times, Saturday Evening Post* and *National Geographic*. As a consequence, Gilbert Grosvenor of the *Geographic* offered to devote an entire issue to the grandeur of the West, and for it Albright gathered photos and wrote copy. During the summer of 1915 Mather and Albright went on the road again, taking a number of conservationists, editors and congressmen on a two-week camping trip into the High Sierra, with an important stop at Yosemite.

In early 1916 the two met frequently with a small group of park friends, lobbyists, intellectuals and politicians to draft a national parks bill. One member of the group was Frederick Law Olmsted Jr., who offered the following key sentence for a bill's first draft: "The fundamental object of these aforesaid parks, monuments, and reservations is to conserve the scenery and the natural and historical objects therein and to provide for the enjoyment of said scenery and objects by the public in any matter and by any means that will leave them unimpaired for the enjoyment of generations."[9]

The bill was introduced in the House by Rep. William Kent, who had previously sponsored park bills that went nowhere. At the same time, Yard flooded the country with favorable park publicity. The special issue of *National Geographic* was sent to every member of Congress. The House Public Lands Committee reported the Kent bill out with two amendments, one that restricted salaries to an overall limit of $19,500 per year and another that allowed private grazing in the parks. Olmsted's language on the mission was left untouched.

Action by the Senate was delayed until July. This interfered with Mather's plans for another Western camping trip, and he left Washington. His departure left Albright to shepherd the bill's progress on Capitol Hill. The Senate passed it on Aug. 5, but without the House grazing provision. So that this issue would not stall the bill, Albright engineered a compromise that permitted grazing except in Yellowstone. On Aug. 15 the Senate agreed to the conference report and seven days later the House did the same. The National Park Service Organic Act became law on the evening of Aug. 25, 1916. The next day Mather emerged from camping in the woods to find a telegram waiting at his hotel: "Park service bill signed nine o'clock last night have pen used by President in signing for you."[10] Compared to the monumental struggles we see today in Washington over landmark legislation, the enactment seems quick and easy; but it would not have been possible without the decades of prior lobbying and publicity by the conservation movement.

Building the Institution

Over the next two decades Mather and Albright worked together to bring the National Park Service into being and place it on a firm footing. The going was not easy. Mather appointed an official from Geological Survey as interim director of the Park Service who turned out to be a bad choice and had to be dismissed. In January 1917 Mather himself was sidelined by an attack of clinical depression and had to return to Chicago. As in the previous summer, Albright took over in an acting capacity. Unfortunately, he then proceeded to stumble by removing the Army from Yellowstone without consulting Congress, making an enemy of the chair of the House Appropriations Committee. Albright learned from his mistake and humbly sought political atonement; as a result he soon secured the Park Service's first appropriation. It was used to hire a small Washington staff, and the NPS began operations in a fourth-floor space in Interior's new building at 18th and E Streets (now occupied by the General Services Administration).

Mather returned to duty the following November. He was appointed the first regular Park Service director and served in that capacity until 1929. His accomplishments included forming a nonpartisan, professional corps of park rangers, setting a tradition of nonpolitical appointments at the top, and establishing good long-term relations with Congress. To encourage park visitation, Mather pulled his old trick of cultivating media support and collaborated with the railroads to encourage tourism in the West. Lodges and access roads were constructed in the parks and contracts were signed with concessionaires to operate the facilities. Using his business connections to good advantage, Mather was able to secure corporate donations to the infant agency to compensate for its minimal budget. Ever the imaginative entrepreneur, he entertained the possibility of spanning the Grand Canyon with a cable car but resisted building a tramway from Yosemite's valley floor to Glacier Point.

Working side by side with Mather in these years was Albright, who complemented Mather's external relations genius with a practical competence at internal administration. As before, Mather continued to suffer occasional mental health breakdowns, at which times Albright would assume the reins. In 1919 Albright fulfilled a long-time dream by being appointed, at age 29, superintendent of Yellowstone. After the close of the summer season he toured other parks as a de facto NPS director of field operations.

After Mather's final departure in 1929, Albright was named the second director of the National Park Service, a position he held until 1933. While his seminal achievements obviously went beyond the four years he was director, during his tenure he elevated historic preservation within the mission and prepared the way for consolidation of all federally owned parks, memorials, battlefields and cemeteries into a single managed system, accomplished under the Reorganization Act of 1933.[11]

National Parks, the New Deal and the Postwar Period

The national parks were strongly affected by the New Deal in the 1930s and wartime events in the 1940s. FDR's Civilian Conservation Corps was administered by the NPS, and many of the buildings, picnic shelters, campgrounds and roadways we see today were built by its recruits. During World War II a period of great retrenchment for the agency occurred in terms of both manpower and money. Its headquarters were actually moved to the Merchandise Mart in Chicago in order to free up office space for mobilization agencies in Washington. Mount Rainier National Park was given over to mountain warfare training, Joshua Tree National Monument to desert training, and Mount McKinley (now Denali) National Park to testing military equipment under arctic conditions.[12]

Since the end of World War II the national park system has grown enormously, a long and interesting story told by many.[13] The number of park units more than doubled, the number of park visitors increased by twentyfold and the agency's budget escalated from millions of dollars to billions. Congress enacted numerous additional statutes over the years, expanding greatly NPS responsibilities. Unlike many federal bureaus, Mather's idea of promoting agency careerists to its top ranks became a habit that lasted many years. Twelve of the 17 directors who served after Albright were Park Service careerists, often with years of field experience as a park ranger or superintendent.

Two directors in the post-founder period warrant discussion. One is Conrad L. Wirth, who served from 1951 to 1964. Wirth's legacy was to undertake a vast enhancement of the system's physical infrastructure. In 1953 widespread attention was drawn to postwar deterioration of the parks when Bernard DeVoto published an article in *Harper's Magazine* under the provocative title "Let's Close the National Parks." With tongue in cheek, DeVoto demanded that Yellowstone, Yosemite, Rocky Mountain and the Grand Canyon be shut down unless something drastic were done about their aging facilities.[14] Wirth responded with a far-reaching capital spending project that eventually invested $1 billion, a huge sum at the time, to upgrade park roads, buildings and visitor structures over a 10-year period. Called Mission 66, construction under it culminated in 1966, the fiftieth anniversary of the Organic Act.[15]

The other National Park Service director deserving special mention is George B. Hartzog Jr., who followed Wirth in 1964 and served until 1972, when President Richard Nixon forced him out of office. His crime was to revoke a special use permit that allowed Nixon's crony Charles G. "Bebe" Rebozo to dock his private boat at Biscayne National Park in Florida. Born and raised in poverty in South Carolina, Hartzog struggled mightily as a young man to pass the state bar exam by reading law alone and obtaining a bachelor and master's degree at night school. He landed his first job in the National Park Service as an attorney in the Chicago office. His big opportunity came in 1959, when he was named superintendent of the new Jefferson National Expansion Memorial National Historic Site in St. Louis, Mo. In this capacity he made it possible for that city's famous Gateway Arch to be built. The achievement impressed Secretary of the Interior Stewart Udall so much that he named Hartzog the next NPS director. The charge Udall laid down was for Hartzog to follow up Wirth's infrastructure contribution with one evoking the spirit of Lyndon Johnson's Great Society.[16]

This was done in several directions. One was to make outdoor recreation a principal Park Service function along with preservation of the nation's natural treasures and historic legacy. This was not a new idea, but it now became a stated extension of the agency's mission. Another new emphasis was adoption of an urban focus, a theme already familiar to Hartzog from his St. Louis work. New downtown parks appeared in Boston, Providence and the District of Columbia. The Park Service took a lead role in building the John F. Kennedy Center for the Performing Arts and the Wolf Trap Foundation for the Performing Arts outdoor theater in Washington, D.C. Still another city-oriented innovation was the bundling together of separated urban park properties; two such projects resulted, Golden Gate National Recreation Area in San Francisco and Gateway National Recreation Area in the port area of New York and New Jersey. Not to neglect new park activity in rural areas, Hartzog also oversaw establishment of the Ozark National Scenic Riverways system in Missouri and the Appalachian National Scenic Trail that stretches from Maine to Georgia. A final realm of Park Service expansion he achieved was to secure passage of the 1971 Alaska Native Claims Settlement Act, which enabled millions of acres of Alaskan lands to be set aside for national parks, wildlife refuges and protected wilderness.[17]

Hartzog is considered by many to have been the boldest, most creative and strongest administrator in modern Park Service history. His tenure is still remembered as a model of leadership, vision and political courage. After his retirement in McLean, Va., in 1973, Hartzog remained a force to be reckoned with throughout the national parks community as he applied his fierce dedication to Park Service ideals to current policy issues. The entire system mourned when he passed away on June 27, 2008.

TODAY'S NATIONAL PARK SERVICE

Today the National Park Service is responsible for the most famous national park system on Earth. It encompasses 84.3 million acres of land (3.5 percent of the country), 4.5 million acres of water, 85,000 miles of rivers and streams, 68,500 archeological sites, 27,000 historic structures, 21,000 buildings, 12,250 miles of trails and 8,500 miles of roads.[18]

The agency's jurisdiction and responsibilities have increased over the years by passage of many statutes, including the Historic Sites Act of 1935; the Park,

Parkway and Recreational Area Study Act of 1936; the Wilderness Act of 1964; the National Historic Preservation Act of 1966; the National Parks and Recreation Act of 1978; and the Archeological Resources Protection Act of 1979. Presently, the national park system comprises 391 units, all of which have the word *national* placed first in their designation. These include 58 parks, 20 preserves or reserves, 74 monuments, 119 historic sites, 29 memorials, 24 battlefields, 18 recreation areas, 10 seashores, 4 lakeshores, 15 rivers, 4 parkways and 3 trails. At least one NPS unit exists in all states but Delaware. It is a system of superlatives, containing the largest gorge on Earth (Grand Canyon), the longest cave system on Earth (Mammoth Cave), the world's largest carnivore (Alaskan Brown Bear), the world's tallest living thing (Giant Sequoias), the highest point in North America (Mt. McKinley) and the lowest point in the Western Hemisphere (Death Valley).

The American invention of the national park has become such a popular instrument of U.S. public policy that a steady political pressure to create new ones has existed for well over a century. Statistically, on average of 2.9 new units have been added per year since Yellowstone's designation in 1872, and 3.5 since the Antiquities Act authorized creation of national monuments by presidential declaration in 1903. While writing this chapter, three newcomer units were added to the list: the African Burial Ground National Monument in Manhattan, Carter G. Woodson Home National Historic Site in Washington and Sand Creek Massacre National Historic Site in Colorado.

Almost 100 years of quantitative system expansion has been accompanied by growing park popularity. In 1920 there were 1 million recreational visits. Over the next four 20-year periods up to the year 2000, the number increased to 17, 79, 198 and 286 million. In 2008 it stood at 275 million people, a figure that calculates as 90 percent of the U.S. population. A Roper poll that year found that 79 percent of Americans perceive the National Park Service in a "highly favorable" or "favorable" way, a rating higher than that given the Forest Service, Centers for Disease Control and Protection, FBI, NASA and the Federal Aviation Administration.[19]

NPS as a Federal Bureaucracy

The National Park Service is an institution of intermediate size compared to other federal bureaucracies. Its overall budget authority is $2.7 billion (2010). It employs 22,000 men and women, of which approximately 16,000 are permanent appointments, 3,000 seasonal and 1,250 term. The efforts of employees are assisted by nearly 167,000 volunteers, who donate about 5.4 million hours annually. The NPS is the largest agency among our six in terms of employment, but not funding (note appendix).

The Park Service is a component of the Department of Interior, which also includes the Fish and Wildlife Service, Geological Survey, and Bureaus of

Reclamation, Land Management and Indian Affairs. It is the largest of these, and receives about 22 percent of the departmental budget and employs approximately 32 percent of its personnel.[20] Because the secretary of the Interior serves in the president's cabinet, the NPS is a bureau considered to be directly within the presidential reach of executive authority. Officially it receives this executive oversight via two administration political appointees, the Assistant Secretary for Fish, Wildlife and Parks and, at a more operational level, the Deputy Assistant Secretary for Fish, Wildlife and Parks.

In Congress, the four most important committees for the NPS are the House Subcommittee on National Parks, Forests and Public Lands, a component of the Committee on Natural Resources; the Senate Subcommittee on National Parks of the Committee on Energy and Natural Resources; and the appropriations subcommittees on Interior, Environment and Related Agencies for each chamber. Typically, their chairs represent Western states.

For many years the NPS director was appointed by the secretary of the Interior, without Senate confirmation. In 1996 the law was amended so that a nomination is submitted by the president to the Senate for confirmation. This change was significant for the agency in that whereas previously it was assumed directors could serve multiple administrations in a relatively nonpartisan way, now each one speaks for the administration of the current president. Bill Clinton nominated the first African-American to the post, Robert Stanton, and George W. Bush the director of state parks for Florida under Gov. Jeb Bush, Fran Mainella. President Barack Obama named to the post Jon Jarvis, a 34-year careerist and most recently director of the Pacific West regional office.

National Park Service Organization

The national headquarters of the NPS, temporarily located in a rental property on Eye Street in Washington, are nicknamed WASO, for Washington Administration Support Office. At its head is the director. He or she is assisted by two deputy directors, one for support services and the other for operations. The first is responsible for partnerships, visitor experiences, information services, American Indian liaison, international affairs, policy development, strategic planning, state and local assistance programs, and park initiatives. The deputy director for operations (DDO) oversees four associate directors, one each for (1) natural resources, stewardship and science; (2) cultural resources; (3) visitor and resource protection; and (4) park planning, facilities and lands. Field organization is built on a system of seven regional directors who supervise park superintendents in their respective regions, namely: Alaska, headquartered in Anchorage; Intermountain, in Denver, Colo.; Midwest, in Omaha, Neb.; National Capitol, in Washington, D.C.; Northeast, in Philadelphia, Penn.; Pacific West, in Oakland, Calif.; and Southeast, in Atlanta, Ga.

Something of an anomaly in the NPS organization chart is the United States Park Police. Formed by George Washington, its history goes back to 1791. It does not have general jurisdiction in the parks around the country but only NPS properties in the District of Columbia, New York City and San Francisco. In recent years the Park Police has been troubled by mismanagement, low morale, firings and resignations, and is something of an institutional orphan child.

The NPS director, deputy directors, associate directors, assistant directors, regional directors, comptroller, chief of staff, chief information officer and Park Police chief collectively form what is called the agency's National Leadership Council (NLC). This group meets monthly and passes on major matters of policy and program. When initiatives are brought forward by staff they are allotted a place on that month's agenda. The NLC is said to possess genuine power as a deliberative body, rather than being a rubber stamp or having a ritual function like the cabinet of most presidents. All NLC positions are considered political appointments, although those filling them are often long-term or former careerists.

The management of each national park is in the hands of a superintendent, with small nonpark units headed by a manager. At one time superintendents operated relatively autonomously, but today they must also act in accord with a three-tier system of directives. This consists of a bound book of *Management Policies,* rewritten every few years; the Director's Orders, which provide supplemental operational directives and procedures; and a variety of specialized handbooks and reference manuals. Park superintendents and other unit managers are all NPS careerists, although new appointments at pay grade GS-15 and above are cleared for acceptance of administration policy goals.

THE PARK SERVICE MISSION

The operant feature of the mission mystique agency is its permeation by a vital belief system anchored in a compelling concept of mission. Cell 1 of the mission mystique template deals with mission purpose. The mission of the National Park Service springs from its Organic Act of 1916, Section 1:

> Be it enacted by the Senate and House of Representatives of the United States of America in Congress assembled, That there is hereby created in the Department of the Interior a service to be called the National Park Service. . . . The service thus established shall promote and regulate the use of the Federal areas known as national parks, monuments, and reservations hereinafter specified by such means and measures as conform to the fundamental purpose of the said parks, monuments, and reservations, *which purpose is to conserve the scenery and the natural and historic objects and the wild life therein and to provide for the enjoyment of the same in such manner and by such means as will leave them unimpaired for the enjoyment of future generations.*[21]

Bifurcated Mission?

What we have here is a clear example of a specified agency mission, in that the NPS mandate is laid out in the founding statute. The italicized words are similar to Olmsted's draft with the exception that he said public enjoyment should be allowed "in *any* manner and by *any* means," implying a more unlimited interpretation of public use than "in *such* manner and by *such* means"—in other words, as judged by the agency. Taking note of this kind of nuance and its possible implications typifies how later generations of the national park community have debated endlessly what on its surface seems to be a perfect example of mission clarity.

At stake in this debate is the issue of whether the goal of enjoyment by the public means *true* preservation for future generations. Those who raise this question tend to be environmentally oriented voices who insist on maintaining *natural* ecological integrity and continuity. They insist that any public presence that interferes with such integrity contradicts the idea of real preservation. Those who take the opposing view argue that the very idea of a *national* park is a place that is open to all of democracy's citizens, for purposes not only of mass enjoyment and education but something as fundamental as identification with the nation. They believe that careful management allows this to happen without jeopardizing the parks' presence as a national treasure.

The official Park Service position on the matter is that conservation must always come first, in that if excessive development occurs there will be no wilderness or cultural ruins left for the public to enjoy, the very reason for having the nation take over untouched lands and ancient sites in the first place. An early statement of this doctrine is contained in a letter ostensibly written by Secretary of the Interior Lane to Director Mather on May 13, 1918 (but drafted by Horace Albright) that announced the principles by which the parks should be administered:

> First, that the national parks must be maintained in absolutely unimpaired form for the use of future generations as well as those of our own time; second, that they are set apart for the use, observation, health, and pleasure of the people; and third, that the national interest must dictate all decisions affecting public or private enterprise in the parks. Every activity of the Service is subordinate to the duties imposed upon it to faithfully preserve the parks for posterity in essentially their natural state.[22]

The official manual of NPS rules, *Management Policies,* deals with the issue this way: "conservation will be predominant when there is a conflict between the protection of resources and their use." In support of this position, NPS training programs align themselves with the precept that "indisputably preservation comes first in law" and cite specific federal court cases to support that contention. The

Policies also states that whether an external impact on a resource constitutes "impairment" depends on what is affected, the severity of the effect, its duration and timing, direct as well as indirect effects, and whether these consequences accumulate.[23] In other words, decisions on preservation versus public use require prudent, reasoned, professional judgment. Making them is not always easy. Recreational sports exist today that were unheard of in 1916, e.g., use of trail bikes, snowmobiles and all-terrain vehicles; should they be permitted in the parks? Unintended consequences arise that produce unforeseeable dilemmas; should managers of the Blue Ridge Parkway cut back roadside trees to renew vistas even though it would destroy the habitat of flying squirrels that invaded them during low-budget years? Long-accepted doctrines about how nature works are shattered by new research; should the public be allowed to stand next to giant sequoias when the compacted earth causes surface erosion but also seals in ground moisture?[24]

Thus continued uncertainty confronts Park Service decision makers in administering a specified mission that is (1) on the surface clear, (2) inherently ambivalent at an intellectual level, and (3) seemingly resolved in favor of one side of a duality yet leaves the consequences open to interpretation and hence disagreement. Looked at from the standpoint of Stephen White's notion of weak ontologies where contestation is always possible, this definitional mess may be a blessing more than a curse. It creates an internal, automatic axis around which debate can occur on philosophies of natural resource management that will always be competing. While many insist there is no "real" duality here in terms of inherent contradiction, there is without doubt a difference in worldview that is deeply ingrained in the NPS. Should we be sympathetic with the philosophy of Muir and roam alone in the wilderness? Or should we build automobile roads into every park, as Mather insisted? With this kind of basic value difference, the Park Service belief system is seldom free of uncontested orthodoxy.

Mission Growth and Expansion

In recent decades the number of park units has increased tremendously, and now nears 400. This growth was not rationally planned, but is the accumulated outcome of a heavily political process involving pressures from members of Congress, urgings by various movements and private groups, and appeals by state and local governments and their allied business interests. By the 1990s a "thinning of the blood" critique of the NPS had emerged that contended topsy-turvy growth of the park system had little to do with the original mission, was lowering the standards as to what is protected, and was diluting agency resources. Various measures to correct the situation have been discussed, including thematic planning of new-park needs, capping permanently the number of parks, and enacting a decommissioning statute like the one used to close military bases.[25] Of the agencies studied in this book, only the CDC has experienced more mission expansion.

Although there is no way to squelch the politics involved, the Park Service has established criteria for selecting new units to recommend to the president and to Congress. Practical factors include whether the resource is redundant to the existing set of parks, big enough and configured right to be included, supported by local landowners, of economic benefit, and capable of efficient administration at reasonable cost. Inherent worth standards are whether the resource is nationally significant, relatively unspoiled, an outstanding example of its type, or offers superlative opportunities for public enjoyment or scientific study.[26]

Growth in the number of park units is partly due to an expansion of the definition of what constitutes a national park. This has been accomplished by amendments to the Organic Act, the passage of additional statutes and amendments to these, court decisions and the issuance of updated *Management Policies,* most recently done in 1997. Further, under the National Environmental Policy Act in 1969 and related "green" statutes, the concept of preservation is redefined to include not only protection of the land and manmade objects but preservation of less tangible necessities such as species survival, ecosystem integrity, and clean skies and water. This step, of course, only stimulates further the long-standing debate over preservation versus public use.

Movement in the opposite direction is laws such as the Urban Park and Recreation Recovery Act of 1978. These have resulted in creating extensive land areas devoted primarily to public use, many of them containing almost as much privately owned property as federal. Two such areas, Golden Gate around San Francisco and Gateway in New York and New Jersey, incorporate scattered separate parcels; thus they are not "a" contiguous park at all.

Departing still further from the conventional definition of a national park are the National Heritage Areas, of which there are now 24, with more waiting to be authorized. These entities, created under pressure from local governments and chambers of commerce, are tools for promoting tourism and regional economic development, a mission having nothing to do with the original 1916 mandate. They too are scattered parcels of private land, loosely linked by a theme such as the beginnings of industrialized agriculture (in Iowa), automobile-related historical places and events (in Michigan) and creation of the Creole culture (in Louisiana). The areas are designated by acts of Congress and involve a contract with the secretary of the Interior; however, they are managed by local nonprofit groups largely for their own purposes, while benefiting from affiliation with the National Park Service and receiving from it up to $1 million in initial funds, locally matched.[27]

PEOPLE OF THE PARK SERVICE
The State of Motivation

The work of T. Zane Reeves, discussed in Chapter 1, points to a secularized missionary identity that embraces clear purpose, shared values, a proclivity for action and high morale. Hal Rainey and Paula Steinbauer talk of mission motivation, by which they mean belief in the inherent importance of the work. These are ways of characterizing how employees of the mission mystique agency are propelled by strong commitment, the subject of cell 4 of the template.

Duke scholar Julie Elmore conducted survey research on 2,500 NPS employees in 2005 with respect to motivation in the Park Service. In response to the statement "I believe the Park Service mission is important," 97 percent answered in a positive manner. The item "I believe that the work I do is important" elicited a positive response from 95 percent. In contrast, much less positive responses, in the range of 57 to 61 percent, were received on references to whether "my opinion seems to count," whether the resources are available "to do my job right," and if recognition is received "for doing good work." Elmore found that the higher you go in the organization the less commitment there is to quality work and success in preserving park resources. Problems identified in open-ended survey comments, interviews and focus groups included lack of funds to carry out the mission and poor mission management by senior agency officials.[28]

This mixed picture of dedication to the mission but criticism of how it is being carried out also comes through in employee responses to the biennial Federal Human Capital Survey, a governmentwide, anonymous, computer-administered questionnaire survey run by the U.S. Office of Personnel Management. A subset of the questions and positive response rates by NPS employees is shown in Table 2.1. The first two statements in the table relate to attitudes toward the work itself: "The work I do is important" receives positive responses in the 90s, although not as high as Elmore's findings. "I like the kind of work I do" elicits a somewhat lower response, yet both sets of percentages are relatively stable and slightly higher than aggregates for the government as a whole.

However, the next two statements, pertaining to recommending employment in the NPS and degree of satisfaction with it, are in the 60s and 50s, respectively. In both instances they fell from 2002 yet showed an uptick in 2008. The final pair of queries, which yielded responses in the 20s and 30s, suggests that a prime reason for this dissatisfaction is disapproval of the organization's leadership for its failure to motivate and for the quality of its decisions. In short, there is strong belief in the mission but all is not well in the house of national parks.

While I was working on this book I belonged to an independent listserv sponsored by the Coalition of National Park Service Retirees (it has had various names, including parklandwatch, parklandsupdate and protectnationalparks).

Table 2.1 NPS Employee Responses to FHCS Questions, 2002–2008

		Percent Positive	
		NPS	All Government
The work I do is important.			
	2002	93.1	
	2004	91.9	
	2006	91.7	
	2008	91.6	90.4
I like the kind of work I do.			
	2002	84.6	
	2004	84.9	
	2006	86.3	
	2008	86.4	84.2
I recommend my organization as a good place to work.			
	2002	67.9	
	2004	65.1	
	2006	61.6	
	2008	63.8	66.4
Considering everything, how satisfied are you with your organization?			
	2002	57.3	
	2004	53.5	
	2006	50.8	
	2008	53.7	59.7
In my organization, leaders generate high levels of motivation and commitment in the workforce.			
	2002	32.6	
	2004	25.1	
	2006	27.8	
	2008	30.3	41.3
How satisfied are you with the policies and practices of your senior leaders?			
	2004	27.2	
	2006	31.0	
	2008	34.8	43.8

Source: Office of Personnel Management, *Federal Human Capital Survey,* 2006 and 2008, items 6, 8, 20, 38, 58 and 63. Positive responses are "strongly agree" and "agree" or "very satisfied" and "satisfied."

In the days following release of the 2006 Federal Human Capital Survey, many comments were exchanged on this network. Some said that morale has dropped in recent years because top management became oriented toward largely irrelevant performance measures and ignored the concerns of subordinates.

Dissolution of a formerly close-knit NPS "family" feeling was also mentioned. An issue frequently raised was shortfalls in operational funding and capital investments during the second Bush administration, a subject we touch on later. Yet despite the complaints, throughout the discussion a fundamental faith in the importance of the mission was expressed. One correspondent wrote:

> Most park service people, in all areas of work, have come to work over the years EXHILARATED to work for the National Parks and programs. . . . The only time they would become depressed is when they would see the Mission compromised or important opportunities missed. . . . They have zeal because of the Mission, and feel thwarted when they cannot help the parks in the ways they expected when they joined.[29]

In my field interviews, NPS employees clearly demonstrated a strong commitment to the agency's mission and to the importance of their work in behalf of that mission. One clue to such an attitude is what respondents said when I asked why they joined the Park Service in the first place. Almost always they begin talking about family memories from childhood. A division head told how when he was eight years old he took a lengthy hike in a park with a ranger. Because there were only the two of them, he was able to observe and converse at length with this articulate, uniformed man. After narrating the story in detail, the interviewee pointed to a snapshot on his desk of himself as a little boy alongside the ranger. Next to it was another photo, of himself as an adult in the NPS uniform, out on the trail with his own son.

On another occasion my wife and I went on an extended motor tour at Yosemite conducted by a female ranger in her twenties. After thanking her for her narrative comments on the trip, I asked if she would write an e-mail paragraph for me on why she joined the Park Service. She did so, and in it recounts how as a little girl she went on hunting trips with her father. This experience opened up the world of migratory birds to her, spurring an interest in the cycles of nature. She then decided to devote her life to protecting such processes and eventually accepted a job in the NPS. She ends with the comment, "I hope there is a way that we can enjoy natural places and leave them intact for the next person to enjoy."

Another theme one frequently encounters among NPS men and women is the innate satisfaction they receive from doing work in which they fervently believe. A veteran ranger wrote in a listserv retirement message, "It has been a wonderful career filled with good memories and much satisfaction. I can honestly say that there were few, very few days in the past 32 years when I got up in the morning and did not look forward to going to work! I have been proud to call myself a Park Ranger." A current employee I ran into while riding on a bus at the Grand Canyon told me he came to the Park Service late in his career after working in the aerospace industry. He said he liked the NPS for two reasons: one, it is more careful in spending taxpayer money than government contractors; and two, in the Park Service you are giving something back by protecting the country's natural resources, as well as keeping America beautiful.

A final theme in the interviews was that, though the Park Service spirit remains vibrant, it has dimmed in recent years—a feeling expressed not in anger but regret. One superintendent told me that funding in the Bush years was so bad that he felt "hanging by a thread" in keeping up with the needs in his 864,000-acre park; each year he had to limit himself to doing a tiny number of must-do projects while leaving everything else in the "undone" category. A recently retired ranger described the sense of loss he felt in collegial closeness when NPS-owned residential compounds were phased out in favor of owner-occupied housing. Another interviewee opined that while the old Park Service ethos is not dead, it is wounded—due in part to partisan policy pressures from the Bush administration that cause management-level personnel to be cautious about what they say and do. He also mentioned the effect of the takeover by large corporations of what were once family-run park concessions, with the result that commercial interests are now superseding mission values. The very fact that NPS veterans miss the "old days" as times change reveals once again the depth of their commitment.

Occupational Roles: Superintendent

The workforce of more than 22,000 includes, as one might expect, almost every conceivable kind of occupational specialist: botanist, wildlife specialist, geologist, anthropologist, forester, landscape architect, historian, accountant, attorney and so on. Two occupational roles stand out, however. The most coveted is that of park superintendent. The very first superintendent, Nathaniel Pitt Langford, was called "National Park" Langford because of his initials. Despite receiving no salary or funds, he theoretically managed the huge Yellowstone Park. As noted, Albright eagerly sought the Yellowstone superintendence himself shortly after he helped create the agency. Over time certain superintendents became legendary because of their colorful personalities and individual styles of operating their distant fiefdoms. In recent years, however, these positions are carefully filled by organization men (and now women) approved by WASO who have risen through the ranks. They are supervised by regional directors and, while exercising considerable autonomy in interacting with nearby "gateway communities," must follow *Management Policies* like all employees. Seven of the Park Service's 19 directors served previously as park superintendents, including the present incumbent, Jon Jarvis. In 2008 an academy for new superintendents was set up at WASO in Washington, but it has yet to achieve a reputation for true worth.

Ed W. Clark, superintendent of Manassas National Battlefield Park, 20 miles west of Washington, D.C. This was the site of the first and second battles of Bull Run in the Civil War. National park superintendents are the most important leadership element in the National Park Service.

Source: Photo by the author.

Occupational Roles: Ranger

The second revered role in the Park Service is that of ranger. In the early days these men "ranged" alone on horseback over the territories of Western parks, hence the name. Their isolation and resourcefulness won them a reputation for courage, fortitude and an ability to tackle any task: break a horse, catch an outlaw, rescue a climber, treat a snake bite, name a plant, fight a fire, clean a latrine, teach a history lesson. Mather, in a famous quote, said it this way: "If a trail is to be blazed, send a ranger, if an animal is floundering in the snow, send a ranger, if a bear is in a hotel, send a ranger, if a fire threatens a forest, send a ranger, and if someone needs to be saved, send a ranger."[30]

Perpetuating the reputation of this Renaissance man are many books that recount the adventures of rangers in embellished form. With titles like *Hey Ranger! True Tales of Humor and Misadventure from America's National Parks,* they draw inspiration from the fabled story-telling skills of rangers and are made available to newly hired rangers at NPS training centers.[31] Even today the ranger myth is not forgotten; it was invoked with nostalgia in the Burns documentary on the national parks, complete with the Mather quote. After former president Gerald Ford, who had a summer seasonal position at Yellowstone at age 23, died in late 2006, quotes by him were recalled in which he said he experienced "one of the greatest summers of my life" riding armed guard on the bear-feeding truck and greeting VIPs at the lodge.[32] Each year on July 31 the International Ranger Federation, a global confederation of ranger associations, celebrates World Ranger Day, marked in 2007 by multiple showings of an Australian documentary, "The Thin Green Line."[33]

Today two Park Service job classifications carry the name of park ranger, one for protection and the other for interpretation. Protection rangers meet the legal definition of a "federal law enforcement officer," meaning they routinely carry arms, have the power to arrest and may retire after 20 years like other federal law officers. In the large Western parks these rangers are headquartered at the Park Police station, sometimes designated "ranger operations." They are trained at the Federal Law Enforcement Training Center at Glynco, Ga., along with officers of the Forest Service, Fish and Wildlife Service and the Bureau of Land Management. Although socialized to wield their coercive authority under clear rules and a unified command, in the NPS they operate in a civilian government agency that is not organized in paramilitary fashion, which can lead to some resentment and frustration by receiving mixed signals from above.

By contrast, interpretive rangers represent the "friendly" face of the Park Service to tourists and visitors. True to their job title, they are engaged in interpretive and educational programs that include, but are not limited to, manning visitor centers, conducting trail walks, visiting school classrooms, and organizing Junior Ranger programs for children and ProRanger internships for college students. At national monuments and other smaller sites they can be a kind of jack-of-all-trades.

Most young people entering NPS careers apply for the interpretive ranger position. To be eligible they must be college graduates with 24 credit hours of coursework in a field related to natural resource management. Upon entry they assume the civil service rank of GS-5 and rise as high as GS-9. Unlike their protection colleagues, interpretive rangers do not go through a professional academy; their training consists of short courses at two in-house educational facilities, the Horace M. Albright Training Center at Grand Canyon National Park and the Stephen T. Mather Training Center at Harpers Ferry National Historical Park. Educational offerings there cover such topics as NPS fundamentals, resource stewardship, communication skills, problem solving and individual development. In addition, on-line courses are available to all employees. Some are critical of the NPS for sending protection rangers to Glynco while having no specialized academy for the interpreters.

PARK SERVICE CORE VALUES

In contemporary public administration one often sees reference to "core values," but often they are ignored as window dressing. At the Park Service, however, such summaries of the culture are taken seriously—another sign of a vibrant belief system. The agency distributes to all employees a "core values" brochure and a plastic card suitable for carrying in a wallet, and at training sessions their contents are discussed. On the card is a list of five such values, to wit: shared stewardship, excellence, integrity, tradition and respect; their meanings

---

Box 2.1 National Park Service Shared Values

Shared Stewardship. *We share a commitment to resource stewardship with the global preservation community.* We are proud that national leadership in resource preservation is the National Park Service's essential public trust. We know that we do not have all the answers to every challenge, yet we champion heritage preservation throughout the United States and the world. The insights and knowledge obtained from all such efforts contribute to our collective success.

Excellence. *We strive continually to learn and improve so that we may achieve the highest ideals of public service.* We encourage creativity, innovation, and vision so that we may achieve excellence as we fulfill the mission of the National Park Service. As caretakers of the natural and cultural resources of the United States, we individually and collectively collaborate to be worthy of the trust given us by the American people.

Integrity. *We deal honestly and fairly with the public and one another. We take responsibility for our actions and their consequences.* We do so in ways that are ethically based and represent the highest standards of public service. Through our actions we aim to earn the trust of those we work with and serve. We are accountable to the public and each other.

Tradition. *We are proud of it; we learn from it; we are not bound by it.* We use only the best from our past to meet the challenges of the future. The continuum between the past, present, and future sustains us as a vital agency. We hold the mission and the traditions of the National Park Service in our thoughts and actions so that it is apparent in our work and interactions with one another and the public.

Respect. *We embrace each other's differences so that we may enrich the well-being of everyone.* We value the ever-changing diversity of our employees, visitors, sites, and the stories of our heritage. We learn from each other's creativity and talents to become richer individuals. We base our actions on the principles of inclusion, empathy, and dignity.

Source: National Park Service brochure, "Core Values," 2001.

---

are spelled out in Box 2.1. The wording of these is said to have resulted from employee workshops held at all levels of the organization, from which a "surprising and gratifying" similarity of views emerged. They are considered by the Park Service as not simply cultural norms, but ideas that "clarify who we are," "articulate what we stand for," "guide us in making decisions," "underpin the whole organization," and "require no external justification."[34]

Shared Stewardship

The core value of shared stewardship highlights the international as well as national leadership of the National Park Service in resource preservation. The agency's Office of International Affairs invites interested persons from around the world to come to the United States to study and experience the national park system. It also administers the World Heritage Convention, which maintains a list of park sites located in signatory nations that should be protected as being of universal value, of which 23 are in the United States. Technical assistance and personnel exchanges are also carried on with foreign national park staffs, and sister park relationships are established from time to time.[35]

The word *shared* in the first core value suggests that resource stewardship should be collaborative. Forming partnerships is endemic to the NPS culture and specifically mentioned in the current mission statement. This is reprinted on the inverse side of the wallet card and reads:

> The National Park Service preserves unimpaired the natural and cultural resources and values of the national park system for the enjoyment, education and inspiration of this and future generations. The Park Service cooperates with partners to extend the benefits of natural and cultural resource conservation and outdoor recreation throughout this country and the world.

That this agency, one of the most famous in government, would place such stress on the use of partners in carrying out its mission speaks to its awareness of current acceptance of collaboration and networking over unilateral administrative action. Indeed, whole sections in *Management Policies* are devoted to the topic, a degree of conscious emphasis not found in the other agencies studied. The authorized partners span the organizational spectrum: other federal agencies, state park departments, local governments, tribal governments, foreign governments, international organizations, private landowners, business firms, nonprofit organizations, recreation and conservation groups, and volunteer associations. Activities sanctioned include educational programs, search-and-rescue operations, preserving scenic views, control of artificial lighting, scientific research, sharing data and expertise, habitat restoration, establishing wildlife corridors and ecosystem management. In justifying such wide collaboration, it is pointed out that natural ecosystems do not, after all, stop at park boundaries; the same can be said with respect to cultural and historical resources, especially if they pertain to early peoples whose borders had nothing to do with today's maps.[36]

At the same time, *Management Policies* warns that the NPS mission must not be compromised by such activity. Superintendents are instructed to monitor all land use proposals and planned external activities adjacent to national parks. If it is determined that they would be harmful, personnel are instructed to do all in their power to restrain their implementation or mitigate their consequences. "When engaged in these activities," the language continues, "superintendents should fully apply the principles of civic engagement to promote better understanding and communication by (1) documenting the park's concerns and sharing with them all who are interested, and (2) listening to the concerns of those who are affected by the park's actions."[37]

Another use of the term *partnership* extends to donations of time and money. In the early days Mather persuaded wealthy acquaintances to buy land for park purposes, since Congress was not paying for it. John D. Rockefeller purchased Mt. Desert Island and the Grand Tetons for the park system, and Mather himself paid half the cost of what became the Great Smoky Mountains National Park. This practice was suspended in the modern era and replaced by independent affiliates of the NPS such as the National Park Service Foundation, which over the years has successfully solicited or channeled much private philanthropy.

Late in his second term President George W. Bush, at the urging of his wife, Laura, launched the Centennial Challenge, an initiative to commemorate the forthcoming hundredth birthday of the National Park Service. It was intended to raise $3 billion for park projects by a combination of appropriations and gifts over the 10-year period prior to the 2016 anniversary. As the Bush presidency wound down, however, only about $30 million in new money came from Congress, and slightly more than $50 million via the matching side of the program. Park advocates believed the fund-raising program had adverse effects, in that the projects selected for private funding were skewed to donor preferences while adding to future maintenance costs.

Excellence

The core value of excellence, with its attention to learning, continuous improvement, creativity and innovation, is directly relevant to cell 9 of the mission mystique template. The Park Service has shown capacity for significant renewal and change in the past, as in Wirth's Mission 66 and Hartzog's expansion of the park concept. With respect to the current time, two pertinent questions in the Federal Human Capital Survey are not promising from the standpoint of employee attitudes—perhaps a consequence of low morale during the Bush years. Only 58.4 percent responded positively to "I feel encouraged to come up with new and better ways of doing things," and a mere 37.9 percent to "Creativity and innovation are awarded." Both scores are several points below the all-government average.

Yet the institution as a whole, along with its allied organizations, has not remained averse to new ideas. "It is quite extraordinary how much and how frequently the NPS emphasizes the need for it to change and adapt," one listserv participant said.[38] The principal mode by which this self-examination is accomplished is periodic conferences. Annually or even more often, a meeting is held of high-level personnel, park advocates or academic experts on an aspect of the agency's need for improvement. Some of these sessions concentrate on how to solve problems, or "single-loop learning," as the literature terms it. An example is a 2008 "summit" in Snowbird, Utah, that sought ways to reconnect Americans with their national parks and develop new leaders for the organization. At other conferences double-loop learning is attempted, i.e., altering norms and practices so as to avoid identified problems. In 2001, following a year of meetings, the National Park System Advisory Board released a report entitled *Rethinking the National Parks for the 21st Century.* It proposed that the agency teach Americans more about history, biodiversity, sustainability and the Indian heritage.[39]

On occasion the rhetoric, if not the reality, of triple-loop learning—i.e., to become more "future-ready"—emerges. At a regional resource management conference held in Tucson in 2008, a former NPS employee urged those present to "be more introspective, think bigger thoughts, think outside the box, envision a future National Park Service unfettered by the patterns of yesterday." A discussant at Tuscon went on to say the agency must escape "a culture of organizational poverty":

> Think about what a culture of organizational poverty means. A culture is a set of perceptions, assumptions, and beliefs so deeply ingrained that we are not even aware of when and how it governs our behavior. Essentially, it means we have reached a point at which we accept, cooperate with, and participate in our own impoverishment and oppression. We reached this point by more than three decades of adjusting to thousands of large and small budget and political "realities." That all happened rationally, and most of it honorably, but to remain in this situation after we have fully recognized it would be shameful.[40]

In 2009 the National Parks Second Century Commission, an independent group composed of 30 national park leaders and experts convened by the National Parks Conservation Association, sought to think deeply about out how the NPS can be improved in the coming decades. Among their recommendations were a six-year term for the director, allocation of 4 percent of the personnel budget to professional development, and creation of a youth corps. Recommendations directly related to triple loop learning were: create a center for innovation to identify lessons and models for future consideration; establish an institute to nurture a culture of organizational learning; and adjust management systems to encourage risk-taking, adaptation and collaboration.[41]

Integrity

The attributes stressed in the core value of integrity are honesty, fairness, responsible and ethical action, representing the highest standards of public service and earning public trust. These would appear to be "motherhood and apple pie" qualities that would apply in any good organization. One might wonder why they are isolated for special emphasis in a wallet card carried by employees. Possibly this stems from past charges that Park Service personnel can exhibit intransigence and even arrogance when asserting the importance of the NPS mission to the public. The prior discussion of thwarting adverse impacts on adjacent land alerts us that the agency is aware of the problem. An NPS report published in 1991, commonly referred to as the Vail Agenda, mentions a sense of personal proprietorship over "my park" and commitment to the ranger's *own* image of the park system as prevailing features of the culture.[42]

In exploring this theme I asked interviewees explicitly about signs of NPS arrogance. One interviewee, the former mayor of a small town in Michigan, recounted how a park superintendent refused to participate in the planning of a new water reservoir for her municipality and yet, after one citizen objection was raised, demanded its already begun construction to cease. In another instance, federal grants for an industrial park that had already been approved were blocked by local NPS officials because it was to be located next to the barren site of an undeveloped national historical park. An instructor at the Albright training center told me he often encountered an excessive sense of "mission superiority" among NPS personnel.

Historically, there were times when the agency brutally forced relocation of long-standing residents from lands acquired for parks. When Yellowstone National Park was formed, Crow, Shoshone and Bannock tribes were forced out of the territory, and at Yosemite it was the Yosemite tribe and in Glacier the Blackfeet. Mark Spence, in his book *Dispossessing the Wilderness,* points out that such actions simultaneously removed Native-Americans from their ancestral homes and isolated them in sterile reservations.[43] In his documentary Ken Burns mentions that when the Great Smoky Mountains National Park was being created in the 1920s, Horace Albright—in the face of cries of outrage and grief—insisted that all backwoods families depart immediately but leave behind their cemeteries. Scholar Katrina Powell obtained access to an archive of letters written by mountain families displaced when Shenandoah National Park was formed in the 1930s; she found that any expressions of frustration or resistance were met by NPS officials with "derision at worst and condescension at best."[44]

To investigate whether "mission arrogance" exists today, I tracked 15 controversies actively covered in the press in 2008–2009 that involved NPS interaction with the public. Of them, in 10 the agency's conduct seemed to represent high standards of honesty, fairness and public service; in three this did not appear to be the case; and in two I felt unable to judge.

To illustrate an instance in the second category, when the national memorial to the Sept. 11, 2001, crash of United Flight 93 in Pennsylvania was being planned, two-thirds of the needed property was purchased without difficulty, but owners of the remaining 500 acres balked. The local superintendent informed the holdouts without warning that he was initiating condemnation proceedings against them. An uproar ensued, with the owners insisting that the compensation being offered by the NPS did not take into consideration true value factors such as rights to natural gas, coal and timber. The superintendent refused to engage in negotiations or even direct discussions with the recalcitrant landowners. Eventually, Pennsylvania senator Arlen Specter and Secretary of the Interior Ken Salazar came personally to the scene to deal with the situation. Salazar told the owners he understood how hard it is to give up farm property, in that his family has lived on the same plot of Colorado ranchland for 150 years. The needed acreage was subsequently acquired without significant controversy, and groundbreaking took place in November 2009.[45]

An incident in the first category that illustrates a more constructive NPS attitude concerns reconstruction of parkland at the foot of the Jefferson National Expansion Memorial, the famous Gateway Arch in downtown St. Louis that Hartzog shepherded. In 2007 former senator John Danforth of Missouri, a prominent and wealthy figure in St. Louis civic life, proposed that a pedestrian bridge to the park be built along with a museum at the foot of the arch. Without telling the NPS, his family foundation had spent two years planning the changes and was prepared to donate $50 million to the project. Park Service personnel learned about Danforth's efforts only after spending months themselves holding open houses to discuss changes. Rather than fight Danforth, the agency proposed that alternative ideas be framed for a public vote. Its only reservations were that character-defining elements of the monument not be disturbed and that, as owner of the land, it must have final say. At this writing the issue has been largely defused, and an international design competition is under way for a final proposal.[46]

Tradition

The fourth core value of tradition envisions a learning continuum that connects the agency's past, present and future and thereby sustains the agency's vitality. This reminds us of Perry Pascarella and Mark Frohman's notion of steering the organization forward based on awareness of its past. We have already mentioned several Park Service traditions that, in the words of its training manual, "clarify who we are" and "articulate what we stand for." These include designation of the site of the Roosevelt-Muir campsite in Yosemite, encouraging circulation of tales of the rangers of old, naming the two training sites after founders Mather and Albright, and activities in anticipation of the hundredth anniversary of the Organic Act.

Another illustration is physical markers of the Park Service past found across the country. Several years ago bronze plates were distributed to all national parks for permanent display. They bear a profile of Mather's head and the following inscription:

> Stephen Tyng Mather, July 4, 1867–January 22, 1930. He laid the foundation of the National Park Service, defining and establishing the policies under which its areas shall be developed and conserved unimpaired for future genera-tions. There will never come an end to the good that he has done.

Entrances to the large Western parks sometimes bear a notable reference to the past—for example, the representation of an Indian chief in headdress at Sequoia National Park. Museums are found at many larger parks that contain not only artifacts representative of the peoples that once lived on their lands but material on the history of the park itself. Just outside the North Gate of Yellow-stone is a Heritage and Research Center that contains an archive of 20,000 books and manuscripts, 3,000 feet of historical records and 90,000 old photo-graphic prints, many of which were used in the Burns documentary. Efforts to create a national NPS museum in Washington in time for the centennial are under way.[47]

The agency's official emblem is the familiar arrowhead, conceived in 1949 and introduced in its present form in 1952. It is found on signs, publications and office stationery. A previous logo was circular, with representations of a sequoia tree and two branches in the center. The present version has a sequoia tree and bison to represent the vegetation and wildlife that are conserved, and the snow-capped mountain and patch of ice or water signify values of scenery and recre-ation. The arrowhead itself may be thought of as a token of respect for the original Americans that once lived in the Western parks.

The Park Service uniform, the most visible physical conveyance of the agen-cy's culture, goes back many years. The first ranger uniforms were authorized in 1911, when the Army cavalry was patrolling the Western parks. After the agency was formed it adopted its own design, in keeping with Albright's desire to instill a military-style *esprit de corps*. The uniform of the 1920s became the basis for today's heralded force of "green and gray," so designated because of dark-green trousers, jacket, and tie with gray shirt. After some experimenta-tion, distinctions between "officers" and "men" ended in 1928, and differences in the uniform worn by administrators and rangers were erased. When women were first hired in ranger jobs they were required to wear skirts and jackets similar to airline stewardesses, but that distinction was eliminated as well.

The uniform is topped off by a headgear affectionately known as the "flat hat." It dates to 1920 and was inspired by a military campaign style popular at the time. The hat worn by Canadian Mounties has also been said to offer inspiration. The hat comes in felt for the winter and straw for the summer, with a hatband decorated by sequoia cones. The importance of this element in the

Horace Albright's hat

Hat worn by Horace M. Albright, cofounder with Stephen T. Mather of the National Park Service. This memorabilia exhibit is at the agency's Horace M. Albright Training Center at the Grand Canyon. He made passage of the National Park Service Organic Act possible in 1916.

Source: Photo by the author.

Park Service's culture is difficult to overstate; most field personnel proudly appear in full uniform when meeting the public. Officials at national and regional headquarters do so when attending formal meetings and public events, but otherwise work in civilian clothes. A revered object on display at the Albright Training Center is the badly crumpled "flat" hat once worn by Director Albright.

Respect

Respect, the fifth core value, embraces all kinds of diversity, especially among NPS personnel and park visitors. The admission of women to the NPS workforce began in earnest in the 1960s. At first, female staff were confined to office work and not sent into the field. After receiving vocal protests from new female recruits, this policy was changed and they are now given the same training and job assignments as men, including armed law enforcement. By 2001, 31.6 percent of agency employees were female, compared to 45.2 percent in the national civilian workforce. By 2007 the figure climbed to 36.1 percent.[48] At a class I attended at Albright, 11 out of 27 trainees present were female. Two directors of the agency have been women: Fran P. Mainella (2001–2006) and Mary A. Bomar (2006–2009).

The record of progress in hiring members of racial and ethnic minority groups has been mixed. In 2001, 10.6 percent of Park Service personnel were African-American, 5.3 percent Hispanic, 3.2 percent American Indian or Alaskan Native, and 2.1 percent Asian and Pacific Islander. By comparison, national civilian workforce percentages for that year were 10.3, 8.5, 0.7 and 2.3, respectively, showing a low proportion of Hispanics and high of native peoples. Percentages for 2007 were 7.9 African-American, 4.6 Hispanic, 2.9 Indian and 2.2 Asian. These indicate losses in all categories except Asian.

Another diversity aspect of concern to the agency relates to park visitors. Although figures on the subject are not kept, the common perception is that those coming to the parks are disproportionately white, educated and middle-class citizens, often travelling in families. The NPS is eager to attract more minorities, immigrants and youth. Indeed, *Management Policies* states that the very future of the National Park Service depends on understanding "why people do or do not visit—or care—about national parks. It is vital that the Service help those who do not visit to understand and support their national park system."[49]

A major step in this regard has been to establish park sites of special interest to African-Americans and American Indians. The three most recent additions to the park system, mentioned earlier, are of this nature. The African Burial Ground monument is an 18th century black cemetery in Manhattan. The Carter Woodson Home was the Washington residence of the father of African-American history. Sand Creek Massacre National Historic Site is the locale of an 1864 attack by Colorado volunteers on a Cheyenne village. Three national historic trails perform a similar function: the Trail of Tears in New Mexico, the Nez Perce trail in Montana, and the Selma to Montgomery route in Alabama. Not a piece of land at all is the National Underground Railroad Network to Freedom, established by Congress in 1998. In a scattered set of sites it promotes commemorative programs and helps organizations interpret this important heritage.[50]

THE MISSION UNDER STRESS

While the mission of the NPS as "caretaker of America's best idea" has never lost its appeal, during the George W. Bush administration its implementation underwent a great deal of stress—more than for any of the other federal agencies we are studying—as a result of administration philosophies. From 2001 to 2006 the secretary of the Interior was Gail A. Norton of Colorado, a former attorney general of that state who was once active in the Libertarian Party and associated with groups supporting private property rights in the West and opposed to the environmental movement. Her deputy secretary at Interior was J. Steven Griles, who became embroiled in the Jack Abramoff scandal and eventually went to prison. Julie A. MacDonald, a deputy assistant secretary, was accused of doctoring scientific findings with regard to endangered species. Paul Hoffman, a Wyoming protégé of Vice President Dick Cheney, served as deputy assistant secretary for Fish, Wildlife and Parks, thus directly administering the Bush agenda at the National Park Service. We examine four examples of the outcome.

Mission Betrayal

Hoffman's views on the parks attracted attention early at the NPS when he over-ruled a decision by the superintendent at the Grand Canyon to remove religious plaques on display at the South Rim. He also instructed that a book be available at the park bookstore that presents a creationist rather than geological explana-tion of how the canyon was formed. Meanwhile, a more long-term project was on his mind. Without telling the Park Service, over a two-year period Hoffman led an effort to redraft radically its *Management Policies,* a new version of which had been issued as recently as 2001. A memo he wrote on the subject called for discarding basic assumptions of the Organic Act and decades of other law and policy by saying, in effect, that the standard for leaving resources "unimpaired for the enjoyment of future generations" does not forbid near-term damage that can later be reversed. Moreover, it is not necessary that such impairments be elimi-nated, only mitigated. Other features of the rewrite called for relaxing rules on cell phone towers in parks, low-flying tour planes, snowmobile use, grazing and mining, and environmental protection.[51]

Interior officials presented Hoffman's proposed new *Policies* language to Director Mainella in July 2005, who forwarded it to the regional directors for comment. They responded with a searing indictment. Mainella then convened a group of 16 long-term NPS employees to determine if the draft could be modi-fied sufficiently to make it acceptable. They said there was no way to make it satisfactory. In August a text of the draft was leaked to the Coalition of National Park Service Retirees, which called a news conference to denounce the proposal in scathing terms.[52] At his home in McLean, Va., Hartzog learned what was going on and began telephoning his contacts around the country. Soon the mainstream press was denouncing the project; stunned by the reaction, Interior officials backed off and downplayed the draft as merely an attempt to launch a dialog. The version of *Management Policies* issued in 2006 departed completely from Hoffman's wording and reinstated existing policy.

Snowmobiles

Meanwhile, another fight with the Interior high command was brewing. Sports-men from Wyoming and nearby states loved to operate their snowmobiles dur-ing the winter at Yellowstone, Glacier and other national parks. Hikers and environmentalists, however, detested the noise and pollution. In 1990 the administration of George H. W. Bush had set a threshold for maximum snowmobile use at Yellowstone. This triggered a series of lawsuits, countersuits and environmental impact studies. At the close of the Clinton administration, Yellowstone authorities phased out snowmobile use entirely.[53]

When George W. Bush came to office the issue flared up again. A federal judge ordered the Park Service to conduct yet another study, but before it was completed Secretary Norton approved an interim policy that allowed up to 720 snowmobiles in Yellowstone per day, provided the machines were propelled by four-stroke engines instead of two and outings were accompanied by guides. Back in McLean, this ruling again riled Hartzog, who contacted the other living ex-directors of the NPS, all of whom signed a letter of protest to *The New York Times.*

The letter was never published, but its contents were widely covered by the media, especially in the West. Six environmental groups argued that Norton's quota of 720 was illegal. The Yellowstone superintendent, with WASO approval, reduced the quota to 540 snowmobiles, a number that had been surpassed only once before. Still, recreation groups and the state of Wyoming objected strongly. Then, in fall 2008, a federal district judge for the District of Columbia nullified the 540 order on grounds that it elevated use over conservation, and three weeks later a second federal district judge in Wyoming reinstated the 720 number. Accordingly, the park returned to that level until Barack Obama became president, at which time the limit was reduced to 318, where it stands at this writing.[54]

Guns in the Parks

In March 2006 Gail Norton stepped down as Interior secretary and Hoffman was shifted to another post in the department. This did not mean the end of mission stress for the Park Service, however. A second threat—at least perceived that way within the agency—was a move to permit loaded and accessible rifles and handguns to be carried into the national parks. NPS policy since the Reagan administration had been to allow transportation of firearms through the parks, but unloaded and stored in racks or car trunks.

For some time state wildlife commissioners in the West had urged the NPS to allow volunteer hunters to cull excessive herds of elk in the parks. In August 2007 President Bush signed an executive order directing federal land management agencies to "expand and enhance hunting opportunities" in national forests, wildlife refuges and range lands. The following January, 47 senators from both parties publicly urged that NPS regulations be relaxed to allow legal gun owners to take guns into the parks "in accordance with the laws of the host state." This would end, they said, inconsistencies among federal land agencies and also terminate discrimination against citizens with valid concealed weapons permits.[55]

A furious national debate erupted between the hunting community and conservation forces. Proponents of the change argued that possessing firearms affords greater personal safety to hikers and campers and upholds Second Amendment rights. Opponents contended that no legitimate reason exists for having loaded handguns and rifles in parks, that it could lead to shooting accidents and deadly violence, and that such a step would be contrary to the concept of the park as a sanctuary. NPS protection rangers worried that the change in policy would lead to poaching and complicate the task of law enforcement. On April 3, 2008, four months before the end of his life, Hartzog and his fellow ex-directors again went into action by signing a letter to the Interior secretary praising the current policy for serving the public well; not only does it prevent the unlawful killing of wildlife, they wrote, but enforcing the unloaded-and-stowed rule gives rangers a reason to search suspicious vehicles carrying guns.[56]

Soon a draft rule appeared in the *Federal Register* proposing that individuals could carry concealed weapons into national parks and refuges "to the extent that they could lawfully do so on analogous state-administered lands." Later, however, the rule was altered to allow guns in national parks even when the adjoining state did not allow guns in its parks, as long as it issued concealed weapons permits.[57] Following suits challenging the regulation by the National Parks Conservation Association and the Brody Campaign to Prevent Gun Violence, a district judge overturned the rule on grounds that the department's rulemaking process was "astoundingly flawed" and failed to evaluate the public safety and environmental consequences. Not waiting for the litigation process to play out, western senators attached a rider to a credit-card reform bill that opened all national parks and refuges to guns. An identical move was made in the House, and the bills passed with substantial majorities. President Obama signed the law without comment, and it took effect in February 2010.[58]

Hard Times

The most serious mission damage sustained by the National Park Service in the years of the second Bush administration was not from policy changes but lack of funding, a problem that affected other federal agencies as well. During this period total appropriations dropped from $2.8 to $2.4 billion, a figure that includes irregular expenditures for fixed purposes such as land acquisition and facility construction, as well as running the parks. The operations budget grew during the period, but by only 3.3 percent a year, compared to 5.1 under Clinton and 8.7 under Bush I. This, however, was not sufficient to overcome the effects of inflation, mandated federal salary increases and the costs of post–Sept. 11, 2001, security measures. The Government Accountability Office (GAO) calculated that, in constant dollars, allocations for park operations dropped by $10 million between 2001 and 2005. In a separate budget analysis I found this was accompanied by a loss of 868 NPS career positions calculated on a full-time equivalent (FTE) basis. In surveying the consequences of the budget squeeze on a sample of parks, GAO investigators reported that funding inadequacy forced Bryce and Yellowstone to reduce backcountry patrols, Grand Canyon to cut interpretive programs, and Yosemite to leave several ranger-protection positions vacant. Zion reduced restroom cleaning from twice a day to once, resulting in many visitor complaints.[59]

Other outside groups came to similar conclusions. A 2008 study by the National Academy of Public Administration concluded that cultural resource staffing had fallen to its lowest level in years, that 2,811 historic structures were in poor condition, and that interpretation programs had remained static while the number of parks had grown.[60] The National Parks Conservations Association, in a 2008 report on *The State of Our National Parks,* gave the following grades to NPS performance: overall natural resource management = C-; ecosystem extent and function = D; overall cultural resource management = D-; ethnography = F. The report came to the conclusion that "chronic under-funding is compromising the ability of the National Park Service to preserve and protect irreplaceable elements of our nation's natural and cultural heritage."[61]

At the same time, visitors to the parks were experiencing more and higher entrance fees, shabby site maintenance (as on the National Mall) and fewer rangers. Because of a shortage of staff positions, superintendents depended more on volunteers and contractors for serving the public. As of Jan. 10, 2006, the total number of people working in the national parks (actual numbers, not FTE) was 198,722, of which 24,679 were federal employees, 137,000 volunteers, 1,402 park foundation workers, 23,799 concession staff, 11,296 contract personnel and 546 student interns. From this standpoint, national park service activity is, for all practical purposes, 88 percent privatized.[62]

THIS INSTANCE OF MISSION MYSTIQUE

The National Park Service, one of the United States' most famous civilian agencies of government, serves a mission that emanates from the treasured nature of the parks it administers. The commitment of its personnel is obvious despite misgivings during the Bush II years, and its public reputation remains high despite differences of opinion regarding park use. Overall, how does the NPS measure up to the nine elements of the mission mystique belief system template?

Cell 1: Mission. This agency possesses a special aura of respect in the United States, primarily because the Western parks are beloved as grand images of wilderness and locales of satisfying personal experiences for many Americans. The mission of the Park Service is of the specified type, laid out in the Organic Act of 1916. It has dual emphases: conservation and public use. The phrase "unimpaired for future generations" brings together the two ideas intellectually but does not end debate over what should be done in specific instances. Also, the mission has grown significantly over time in terms of numbers and types of parks, including some that stray far from the agency's basic purpose, such as promoting local economic development.

Cell 2: Need. It would be difficult to argue that the need for national parks is urgent. The physical health or safety of citizens is not at stake. Yet their well-being is certainly affected. The great Western parks, as interpreted by Olmsted and Muir, bring the solace of nature to their visitors, and contemporary admirers see them as spiritual embodiments of the nation. Historical parks and national monuments preserve the history of the nation, and recreation areas and national trails, rivers and seashores provide healthful outdoor outlets for millions. Yet, as recognized by the Park Service itself, there are millions of Americans to whom the national parks are not of particular interest.

Cell 3: Reputation. The NPS is an exceedingly well-known agency, domestically and internationally. Indeed, it may be the closest thing the United States has to a noncommercial "passionbrand." Aggregate annual visitation numbers approach the population size of the country. Polls rank it high in public esteem. The agency's image in legislative bodies at all levels of government is such that new additions to the park system are advocated every year, more than can be handled with available staff and funds. The only defect in the image is a reputation for excessive zeal in protecting and acquiring land, although this perception may be exaggerated as the agency seeks to improve its civic conduct.

Cell 4: Motivation. Surveys indicate that almost all NPS employees think the work they do is important. It is clear that the vast majority believe wholeheartedly in the mission, even while having differences on priorities related to occupational role or mission emphasis. Time and again one runs into careerists who were attracted to the NPS because of childhood experiences at the parks. This deeply implanted dedication to the mission suffered in the recent past because of feelings that the Bush II administration was unsympathetic to the mission. Funding shortfalls, position shortages and policy decisions on guns and snowmobiles have been dimly received by career employees.

Cell 5: Culture. The culture of the organization is strong. The ethos of stewardship is focused not inward, to preserving a collective tradition, but outward, to safeguarding the nation's resource heritage. The green and gray uniform, flat hat, and arrowhead emblem are tangible symbols within the cultural frame. So too are the *Management Policies* and wallet card, with its mission statement and core values. New leadership, following the adversities of the eight Bush II years, is reigniting the mobilizing power of this culture. This is the aim of new director Jon Jarvis, a career veteran who is nudging the organization ahead in the aftermath of the Burns documentary and the work of the Second Century Commission.

Cell 6: History. Nonetheless, the Park Service is very conscious of its past. Numerous books have been written on the history of the parks and the Park Service, and the agency publishes its own short version as well.[63] Founders Stephen Mather and Horace Albright are memorialized in many ways, including the names of the agency's training centers, where every enrollee is made well aware of their achievements. Emergence of the national park idea in the 19th century and passage of the Organic Act in the 20th century are absorbed in the collective memory, along with sagas about legendary rangers and famous superintendents. Every quarter-century the founding is institutionally celebrated, as with Mission 66 at 50 years, the Vail Agenda at 75, and the pending centennial festivities at the one-century mark.

Cell 7: Contestation. At the level of mission emphasis, e.g., conservation versus public use and interpretation versus scientific study, disagreements are aired frequently, both at the everyday level of action and the conceptual level of debates at retreats and conferences. During the Bush II years internal dissent on day-to-day policy was muffled and, in fact, Interior Department political staff regularly monitored NPS press conferences and congressional testimony. During those years the Coalition listserv performed as an influential medium for anti-administration grumbling, although its contributors were mainly retirees. Under the Obama administration and the leadership of Director Jarvis this tension is being relieved.

Cell 8: Autonomy. Politically, the agency is bolstered generally by its fame and the wide appeal of its mission. During the Bush II years it had sufficient clout to overturn efforts at the secretary of the Interior level to subvert the organization's basic mission. Yet the institution could not save itself from serious underfunding, which is why the somewhat dubious value of corporate donations in accord with the Centennial Challenge initiative had to be welcomed. Events in the snowmobile and guns-in-the-parks battles show that even when national park values are being trampled upon, the agency's leadership remains loyal to political direction from the White House, as well as instructions from Congress and the courts. By no means does the agency try to break loose from its constitutional bounds.

Cell 9: Renewal. Federal Human Capital Survey results in 2002–2008 showed Park Service personnel feeling little encouragement to innovate or be creative. This is likely due to the conservative and controlling governmental climate during the Bush II administration. Yet, even during this period, the institution continued a long-standing cultural habit of holding, sponsoring or being receptive to periodic conferences on the topic of sweeping change. It is as if the agency is accustomed to "thinking big" no matter who is in power. Its insiders and outsiders meet time and again to work out solutions to problems and consider how they can be avoided in the future. Going beyond that, they reflect thoughtfully on how to make the organization more inventive, such as institutionalizing organizational learning and "going to where the puck will be," as Wayne Gretsky advised.

As mentioned in Chapter 1, the National Park Service was the inspiration for writing this book. The foregoing review indicates that, with the exception of cell 2, it fits quite well into the template of the mission mystique ideal belief system. As we will see, some of the remaining agencies to be studied do as well, while others match it to a lesser degree.

3

U.S. National Weather Service

Daily Companion and Watchful Guardian

THE STATE OF THE WEATHER AFFECTS US EVERY DAY: how we feel, what we wear, what we do, how long it takes to get to work. No wonder we consult routine weather forecasts so often. The organization that makes them, the National Weather Service (NWS), is like a personal companion in our daily lives. And on unusual days when the prediction is for a blizzard, tornado, hurricane or flash flood, it can become the guardian of our lives. Rivaled only by the U.S. Postal Service, the NWS is the federal government's most frequent visitor to our homes.

KATRINA, THE PERFECT STORM

The National Hurricane Center (NHC) in Miami is the Weather Service's most famous focal point for its watchful guardian role. The center's meteorologists, hurricane specialists and storm surge experts occupy most of a large concrete building on the edge of the campus of Florida International University. This fortress-like structure, faced with square columns and topped with a catwalk, is built to withstand winds up to 130 miles per hour. The center's mission is to forecast and issue warnings of hurricanes and other hazardous weather heading for American shores. These forecasts are prepared in its operations room, a large space equipped with numerous computer consoles and large wall maps. Another room is a studio for teleconferences with emergency management officials. A third is for coordinating Hurricane Hunter flights into the eye of storms to measure their intensity and direction.

The Hurricane Center's director from 2000 to the end of 2006 was Max Mayfield, an internationally known meteorologist and hurricane specialist who began

National Hurricane Center, Miami, Fla. This building, constructed to withstand winds of up to 130 miles per hour, is where the National Weather Service watches for dangerous storms in the Atlantic and Pacific Oceans, Caribbean Sea and Gulf of Mexico. Thus it is a focal point for the NWS watchful guardian function.

Source: Photo by the author.

his career in the National Weather Service in 1972. His skills were tested to the full in a sequence of events that began at 4 p.m. central daylight time on Tuesday, Aug. 23, 2005, when the forecasting staff took note of a tropical storm cell developing in the Bahamas. They christened it Tropical Depression 12 and issued a routine weather advisory that predicted it would probably make landfall on the south Florida coast that night, off Fort Lauderdale.[1]

Over the next two days, the NHC kept increasingly careful watch on the storm as it passed across the Florida peninsula into the Gulf of Mexico. There it elevated in intensity and was designated Tropical Storm Katrina. The Hurricane Liaison Team, a standby coordinating arrangement established in 1996 to foster communication with the Federal Emergency Management Agency (FEMA), held many urgent conversations in the teleconference studio with emergency management officials. The Hurricane Hunter coordinators tasked one of the huge WC-130J aircraft to take off at Keesler Air Force Base in Biloxi, Miss., to check out the storm at 10,000 feet. With its specialized instruments and drop-sondes (16-inch tubes released in the air), measurements were taken of wind speed, precipitation, air pressure, temperature and dew point.

This information plus radar and satellite images made it clear the storm was growing in intensity. An advisory issued at 4 p.m. on Thursday, Aug. 25, stated that what was now Hurricane Katrina was headed for the Gulf of Mexico's loop currents and could reach Category 4 before landfall. At 10 p.m. an advisory was issued that anticipated landfall on the eastern Gulf Coast near the Louisiana–Mississippi boundary. The most likely spot was estimated to be the town of Buras, La., near Fort Jackson.[2]

On Saturday, Aug. 27, activity intensified at the Hurricane Center. At 10 a.m. a formal hurricane watch was declared for southeastern Louisiana, including metro New Orleans and Lake Pontchartrain. By this time Katrina was a Category 3 hurricane with 115 miles per hour winds. The watch indicated that attainment of Category 4 before landfall was possible and a Category 5—the most intense hurricane ranking—not out of the question. At 4 p.m. the watch was extended all the way to the Florida line. Teleconferences continued between NHC managers and all levels of FEMA.

As Saturday evening unfolded, Mayfield became so concerned about an eminent catastrophe in the low-lying, levee-protected city of New Orleans that he personally telephoned Mayor Ray Nagin, Louisiana governor Kathleen Blanco and Mississippi governor Haley Barbour. This action went beyond the normal protocol, but Mayfield was willing to go out on a limb because of the magnitude of the threat. Mayor Nagin immediately ordered the evacuation of the city, later telling reporters that Mayfield's call had "scared the hell" out of him. Meanwhile, the NHC director went on local radio and TV to warn the affected populace. Robert Ricks, the meteorologist in charge of the Slidell, La., Weather Forecasting Office (WFO), did the same. At 10 p.m. the Hurricane Center took the ultimate step by reclassifying the watch as a warning and describing the threat as highly dangerous. Eleven minutes later Ricks at Slidell issued the following ominous message to the public and media:

DEVASTATING DAMAGE EXPECTED [FROM] HURRICANE KATRINA. . . . A MOST POWERFUL HURRICANE WITH UNPRECEDENTED STRENGTH . . . RIVALING THE INTENSITY OF HURRICANE CAMILLE OF 1969.

MOST OF THE AREA WILL BE UNINHABITABLE FOR WEEKS . . . PERHAPS LONGER.

AT LEAST ONE HALF OF WELL CONSTRUCTED HOMES WILL HAVE ROOF AND WALL FAILURE. ALL GABLED ROOFS WILL FAIL . . . LEAVING THOSE HOMES SEVERELY DAMAGED OR DESTROYED.

THE MAJORITY OF INDUSTRIAL BUILDINGS WILL BECOME NON FUNCTIONAL.

PARTIAL TO COMPLETE WALL AND ROOF FAILURE IS EXPECTED. ALL WOOD FRAMED LOW RISING APARTMENT BUILDINGS WILL BE DESTROYED. CONCRETE BLOCK LOW RISE APARTMENTS WILL SUSTAIN MAJOR DAMAGE . . . INCLUDING SOME WALL AND ROOF FAILURE.

HIGH RISE OFFICE AND APARTMENT BUILDINGS WILL SWAY DANGEROUSLY . . . A FEW TO THE POINT OF TOTAL COLLAPSE. ALL WINDOWS WILL BLOW OUT.

AIRBORNE DEBRIS WILL BE WIDESPREAD . . . AND MAY INCLUDE HEAVY ITEMS SUCH AS HOUSEHOLD APPLIANCES AND EVEN LIGHT VEHICLES. SPORT UTILITY VEHICLES AND LIGHT TRUCKS WILL BE MOVED. THE BLOWN DEBRIS WILL CREATE ADDITIONAL DESTRUCTION. PERSONS . . . PETS . . . AND LIVESTOCK EXPOSED TO THE WINDS WILL FACE CERTAIN DEATH IF STRUCK.

POWER OUTAGES WILL LAST FOR WEEKS . . . AS MOST POWER POLES WILL BE DOWN AND TRANSFORMERS DESTROYED. WATER SHORTAGES WILL MAKE HUMAN SUFFERING INCREDIBLE BY MODERN STANDARDS.

THE VAST MAJORITY OF NATIVE TREES WILL BE SNAPPED OR UPROOTED. ONLY THE HEARTIEST WILL REMAIN STANDING . . . BUT BE TOTALLY DEFOLIATED. FEW CROPS WILL REMAIN. LIVESTOCK LEFT EXPOSED TO THE WINDS WILL BE KILLED.

AN INLAND HURRICANE WIND WARNING IS ISSUED WHEN SUSTAINED WINDS NEAR HURRICANE FORCE . . . OR FREQUENT GUSTS AT OR ABOVE HURRICANE FORCE.ARE CERTAIN WITHIN THE NEXT 12 TO 24 HOURS.

ONCE TROPICAL STORM AND HURRICANE FORCE WINDS ONSET . . . DO NOT VENTURE OUTSIDE![3]

At approximately 1 a.m. Sunday, Aug. 28, the Hurricane Hunters reported winds of 145 miles per hour. Shortly after 6 a.m. Katrina was elevated to Category 5; winds of 160 miles per hour were reported at daybreak and 175 miles per hour by 10 a.m. The state of affairs was thoroughly reviewed with Florida and FEMA personnel. At noon Mayfield briefed President George W. Bush by videoconference at his ranch in Crawford, Texas. Secretary of Homeland Security Michael Chertoff and FEMA director Michael Brown were also present, along with state officials. Mayfield told them in no uncertain terms that Katrina posed a catastrophic threat to New Orleans and the Gulf Coast. "This hurricane is much larger than Hurricane Andrew ever was," he said. "I also want to make absolutely clear to everyone that the greatest potential for large loss of life is still in the coastal areas from the storm surge." The president responded, "We are fully prepared to not only help you [state officials] during the storm, but we will move in whatever resources . . . we have at our disposal after the storm."[4]

At 1 p.m. warnings were issued of significant surge flooding. At 2 o'clock it was advised that Katrina was moving toward a Louisiana landfall at 13 miles per hour, and would hit as a Category 4 or 5, with winds that could create water surges that would overtop levees. At 10 p.m. it was again warned that preparations to protect life and property be rushed to completion.

On Monday, Aug. 29, additional dire proclamations were issued at 4 and 6 a.m. Katrina, now classified Category 4, hit southeastern Louisiana at 6:10 a.m., with the midpoint of contact only 18 miles from Buras, the point predicted 56 hours earlier. Official watches had been issued 44 hours before this moment and warnings 32 hours previous.[5]

This "perfect storm" had been almost perfectly predicted. As forecast, it wrought frightful damage and became a natural disaster of historic proportions. The subsequent storm surge, waves and rains caused the levees to overtop. The cascading water then scoured out their foundations on the lee side, causing them to collapse. Although levee collapse was not specifically predicted by Mayfield, President Bush's later comment that "I don't think anybody anticipated the breach of the levies" rang hollow. Eighty percent of New Orleans was inundated and about half of its homes and buildings destroyed. Tens of thousands of its citizens were seen on television marooned on rooftops and huddled in the Superdome and Convention Center. An estimated 1,000 persons perished in New Orleans and about 600 elsewhere. Yet, because of the credibility and timing of the NWS forecasts and Mayor Nagin's evacuation order, 80 percent of the city's population had gotten to safety, a high proportion in such situations. Without the work of the Hurricane Center and Slidell WFO, fatalities would no doubt have been many times greater. In the following days and months, FEMA and the Bush administration, along with many state and local officials, received withering criticism for mishandling the aftermath of Katrina. High praise was received, however, by the Weather Service and the Coast Guard, which did heroic work in the aftermath.

A LONG AND VARIED HISTORY

Public agencies have long been at the forefront of meteorology in the United States. During the War of 1812 the Medical Department of the U.S. Army created the first weather recordkeeping network in the country. The Army surgeon general ordered all post surgeons to maintain weather diaries in order to investigate the influence of weather on disease. In 1817 the General Land Office encouraged daily observations at its numerous local offices in the West. Back in Washington, in 1841 the Patent Office began accumulating weather data, and the Naval Observatory received reports on storms at sea. The state governments of New York, Massachusetts, South Carolina and Pennsylvania also set up data collection networks.[6]

Early Technology Aids Weather Bureau Forecasting

The advent of the telegraph—humankind's first breakthrough in conquering long distances for communication—meant that weather reports could be obtained and distributed quickly throughout the nation. A foremost innovator in this realm was Joseph Henry, an eminent 19th century scientist and early experimenter with telegraphy. When the Smithsonian Institution was founded in 1846, Henry was appointed its first secretary. He made the new Smithsonian Castle a center for national weather reporting. Private telegraph companies wired in information daily, and by 1860 some 300 observers were sending information to the Smithsonian. The data were recorded and charts drawn of temperature and precipitation patterns, which were displayed in the Castle's hall. A sign at the top of the Smithsonian tower summarized the current outlook.[7]

Meanwhile, meteorology as a science was beginning to develop. Weather pioneers such as Cleveland Abbe in Cincinnati set up forecasting centers in various regions of the country and sold predictions commercially. Other meteorological entrepreneurs favored this approach as well, but a sudden public emergency redefined the weather world. The 1868 and 1869 shipping seasons on the Great Lakes were plagued by storms that sank scores of vessels and led to the loss of more than 500 seamen. Increase A. Lapham, a Wisconsin naturalist, surveyor and geologist, proposed a nationwide weather service to protect Lakes shipping, although not necessarily in the hands of government. He approached Milwaukee representative Halbert E. Paine, who agreed to sponsor legislation, but insisted that such a service be a function of the federal government. Furthermore, he wanted it placed within the military establishment, whose discipline he admired.[8]

On Dec. 6, 1869, Paine introduced a joint resolution in the House that authorized and required the secretary of war "to provide for taking meteorological observations, at the military stations in the interior of the continent, and at other points in the States and Territories of the United States, and for giving notice, on the Northern Lakes and on the seacoast, by magnetic telegraph and marine signals, of the approach and force of storms."[9] The measure passed and was approved by President Ulysses S. Grant on Feb. 9, 1870. Secretary of War William W. Belknap assigned the program to the Army's Signal Service, an organization of about 100 men that had been established 10 years earlier as the Signal Corps (a name later restored). Col. Albert J. Myer, its commander, set up a Meteorology Division in his organization, pleased to expand its mission beyond stringing telegraph lines and coordinating flag signals for marine use. This 19th century beginning makes the NWS the oldest agency studied in this book (see appendix).

Colonel Myer (later General) wasted no time becoming the father of what was popularly known as "the weather bureau." On Nov. 1, 1870, at 7:35 a.m., 24 observer-sergeants simultaneously sent their reports to Washington by existing military telegraph lines, officially beginning the bureau's work. A week later Myer hired Lapham as head forecaster for the Great Lakes, operating in Chicago. That very same day Lapham issued his first storm warning, which forecast "high winds probable along the Lakes." In December Myer recruited Cleveland Abbe as well, who was named special assistant to the chief signal officer. On Feb. 19, 1871, the first of a continuous stream of tri-daily weather reports was issued by Abbe, each of which was called a "Weather Synopsis and Probabilities."[10] The War Department appropriation for 1872 extended the jurisdiction of the Signal Service's Meteorology Division from the Great Lakes and seacoast to the entire nation, "for the benefit of commerce and agriculture." Within a few years the number of observer field stations was expanded to hundreds and then to thousands, assisted by absorption of the data-collection networks of the Army Medical Department and Smithsonian Institution, together with several state reporting systems.[11]

For 20 years station observers around the country used simple instruments to report conditions to the Army's weather bureau in Washington. Barometers, thermometers, hygrometers, anemometers, a wind vane and a rain gauge were used to measure air pressure and temperature, relative humidity, the direction, velocity and pressure of the wind, and the nature and amount of cloud formation. The incoming information was received in standardized code at the central office, where one man read the telegrams aloud while others punched the information in symbolic form onto metal plates. These plates were inserted into slots on a metal outline of the United States. The platen of a specially designed printing press then pressed paper against this surface to produce a national weather map. Copies were given to a team of four forecasters, who wrote weather bulletins for different parts of the country. These were immediately telegraphed back to the observers and to railroad stations, post offices and the Associated Press. Although newspaper editors were initially skeptical of the venture, they soon realized that their readers devoured the daily weather report. In 1876 a *New York Tribune* editorial commented that the work of the Signal Service had acquired the status of a national institution.[12]

From Military to Civilian Control

Despite a positive public image, by its second decade the Weather Bureau was suffering from internal and external discord. General Myer died in 1880, and his successor was less skillful as an administrator and not without political enemies. Agency morale was undermined by complaints of too much discipline in an essentially nonmilitary organization, and the rest of the Army was jealous of the unit's large officer allotment. A highly publicized case of embezzlement on the part of one officer further eroded the agency's standing. A consensus emerged on Capitol Hill that the government's weather function should be placed in civilian hands. This occurred on Oct. 1, 1890, when it was transferred by statute to the Department of Agriculture. Secretary of Agriculture Jeremiah M. Rusk was the only cabinet officer who wanted it.[13]

The statute of transfer, which with minor changes still stands as the organic act of the National Weather Service, was much more detailed than the resolution signed by President Grant 20 years earlier. It reads:

> The Chief of the Weather Bureau . . . shall be charged with the forecasting of weather, the issue of storm warnings, the display of weather and flood signals for the benefit of agriculture, commerce, and navigation, the gauging and reporting of rivers, the maintenance and operation of sea-coast telegraph lines and the collection and transmission of marine intelligence for the benefit of commerce and navigation, the reporting of temperature and rainfall conditions for the cotton states, the display of frost and cold wave signals, distribution of meteorological information in the interests of agriculture and commerce, and the taking of such meteorological observations as may be necessary to establish and record the climatic conditions of the United States.[14]

Now named the United States Weather Bureau, the civilian agency commenced operations in 1891. Secretary Rusk replaced the general who had been running it with Mark W. Harrington, a professor of astronomy at the University of Michigan. The four forecasters in Washington who produced the national forecasts were retained. Sergeant observers around the country were honorably discharged and rehired as civilian employees of the government. The organization's activities and resources proceeded to expand, and by 1894 the staff of forecasters rose to 40. In the field, district offices were established and local forecasters were permitted to modify, with approval, predictions made in Washington. The bureau's appropriation rose from a base of approximately $1 million to $1.6 million in 1913, $2.1 in 1921, $4.5 in 1932, $7.8 in 1942, $21 in 1947 and $39 million in 1956.[15]

20th Century Advances

As the 20th century unfolded, a rush of scientific and technological advances affecting weather forecasting took the organization in a number of new directions. Wireless telegraphy was invented, meaning that dependence on telegraph lines ended. Text-copy transmissions of weather bulletins began in 1913 and broadcasts by voice commenced in 1921. In 1928 the teletypewriter became the principal means of communicating weather information.

Another major innovation was air mass analysis, a science imported from Norway whereby not just conditions on the ground are considered but the movement of atmospheric air masses and fronts. Beginning in the late 1930s, upper-air data collection was no longer done by kites but by balloon-mounted radiosondes, devices that automatically collected and radioed to ground high-atmosphere information on air temperature, pressure and humidity. These are still in use today, equipped with more sophisticated microsondes that also gather data on wind and report their GPS position. This information is received by an antenna at the balloon liftoff station, digested and coded locally, and then entered into the national weather information system.[16]

The dawn of powered flight created a compelling new need for forecasting accuracy. In 1920, to support the initiation of cross-continental air service, the Weather Bureau created flight forecast centers in Washington, Chicago and San Francisco. In 1926 Congress laid the legislative basis for the emerging aviation industry by passing the Air Commerce Act, one of whose provisions made the Weather Bureau officially responsible for providing meteorological support as well as conducting supportive research.

The new air mass research from Norway was crucial to aviation. A naval officer and pilot who became interested in meteorology, Francis W. Reichelderfer, obtained a master's degree in the subject in that country. When he returned to the United States he was imbued with air mass theories and became head of the Navy's weather service. When in 1938 the Weather Bureau chief suddenly died of a heart attack, Commander Reichelderfer was appointed his successor. "Reich" remained in this post until 1963, achieving the longest tenure of any director in the agency's history.[17]

By the end of the 1930s, the need for successful weather forecasting for aviation surpassed that for agriculture, in that its prediction is a matter of life or death to pilots and their passengers. The weather chief was himself a pilot, and the aviation industry's new promotional bureaucracy, the Civil Aeronautics Authority, had been established in the Department of Commerce. The Weather Bureau was transferred to that department by a reorganization plan effective June 30, 1940, and has remained there since.

The name "United States Weather Bureau" was changed to "National Weather Service" in 1967. This was done in association with an administrative reorganization in the Commerce Department. A short-lived "holding company" organization, the Environmental Science Services Administration (ESSA), was established in the department, and included the Weather Service and other agencies.

In 1970 Reorganization Plan No. 4 abolished ESSA and transferred its entities to a substitute conglomerate, the National Oceanic and Atmospheric Administration (NOAA). The declared intention of the change was to create a balanced and overarching consolidation of activities that deal with bodies of water, marine life and the weather. Departments other than Commerce also contributed to the newly created NOAA, bringing together programs as varied as marine sport fishing from Interior to the Navy's National Oceanographic Instrumentation Center.[18]

The National Weather Service now had its present name, its present departmental home and its present supervisory organization. We can now turn to its present status and work.

TODAY'S NATIONAL WEATHER SERVICE

The National Weather Service budget for FY 2009 was $959 million, a third of the National Park Service's figure. Its personnel number was 4,700, compared to 22,000 in the Park Service. Known as one of the best-managed agencies of the federal government, in 2001 it was reported by the Maxwell School of Syracuse University as the only one among 27 studied to deserve an "A" ranking in all four areas of finance, personnel, IT and management of physical assets.[19]

Essentially an applied science organization, NWS employees include 2,300 meteorologists, 300 hydrologists and 1,800 physical scientists, computer scientists, engineers, technicians and management analysts. This workforce depends for success on mammoth-scale sensing and communication systems, requiring heavy public investments in technology. The scientific specialization and technologic orientation of the NWS, along with a mission crucial to human life, provide the basis for the mystique of this relatively small agency. Like the Park Service, America's Weather Service is an international leader in its field; in opposition to it, the NWS does not protect nature from man but man from nature. The agency's headquarters are in Silver Spring, Md., outside Washington, D.C.

Organization Leadership and Hierarchy

The Weather Service is headed by a nonpartisan director not automatically replaced by each incoming administration. In the agency's first century of history directors were appointed, successively, by the secretaries of war, agriculture and commerce. Since 1979 the administrator of NOAA, a political appointee of the president, has possessed this authority. Since civilian status was attained in 1890, the directorship has been filled by 12 men, making the average tenure 10 years. For long stretches of time leadership was more stable than this figure indicates, however. Four directors were in office for an aggregate total of 78 years, almost two-thirds the life of the organization: Professor Willis F. Moore (1895–1913), Professor Charles F. Marvin (1913–1934), Dr. Francis W. Reichelderfer (1938–1963) and Dr. George P. Cressman (1965–1979). All post-1890 directors came to the position with an academic background in meteorology and/or high-level managerial experience in the field.[20]

The director from 2004 until 2007 was David L. Johnson, a career Air Force officer who, before retiring from the military in 2003, accumulated more than 3,800 hours as a fighter and transport pilot. As he held successive command positions he rose to the rank of brigadier general. Johnson became director of weather for the Air Force in 2000 and was appointed NWS director four years later; the Weather Service staff universally referred to him as "General Johnson" or, when not in the room, "D. L." Dr. John L. "Jack" Hayes replaced Johnson in 2007. Also a career Air Force officer, Hayes held Johnson's prior job of heading the Air Force weather agency for a time. As a civilian he worked in several other top weather positions at Litton Industries, the World Meteorological Organization, the Weather Service and NOAA.

The NWS hierarchy below the level of director consists of directors of four program offices that provide top-level oversight to the weather enterprise. Their jurisdictions cover climate, water and weather services; operational systems; science and technology; and hydrologic development. Also reporting to the director are six region directors, whose jurisdictions are the Central, Eastern, Southern, Western, Alaska and Pacific regions. Other high positions are those of deputy director and chief financial officer (also chief administrative officer); although not line officials, their occupants are second and third in the order of leadership succession in case of the absence or death of the director.

Comparable to the National Park Service's National Leadership Council, the National Weather Service's corporate board provides an opportunity for shared influence in agency governance. Sitting on it are the officers just named plus two staff heads and the director of the National Center for Environmental Prediction, an umbrella organization for several specialized technical units located in Camp Springs, Md. Although inactive in prior years, the board is now a key decision-making and governance body, complete with committees dealing with such matters as finance, research and acquisition. It meets at least quarterly and is a mechanism for representation of all viewpoints and interests—thus being "corporate" in the collective rather than business sense.

Integration: "Big Eye" and "Little Eye"

Components of the National Center for Environmental Prediction are the Climate Prediction Center, Environmental Modeling Center, Hydrometeorological Prediction Center, Ocean Prediction Center, Aviation Weather Center (located in Kansas City, Mo.), Storm Prediction Center (in Norman, Okla.), Tropical Prediction Center (in the National Hurricane Center building in Miami) and Space Weather Prediction Center (in Boulder, Colo.).

This is not the end of "center" pluralism in the NWS structure. Six regional climate centers analyze long-term climatic trends, covering the High Plains, Midwestern, Northeast, Southeast, Southern and Western regions. The Aviation

Weather Center, Ocean Prediction Center and Spaceflight Meteorology Group forecast for specific audiences. Other entities assemble and disseminate special kinds of weather information, like the National Data Buoy Center (sea conditions), Hydrologic Information Center (flooding) and National Operational Hydrologic Remote Sensing Center (snow coverage).

Collectively, these organizations conduct program activities at the macro level of the weather prediction system and are thus thought of as comprising the "Big Eye" of forecasting, concentrating on overview observations and long-term trends. The field-level "Little Eye" of the Weather Service is the micro component that prepares individual ground and area forecasts. The principal organizational unit here is the Weather Forecast Office, of which 122 exist across the country. It is mostly they that generate the routine forecasts we receive several times a day and the warnings of storms and floods that occur suddenly. Big Eye and Little Eye observations and analyses integrate at their own levels and with each other via a remarkable, all-encompassing data transmission system operating through a central telecommunications operations center in Silver Spring, known informally as the Gateway. At its heart are two of the largest supercomputers in the world, one to carry on the daily work and the other to stand by in case of sudden breakdown or needed downtime.

Hence the National Weather Service is a tightly integrated yet loosely coupled organizational universe of great complexity. Collaboration within it is structured to some extent by hierarchical authority and the demands of time, yet the system is not "controlled" in the managerial sense. No doubt this would be impossible, anyway, because of the need to incorporate new information almost instantly. To have any chance at understanding nature's chaotic, nonlinear relationships and self-organizing processes, the human organization that tries vainly to do so must itself engage in self-organized, quasi-spontaneous functioning.[21] When I asked a mid-level NWS executive how such a far-flung apparatus could possibly work, he simply said it happens because everyone has the same goal—to produce the most accurate and timely forecasts possible.

NOAA AS INSTITUTIONAL SUPERVISOR

As noted, the National Oceanic and Atmospheric Administration is a component of the Department of Commerce. Except in years of the decennial census, when the Census Bureau grows big, NOAA employs the most people in the department—12,800 as of FY 2009. The budget for Commerce that year was $17.4 billion, of which NOAA received $4.4 billion.

The Weather Service is by far the largest of six line bureaus in NOAA. In FY 2009 it was allocated 23 percent of the budget, and its workforce constituted 37 percent of NOAA personnel. Five other bureaus are in NOAA. The National Marine Fisheries Service regulates commercial fishing and conducts fisheries research in waters up to 200 miles offshore. The National Ocean Service protects coastal waters and shorelines with respect to environmental conditions and safety. An Office of Oceanic and Atmospheric Research studies Earth and climate systems and lake environments. The National Environmental Satellite Data and Information Service, or NESDIS, manages the 16 active satellites used by all components of NOAA. The final component is the Office of Marine and Aviation Operations, which provides reconnaissance aircraft and research ships to support NOAA missions. These planes and ships are manned by members of the NOAA Commissioned Officer Corps, a force of 299 uniformed officers whose roots can be traced back to 1807, when President Thomas Jefferson created the Coast and Geodetic Survey.[22] Physically, NOAA activities are directed from two locations in the national capital area—the imposing Department of Commerce building on 15th Street downtown in Washington, D.C., and a cluster of four office structures in Silver Spring. The downtown location is appropriate, since the NOAA administrator simultaneously holds the position of undersecretary of commerce for oceans and atmosphere. For top-level meetings NWS administrators must endure the long Metro ride down to the Commerce Department, accentuating a "we versus they" relationship between NOAA and the Weather Service.

NOAA has had nine administrators in its 40-year history. The eighth was Vice Adm. Conrad C. Lautenbacher Jr., U.S. Navy (Ret.), who was appointed by President George W. Bush in 2001 and served until December 2008. Because of prior staff assignments with the chief of naval operations in Washington, Lautenbacher assumed the position with close knowledge of program planning, operations analysis and financial management. The ninth and current administrator is Jane Lubchenco, a well-known professor of marine biology from Oregon State University.

The Integration of NOAA Agencies

Since NOAA's creation in 1970 it has become increasingly clear that, unlike ESSA, the administration is not a mere holding company. Many linkages exist between NOAA and its constituents. The Weather Service director is simultaneously assistant NOAA administrator for the National Weather Service, parallel to the NOAA administrator's duplicate role as undersecretary of commerce. Another tie is a set of top NOAA executives who supplement the agency's vertical hierarchy by overseeing separate mission goals and support areas, creating a matrix of authority by which the bureaus are supervised from two directions. These goal areas are ecosystem, climate, weather-water and commerce-transportation; mission support areas are satellite services, fleet services, modeling and observing infrastructure, and leadership and corporate services. The Weather Service falls under the jurisdictions of all but one or two of these.

Another integrating tool is an NOAA executive council, a corporate leadership board comparable to the Weather Service's corporate board. The NWS director, along with the other bureau chiefs, is a member. Also, in the personnel area, an NOAA-wide human capital council coordinates the employment practices of all bureaus, in accord with a unified strategic human capital management plan. In a feature of the plan that reveals NOAA's interest in having its bureau chiefs be "team players," the most heavily weighted criterion (40 percent) for evaluating the performance of senior executive service personnel is "support of corporate NOAA."

Even so, the NOAA bureaus interact daily on an operational basis, hence much technical coordination takes place in any case. For example, NOAA's climate center exchanges data and insights with NWS climate centers. The Weather Service depends on pilots from NOAA's commissioned officer corps when its Air Force Hurricane Hunters are overwhelmed. Without the weather satellites operated by NESDIS, the NWS could not forecast the weather.

The Push-Pull Relationship between NWS and NOAA

Despite (or because of) all these existing ties among elements of the nation's ocean-atmospheric bureaucracies, in recent years a struggle has emerged between the top commands of NOAA and the Weather Service. It developed in particular between 2004 and 2007, a period when the tenures of Admiral Lautenbacher at NOAA and General Johnson at the NWS overlapped. These two strong-minded former military officers clashed over the issue of whether or not NOAA should ascend in bureaucratic status and centralize its power vis-à-vis the bureaus, particularly the NWS. The admiral was adamant that NOAA should become as politically potent and prominent as possible, perhaps even reaching the fame of the National Aeronautics and Space Administration (NASA). By the same token, General Johnson was equally firm in his insistence that the Weather Service, NOAA's largest and best-known bureau, not lose its autonomy and visibility at the expense of tighter NOAA controls and integration. Furthermore, a shift of mission emphasis in the direction of the "Oceanic" in NOAA's name and away from the "Atmospheric" could cost the Weather Service its share of funding resources and new technologies. On top of it all, Lautenbacher's association with the Navy and Johnson's with the Air Force could not help but add to the tension.

An early objective floated by political allies of NOAA was to have it attain independent agency status like NASA, outside the Commerce Department. This idea was soon discarded as unrealistic. Lautenbacher then advocated the more modest step of replacing the 1970 reorganization plan that created NOAA with a true organic act, as a way of reaffirming the agency's legitimacy and recasting its image. A pro-NOAA ocean policy commission took on the task of drafting a bill, and it produced one that tilted strongly in favor of the acronym's "O" over its "A." The White House was not enthusiastic about the initiative, but OMB cooperated by coming up with a more balanced draft that emphasized the ecology and the environment, while still stressing oceanic concerns more than weather. Neither bill made headway in Congress, however, and the idea was dropped.[23]

If organizational or statutory means to build up NOAA were not available, management policies were. One of these was in the area of financial management. Unlike the old days, when the NWS presented its own budget to Congress, Lautenbacher required that all appropriation estimates and proposed capital projects be funneled through NOAA's Office of Program Planning and Integration. The unit's Planning-Programming-Budgeting-Execution (PPBE) system mirrored what the admiral worked on at the Pentagon in his Navy days. Using the PPBE format instead of the "seed corn" slides Johnson liked to use to present new projects, the general was reduced to defending his agency's funding requests before the NOAA executive council, where he was automatically outnumbered by the multiple ocean bureau chiefs.

Completed budget estimates were now incorporated into a joint NOAA budget, defended before congressional appropriation subcommittees by the NOAA administrator without the presence of bureau heads. Although Johnson often went to Capitol Hill to meet informally with committee staff, he was permitted to testify before Congress only upon request. When doing so, he was accompanied by an "escort" from NOAA to detect any disloyalties to the supervising institution's interests.

As an example of the admiral's sensitivity about Johnson's communications with Congress, the general was invited to appear before the House Science Committee on the success of his agency's forecasts of Katrina. In the course of testifying on the subject, he commented on how additional funds could better equip the Hurricane Hunter WC-130Js. A subsequent tour of the National Hurricane Center for President George W. Bush organized by NOAA did not include Johnson among the welcoming officials—an act the NWS director interpreted as retaliation.[24]

A second area of management policies used to integrate the NWS more fully into NOAA was to increase the public visibility of the supervising agency at the expense of the Weather Service. Its official name was changed to "NOAA's National Weather Service," and when NWS receptionists answered the phone they were expected to use that phrase. In correspondence and documents General Johnson's primary title was now "Assistant Administrator [of NASA] for Weather Services." The NWS website was closed down and replaced by the NOAA website, with a link to the Weather Service home page. At NWS news conferences, the name and seal of NOAA, not the NWS, was now on the wall behind the speaker. Emergency weather radios were renamed "NOAA Weather Radios." Weather forecasting office buildings around the country were adorned by the NOAA seal on the outside wall, and the NWS seal—if visible—was relegated to a front floor mat. Weather Service T-shirts and caps were theoretically banned from NWS offices in favor of NOAA-marked items. When on the job administrators were supposed to wear an NOAA lapel pin on their suit coat, not the NWS counterpart—a practice D. L. refused to follow.

The crowning act of Lautenbacher's campaign to build up NOAA was a two-century birthday celebration for the agency in 2006–2007. The rationale given for celebrating the 200th birthday of an agency created in 1970 (a century after the NWS' beginnings) was that Jefferson's 1807 Survey of the Coast led to creation of the Coast Survey, later called Coast and Geodetic Survey (now part of the National Ocean Service). The anniversary's theme was "200 Years of Science Service, and Stewardship"; its observance cost $1.5 million, a sum several bureau administrators strongly felt could have been better spent on programs during a tight budget year.[25]

SAVING LIVES AND LIVELIHOODS

As we know, cell 1 of the mission mystique template calls for a central mission purpose that permeates the agency's belief system. The closest thing to an organic act for the National Weather Service is the 1890 statute that transferred the Weather Bureau from the Army to the Commerce Department. In essence, the law's charge at that time was to forecast weather and river conditions, inform the public of impending storms and floods, and maintain "sea-coast telegraph lines" and other meteorological assets. The first task corresponds to what we term as the daily companion role of the NWS, the second to the watchful guardian role, and the third to an underlying stewardship obligation to maintain the forecasting infrastructure that has become infinitely more complex in the modern era. Stated as it is, the mission is classified as specified in terms of our study. While not unitary, the three purposes are clearly intertwined: weather conditions must be predicted continuously in order to uncover looming dangers, and for that to happen the equipment must be working well.

Even though the NWS does not possess a modern-day organic act, it does have a formal mission statement:

> The National Weather Service provides weather, hydrologic, and climate forecasts and warnings for the United States, its territories, adjacent waters and ocean area, for the protection of life and property and the enhancement of the national economy. NWS data and products form a national information database and infrastructure which can be used by other governmental agencies, the private sector, the public, and the global community.[26]

The duality of "forecasts" and "warnings" in the initial sentence captures the first two of the 1890 trio of purposes, and "a national information database and infrastructure" in the second sentence is the present-day equivalent of observing instruments and telegraph lines. Yet the statement is lengthy and dull, and fortunately more arresting and compact language is often used. "Working Together to Save Lives" is the theme of the NWS strategic plan covering the years 2005–2010.[27] In his public speeches, General Johnson liked to use the phrase "saving lives and livelihoods" to convey the urgency of the watchful guardian role. To make that possible, he would often add the phrase that the agency must "be heard, be understood, be believed and be acted upon."

Both the strategic plan's title and General Johnson's words give much credence to the elemental public-protection function. This is a powerful concept, equal in weight to the heavy public safety responsibilities borne by police and fire departments. Yet to the average citizen the image of the Weather Service is one of issuing routine daily forecasts, a process that is so much a part of daily life that it is taken for granted. But almost every day serious storms or floods are being experienced somewhere in our large country, and without continuous meteorological monitoring watching out for them would be impossible. The net consequence is that, to outside eyes, society's urgent need as called for by cell 2 of the template is downplayed.

Also, citizens may forget the essential contribution the NWS makes to the economy. That has not escaped the attention of meteorologists and elected officials over the years, however. The 1890 statute mentions advantages to agriculture, commerce and navigation. The current mission statement speaks of protecting property and enhancing the national economy. General Johnson pointed out that livelihoods as well as lives are saved. Inarguably, the benefits of weather prediction are indispensable to safe transportation and a host of other economic activities, and entire books have been written on the subject.[28]

Moreover, weather information is itself a raw material for economic production. The agency's enormous daily output provides a cornucopia of planning and research information for corporate, academic and international users, who obtain NWS products free of charge electronically. Weather data are a public good that is distributed everywhere: to armies, navies, air forces, meteorologists, researchers, foreign and international weather agencies, and the private U.S. weather industry. The weather bureaus of many countries are not so generous, and charge significant fees for data services.

A final mission theme for the NWS that has gained significance in recent years is enlarged understanding of the implications of climate change for our planet. For decades the NWS and NOAA climate centers have been collecting and analyzing data on the subject. One of the Weather Service's strategic plan goals is to "understand climate variability and change to enhance society's ability to plan and respond." NOAA publicly anticipates that, over the next 20 years, "fundamental, long-term research on a broad range of global change issues will remain a high NOAA priority."[29] The issue is not whether global warming is happening, or whether research on it should be done, but who shall be the lead in doing it; at times the NWS has felt NOAA is trying to steal the global warming thunder, and in turn NOAA officials have suspected NASA of attempting to do the same. Ah, bureaucratic politics!

WORLD-CLASS WEATHER FORECASTING

A thesis of this book is that mission mystique emanates from the agency's work. The work of the NWS is to forecast the weather. We have discussed the extensive array of organizations and functions involved in this activity, without saying much about how it is actually done. Yet it is the unusual and even bizarre nature of weather prediction itself that makes it fascinating to those who do it. To appreciate this magnetic attraction, we need to learn more about how modern weather forecasting is accomplished.

A good starting point is to look at the local Weather Forecasting Office. Prior to the 1980s, weather prediction offices were situated in main cities or at county seats, like most field offices in government. Today's WFOs, however, are situated not in relation to population or government centers, but in accord with technical aspects of radar location. Each "county warning area"—a term held over from the old days—consists of a circular area roughly 300 miles across, with a Doppler radar tower planted at the center. The continental United States, Alaska and offshore areas are dotted with such installations; although most are operated by the NWS, some have been built and are manned by the Department of Defense or the Federal Aviation Administration (see Figure 3.1).

Each WFO is headed by a meteorologist-in-charge (MIC), comparable to a unit commander in the military. Second in command is the warning coordination meteorologist, who supervises the issuance of storm watches and warnings. Third in line is the science and operations officer, who keeps abreast of new equipment and conducts staff training. In addition, during any given eight-hour shift three operational personnel are on duty: the senior forecaster, who heads that shift's team; the general forecaster, who has main responsibility for the substance of forecasts; and the hydro-meteorological technician, the primary technician on hand.

The heart of the WFO building is its operations room, a usually placid space that can be transformed into a kind of "war room" atmosphere when a storm looms and a sense of urgency permeates the entire WFO. To have an idea of what actually goes on in this room, it is necessary to recount the revolutionary changes adopted in American weather forecasting practices just a few years ago. In a massive modernization program that cost billions of dollars and took more than a decade to accomplish, the U.S. system achieved world-class status. Five interlocked components were developed in this project, and by reviewing them the essentials of the forecasting process become visible.

Figure 3.1 National Doppler Radar Sites

Doppler radar sites are placed throughout the country and in outlying areas so as to give full weather forecasting coverage to the nation. Their positioning, based on radar range and terrain conditions, determines where weather forecasting offices are found, an unusual way to select where administrative field offices should be.

Source: National Weather Service, http://radar.weather.gov/.

Note: Some of these sites are operated by the Department of Defense or Federal Aviation Administration.

The Modernization of American Weather Forecasting

The first component is adoption of an advanced version of Doppler radar. Radar was first used to detect German aircraft headed for Britain during World War II. Following the war, radar equipment developed for the military was adapted for weather forecasting. However, its reflected waves produced scope images that revealed only the existence and rough outlines of rain formations or tornadoes. Doppler radar, invented later, in effect turned this still picture into a moving, three-dimensional one by detecting also the depth and motion of objects. This was achieved by making use of the Doppler effect: like the sounds made by fast trains, reflections received from objects moving toward the antenna register a higher wave frequency, and those moving away a lower one. This feature, along with high-resolution reflectivity, allowed the new radars to "see," in depth, objects as small as hail or even birds.

To use the new technology, known popularly as NEXRAD (Next Generation Radar) and technically named WSR-88D (Weather Satellite Radar-1988 Doppler), 159 ninety-foot towers were eventually built around the country, topped by 32-foot white spheres that can be seen for miles. The 28-inch dish antenna inside sweeps the horizon, and the captured data stream travels down the tower legs by cable into a bank of computers at the base, where it undergoes preliminary processing. It is then transmitted to the associated WFO by underground fiber optic or copper cable.

A second component of the modernization program was installation of automated information reporting systems at strategic points on the ground. These unmanned stations provide data on temperature, air pressure, humidity, wind speed and direction, visibility, precipitation and cloud heights up to 12,000 feet. They are often located at airports; one is adjacent to the Virginia Tech airport in Blacksburg and looks like a dirt mound about 15 feet high with protruding pipes. Nearly 1,000 ASOS (Automated Surface Observation Systems) around the country make and transmit measurements once a minute, and 1,300 less-advanced AWOS (Automated Weather Observation Systems) do so every 20 minutes.[30]

The third element was to integrate fully the detection capabilities of weather satellites into both Big Eye and Little Eye weather analyses. The weather space age began in 1960 with NASA's launch of Tiros I, the first successful weather satellite, in coordination with the weather and military communities. The technological aftermath of that step is currently embodied in two types of weather satellites. The Polar Orbiting Environmental Satellite, or POES, orbits at an altitude of

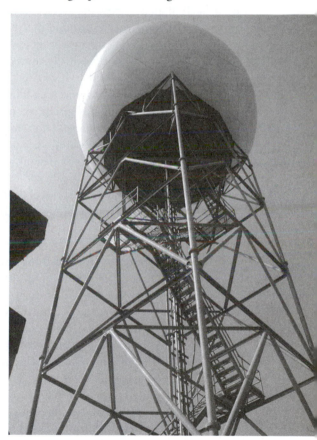

Doppler radar tower, Floyd County, Va. This is one of 159 such towers around the country, each of which is 90 feet high and has within its white sphere a rotating radar dish that "sees" up to 254 nautical miles. It is part of the NEXRAD forecasting system, mostly built in the 1990s.

Source: Photo by the author.

450 miles and passes over every square mile of the Earth's surface twice a day; with two of them operating, a total of four comprehensive swings occurs every 24 hours. The second type is the Geostationary Operational Environmental Satellite (GOES). Instead of orbiting the Earth, it remains in a fixed position relative to our planet at an altitude of 23,300 miles. One of the two GOES observes part of North America, all of South America and much of the Atlantic Ocean; the other covers the remainder of North America and the Pacific Ocean.[31]

A fourth technological breakthrough is the application of numerical modeling to weather forecasting. Prior to this achievement, weather prediction was largely a hit or miss process of extrapolating how and when fronts and other conditions would likely migrate across the surface of the land or sea. Ground readings of temperature, barometric pressure and precipitation assessed the progress of these movements. The resulting forecasts were essentially based on human observation and calculation, and were individually composed by each local forecaster. Numerical modeling changed all of that. It was developed in the decade following World War II by the "Meteorology Project," a kind of interagency Manhattan Project for weather. Predictions are now produced not by human beings directly but by their interaction with computers. These machines process incoming digitized data using complex mathematical models of weather situations that are derived from a combination of existing conditions and past experience. The models are dynamic and evolve constantly as data come in. The forecaster "tweaks" the models by altering assumptions on the basis of professional judgment and what nearby WFOs are predicting. Typically, four models operate simultaneously, allowing the forecaster to accept the scenario that seems most likely.

The fifth and final component of weather modernization that makes all this possible is the Advanced Weather Information Processing System (AWIPS), which consists of a vast digital communications network operating by high-speed wireless transmission and fiber optic cable. Current and predicted information flows in from myriad sources, is subject to analyses of various kinds, and then is deposited in an enormous, integrated National Digital Forecast Database (NDFD). It then turns around and feeds the outgoing forecasting process. As mentioned earlier, the funnel through which all communication passes is a central data-switching center in Silver Spring, Md., known as the Gateway.

From the perspective of the WFO, in its operations room forecasters observe consoles of four computer screens that show continuously shifting maps, graphics and numerical data that predict, based on NDFD data, how different models armed with slightly different assumptions forecast that county warning area's weather seven days ahead, based on the latest updates on current conditions. Weather reports derived from these data are automatically composed in written and voice form and distributed by the Internet, press wire services, commercial broadcasters, weather companies and special users like airports and shipping companies. If an emergency is looming it is also transmitted on NOAA All Hazards Weather Radio.

The moment of truth in forecasting comes when the forecaster has completed tweaking the models and, with his or her computer mouse, clicks on "publish to official" to lock in place the local input to the national NDFD grid and then hits "run/dismiss" to send it to Silver Spring and hence the world. That moment looms considerably larger when a dangerous weather condition is approaching and the mouse is placed on "send" and then, after confirming this is a real situation and not a practice, a watch or warning goes out that may indeed save lives and livelihoods.

THEMES IN THE NWS BELIEF SYSTEM

The makeup of the National Weather Service institutional belief system is a direct consequence of this sophisticated analysis and communication network and its operation. Within it several themes can be detected.

Intense Technical Dedication

The intrinsic motivation called for in cell 4 of the mission mystique template is palpably noticeable in Weather Service career professionals. It takes the form of a pattern commonly found among engineers and computer people—a "geek"-like obsession with things technical. For Weather Service personnel this obsession is meteorological. Forecasters eat, sleep and drink weather prediction. Often this fascination dates since childhood. Forecasters are fixated on the equipment and its continuous improvement. They talk weather all the time with each other. Their professional world is one of weather balloons, ASOS, AWOS, Doppler images, satellite passes and modeled systems of the moving atmosphere. Epistemologically and ontologically, they think objective measurement, traceable causation, statistical probability, the fickleness of Mother Nature and the progress of knowledge in solving her mysteries. When weather people go home after their shift or on weekends they delight in tinkering with personal weather equipment and checking to see if that day's forecasts were on target. But when serious storm conditions brew, they rush back to the WFO operations room, where they stand ready to work frantically around the clock.[32]

As for educational background, weather professionals are typically trained in meteorology and hydrology, along with substantial helpings of computer science, earth sciences, electrical engineering and statistics. Favored for permanent positions are those who hold degrees from universities with strong meteorology programs, such Penn State, Oklahoma, Missouri and North Carolina at Asheville. Many come to the NWS with prior service in weather services of the Armed Forces, especially the Air Force, Navy and Marine Corps. Truly serious careerists may go to European universities with famed meteorology departments for graduate study, as "Reich" Reichelderfer did in the 1930s. Whether educated abroad or at home, many attend and give papers at annual meetings of the American

Meteorological Society, National Weather Association, American Institute of Hydrology or World Meteorological Organization.

Residual Military Culture

The effects of the NWS' early military legacy linger to this day, tucked in the interstices of the American public weather enterprise. Of the agency's 140 years of existence, for 112 years, or 80 percent of its lifetime, it has been headed by high-ranking military officers, on active duty or retired.[33] Many field personnel have extensive military experience as well, often in a weather unit of the Armed Forces. New forecasting technologies have in several instances been inherited from the military or developed in conjunction with the Pentagon. Most Hurricane Hunters are manned with Air Force crews, with the remainder by uniformed members of the NOAA commissioned officer corps.

The military discipline sought by Representative Paine at the organization's founding is, to a substantial extent, still present in the institution. The MIC who heads each Weather Forecasting Office has authority akin to that of a company commander. He or she customarily conducts a "station meeting" each workday morning. WFO shift teams resemble the infantry squad in terms of size, organization, team spirit and comradeship. The Armed Services' habit of rotating upper-level leaders among posts is followed to some extent. Acronyms are incessantly utilized, as they are in the military culture. Following weather incidents where loss of life or unusual property damage have occurred, the performance of all relevant NWS personnel is reviewed in what is called a *hot wash,* a military term for a post hoc investigation that occurs after airplane crashes or similar events. Although medals are not given out for bravery, bronze, silver and gold awards are granted to units that perform admirably under emergency conditions. When General Johnson toured WFOs and the specialized NWS centers, he followed the military custom of "palming" merited personnel, i.e., transferring when shaking hands a large commendation coin with the NWS seal on one side and the NOAA emblem on the other.

An Ahistoric Outlook

Despite the Weather Service's rich history as an institution, its leadership does not show serious interest in celebrating it, as required by cell 6 of the template. Two books on the history of the NWS have been privately written, but they are 40 years old.[34] No official agency history exists, and no directors have seemed to publish their memoirs. There are no historic photographs in lobbies or offices, and no historic plaques, monuments or building names of which I am aware. I have not encountered evidence of anniversary celebrations of either the 1870 or 1890 founding. The agency has no national museum and only a few individual collections of old equipment. In my talks with NPS personnel I have encountered little knowledge of the weather enterprise's key figures, such as Joseph Henry, Cleveland Abbe, Increase Lapham, Halbert Paine or Albert Myer. The training of Weather Service employees, which is extensive and ongoing, does not include significant coverage of the agency's past. The curriculum of the NWS training center in Kansas City covers many management, leadership and technical topics, but the only aspects of agency culture that are conveyed derive from asking participants to tell stories about employee experiences that seemed to hold a lesson.

In short, the Weather Service lives in the present as it prepares tomorrow's forecasts, and in the future as it adopts new technologies and studies climate change. It is unfortunate that memories of early events like weather signs on the Smithsonian Castle, fatal storms on the Great Lakes and air mass theories from Norway are not introduced to help define institutional identity and reinforce employee pride. The Weather Service is unique among our six agencies in the degree to which its history is neglected; perhaps this characteristic is simply an outgrowth of a culture that is skewed in a "hard" technical direction rather than a "soft" humanistic one.

A Penchant for Improvement

By contrast, the penchant for looking ahead, relevant to cell 9, exerts a very strong influence. A number of single-loop organizational learning activities take place in WFOs on a continuing basis. Generally once a week the science and operations officer gives a lesson to all staff on new equipment and procedures. In effect, he or she is the resident teacher, solving technical problems whenever they come up. As for the WFO leadership team, the meteorologist-in-charge conducts a periodic learning exercise called "360 degree feedback." The MIC meets privately once a quarter with each supervisor to discuss, in frank terms, current issues of the workplace and the conduct of both parties regarding them, including that of the MIC. Any significant items that emerge from this mutual exchange are then noted for remedial action and follow-through if needed. If appropriate, the issues so identified are brought up for discussion at one of the morning station meetings, with names withheld if necessary.

On the quality of work itself, during benign-weather days many man-hours at the WFO are devoted to evaluating the accuracy of predictions made in the recent past. This is done by comparing forecasts issued with subsequent weather conditions. This process of self-checking is known as validation; the results are compiled and sent forward for inclusion in consolidated reports from throughout the national system. Breakdowns of the data are then distributed throughout the organization, allowing each WFO to see how it compares in performance. Noticeably low verification figures result in corrective action.

Table 3.1 NWS Performance Summary for FY 2008

	Target	Actual
Lead time for tornado warnings (minutes)	11	14
Accuracy of tornado warnings (percent)	67	72
False alarm rate on tornado warnings (percent)	74	75
Lead time for flash flood warnings (minutes)	48	77
Accuracy of flash flood warnings (percent)	90	91
Error in predicting hurricane track, 48 hours prior (nautical miles)	110	86
Error in forecasting hurricane intensity, 48 hours prior (knots)	14	14
Accuracy of next-day precipitation forecasts (percent)	29	33
Lead time for winter storm warnings (hours)	15	17
Accuracy of winter storm warnings (percent)	90	89

Source: GPRA performance measures given in NOAA Blue Book (Budget Summary), chap. 1, 1–22, obtained online at www.corporateservices.noaa.gov/nbo/FY10_BlueBook/.

Table 3.1 indicates agency-wide performance data for FY 2008, prepared in this instance for compliance to the Government Performance and Results Act. It should be noted that targets were met or exceeded in all computations with exception of the tornado false alarm rate and the accuracy of winter storm warnings. The results of such measures are kept over time in order to identify long-term trends. Between 1978 and 2002, for instance, the average lead-time for tornado warnings rose from three to 13 minutes and for severe thunderstorms from six minutes to 18. In the same period, the accuracy of warnings went up from 22 to 72 percent for tornadoes, and from 25 to 65 percent for severe thunderstorms.[35]

With respect to double-loop organizational learning in which the source of problems is sought out, a Weather Service example is the service assessment. The purpose of this learning tool, a formalized kind of hot wash, is to conduct an independent investigation of a weather-prediction incident in which fatalities were significant or property damage was heavy. A team is assembled composed of an experienced MIC and other NWC personnel who were not involved, along with professionals from other federal agencies and/or state and local governments. A final report is prepared that describes the event, states findings of fact, provides recommendations for improvement and lists "best practices"—i.e., corrective behaviors that would keep the problem from happening in the future. The final report is widely distributed.

Two examples illustrate. One such report dealt with a multiple outbreak of tornadoes in the Midwest and Southeast on Veterans Day weekend in 2002. Seventy-six separate funnel clouds killed 36 people in 17 states. Although the assessment concluded that NWS personnel performed well overall, because of the concentration of storms the principal forecaster at the Storm Prediction

Center was unable to authorize watches with sufficient lead times. The report recommended altering the rules so that the approval of watches could hereafter be made by multiple senior forecasters.[36]

A second service assessment dealt with the results of wind-driven forest fires that broke out on the coast of Southern California in fall 2003. Twenty-two people were killed and 740,000 acres blackened. Prior notification of citizens and firefighters was adequate, but because crucial Weather Service buildings were consumed by the fire, the public was not adequately informed about shore wind patterns, and much confusion resulted. The report recommended that in the future dry brush near NWS facilities be removed and a supplemental teleconference studio be made available in Los Angeles.[37]

The National Weather Service is committed to a change-anticipating philosophy as well, in keeping with triple-loop organizational learning. As one would expect, this future orientation relates to new technologies. With respect to Doppler radar, a near-term innovation being sought is what is called dual polarization, an advance that would capture images on a vertical plane as well as horizontal. A more long-term hope is to introduce phased-array Doppler radar, which—instead of projecting a single beam at successive layers—would emit, simultaneously, multiple beams at varied frequencies, thus "seeing" like a fly's composite eye.

In addition, several over-the-horizon innovations are being discussed. Eventually forecasters want hurricane storm modeling to incorporate internal winds at all levels, the rate of vortex air circulation, and ocean wave action and temperature. Another proposal is to send drones into hurricanes when it is too dangerous for a WC-130J. Other wish-list items are airport-specific forecasts that cover icing, turbulence, low ceilings and visibility, and a capacity to detect lightning strikes thousands of miles away.[38]

A Citizen Army

In the book's opening chapter I noted that no contradiction exists between dedicated bureaucracies and their strong ties to networks and partners. As with the National Park Service, the point definitely applies to the National Weather Service. A large manpower force, numbering approximately 11,800 volunteers, assists the Weather Service across the country each day. It is a trained and disciplined group of unpaid citizens to whom the government loans equipment to perform small but important actions on behalf of the weather enterprise. Traditionally, these volunteers have been called Cooperative Weather Observers, a name in the process of being changed to NERON, or NOAA Environmental Real-Time Observation Network.

The job of these observers is to see to it that temperature and precipitation information in their immediate vicinity is reported to the nearest WFO each day.

Most are retired senior citizens or persons who carry out their duties before going to work. Others are employees of local governments who report in while on the job. At one time, observers used a mercury thermometer, glass rain gauge and snowboard, and telephoned the readings in personally by 7 a.m. Now most supervise data collection by an electronic temperature sensor and Fisher Porter Rain Gauge; the latter, which looks like a missile with its nose cone removed, is nicknamed the "white rocket" and weighs the liquid that enters its mouth every 15 minutes.

Many weather observers have been performing their duties for years, and close relationships develop between them and WFO technicians. Bonds are sometimes reinforced by publication of an observer newsletter and the distribution of Weather Service coffee cups, key rings or service pins. Each year the weather observer of the year is selected to receive the Thomas Jefferson Award for Outstanding Service. Ideally, observers are spaced across the country on a grid of one every 25 square miles, with an average of just under 100 volunteers per county warning area. The collection of such local observations is done in order to become aware of micro weather events that occur briefly in only one small place.

This citizen army consists of more than weather observers. Thousands of weather spotters, alternatively called storm warners, are trained to report any thunderstorms, tornadoes or flooding they encounter in their daily movements. Typically, the spotters are law enforcement officers, firefighters or EMS responders. Another complement to the army is ham radio operators who, in the event of a breakdown of all other forms of weather communication, are prepared to relay emergency information to and from the NWS and local first responders. In addition, local farmers inform NWS hydrologists on flooding conditions and the water permeability of the soils on their land.

An Industry Partnership

Organizational partners of the Weather Service include other weather-involved public agencies and organizations in the private weather industry. As mentioned earlier, NWS products are available free to the private sector, as well as to academic and international users. Much moneymaking potential lies in this free good, and it is not surprising that private enterprise has enthusiastically entered the field.

One role of the private weather industry is to be the principal disseminator of weather information and warnings to the American public. Television stations, newspapers and online forecasting services receive most of their underlying data from the NDFD, whose mammoth mosaic of weather information is designed so that users can freely manipulate data according to desired categories or formats.[39]

In large part because of the open policy of the NWS, another component of the private weather industry is the more than 400 companies that offer tailored predictions to agriculture, transportation, utilities, the energy sector and the insurance industry. Various enterprising firms have filled other niches as well. AccuWeather transforms NWS data into different formats, Digital Cycle sends localized weather maps and storm warnings to hand-held wireless devices and Oceanroutes produces forecasts for cruise lines. Weatherbug couples NDFD data with its own data sources to provide hourly, three-square-mile forecasts to paying customers. The Weather Channel, founded in 1982 and recently sold for $3.5 billion, can be seen on cable by 97 percent of American homes.[40]

The development of a weather industry that at times generates its own predictions raises public policy questions. Conservatives have argued that by continuing to perform its function of weather forecasting, government is competing unfairly with business. A more reasoned position, adopted by the NWS, is to welcome private enterprise to be the daily companion side of its work but not the watchful guardian side. Multiple predictions in a weather emergency could discredit all warnings, create uncertainty and cause hesitation in taking cover or evacuating a city. No longer would there be an authoritative voice that is heard, understood, believed and acted upon, in the words of General Johnson. Even NOAA has insisted that a ground rule of public-private weather collaboration must be that "government and industry designate the National Weather Service as the single official voice in the critical areas of severe weather, such as hurricane, flood and tsunami."[41]

THE PERILS OF A BIG PROJECT

Cell 8 of the template stipulates that the mission mystique agency possess sufficient autonomy to undertake policy innovation. As a technology-oriented, forward-looking institution, the Weather Service is continuously looking to improve the nation's meteorological infrastructure. This can involve very expensive and thus controversial projects, and it is in this realm that we can best assess the agency's degree of policy autonomy. The modernization project was, by far, the biggest single investment in Weather Service history, and hence its best test. It was initiated in 1989 by Dr. Elbert W. "Joe" Friday Jr., NWS director from 1988 to 1997. Informally known as NEXRAD but formally titled the Modernization and Associated Restructuring (MAR) project, Friday conceived of it as a "meteorological revolution" that would be comparable to the information revolution itself.[42]

A Slow and Expensive Meteorological Revolution

The undertaking was expected to take 10 years and cost $4 billion. It required close interaction with the Federal Aviation Administration and the Department of Defense. The antigovernment, budget-cutting administration of Ronald

Reagan, coming to a close at the end of 1988, had not been a supportive atmosphere for big steps forward in the weather realm; indeed, it had attempted to sell the Landsat satellite system to private enterprise, a step blocked by Congress.

The incoming Republican presidency of George H. W. Bush, however, was persuaded by the soundness of the proposal. The Department of Commerce and NOAA (not yet headed by Admiral Lautenbacher) supported it. On the Hill, Friday convinced the NWS legislative and appropriations subcommittees of the value of the investment. He argued that it would not only help the American economy but require fewer government employees as a result of productivity gains. The main opponent was the NWS Employees Organization, which said that MAR ignores the human factor in forecasting, continues the march toward privatization and will lead to lower operational budgets.[43]

Initial development of the NEXRAD system was begun in 1989 at the National Severe Storms Laboratory in Norman, Okla., with Sperry Corporation as lead contractor. After lengthy delays, cost overruns and disputes with a subcontractor, an experimental WSR-88D Doppler radar tower was linked to the Oklahoma City WFO. The results in terms of an improved radar view were described as "incredible" by the Oklahoma MIC. On one occasion his forecasters spotted a nascent tornado 20 minutes before it hit Kingston, Okla., 90 miles away, with the result that the only damage inflicted was minor injuries from flying glass.[44]

The first fully operational NEXRAD installation was completed at Sterling, Va., in 1992, adjacent to Dulles Airport. Over the next five years a network of 159 installations was built. During this period technical delays in AWIPS development were also encountered, along with some political flak. The GAO leveled the criticism that power backup systems for the towers were inadequate; a House subcommittee complained that MAR funds had been diverted to NWS operations during a budget squeeze. Then in 1997, after Director Friday took the dangerous step of warning that without additional appropriations the agency would have to delay modernization and lay off personnel, he was fired.[45]

Discontent Leads to the Weather Service Modernization Act

Yet the biggest political challenge to face the modernization program came from another source: towns that felt they were being left out of the Weather Service's augmented guardian role. From the earliest days of the program, community leaders told their members of Congress that the success in distant tornado forecasting achieved in Norman would not work in hilly country. As a consequence, several representatives opposed decommissioning of existing weather stations in their districts on grounds that this would leave their constituents unprotected. Friday responded that as new WSR-88D facilities came on line they were greatly enhancing prediction range and capacity, and that the total impact of the system must await completion of all its parts.[46]

Even though all informed parties agreed that the modernization project would eventually greatly improve weather forecasting, in 1992 a group of legislators bombarded by constituents convinced their colleagues to pass a law intended to hobble if not halt the modernization project. Euphemistically named the Weather Service Modernization Act, the statute is a model of congressional interference in a major technology project of the executive branch. The law required (1) each year's budget submittal by the Commerce Department to contain a detailed update on NEXRAD implementation plans; (2) certification by the commerce secretary that any closed NWS offices are not leading to degradation of local service; (3) review of such certifications by a special transition committee; (4) a report within six months on the size, coverage and type of all weather radars; (5) no added decommissions be allowed before Jan. 1, 2006; and (6) the National Research Council of the National Academy of Sciences be asked to review the project and report its conclusion on the alleged degradation problem.

The council accepted the assignment and recommended further study be made of forecasting coverage in parts of five states. The Commerce Department responded by forming a team of departmental and NWS representatives, which recommended that additional WSR-88Ds be built in five additional locations. By the time the NEXRAD network was completed in 1997, they were in place at or near all five sites.[47]

The modernization project, then, endured enormous difficulty and harassment over its lifetime. Even as late as 2005 a reporter for the *Miami Herald* was ridiculing the project as "rife with stumbles."[48] Yet, taking the long view, it was an astounding success. It took two years longer than expected and cost $4.5 billion instead of $4, but it revolutionized the art and science of weather forecasting. With the leadership of Joe Friday and the support of numerous key stakeholders, enough policy autonomy was carved out to bring together all of the elements of an immensely complex technologic system. Despite a concerted campaign against its presumed consequences by certain members of Congress, it would be difficult to argue that the autonomy that prevailed overrode the will of elected officials; the interfering statute was complied with at least minimally, and recommended adjustments in Doppler location were satisfied.

THIS INSTANCE OF MISSION MYSTIQUE

The National Weather Service met or did not meet the standards of mission mystique in the following ways.

Cell 1: Mission. The agency's mission is spelled out, albeit in archaic language, in the 1890 law that transferred the weather bureau from military to civilian hands. The mission's content is thus classified as specified. It consists of three interrelated components: what we are calling the daily companion forecasting role, the duty to be a watchful guardian against dangerous storms, and maintenance of the meteorological infrastructure. As time has gone by, the last-named task has expanded from keeping telegraph wires intact to building and operating a mammoth integrated system of weather observation and analysis. The crisp phrase "saving lives and livelihoods" elevates these purposes to the level of a critical and internally consistent mission.

Cell 2: Need. Yet it is easy for the general public to overlook the agency's importance. The need for daily weather forecasts is one of those quiet, bedrock services of modern government that stay in the background as long as they are well performed, much like delivery of mail. Minimizing the chance that people are caught on ice-covered highways, lost in snowdrifts while hiking, killed by a sudden tornado or drowned while boating is obviously of enormous significance. Yet when such conditions arise, subsequent attention goes to responding to the emergency, not the advance warning that mitigated its cost. This quasi-hidden character of the forecasting contribution applies as well to how it underpins the economy.

Cell 3: Reputation. The United States possesses a world-class weather forecasting enterprise. This is realized mainly by academic meteorologists, the private weather industry, civil and military aviation, and American agriculture. Weather experts around the world know how sweeping and far-sighted the NPS modernization program was and look to the day when the next phase of NWS leadership in the field can take place. While you and I often complain that "the weatherman" was wrong again for not forecasting rain today, we tend to be unaware of the remarkable gains in forecasting that have occurred in the past quarter-century: increasing the accuracy of thunderstorm warnings from 25 to 65 percent, for example, and advancing the lead time for tornado warnings from three to 13 minutes.

Cell 4: Motivation. NWS professionals eat, drink and sleep weather forecasting. They are technologic geeks who are passionate about their jobs, love their equipment and are turned on by how they can anticipate the chaotic behavior of Mother Nature. When major storms loom, they are ready at a moment's notice to abandon their homes for long shifts in the operations room. A level of discipline reminiscent of the military is present in the workforce that accentuates a "can do" attitude, and individuals and units are awarded for outstanding service. At the system level, thousands of meteorologists, hydrologists, computer scientists, researchers, managers, technicians and Hurricane Hunter crew members join together to keep a highly differentiated and physically decentralized enterprise working in a remarkably integrated way.

Cell 5: Culture. The agency's culture emanates from its unusual mission and does not depend on social markers like uniforms, flags or ceremonies. Instead, the culture is built around the applied science of meteorology and its rituals. These consist of issuing the seven-day forecast, disseminating watches and warnings, releasing weather balloons at 6 a.m. and 6 p.m., validating the accuracy of forecasts, training weekly at the WFO and interacting with industry partners, citizen observers and emergency managers. The operant symbols of the weather culture are the AWIPS console, Doppler tower, Fisher Porter gauge, ASOS-AWOS sensor stations, POES and GOES satellites, and the Gateway supercomputer through which all pass. The culture is, in short, distinctive for its reliance not on sentiment and status but on science and its tools.

Cell 6: History. Along the same line, the organization is absorbed by the exigencies of the present and the technologies of the future rather than wrapped up in memories of the past. The institution's founders are barely known by its current employees, and achievements of later leaders like Reichelderfer and Friday are not discussed. Museums of early forecasting relics are few and histories, memoirs and biographies seldom written. The identity of the institution lies not in the glories of the past but its self-acknowledged preeminence as a cutting-edge actor in today's meteorology. Hence in cell 6 of the mission mystique template the National Weather Service does not score well.

Cell 7: Contestation. The NWS does not encourage dissent at the employee level. Aside from an NOAA-wide online employee survey and the 360-degree feedback exercise for WFO leaders, there are no official channels for dissent. At the institutional level, the main source of opposition is the supervisory posture of NOAA. During the overlapping tenures of Admiral Lautenbacher and General Johnson, the former was a strong counterforce to the latter, and vice versa. Moreover, as NOAA sought to intensify organizational absorption of its constituent bureaus, NOAA supervision moved from being purely external to a semi-internalized check on the Weather Service. Probably the most significant restraints on NWS ambitions are the huge costs of desired infrastructure projects.

Cell 8: Autonomy. Over the years the NWS has enjoyed a considerable degree of policy autonomy, if for no other reason than the highly technical nature of its work. Most outsiders felt out of their league in trying to second-guess world-class experts. As the agency's reputation grew, so did an aura of respect for the institution's standing and credibility. It is precisely this attribute that allowed Friday to overcome all the obstacles thrown in the path of the modernization project. The great success of that achievement both demonstrated and reinforced the organization's ability to get things done. Although Congress insulted the agency by its "degradation" legislation, it did not threaten the project.

Cell 9: Renewal. Organizational learning and renewal are not occasional but ongoing in the Weather Service. The agency operates in an applied science field where the forward progress of knowledge is assumed and room for self-satisfied hubris or status-quo conservatism does not exist. A military type of habitual self-assessment is also present, as well as a parallel devotion to continuous training. Sufficient professionalization exists in the workforce that meteorologists and hydrologists attend national conferences in their fields, and the agency's national leaders take graduate degrees and can be internationally known. At the system level of performance, the organization continuously looks for new technologies and techniques to procure and deploy, should the requisite resources become available.

In conclusion, the National Weather Service falls short in varying degrees to the expectations of cells 2, 6 and 7, but excels distinctly in the remaining template attributes of mission mystique.

U.S. Centers for Disease Control and Prevention

Stewards of the Public Health

THE CENTERS FOR DISEASE CONTROL AND PREVENTION, or "CDC" as it is commonly called, is considered the lead federal agency for promotion of the health of the American public. It is staffed by people who, in the public health tradition, see themselves as being the good doctor not to individual patients but to whole communities and peoples. In carrying out this function, they pride themselves on their passion, determination and sense of responsibility. A quote exhibited prominently at the agency's headquarters in Atlanta, Ga., reads, "Think one hundred years in the future and ask, what will people wish we had done?"[1]

A BIOTERRORISM ATTACK

On Sept. 27, 2001, 16 days after the Sept. 11 terrorist attacks, 63-year-old Robert Stevens and his wife, Maureen, drove from Boca Raton, Fla., to Charlotte, N.C., to visit their daughter. As a photo editor for the *National Enquirer,* Weaver retouched pictures to accompany the tabloid's flamboyant stories.

While in North Carolina, Weaver and his wife hiked in Chimney Rock State Park, a promontory known for its spectacular sights of landscape and migrating birds. The next day he did not feel well, and on the trip home that night was sick to his stomach. By the time they got to Florida, he was running a fever and becoming incoherent. Maureen took him to a hospital emergency room in Palm Beach at 2 a.m. Thinking he might have meningitis, doctors ordered a spinal tap. But upon examining slides of the fluid they found what they suspected to be *Bacillus anthracis,* a bacterial organism routinely found in livestock but highly dangerous to human beings, especially when inhaled. On Thursday, Oct. 4, a state lab report confirmed the diagnosis of anthrax inhalation.

The CDC was immediately called, in keeping with the agency's established practice of providing federal assistance to state health departments on an immediate-response basis. Within hours a CDC investigative team was on its way from Atlanta, headed by Bradley Perkins of the agency's National Center for Infectious Diseases. The team's first objective was to locate the source of infection. Team members checked out his daughter's house in Charlotte, searched Chimney Rock for dead animal carcasses and telephoned hospitals in the Palm Beach area for reports of suspicious respiratory illnesses. They hit pay dirt when a call to Cedars Medical Center in Miami turned up a man in his 70s named Ernesto Blanco, for whom a nasal swab indicated the presence of anthrax. Blanco did not know Stevens socially, but he worked in the mailroom of the building occupied by the *Enquirer*. The team investigated and found the paper's mail bin to be contaminated with anthrax spores.

By Friday, Oct. 5, Stevens had fallen into a coma. He died that afternoon. An attending doctor quickly telephoned the CDC, where Sherif Zaki, pathology chief at the Infectious Diseases Center, was waiting for the call. Early the next morning he and fellow autopsy specialists were on their way to Palm Beach. Together with local medical examiners, they carefully opened Stevens' chest cavity to find it filled to the brim with a bloody fluid saturated with anthrax cells. Since such cells when exposed to the air turn into easily inhaled deadly spores, the doctors had donned protective suits and masks. At the conclusion of the procedure the instruments used were packed into the body cavity for cremation. Hours were spent afterwards decontaminating the autopsy room and its contents.[2]

An Investigation Mobilizes

On Monday, Oct. 8, Perkins and his team began a systematic investigation of the *National Enquirer* building. They swabbed surfaces, collected air filters and interviewed employees. One employee of the paper recalled that on Sept. 19 Stevens was seen examining, close to his face, a letter covered with fine, white, talcum-like powder. On Thursday, Oct. 11, the team looked for signs of an anthrax presence at area post offices. Some contamination was found, but no postal workers had reported in sick; nonetheless, antibiotics were offered to the 32 workers most likely to have handled *Enquirer* mail, even though by this time the incubation period for anthrax had passed.[3]

Meanwhile, the matter was building as a national news story. It was discovered that anthrax-laced letters had been received by four additional media companies, all located in New York City. These were the *New York Post* and the

ABC, CBS and NBC broadcast networks. A later reconstruction of events revealed that these pieces of mail, as well as the Stevens letter, had been placed in the mail stream at Trenton, N.J., on Sept. 18, and thereafter processed at the Trenton Postal Distribution Center. Two Trenton postal workers and several media employees became sick, but because they had been exposed only through the skin they survived.[4]

As this larger crisis unfolded, the CDC mounted the most extensive epidemiology effort in its history. Some 2,000 employees, nearly a fourth of the agency's staff, were enlisted. An emergency operations center was established in Atlanta to set agency policy, coordinate field operations, and provide 24-hour information and triage services. In addition to Florida, field teams were sent to New Jersey, New York, Connecticut, Maryland and Virginia. Groups were established back at Atlanta to support field operations in diagnosis and treatment, environmental contamination, laboratory testing and liaison with other agencies. The CDC's national network of public health laboratories and the National Strategic Stockpile of drugs and medical supplies were also brought to bear.[5]

Anthrax in the Senate

On Oct. 15 the anthrax crisis escalated to yet another level when, at 9:45 a.m., a female aide for then Senate Majority Leader Tom Daschle opened a taped envelope addressed to the senator at his office in the Hart building. It had been mailed Oct. 9 at Trenton and the return address was given as "4th Grade, Greendale School, Franklin Park, N.J. 08852." A letter, covered with a white powdery substance, said:

09-11-01

YOU CAN NOT STOP US.

WE HAVE THIS ANTHRAX.

YOU DIE NOW.

ARE YOU AFRAID?

DEATH TO AMERICA.

DEATH TO ISRAEL.

ALLAH IS GREAT.[6]

Senator Daschle's assistant, alert to terrorism dangers so soon after Sept. 11, carefully placed the letter on the office floor and called the Capitol police.

Officers arrived within minutes, and soon thereafter a Hazmat crew was present to secure the senator's office. It conducted initial anthrax testing, with positive results. Capitol medical personnel swabbed the noses of all occupants of Daschle's office and of Sen. Russell Feingold's nearby, and distributed Cipro antibiotic pills to all present. The aide who opened the letter was ordered to change clothes and decontaminate with soap and water. Because of these quick reactions, no one became sick.[7]

Over the next several days all congressional office buildings were closed and searched. The Senate did not convene and the House recessed early. Members and staff were moved to temporary offices near Capitol Hill or told to stay home. Tests conducted at the Capitol itself were negative, and the same was true with the Supreme Court and the White House. Traces of anthrax contamination were found, however, in several nearby mail-handling facilities of the government.[8]

While no further poisoned envelopes were immediately identified, in mid-November another anthrax letter was discovered in a drum of decontaminated mail intercepted in October. Also postmarked Oct. 9 and cancelled in Trenton, it was addressed to Sen. Pat Leahy of Vermont and contained a message similar to the one sent Daschle.

Another shoe fell on Oct. 19, when a worker at the U.S. Postal Service Processing and Distribution Center on Brentwood Road in northeast Washington was diagnosed with inhalational anthrax. This development was significant because this facility is the central receiving point for incoming mail to the government in Washington, D.C. Brentwood employs more than 2,000 people who process 3.5 million pieces of mail a day.

Despite the Brentwood discovery and two sick postal workers in Trenton, the Postal Service underplayed the threat. Postmaster General John Potter assured postal workers that large-scale "upstream" testing of mail for anthrax was unnecessary. The basis for this conclusion was that the CDC believed anthrax spores are too large to escape from sealed envelopes, making the opening rather than the processing of mail dangerous. This theory evaporated Oct. 21–22 when two more Brentwood postal workers, Joseph Curseen, 47, and Thomas Morris, 55, became sick and were taken to hospitals where they soon died of what was diagnosed as inhalant anthrax poisoning. The spores were obviously getting loose. Meanwhile, several other Brentwood workers also exhibited anthrax symptoms, as well as postal employees in New Jersey and elsewhere.[9]

It was not until Oct. 24, 20 days after the CDC responded to the Florida outbreak, that the CDC came into possession of a key piece of information that might have made it possible to avoid the deaths of Curseen and Morris. The FBI had taken a sample of the spores from the Daschle envelope to the Army's bioterrorism center at Fort Dietrich, Md., innocuously called the United States Army

Medical Research Institute of Infectious Diseases (USAMRIID). Scientists there found that this particular strain of anthrax was similar to one being worked on at Fort Dietrich itself. One of its qualities is that its spores are so tiny they can pass through paper and float in the air like a gas. Knowing this fact would have enabled the CDC and USPS to realize that postal workers can be infected by unopened envelopes, especially when squeezed by sorting and canceling machines.[10]

Disseminating Information

The public, too, was being kept in the dark. Journalists complained they were finding it impossible to get officials to talk about the subject, even without attribution. The reason was a post–Sept. 11 policy of the George W. Bush administration that all releases of information concerning national security matters must come exclusively from the White House or from cabinet secretaries. Secretary of Health and Human Services Tommy Thompson had authorized only one person, Anthony Fauci of the National Institute of Allergy and Infectious Diseases at NIH, to speak for the department. He appeared on talk shows several times while the CDC, chief responder to the crisis and the logical source of information, was banned from doing so. The agency felt this was not only a counterproductive gag order but a slap in the face; CDC officials suspected that Claude Allen, Thompson's deputy, was behind the move because of his hostility to its programs on safe sex and family planning.[11]

As dangers of widespread infection from these particular spores became known, information channels began to open up. Thompson ordered frequent televised briefings on the crisis, and for a time they featured, in addition to Fauci, CDC director Jeffrey Koplan. After a few televised briefings Koplan asked the CDC person most informed on the crisis to speak for the agency. This was Julie Gerberding, a relative newcomer to the CDC who was directing the agency's overall anthrax response. On television she combined a technical grasp of the problem with a remarkable degree of poise and speaking skills. Her performance was noticed by Secretary Thompson and President Bush, and the following year she became the next CDC director.

In the ensuing weeks, after thorough campaigns of decontamination and extensive investigation, the anthrax scare wound down, though the investigation did not close until February 2010, when the Department of Justice identified the late Bruce Ivins from USAMRIID as the culprit. All told, the attacks killed five people, sickened 17, involved distributing 30,000 doses of antibiotics and cost hundreds of millions of dollars. It also frightened a jittery nation into thinking a second Sept. 11 was under way. On Nov. 8, 2001, Homeland Security adviser Tom Ridge and President Bush toured the CDC campus in Atlanta and praised its personnel as "new heroes in America."

WARTIME MALARIA CONTROL

Whereas in nature anthrax seldom infects human beings, millions die from malaria every year. The reason is that malaria is borne by man's ubiquitous enemy, the mosquito. Battling this plague and its perpetrator was how a predecessor to the Centers for Disease Control and Prevention was brought into existence. On April 27, 1942, Dr. Joseph W. Mountin, director of the Bureau of State Services in the Public Health Service (PHS), instigated the creation of a program to conduct mosquito abatement and battle malaria in the southeastern United States so that military training camps, supply depots, shipyards and factories in the region would not be hobbled by the disease. The program was called Malaria Control in War Areas (MCWA), and reported administratively to Mountin's Bureau of State Services. The first director he chose for the MCWA was Dr. Louis L. Williams, the top PHS specialist in malaria.[12]

Within the 15 southeastern states of MCWA's original jurisdiction (plus Puerto Rico and the Virgin Islands), some 900 "war establishments" or pieces of territory were identified for action. These were grouped into 250 "war areas," each of which was supervised by an area supervisor who in turn reported to a state MCWA administrator. For the task Williams assembled a workforce that eventually numbered 4,300. This included 300 members of the PHS commissioned officer corps, a small, uniformed service comparable to the one noted in the National Oceanic and Atmospheric Administration.

Two professional groups dominated the project: engineers, who oversaw the digging of ditches and the draining of swamps, and epidemiologists, who tracked cases of malaria infection by anopheles mosquito and devised programs of control. Since epidemiology was a new science at the time, MCWA established a training program in the field, and obtained surplus trucks from the Navy and picks and shovels from the now-defunct Works Progress Administration. Office space for the MCWA's central office was not available in wartime Washington, so Surgeon General Thomas Parran placed it in Atlanta, in parts of two downtown office buildings.

This temporary wartime agency succeeded in its mission. Within two years malaria was no longer a threat to the war effort. In the wake of this success, Williams and two successor MCWA administrators—his brother C. L. Williams and then Mark D. Hollis, a PHS civil engineer—looked for new worlds to conquer. They took on another mosquito, aedes, the vector of dengue and yellow fevers. A program on typhus in Washington was transferred to Atlanta. As transcontinental aviation expanded they inaugurated a spraying program for commercial aircraft landing at Atlanta. When dysentery broke out in a mental hospital in Alabama, an investigative team was sent in to deal with the event and a public education program was launched to warn citizens not to let larvae breed in rainwater standing in barrels and old tires.

An overseas dimension to the MCWA emerged as well. Louis Williams was sent by the War Department to Algeria to devise plans on how to reduce the incidence of infectious disease among troop units that would soon be invading Italy. While in North Africa he ran into Justin Andrews, the Army's foremost expert on malaria. One day the two found themselves sitting under a palm tree discussing the possibility of creating a permanent public health agency in the federal government after the war was over. Their idea was that it would be devoted to the abatement of all communicable diseases. Since Atlanta was already Williams' home base and Andrews had ties with Emory University, they agreed that this city would be the ideal location for such an institution.[13]

ESTABLISHING THE CDC

The concept of turning MCWA into a permanent communicable disease agency was met with enthusiasm by Mountin back in Washington. As it happened, he

Poster for a malaria abatement program in the U.S. South during World War II. Based in Atlanta, the MCWA successfully protected Army camps and defense factories. This inspired federal public health officials to create a permanent peacetime equivalent to battle infectious disease.

Source: Photo by the author.

too was thinking about a postwar MCWA. He advocated in memos within the PHS that several centers be created around the country to advance, in a comprehensive way, the health of the general public. He proposed Atlanta as the ideal headquarters location. His aim was to continue the MCWA's combination of laboratory science, control of infectious disease and environmental sanitation. The National Institutes of Health (NIH), proud of its lead role in medical research, had to be persuaded that the new entity would not do basic medical research and thereby invade its turf. In deference to NIH, Mountin and Mark Hollis dropped their earlier thought of naming the new

THE FOUNDING
OF CDC–1946

COMMUNICABLE DISEASE CENTER

Exhibit honoring Joseph W. Mountin, founder of the CDC. It is located in the communication building of the agency's headquarters in Atlanta, Ga. A Rear Admiral in the Public Health Service Corps of Commissioned Officers, Mountin's uniform, sword, and microscope are displayed.

Source: Photo by the author.

entity an institute and instead called it a center. On July 1, 1946, Surgeon General Parran signed an administrative order establishing what was called the Communicable Disease Center. As an internal unit within the PHS, no organic statute was necessary.[14]

Hence Rear Adm. Joseph W. Mountin of the Public Health Service Corps of Commissioned Officers must be considered founder of the CDC, even though he was never employed by the organization. Born in 1891 and active until his death in 1952, Mountin spent the first part of his career in the PHS quarantine service, later worked in state health departments, and as a sideline published a number of academic papers. In 1931 he returned to Washington and in a few years became head of the PHS Bureau of State Services. Today an exhibit containing photographs and Mountin's uniform and sword is found in an agency museum at CDC headquarters.

Initially, the CDC was the MCWA with a different name. Hollis was named director. He left office in a few months and was replaced by Raymond A. Vonderlehr, former chief of the PHS' vaunted Venereal Disease Division. At that time syphilis and other venereal diseases were a top priority in the federal public health world, and this appointment gave the infant agency some stature. When Vonderlehr departed in 1951 he was replaced by Justin Andrews, who had, along with Williams, dreamed in North Africa of what would become the CDC.

The CDC's activities, including an emphasis on malaria control, continued to be directed from Atlanta. Yet, as with its wartime antecedent, programmatic restriction was not in the new agency's blood. The CDC began to extend its epidemiologic purview to all diseases of zoological origin, including amebiasis, filariasis, hookworm, plague, sand-fly fever, and forms of diarrhea and dysentery.

Before his death Mountin was urging an even broader scope to the agency's work—coverage of every communicable disease other than tuberculosis and venereal diseases, whose programs were presumably immovable from Washington. In a few years these too would migrate to Atlanta, as typhus had done in the MCWA days.

Program growth required more space. When a large new federal building was erected in Atlanta, the CDC took over an entire floor. Beyond Atlanta, by 1949 the CDC occupied structures in Montgomery, Ala., and Savannah, Ga. Despite the objections of turf-conscious NIH, the importance of high-quality, in-house laboratory research led to creation of a Laboratory Division, which, along with the Epidemiology Division, became the heart of the agency in its early days. Meanwhile, the MCWA tradition of a widely dispersed field presence was attained; by 1956 CDC staff worked in 31 states and Puerto Rico, and close ties were maintained with state and local public health departments.[15]

The Epidemic Intelligence Service

The early MCWA commitment to epidemiological training was renewed in 1949 when an associate professor from Johns Hopkins University, Alexander D. Langmuir, was recruited by the CDC. He became head of the Epidemiology Division and remained in that position until his retirement in 1970. In time Langmuir's name became nearly as important to the history of the CDC as that of Joseph Mountin. Struck by the deficiency of epidemiologists available to respond to infectious disease outbreaks, Langmuir created, at Mountin's suggestion, what was called the Epidemic Intelligence Service (EIS).[16]

Ever since, the EIS has been a key institution within the CDC. Similar to the residency following medical school, enrollees are young physicians, nurses, epidemiologists and PhDs who get practical field experience while capping off their professional education. Langmuir demanded three criteria for admission: be as bright as possible, be aggressive in personality even to the point of abrasiveness, and be enthusiastic enough to be ready to go anywhere at any time. Enrollees are hired for a period of two years, with a first-year and second-year class enrolled simultaneously. When they complete the program, in lieu of a graduation ceremony an EIS-sponsored, academic-style conference is held to which public health professionals come from far and wide. Because of their intense experiences together, EIS trainees develop close camaraderie and desire to remain part of the CDC heritage; as a result, each class leaves behind in the agency museum a unique photo montage. EIS alumni take up careers in the CDC but also other public health organizations and positions in academia around the country and world. Three former EIS members have become directors of the CDC, and two have served as surgeon general.[17]

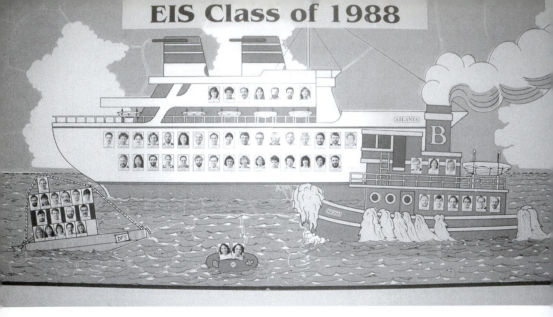

Graduation collage for the Epidemic Intelligence Service, class of 1988. The EIS was founded by Mountin and Alexander D. Langmuir, longtime head of epidemiology at the CDC. It is a demanding two-year practicum in which "disease detectives" learn to respond to sudden outbreaks.

Source: Photo by the author.

Achieving National Fame

Another legacy of Langmuir is a publication known as *Morbidity and Mortality Weekly Report*, or *MMWR*. The origins of this small weekly publication can be traced to 1878, when the Office of the Surgeon General began producing its *Bulletins*. A more immediate ancestor is a weekly report of health data put out by the National Office of Vital Statistics. In 1961 Langmuir persuaded the surgeon general to transfer the publication to the CDC as part of a proactive national disease surveillance system.

A kind of national bulletin board for health information, *MMWR* reports each week the latest disease and death statistics from every state and territory, which are compiled in tabular form. Each issue also includes short articles on current health issues, editorial comments on the public health scene and notices of new studies or publications. The *Report* is distributed widely throughout the world in hardcopy and electronically, and to an important degree has put the CDC on the map as a lead health agency. The agency also publishes a prestigious monthly journal of scholarly articles, *Emerging Infectious Diseases*.[18]

The event that brought fame to the CDC among the general public was its involvement in the poliomyelitis epidemic of the early 1950s. During that frightening episode in American public health history, communities throughout the nation became terrified of lifetime paralysis in children or young parents.

The deadly nature of the disease was dramatized by how serious victims were kept alive in huge iron lungs. In addition to conducting research, the CDC's most famed involvement in the epidemic was through Langmuir's EIS. One of the contributions of its epidemiologists was to discover via systematic surveillance that a favored gamma gobulin treatment is ineffective for true cases of polio, as distinguished from related diseases that cause temporary but not permanent paralysis. Another was to verify the effectiveness of a vaccine discovered by Dr. Jonas Salk that eventually brought the disease under control. When six children who had been given the Salk vaccine contracted polio, EIS teams headed off public dismissal of its efficacy when they found that all six had been inoculated by a serum from one pharmaceutical company, Cutter. The reason was that its output contained live rather than deactivated virus. Continued surveillance by the CDC made it clear that, when properly prepared, the Salk vaccine was not only safe but 75 percent effective.[19]

Thus, in a decade or so, the new CDC had done quite well in establishing itself as a public institution. It had built upon its progenitor's legacy, broadened its portfolio of disease activity, developed significant laboratory capacity, competed successfully with the rival NIH, seduced several federal disease programs to Atlanta, hired the most brilliant epidemiologist in the country, created a unique corps of disease detectives, established the beginnings of a national surveillance system and guided a high-stakes national vaccination program to eventual success. Now only one more thing was needed: obtaining a decent institutional home.

CDC Headquarters

Two Atlanta figures associated with the Coca-Cola Company opened the way for this possibility: Robert C. Woodruff, chairman of the board of the Coca-Cola Company, and Dr. Glenville Giddings, an Atlanta physician, professor at Emory University and medical adviser to Coca-Cola. Giddings had known Mountin and Hollis since the CDC's establishment in Atlanta in 1946, and both he and Woodruff were interested in controlling malaria. As a result of these personal relationships, helped by the fact that the Coca-Cola chairman had been a member of the Emory University board of trustees for many years, the university offered to sell for the token amount of $10 fifteen acres of land next to its campus to the CDC for its headquarters. The offer was snapped up, and the approximately 1,000 persons then employed by the agency each donated a penny toward the purchase cost.

A large headquarters building was planned for the property, along with several allied structures. The needed appropriations from Washington were not forthcoming, however, and a wartime presidential order not to finance government buildings for other than defense purposes remained in effect. After years of inaction and the worsening deterioration of the CDC's scattered buildings, Woodruff telephoned his old golfing partner, President Dwight Eisenhower, and demanded to know why construction was not under way on the donated property. The White House prodded the surgeon general on the matter, and an appropriation was soon enacted. More hurdles and delays stood in the way, however, until Rep. John E. Fogarty, chairman of the relevant appropriations subcommittee, came to Atlanta to see for himself the conditions under which the agency was operating. He declared them "deplorable" and "inexcusable," and soon the funding became available. On Sept. 8, 1960, 13 years after the land donation, a new headquarters building was dedicated.[20]

A MISSION IN FLUX

Unlike the National Park Service and the National Weather Service, the CDC's mission has never been spelled out in law. There is no organic act or other statute that states its purpose. The MCWA was internally created by the PHS as a temporary program and the Communicable Disease Center was established by administrative order of the surgeon general. Although many laws have since been enacted that concern the agency, none fill this void. Hence the CDC's mission is an example of what we are calling the acknowledged rather than specified type. What is being acknowledged in this case is, of course, the public health function, which is performed routinely in public-sector jurisdictions at all levels of American government and around the world, including at the U.S. Public Health Service, the CDC's original parent agency.

One great advantage of an acknowledged over a specified mission is that its coverage is elastic. Over the decades the CDC had taken notable advantage of this feature, and herein lies a fundamentally important characteristic of the CDC as a mission mystique agency. From the very beginning, including the MCWA period, it has been a governmental organization whose mission is in flux. Its stated and unstated purposes have grown over time, very significantly. The effect of this change has been to accumulate new programs while not discarding old ones.

The consequence has been radical mission growth. Scholars often call this "mission creep," which they ascribe to an inevitable tendency in bureaucratic organization. A less disparaging characterization would be "mission in motion," with the motion's direction always being upward. No matter how we describe it, mission expansion is more strongly present in this agency than any of the others studied in the book. Because of its importance in understanding the Centers for Disease Control and Prevention, the next several pages of this book are devoted to recounting important mission-expansion steps taken over the last four decades. This will be done by tracing program developments during the tenures of the three most proactive directors the agency had during this period. They are David J. Sencer, William H. Foege and Julie L. Gerberding.

THE SENCER ERA

David J. Sencer, the ninth director of the CDC, served from 1966 to 1977. A medical doctor once diagnosed with tuberculosis, early in his career Sencer worked to improve the health conditions of migrant workers in Idaho as a member of the PHS commissioned officer corps. Later he joined a project studying outpatient treatment of victims of his own disease in Georgia. Following a stint in the PHS Bureau of State Services in Washington, Sencer was transferred to the CDC in Atlanta when the tuberculosis program moved there in 1960. After several years as deputy director, he advanced to the lead position. Known as a consummate bureaucrat with keen intelligence and a prodigious memory, Sencer loved the job, knew the CDC inside and out and ruled it with a firm but benevolent hand.[21]

One of the major aims of Director Sencer's 11-year tenure was to "broaden domestic horizons" at the agency, to use his own words.[22] This was done in several ways. Langmuir's increasingly well-regarded surveillance activity was expanded to include several additional diseases, such as leukemia, ebola, rubella, shigellosis, hepatitis, tetanus, trichinosis and, after it was finally isolated, Legionnaire's disease. Following creation by Congress of a grant program for mass inoculation of children, the CDC was given responsibility for handling measles. Within three years the annual number of measles cases dropped from 262,000 to 22,000. Another innovation was to make a conscious effort to move the organization beyond infectious diseases to chronic ones, such as heart trouble, cancer and diabetes. Efforts to ameliorate the effects of environmental toxins were also made, in such realms as rat control and removal of lead water pipes in urban areas. Still another new thrust was the prevention of disease in the first place; measures in this category included water fluoridation, nutrition surveys and analyses, birth defect research, and anti-smoking education.[23]

It was well understood in Washington that the agency's mission was expanding. In 1968 a departmental reorganization elevated the CDC from being a division of the Public Health Service to individual bureau status within the Department of Health, Education and Welfare. This put it on an equal organizational footing with NIH and the Food and Drug Administration. A temporary name change was made from Communicable Disease Center to National Communicable Disease Center. Then in 1970 the agency was renamed again, so as to recognize how much the mission had transcended communicable diseases; now it was called the Center for Disease Control, a choice of wording that reverted to the familiar initials.

Smallpox Eradication

Another major contribution of Sencer's directorship was to augment the CDC's international reputation. This was done on several fronts, of which the most dramatic was a smallpox eradication program carried out in Africa and other continents. Langmuir, always on the lookout for new horizons, advised one of his newly minted EIS officers, J. Donald Millar, "to keep an eye on smallpox around the world." Millar took this assignment seriously and conducted research and monitored smallpox outbreaks. After a young Canadian man came down with smallpox in New York on the way home from Brazil, Millar was put in charge of an EIS team to collect epidemiologic intelligence in the New York City area. This case and a subsequent confusion of smallpox with chickenpox in the District of Columbia brought the disease's dangers to the attention of the American press.

Then an opportunity arose for Millar's group to try out ways to eradicate smallpox all over the world. The nation of Togo requested assistance in this regard, and the interventions taken by the CDC team enjoyed great success. The accomplishment was recorded in a film entitled *Miracle in Togo*, which circulated internationally. The health ministers of several African countries, aware of the CDC's success in measles vaccination in the United States, expressed interest in a program of immunization for the two diseases simultaneously. Doing both at the same time caused concern, so Sencer supported going ahead with smallpox, in collaboration with the U.S. Agency for International Development (USAID) and the World Health Organization (WHO).

This set the stage for creation of a smallpox eradication program at the CDC. Its goal was the almost unthinkable aim of completely eradicating one of mankind's worst scourges from the developing world. Millar and several other CDC staff, including William Foege, a future director of the agency, began conducting mass vaccination operations in several West African nations. Eventually, 300 CDC personnel were working on the project, including many under the

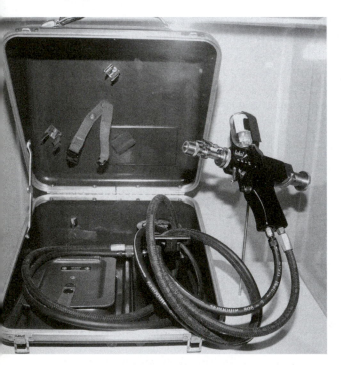

Jet vaccination injector used by CDC field personnel to combat smallpox in Africa and elsewhere in the world. Powered by a foot pump, it penetrated the skin without a needle. As a result of a CDC smallpox eradication campaign, the planet was declared free of the disease in 1981.

Source: Photo by the author.

aegis of WHO. Of great benefit to their productivity was a jet vaccination injector developed by the Army and adapted for the program; powered by a foot pump, it penetrated the skin without need for a needle.[24]

By means of this device and a simple bifurcated needle invented later, more than 150,000 people in Africa, India, Indonesia, Pakistan and Brazil were vaccinated from 1967 to 1972. While the initial strategy was to protect affected populations on a generalized basis, Foege and his colleagues discovered by a fluke that a more concerted approach was superior. In a Nigerian village where a smallpox outbreak had occurred but mass vaccination supplies had not yet arrived, the team went ahead and treated only those who had recently been exposed. To their surprise, the disease was quickly brought to a halt. This strategy, christened "eradication escalation," or E[2], then became the foundation of the rest of the smallpox campaign. On Oct. 26, 1979, the last documented and naturally occurring case was noted in Merka, Somalia. In 1981 the Global Commission for the Certification of Smallpox Eradication pronounced the world free of the disease.[25] It was one of the proudest moments in CDC history. In a speech on the achievement Sencer said:

> Anyone who has had an opportunity to participate in the smallpox eradication program will never forget the thrill of the achievement of eradication—to see that people can work together—all colors, all religions, and all political beliefs—to bring about the complete destruction of a disease. It is a very thrilling thing to have been part of this campaign. I don't think that anyone who has had anything to do with the program will ever forget it.[26]

The Tuskegee Experiments

Along with striking successes such as this, two setbacks occurred during the Sencer era. One was the Tuskegee study of untreated syphilis in African-American men. This project was launched in 1932 in Macon County, Ga., whose county seat is Tuskegee. Raymond L. Vonderlehr, former MCWA head and a 35-year-old officer in the PHS Venereal Disease Division (and later CDC director), specialized in cardiovascular syphilis and served as the project's field director. A hypothesis he wished to test was whether African-Americans were more prone to contracting this form of the disease than whites, and furthermore more subject to neurological damage. The poor, rural county of Macon had a particularly high incidence of syphilis, making it an ideal site for a longitudinal study of the effects of the disease over time, especially in its advanced stages.[27]

The project went on for 40 years, until national publicity forced its end in 1972. For its first 25 years the study was under the Venereal Disease Division of the Public Health Service in Washington, with the CDC in charge during its final 15 years after the VD Division was transferred to Atlanta. Overall, the experiment involved 399 male subjects with syphilis, with 201 in a control group whose members were initially free of the disease. The 399 individuals were not told they had syphilis but only "bad blood," and were subject to extensive periodic physical examinations that included painful spinal taps. Although technically any treatment at all would contaminate the study's assumptions, over time the participants were sporadically given the syphilis remedies available in the 1930s: neoarsphenamine, mercury, iron tonic and pink aspirin. These medications did little or nothing to halt the disease but gave the men the impression that their "government doctors" were helping them.

Contradictions within the study multiplied in 1943 when penicillin became available. It offered a true remedy for the disease but was withheld from the men on grounds that it would invalidate continuing observations. Moreover, even when it became clear that Vonderlehr's hypothesis about racial differences was not supported, he did not end the experiment but added the stipulation that autopsies be done on deceased victims to make sure. Far from keeping the experiment secret, between 1936 and 1973 Vonderlehr and other researchers published 13 professional journal articles from it.

For many years the Venereal Disease Division or the CDC did nothing to halt the project. Questions about the ethics of the project were raised by various parties in 1948, 1956 and 1966, but they met with little response. A second, more forceful complaint by CDC venereal disease interviewer Peter Buxtun in 1966 to William J. Brown, then head of the VD Division, elevated the issue to Sencer's attention. Brown and Sencer convened a panel of physicians who recommended only that the study's methodology be cleaned up and existence of the experiment discussed with members of the Macon County Medical Society.

Buxton did not accept the results. In 1972 he brought the matter to the attention of an Associated Press reporter who, upon telephoning CDC officials for confirmation, broke the story in *The Washington Times*. HEW appointed a citizen panel to investigate, and Sen. Edward Kennedy held hearings on the subject. A cry of moral outrage was heard around the nation. The project was immediately halted, and the CDC offered those participants who were still alive free health care for the rest of their lives. The agency did not apologize, but in 1997 an agency representative participated in a televised White House event in which President Bill Clinton did so, in behalf of the nation.

Rush to Immunization

Another public relations flap hit the agency during the Sencer era. In February 1976, laboratory reports were received on four cases of swine flu among Army recruits at Fort Dix, N.J. This was not the N1H1 strain of influenza that hit the world in 2009, but an earlier version whose properties were as yet unknown. What was so frightening about this disclosure was the possibility that it could lead to a repeat of the immensely deadly pandemic of 1918, which killed an estimated 50 million people worldwide.[28]

No one knew for sure. Under the circumstances, Sencer felt he had to announce the cases publicly and consulted experts inside and outside the agency. A memorandum prepared for HEW secretary David Mathews stated that "a strong possibility" existed of swine flu spreading widely in the coming months. The secretary then communicated to the White House that "projections are that this virus will kill one million Americans in 1976." President Gerald R. Ford quickly assembled a meeting of leading national authorities on the subject, who advised a national immunization campaign be undertaken immediately. Congress granted an emergency appropriation of $135 million, and what became known as the National Influenza Immunization Program was launched, with the aim of inoculating all 215 million U.S. residents.

Don Millar, of smallpox fame, led the program. He formed a task force, had a vaccine developed, acquired sufficient injectors and other supplies, mobilized state health departments, and set up administrative regions in the manner of the MCWA. In the rush of preparations, however, no new cases of swine flu cases appeared. Nonetheless, no steps were taken to reconsider or interrupt the program. To keep the public's faith President Ford received his personal flu shot on television. In 10 weeks nearly 50 million people were vaccinated—the most extensive public health immunization to that point in history.

The CDC continued to monitor for complications. In the third week of November, an immunized Minnesota man suddenly became sick with what was identified as Guillain-Barre Syndrome. This is a rare neurological disease with symptoms like polio, although less severe (it is sometimes called French polio). Within the next few days 30 more such reactions occurred in other states. This incidence rate was initially gauged as statistically insignificant, but further analysis concluded that the flu vaccine had probably caused the Guillain-Barre outbreak.

In March 1977, exactly one year after it had been announced, the massive immunization program was cancelled. New HEW secretary Joseph Califano decided in the aftermath of the affair to replace all his bureau chiefs except at NIH. Sencer's dismissal hit the CDC staff hard, and a futile petition was organized to restore him to office. Califano asked Professor Richard Neustadt of Harvard University to analyze the aborted immunization program so that the CDC and HEW as a whole could learn as much as possible from it. Neustadt's conclusions were hard-hitting. Although the decision makers were praised for their goodwill, high ideals, technical competence and dedication to the public good, excessive credence was given to conclusions based on meager evidence, too much was decided more quickly than necessary, personal agendas of the players interfered, and career employees were excessively zealous in trying to make lay superiors do right.[29]

Thus by the end of the Sencer era the CDC had achieved many fine things, including the worldwide eradication of smallpox. Yet its reputation had been sullied by not stopping the Tuskegee experiments and setting off a premature mass inoculation campaign. In hindsight, however, both disasters eventually did some good: raising awareness of human-subject research ethics and the need to be cautious before launching a nationwide vaccination campaign.

THE FOEGE ERA

William H. Foege replaced Sencer and served as director of the CDC between 1977 and 1983. After attending EIS and receiving the Master of Public Health (MPH) from Harvard, Foege, who planned to be a medical missionary, went to Nigeria to work in a Lutheran medical center. The onset of civil war there forced him to leave the country, and as a result he was recruited by Millar for the Smallpox Eradication Program. Eventually he took the program over and later served in India under WHO auspices. In 1975 Foege moved to Atlanta and became, in effect, Sencer's assistant and protégé. After Foege was fired Sencer recommended him to be his successor.

In his new job Foege faced many challenges: a demanding new Jimmy Carter administration in Washington, fallout from the swine flu debacle and insufficient appropriations to finance the agency's expanded portfolio of programs. Yet the new director received support from the assistant HEW secretary and surgeon general, Julius Richmond, a pediatrician who had founded Head Start. Also to Foege's advantage were his many connections to the world of public health and an outgoing personality that enabled him to attract its leading figures for advice and cooperation. Foege set out to use these resources to go on the offensive—by redefining the disease-prevention aspects of the CDC's work more emphatically and comprehensively.

A New Mandate for Prevention

In July 1977 a planning process was initiated on how the agency could best combat morbidity (sickness) and mortality among Americans. Foege sought recommendations around the country and received several hundred replies. A committee of 16 outsiders, with Millar as chair, drew from these ideas to produce a report entitled *Recommendations for a National Strategy for Disease Prevention*. Bound in a bright red cover and known by everyone as the Red Book, the report listed 12 preventable health problems considered of highest priority: alcohol abuse, cancers, heart disease, drinking water contamination, dental diseases, hazardous workplace exposures, infant mortality, car accidents, unexpected epidemics, hospital infections, smoking and preventable children's diseases. For each problem a strategy of intervention was outlined, such as health education, screening, fluoridation, prenatal services and lower speed limits.[30]

Foege then called for a second study to develop plans for implementing these ideas, this time involving representatives of other federal agencies as well as nongovernmental professionals. This resulted in a long report written in technical language. But Richmond was so impressed with its contents that he had a popular edition prepared, named *Healthy People: The Surgeon General's Report on Health Promotion and Disease Prevention*. (The term "Surgeon General's Report" was intended to equate the document with the highly influential 1964 document, *Smoking and Health*.) In the introduction, HEW secretary Califano noted that while between 1900 and 1970 deaths from major acute infectious diseases had plummeted, those from chronic diseases had skyrocketed. "We are killing ourselves," he said, "by careless habits, pollution of the environment, and allowing poverty, hunger and ignorance to persist."[31]

In effect, the Carter administration licensed the CDC to convert itself from a disease sleuth and technical adviser to the states to an activist policy advocate in the public health realm. Prevention is "an idea whose time has come," the report admonished. It contended that policy action is vitally needed in three areas: health services, such as family planning and reduction of sexually transmitted diseases; health protection, e.g., toxic agent control and fewer car accidents; and health promotion, e.g., reducing misuse of alcohol and drugs and curbing stress and violence. This interventionist manifesto even proposed specific numeric goals for the next dozen years: reduce infant mortality to nine deaths per 1,000 live births, bring adult deaths down to 400 per 100,000, and cut the average annual number of acutely sick days by the elderly to 30.

The third step in Foege's prevention crusade was to formulate specific objectives for ameliorating each problem and meeting each goal. As before, he convened a large body of health experts from the private and public sectors. The ensuing report, *Promoting Health/Preventing Disease: Objectives for the Nation* (1980), was a massive compendium of policy prescription. It analyzed the nature and extent of each of the 12 problems, indicated the prevention or promotion measures available to attack it, declared specific benchmarks of success, explained underlying assumptions and outlined possible tracking data. To illustrate with one example, the plan for reducing gunshot wounds advocated educational programs on firearm safety, improvements in trigger safety locks, use of wax bullets for target practice and standardization of state gun laws. Based on the assumption that fewer people would purchase handguns over the next 12 years, it predicted that the annual number of firearm fatalities would be reduced from 1,800 to 1,700.[32]

Presumably the participants in Foege's plans were sophisticated enough to realize that their mountain of ideas and scores of objectives could only be a starting point in the public policy process. Their true importance lay not in being exact blueprints for actual outcomes but a way to institutionalize a joint reframing of thought. In a retrospective article on the achievements of his administration, Foege spoke of how the staff began to think in terms of such concepts as "redefining the unacceptable" and cutting "the years of potential life lost."[33] The old public health nostrum of "prevention is the best cure" was raised to an elaborate and concrete level. Moreover, the likelihood of controversy was raised to the fore: Should the CDC—and its organizational parent, HEW—surge beyond the safe boundaries of professional medicine and advocate deep societal change? It appears that Califano and Richmond were anticipating precisely this step.

Redefining the Unacceptable

Indeed, a characteristic of the Foege era was a willingness to take on powerful players. When flu-stricken children showed symptoms of Reye's Syndrome, CDC investigators discovered they had all taken aspirin. Dogged pursuance of the matter led to the conclusion that the problem was the salicylates found in aspirin, a determination that infuriated Bayer and other pharmaceutical companies. In another instance, a vague but sometimes fatal set of symptoms that included fever, rash, low blood pressure, vomiting and diarrhea was noted in women of childbearing age. A staphylococcus bacterium was isolated and discovered to be present in tampons, particularly the Rely brand. Manufacturer Proctor & Gamble was forced to remove the product from the market, and the term "Toxic Shock Syndrome" joined medicine's vocabulary.[34] Several other examples can be cited of redefining the unacceptable: studying the effects of Agent Orange on Vietnam veterans; warning mothers against the use of infant formulas; issuing precautions about diet preparations; and pointing to the danger of transmission of measles within daycare centers, preschools, colleges, stadiums and theme parks.

HIV-AIDS

The most significant controversy under Foege had to do with a scourge that concentrated on two classes of social outcast: sexually active gay men and habitual drug users. Identification of the Acquired Immune Deficiency Syndrome (AIDS) and discovery of the Human Immunodeficiency Virus (HIV) that causes it were accomplished by many medical researchers and health institutions, but the CDC had a crucial role.

The problem initially came to the attention of the medical community in 1981, when the CDC received an unusual number of requests for pentamidine, a drug normally used to treat pneumonia. A preponderant number of these requests were for young adult males in New York and California. An EIS officer assigned to the Los Angeles County Department of Health investigated and found all five of the victims were homosexual. Just before the matter was reported in *MMWR*, two physicians in the CDC's Sexually Transmitted Disease Division (formerly the Venereal Disease Division) attended a conference in San Diego and discussed the question with gay physicians at the meeting. The subject seemed serious enough to establish a task force to conduct surveillance in Los Angeles, San Francisco and New York City. EIS officers with connections to the gay community interviewed single men lingering by rundown motels. Meanwhile, back in Atlanta, Dr. Donald Francis, a young hepatitis researcher at the CDC who had done his dissertation at Harvard on feline leukemia, wondered if, like the killer of cats, this disorder might be caused by an immunity-depressing retrovirus, a little-known organism at the time.[35]

Although the disease attracted little attention from the press, the number of cases of this newly recognized disease rose into the hundreds. In addition to gay men, drug addicts and hemophiliacs seemed to get it, as well as Haitian immigrants. It began to dawn on researchers that the disease may emanate not from a VD-like bacterium but could be a blood-borne agent transmitted by used needles and blood transfusions. The Red Cross and blood bank industry rejected this conclusion since it would discourage use of their services. Without proof for the theory, and with a loss of credibility arising from swine flu, the CDC was in a weak position to demand a crash research program into the problem. Budget cutbacks by the Ronald Reagan administration further limited what the CDC itself could do. Research went ahead in Europe, however. Early in 1984 the Pasteur Institute in Paris sent to the CDC two ounces of viral isolate from a patient with symptoms similar to AIDS. It was a retrovirus, just as Donald Francis had suspected. Parallel work in Belgium collaborated the finding. Science now knew what it faced from this new pestilence; it had become possible to mount an adequate response, which when launched became part of a worldwide endeavor of the international public health community.

Reorganization

The CDC's newfound assertiveness under Foege precipitated the need for an internal reorganization. It was happening anyway at the department level. By 1968 the Public Health Service had all but disappeared as a line agency. The surgeon general had been demoted from a bureaucratic power to health educator of the nation. In the wake of this change, Foege reported directly to his friend and fellow advocate Julius Richmond, now assistant secretary for health and scientific affairs and in a good position to make waves. This gave the CDC director the freedom to break away from the agency's long-standing organizational pattern of disease programs plus laboratory support. He remolded the organization by highlighting treatment of chronic diseases and disease prevention, bringing them to the same level of standing as the traditional infectious disease function.

Foege was inspired in part by a thematic approach taken by the Canadians in this regard, which treated public health as consisting of four emphases: biological, environmental, lifestyle and medical care. But an exact replication of Canada's approach would not work. After weeks of discussion with CDC staff, the epidemiology and laboratory programs were fused into a single Center for Infectious Diseases. This action caused considerable acrimony within each of these venerable divisions. Foege then assigned most of the remaining components to one of three new line units: Center for Chronic Disease Prevention and Health Promotion, Center for Environmental Health and Injury Control, and Center for Prevention Services. In another innovation, cross-cutting coordination offices were created for Epidemiology, International Health and Public Health Practice. The National Institute for Occupational Health and Safety (NIOSH), a pro-labor research unit seeking to expand workplace safety, was left as is.

Having converted one center into a family of multiple centers, Foege had the agency's overall "center" designation made plural. In 1992, under Director William L. Roper, the surge of interest in prevention begun by Foege was embodied in lengthening the name as well, by adding the words *and Prevention*. To satisfy demands that this alteration would not destroy the time-honored "CDC" nickname, Congress enacted a statute that required continued use of the initials.[36]

THE GERBERDING ERA

Julie L. Gerberding earned MD and MPH degrees at the University of California at Berkeley. In 1987 she founded an Epidemiology Prevention and Intervention Center at the University of California General Hospital in San Francisco and remained its director until 1998. From there she came to the CDC in Atlanta, where she initially served as director of the Division of Healthcare Quality Promotion and later as acting deputy director of the National Center for Infectious Diseases. Impressed with her performance during the anthrax episode, President George W. Bush nominated her to the Senate as CDC director in 2002.

Gerberding's era of leadership extended the visions of previous directors. She added yet another conceptual goal to the organization's roster of battling and preventing disease: achieving the best possible state of health for the nation. This idea shifts from earlier concentration on illness as a scourge that must be minimized to an emphasis on wellness as a precious resource that should be attained and preserved to the largest extent possible. Following this path goes far to redefine the CDC as society's activist leader in a campaign to seek the maximum possible quality of life, in health terms, for every citizen. This posture was hinted at in Foege's *Healthy People* report, but Gerberding recast the argument from illness avoidance to wellness possession. She stated her philosophy this way:

Each day at CDC, we try to imagine a safer, healthier world. A world where infants are born healthy and cared for—so, as children, they can arrive at school safe, well-nourished, and ready to learn. A world in which teenagers have the information, motivation, and hope they need to make healthy choices about their lifestyles and behaviors. A world in which adults enjoy active and productive lives in safe communities where they can remain independent and engaged with family and friends throughout their senior years.[37]

The Futures Initiative

After a year of study and discussion, Gerberding presented the first aspects of what she called the Futures Initiative. It posits four overall goals for the country. The first is "Healthy People in Every Stage of Life," which sets forth concrete objectives such as the United States ranking among the top five nations of the world in infant survival, a 95 percent rate of very good or excellent health for adolescents, and an increased average lifespan of two healthy life-years for senior citizens. The goal embraces an equity theme and aims to reduce health disparities between genders and among races.[38]

The second goal is "Healthy People in Healthy Places." This refers to having healthy environments for living, working and playing. Among the aims of this goal are to educate homeowners on environmental health (e.g., carbon monoxide, radon gas), to encourage walking and biking paths in communities for exercise, and to promote schools' requiring strict hand-washing procedures and providing fresh fruit and vegetables in lunches.

For many years the CDC has played a major role in the international public health realm, and the third Futures Initiative goal, "Healthy People in a Healthy World," speaks to this role in what Gerberding calls "health diplomacy." It targets health promotion through training health managers abroad and advising foreign governments and nongovernmental organizations, and the detection and prevention of diseases globally through surveillance and vaccination programs. In addition to smallpox, the CDC has responded to many overseas health emergencies, including Severe Acute Respiratory Syndrome (SARS), Lassa fever and the Marburg virus.

The final Future Initiatives goal is "People Prepared for Emerging Health Threats." Gerberding came to this issue via the anthrax crisis, and at the CDC was a loyal member of the Bush administration's team with respect to its war on terrorism, as well as emergency preparedness. The agency staffs 25 quarantine stations at international ports of entry around the country. Under contract to Lockheed Martin Corporation, a CDC Emergency Operation Center is continuously on duty and frequently conducts simulation exercises. Lockheed also maintains the CDC's National Strategic Stockpile, a repository for antibiotics, antidotes and medical supplies that can be drawn upon in an emergency. Located in secret, rotated places, the stockpile is primed to ship supplies to any disaster-stricken area within 12 hours.[39]

A Healthiest Nation

By 2008 Gerberding had developed a second phase of her Futures Initiative: to place on the public health agenda the aim of making America "a healthiest nation," i.e., not be exceeded in that regard by any country. In her speeches she would ask, "What can be accomplished in eight years and 59 days?" Her answer was achieving President John Kennedy's 1961 goal of placing a man on the moon and bringing him home safely before the end of the decade. Gerberding then paraphrased Kennedy's speech that set the moon-shot goal:

> I believe that this nation should commit itself to achieving the goal, before this decade is out, of becoming "A Healthiest Nation" and leading the way so that every Nation on Earth can to share in this endeavor. No single human project in this period will be more impressive to mankind, or more important in the long-range expansion of human development and equity, and none will be so difficult or expensive to accomplish.[40]

She would go on to say that three things may be learned from studying *Apollo*'s success: setting a goal that is audacious, inspirational and yet achievable; collaboration across sectors and among stakeholders; and an inspired workforce, adequate funding and sophisticated management. Gerberding told her audiences the CDC could meet these requirements, but not alone. Accordingly, she called for creation of a private-public "Alliance to make U.S. Healthiest" that would highlight health protection as well as disease care, call for systemic change in the ways of public health, launch a "Bring Health Home America" marketing campaign, and develop a "Healthiness Index" to measure progress.

A final component of her vision was to inventory research needs for achieving a healthiest nation. Gerberding estimated that science has defined interventions to prevent perhaps a fourth of the risk factors associated with leading causes of illness and death. Hence we need "to find tried and true solutions for the other 75%."[41] In 2006 the CDC published a guide on what researchers in all sectors and institutions of the public health enterprise should study through the year 2015. It describes the current state of science in seven thematic areas and outlines what is needed to meet 467 concrete public health objectives over the next decade, along with indicators for measuring progress toward each. Every project identified is cross-referenced to the four Futures Initiative goals. If nothing else, planning in Gerberding's CDC was audacious, elaborate and synoptic—even more so than in Foege's.[42]

Political Controversy

Like the activist directors before her who expanded the CDC's mission, Gerberding faced political controversy. One of her favorite causes was reduction of obesity in America. On one occasion a report issued by the agency stated that obesity contributes to 400,000 deaths per year. In response, an academic researcher in the field told a reporter that his best estimate was a fraction of this amount, about 26,000. A spokesman for a restaurant association told the press, "Americans have been force-fed a steady diet of obesity myths by the 'food police,' trial lawyers and even our own government." The CDC was forced to admit its figure was in error.[43]

A number of cases of food contamination have occurred in the United States in the early 21st century. Bacteria like salmonella, vibrio, E. coli O157, listeria and campylobacter have invaded the food supply, causing highly publicized outbreaks of illness from peanuts, spinach, pistachios, tomatoes, hot peppers and other foods. Members of Congress roundly criticized the Food and Drug Administration (FDA) in the press for being too lax in tracing the source of these infections within the food chain. Hill investigators also questioned whether the CDC was falling down on the job. In response, the CDC explained the science and spread of bacteria and reaffirmed its own credibility by releasing precise statistics it had been collecting on food contamination incidence rates; they showed increases to new levels, which the agency readily admitted were higher than they had previously targeted.[44]

When Gerberding was asked to testify on the health impacts of global warming to the Senate Committee on Environment and Public Works, CDC staff prepared written testimony for advance submittal to the Office of Management and Budget (OMB), as required. After her appearance the press discovered that six of the 12 pages of prepared manuscript were redacted, removing all discussion of the actual effects of global warming. The reporters concluded she had been censored by the OMB because of the Bush administration's refusal to acknowledge man-caused global warming. Gerberding was put on the defensive by this leak and insisted, "I don't let people put words in my mouth."[45]

Other instances of bad press developed from public complaints by a member of the CDC staff. The Federal Emergency Management Agency (FEMA) asked the CDC to study the effects of formaldehyde in trailers provided by FEMA to victims of Hurricane Katrina. The CDC found no such effects in the short term, but confirmed later that over a longer time this preservative could cause respiratory problems and was probably carcinogenic. Christopher De Rosa, head of the office that conducted the study, publicly criticized the CDC's handling of the matter. De Rosa also spoke out that a report in which he was involved on the extent of environmental pollution in the Great Lakes had been suppressed. De Rosa was given an unsatisfactory job performance rating by the agency and transferred to other duties. Combined, the redaction of the global warming testimony and the De Rosa matters created much attention on the Hill from Democrats critical of the Bush administration. Gerberding was lectured sternly, "The agency's conduct has called into question its ability to investigate public health hazards accurately and appropriately in the future."[46]

Managing Controversy

In the obesity and food contamination matters political controversy was defused. In the redaction and De Rosa incidents this did not happen. The CDC takes seriously the political fallout from bad press, and under Gerberding an Office of Enterprise Communication was established to minimize it. Operating at an agency-wide level and within selected centers, the office performs four duties: monitoring internal official messages, reviewing in advance health announcements or research findings, promoting desirable public relations practices generally, and conducting what is called "issues management."

A term borrowed from the corporate world, *issues management* means taking deliberate steps to anticipate bad publicity and thereby be in a position to deflect it by skillful action. In terms of our template, it is pertinent to reputation considerations in cell 3. Aside from controlling communication content, such management involves educating staff on how to talk to outsiders. A wallet-sized Crisis-Emergency Risk Communication card is given to each employee. On it are recommendations on how to deal with the public or press when on a disease surveillance or otherwise in the field. Admonitions given are to "tell the truth," "be transparent," "embody your agency's identity" and "know your organization's policies." Cardholders are also urged to acknowledge uncertainty, explain the process in place to get answers, and be prepared to use the phrase "I can't answer that question but I can tell you. . . ."

Another facet of issues management is "Risk Smart" classes for employees. Their focus is what to do when something questionable is noticed going on in the organization that could damage its reputation. A rectangular "Heat Map" diagram is shown with one axis showing gradations of likelihood and the other degrees of danger. If the incident can be located near the "cool" (rare-insignificant) corner of the diagram, the successive options are not to worry, watch it or be concerned and have a conversation. If the matter lies closer to the "hot" (certain-catastrophic) corner, the options are, depending on proximity to it, take the question up with your supervisor, bring it to the attention of your center's issue management officer or—if very hot—inform the CDC's top leadership, i.e., the director.

The sharpest sword pricking the agency that the Office of Enterprise Communication had to deal with was Alison Young, a reporter for the *Atlanta Journal-Constitution* whose beat was the CDC for some years (she has since left the paper). Her articles were informed, based on inside contacts and a mixture of honest description of the agency's good works and polite but pointed dissection of those works deemed not so good. In writing this chapter her work was one of my few sources of independent insight.

In January 2007, the newspaper learned that the CDC was conducting a "risk analysis" of the *Atlanta Journal-Constitution*'s coverage of the agency. Sources indicated that the Enterprise Communication office had compiled a collection of 4,000 pages of documents related to Young's articles. It was also leaked that the CDC hired a contractor—outside the normal procurement process—to analyze them. The newspaper filed a Freedom of Information request for the contractor report and all associated documents; it was denied, but after the Barack Obama administration entered office the CDC released 46 pages, mostly of published stories. In one of her final articles before leaving the newspaper for another position, Young detailed these events, disclosing the extent to which the agency had become annoyed with her sometimes unflattering coverage.[47]

THE ORGANIZATION TODAY

Compared to the National Park Service and National Weather Service, the Centers for Disease Control and Prevention is a work in progress. It is less an established institution whose contemporary times are dynamic than one whose entire life has been in flux and remains so today. While the CDC's basic character as a steward of the public's health has held steady over time, the nature of that stewardship has altered greatly in scope, style and substance. Hence any description of the organization itself must be tentative; the picture given below is a snapshot at this time of writing and does not lay out the enduring features of a settled institution.

Organizational Basics

As an institution in flux, the closest thing to a formal statement of the current concept of purpose does not say what the mission *is* but what it *involves*, as if its exact nature cannot be reduced to writing: "collaborating to create the expertise, information, and tools that people and communities need to protect their health—through health promotion, prevention of disease, injury and disability, and the preparedness for new health threats." Ways to protect, i.e., maximize, the nation's health are to "monitor health, detect and investigate health problems, conduct research to enhance prevention, develop and advocate sound public health policies, implement prevention strategies, promote healthy behaviors, foster safe and healthful environments, provide leadership and training."[48]

The CDC is considered a world-class agency in health protection. Its international fame is such that health departments of other countries look to it as a model. China even has its own comparable agency, informally known as the China CDC. In a nationwide Harris poll conducted in 2007 in which 2,337 members of the public were asked to rate the performance of 13 federal agencies, the CDC received the best rating. Ninety percent of respondents could identify what the CDC is and 84 percent rated it excellent or pretty good. This compares to a 78 percent rating for the Federal Aviation Administration, 75 percent for the National Institutes of Health, 74 percent for the FBI and 73 percent for the Department of Agriculture. At the bottom of the scale were the Environmental Protection Agency and Internal Revenue Service at 55 percent, and the Social Security Administration at 40 percent.[49] In short, although the CDC's purpose is vague, its fame—the attribute of cell 3—is great.

In terms of overall size, the CDC employs about 8,900 full-time employees. This places it less than halfway between the NPS (22,000) and NWS (4,700). Approximately 6,000 contractor personnel are counted as part of the workforce, compared to 11,000 for the NPS. Adding those to direct employees creates an organization of around 15,000.[50]

With respect to funding, however, the CDC greatly outranks the first two agencies discussed in this book. The CDC's budget submission for FY 2009 was $9.2 billion, compared to under $3 billion for the NPS and less than $1 billion for the NWS. When the infant CDC began in 1942, it was allocated less than 400 people and a $10 million budget. Since that time funding levels have increased almost a thousandfold, and by more than $4 billion in just the last 10 years.[51]

The culture of the CDC and the mystique it portrays is that of an elite, famous and affluent public institution. This picture is projected physically by its growing main Atlanta campus, which as noted earlier is on land obtained from Emory University. Along Clifton Road adjacent to the campus a complex of approximately 15 major buildings has been built, overwhelming the old headquarters structure dedicated in 1960. Officially it is the Edward R. Roybal Campus, named after a former Georgia member of Congress who helped arrange for the needed appropriations. A 12-story administration building (with the director's office on the top floors) is the center of power, and the venue to which the public is admitted is a grandiose communications building containing vaulted lobby, museum, conference facilities and television studios. At the campus security entrance stands an arresting gate sign bearing the familiar initials and agency logo.

Less than half of the workforce is present here, but it is expected that the proportion will grow with time. Several installations exist elsewhere in the Atlanta area. The CDC also has a major physical presence in Cincinnati, Ohio; Pittsburgh, Pa.; Morgantown, W.Va.; Hyattsville, Md.; Spokane, Wash.; Durham, N.C.; Fort Collins, Colo.; and Puerto Rico. Its limited presence in the District of Columbia promotes a feeling of psychological distance from the political machinations of Washington, a feature that was understood by Mountin, Williams and Andrews back in the 1940s. The international character of the organization is also represented from the physical location standpoint; hundreds of personnel engage in operations in some 54 countries, many at CDC Global Disease Detection Centers and projects in collaboration with WHO and the Department of Defense.[52]

Organizational Structure

The CDC is headed by a director, who is appointed by the president with Senate confirmation. This has been the case since 1983; prior to that the appointment was made by the secretary of health and human services. The CDC head is accountable directly to the secretary, without any supervising layer such as the National Oceanic and Atmospheric Administration for the Weather Service. Counting the MCWA years, as of 2010, 19 people have held the position, with an average tenure of three and one-half years. Only two directors—Sencer and Foege—served a decade or more. In keeping with the medical nature of the agency's mission, all have held medical degrees. While not all directors have been CDC careerists, without exception they possessed strong professional credentials in public health circles. No obviously "political" appointee in the nature of an unqualified campaign aide has held the position.

By an odd quirk, the CDC director is not only responsible for this large, famous organization but, by law, simultaneously supervises another very small one. This is the Agency for Toxic Substances and Disease Registry, whose 300 employees assess public health implications of Superfund waste sites and maintain a prioritized list of damaging toxins. As far as the director's big job is concerned, this is to lead a core group of eight national science centers of research and technical expertise that provide the rationale for the organization's plural name. Stated in abbreviated form, these concern environmental health, injury prevention, health statistics, birth defects, chronic diseases, immunization, zoonotic diseases (communicable from animals to man) and HIV/AIDS (see Box 4.1). Of these, environmental health, injury prevention and chronic diseases originated in the Foege era. The Center for Infectious Diseases that he created with much struggle is now broken down into the centers for immunization, zoonotic diseases and HIV/AIDS. Foege's coordinators for public health practice and global health still exist in some form, as does the politically untouchable National Institute for Occupational Safety and Health.

In addition to the organization components under Gerberding, Box 4.1 indicates those under Thomas Frieden, who took office in 2009 (see part of the box on the following page; it will be discussed shortly). The contrast between the two is significant in understanding what has happened to the agency's mystique in recent years.

Directing attention first to the Gerberding table of organization, we note the presence of four coordinating centers and two coordinating offices. To a substantial extent they incorporate the four goals of her Futures Initiative: "healthy people in every stage of life" is reflected in the Coordinating Center for Health Promotion; "healthy people in healthy places" corresponds to the Coordinating Center for Environmental Health and Injury Prevention; "healthy people in a healthy world" is covered by the Coordinating Office for Global Health; and

---

Box 4.1 Organizational Components of the CDC

Under Gerberding

Office of the Director
> The Director
> Office of Chief Science Officer
> Office of Chief of Public Health Practice
> Office of Chief Operating Officer
> CDC Washington Office
> Office of Strategy and Innovation
> Office of Workforce and Career Development
> Office of Enterprise Communication
> Office of Chief of Staff
> Office of Dispute Resolution and Equal Employment Opportunity

Coordinating Office for Global Health
Coordinating Office for Terrorism Preparedness and Emergency Response
Coordinating Center for Environmental Health and Injury Prevention
> National Center for Environmental Health/Agency for Toxic Substances and Disease Registry
> National Center for Injury Prevention and Control

Coordinating Center for Health Information and Service
> National Center for Health Marketing
> National Center for Health Statistics
> National Center for Public Health Informatics

Coordinating Center for Health Promotion
> National Center on Birth Defects and Developmental Disabilities
> National Center for Chronic Disease Prevention and Health Promotion
> National Office of Public Health Genomics

Coordinating Center for Infectious Diseases
> National Center for Immunization and Respiratory Diseases
> National Center for Zoonotic, Vector-Borne and Enteric Diseases
> National Center for HIV/AIDS, Viral Hepatitis, STD and TB Prevention
> National Center for Preparedness, Detection and Control of Infectious Diseases

National Institute for Occupational Safety and Health

"people prepared for emerging health threats" is found in the Coordinating Office for Terrorism Preparedness. Another coordinating center deals with health information (including health marketing, or practitioner training by teleconference, and informatics, meaning electronic health records and computer-aided medical decision making). A final coordinating center for infectious diseases (see bottom of list) is by far the biggest in terms of employees; it covers three of the long-standing infectious disease centers, along with one for epidemiologic surveillance, i.e., detection and control of disease.

Under Frieden

Office of the Director
 The Director
 Principle Deputy Director
 Chief Operating Officer
 Chief of Staff
 Office of Diversity Management and Equal Employment Opportunity
 Associate Director for Program
 Associate Director for Science
 Associate Director for Communication
 Associate Director for Policy
Office of Public Health Preparedness and Response
Office for State, Tribal, Local and Territorial Support
Office of Surveillance, Epidemiology and Laboratory Services
 National Institute for Occupational Safety and Health
 National Center for Health Statistics
 Offices of Surveillance, Epidemiology, Informatics, Laboratory Science, and
  Career Development
Office of Noncommunicable Diseases, Injury and Environmental Health
 National Center on Birth Defects and Developmental Disabilities
 National Center for Chronic Disease Prevention and Health Promotion
 National Center for Environmental Health/Agency for Toxic Substances and
  Disease Registry
 National Center for Injury Prevention and Control
Office of Infectious Diseases
 National Center for Emerging and Zoonotic Infectious Diseases
 National Center for HIV/AIDS, Viral Hepatitis, STD and TB Prevention
 National Center for Immunization and Respiratory Diseases
Center for Global Health

Source: CDC organizational chart, www.cdc.gov/about/organization/orgchart.htm.

The 2004 creation (or augmentation) of these coordinating bodies heavily affected the final years of Gerberding's tenure at the CDC. Each had their own bureaucracy, with staff specializing in finance, travel, logistics, procurement, personnel, training, communications and management efficiency. Thus the coordinators were endowed with real power. This threatened the independence of the national science centers and the autonomy of their directors. Their fears were intensified by two accompanying moves. One was to create new staff offices in the director's office dealing with the influential areas of strategy, the workforce and communication. The other was formation of four coordinating councils by means of which centralizing influence could be exerted. These cut through successive levels of the organization: the executive level, including the director, her staff heads and directors of the coordinating councils; the managerial level, including the chief operating officer and all financial and business managers; and, lastly, councils for center heads and division chiefs.

The national center directors, particularly those leading the scientific centers for infectious diseases, were furious. They viewed the coordinating centers as superfluous, unneeded and an attempt to have details of their scientific work controlled by nonscientists. Further, the formation or enlargement of separate entities associated with Gerberding's Future's Initiative goals implicitly downgraded infectious diseases and epidemiology in favor of her vision. Building up the office of the director and creating the executive and management councils added to the feeling that power was migrating upward to the top of the administration building, away from the scientific and technical talent that gave the CDC its reputation in the first place. The Zoonotic Center director complained, "There is frustration, anger, and a sense of things spinning out of control. . . . The intensity of emotions and commonality of experience across ZVED is both profound and real."[53] The organization's "constitution" of unspoken basic rules, identified by Gary Wamsley and mentioned in Chapter 1, was being broken by violating the primacy of the science-oriented national centers that lie at the core of the institution's mystique.

An uprising occurred against Gerberding that shook the agency internally and sent shock waves out from it externally. Veteran officials of the organization and many of its top scientists began submitting their resignations. By September 2006 no less than 13 had quit or announced their departures out of protest. Alison Young and other journalists around the nation covered the exodus, much to the embarrassment of the CDC leadership.[54]

Earlier, in December 2005, five former directors of the CDC—David Sencer, William Foege, Jeffrey Koplan, James Mason and David Satcher—wrote a joint letter to Gerberding stating:

> We have all gone through periods of change and recognize the difficulties attendant to change. However, we are concerned about the previous and impending losses of highly qualified and motivated staff. . . . We are concerned that so many of the staff have come to us to express their concerns about the low morale in the agency. We are concerned about the inability of many of the partners to understand the direction in which CDC is headed.[55]

After receiving no satisfactory answer to the letter, the five directors requested a joint meeting with her. That was arranged, but its outcome was even less satisfying; one former director told me it felt like being called before the principal at school for a reprimand.

A Changing of the Guard

As late as spring 2008 Gerberding hoped to be retained in office by whomever was elected president that fall. While precedent exists for such a carryover, the Obama transition team requested that Gerberding submit her resignation, and she did so on the day the new president was inaugurated. The Obama administration quickly appointed Richard E. Besser, head of the CDC's Coordinating Office for Terrorism Preparedness and Emergency Response, to serve as acting director.

Besser served in this position during the first half of 2009. With an education in economics and medicine, Besser began his career at the CDC in the EIS, serving as a PHS commissioned officer in Boston. His first assignment there was to investigate a bacterial outbreak that turned out to be caused by E. coli in unpasteurized cider. Before taking over the Coordinating Center for Terrorism, he held two branch chief positions at the National Center for Infectious Diseases. Known for his engaging manner and excellent speaking skills, after completing his acting directorship Besser resigned and joined ABC News as senior health and medical editor.[56]

During Besser's half-year at the helm, the H1N1 swine flu epidemic of 2009 broke out. In late March 2009 a few cases appeared in California and Texas, and within a few days hundreds were sickened in Mexico. Other countries also began experiencing the disease, and the United States declared a public health emergency. In June the CDC officially declared a pandemic to exist. Besser went on television frequently to explain what was happening, and his reassuring yet concerned manner was a deliberate contrast to the panic of the administration during the 1976 swine flu debacle. Gradually supplies of an H1N1 vaccine were produced and distributed to high-risk citizens, particularly children. In another lesson from 1976, the CDC kept a sharp eye out for shot-induced cases of Guillain-Barre Syndrome, but none occurred. By the end of 2009 the incidence of new cases had died down, and experts' worst fears were not realized; however, by the time it was over 18 percent of Americans had caught the disease and over 11,000 died, mostly among the elderly. Many at the CDC compared Besser's calm, clear media persona as on par with Gerberding's during the anthrax crisis—and indeed, many observers hoped he would become her permanent successor.[57]

The appointment instead went to Thomas R. Frieden, commissioner of the New York City Health Department, one of the biggest public health agencies in the world. Like Besser, he began his public health career at the CDC as an EIS officer, although his assignment took him not to Boston but to New York. For five years he led a tuberculosis abatement program there, and later took his anti-TB skills to India. As New York City mayor Michael Bloomberg's health commissioner, Frieden earned the reputation as a health crusader who wanted to ban smoking in restaurants and bars, distribute millions of condoms and make HIV/AIDS testing a routine part of all physical exams. Public health liberals hailed Obama's CDC appointee as a progressive crusader, while conservatives charged that Frieden was better at playing politics than doing good science.[58]

Upon taking over the agency Frieden quickly realized something had to be done about Gerberding's controversial reorganization. He created a team to study the matter and initiated an all-employee survey. Nearly 5,000 responses were received, and he released the results for comment. A description of the conclusions, posted anonymously on the employee blog CDC Chatter, concluded, "Nor surprisingly, overwhelmingly CDC staff, management and outside partners were not favorably inclined to the changes that occurred over the past eight years." While Gerberding's restructuring had merit, the analysis went on, it was poorly implemented and had unintended consequences, such as duplication of processes, a heavy administrative burden, displacement of program staff to coordination assignments, loss of a public health focus and diminishment of the value of science. Other concerns were an atmosphere that discouraged dissent, endless council meetings that aided social networking but not governance, and an excessive use of contractors.[59]

In August 2009 Frieden wrote to all staff that the current organizational structure ill-suited the CDC's mission and that the coordinating centers would be removed. At the same time, he expressed interest in retaining in some way the facilitative contributions of their staffs. The organizational arrangement he came up with is shown in Box 4.1. The coordinating centers are gone, although three "offices" remain that stand between the national centers and the director's office. The groupings involved are not organized around Gerberding's four goals but in accord with the core functions of disease surveillance, noncommunicable diseases and infectious diseases. The eight principal national centers have been retained, while the work of those for health marketing, informatics and preparedness has been absorbed elsewhere. In addition, more organizational attention is paid to field support, another traditional CDC function. In the director's office, the office of strategy and innovation is gone and a deputy director and associate directors for programs and policy have been added, presumably to permit more delegation of line authority below the level of director. In short, the Gerberding era was now over organizationally, and the agency's mission mystique could again center on battling man's plagues, a more concrete reality than visions of ideal wellness.

In January 2010 I discussed the changing of the guard with one of my most experienced CDC sources. He told me that the moment Gerberding had gone and Besser began roaming the halls, employees started smiling again. They were delighted with his warm demeanor and his practice of walking alone without aides. The fact that this was the moment when H1N1 struck turned out to be a happy coincidence, in that under Besser's leadership they could join in a common, urgent cause with an enthusiasm that was lacking earlier. Then, when Thomas Frieden came on board, people had to get used to a more hard-charging New Yorker who liked to micromanage, but nonetheless the institution had become rejuvenated. A page had turned on CDC history, my interviewee assured, and the institution's future was bright.

INSTITUTIONAL COMMITMENT

In this chapter on the Centers for Disease Control and Prevention much has been said, in effect, about mission mystique's purposive aura (cells 1–3 of the template) and vitalizing forces (cells 7–9). The part of the belief system template that has been neglected so far is the commitment thrust, which incorporates intrinsic motivation (cell 4), institutionalized culture (cell 5) and honored history (cell 6). We turn to these subjects now.

To some extent, insights on employee attitudes can be found in results of the Federal Human Capital Survey (FHCS), as was the case with the NPS in Chapter 2. Percentages for six questions are shown in Table 4.1; three of these were also included in Table 2-1, specifically the first two questions on work attitude and the last on leadership policies. It should be noted that all of the years covered are during Gerberding's tenure.

Positive percentages as to the perceived importance of CDC work and how the respondents like it range generally in the 80s, which speaks quite well for commitment to the duties performed. Yet these figures are mostly lower than the all-government level and are a few points below that shown for the National Park Service. As can be seen, responses to the remaining questions are substantially less positive and may provide insights into why these work answers were not higher.

Percentages with respect to feelings of accomplishment, empowerment and involvement range from the 70s to the 30s. Those for feeling empowered and involved were mostly below 50 percent, indicating possible resentment over the concentration of power under Gerberding. The last question, on degree of satisfaction with the policies and practices of senior leaders, yielded responses entirely in the 30s range, seemingly reflective of general dissatisfaction with the actions and manner of Gerberding herself. The five-point drop in responses to that question after 2004 may be an outgrowth of her announcement of the reorganization that year. In short, the nature of the work is good, but there are problems with control and leadership.

In thinking about the content of the CDC culture itself, it is interesting to ponder what might be considered to be the main "thing" around which the mission revolves. In the Park Service this is the beloved national parks themselves. In the Weather Service it is a technologic process, the forecasting of weather. Both of these cultural anchors are tangible, concrete and easy to define. The CDC, by contrast, has as its cultural mooring a broad idea: public health. It is a concept that is far from tangible, concrete and easy to define.

Table 4.1 CDC Employee Responses to FHCS Questions, 2004–2008

		Percent Positive	
		CDC	All Government
The work I do is important.			
	2004	87.6	
	2006	86.4	
	2007	87.3	
	2008	87.6	90.0
I like the kind of work I do.			
	2004	80.1	
	2006	79.6	
	2007	83.0	
	2008	85.2	84.2
My work gives me a feeling of personal accomplishment.			
	2004	68.4	
	2006	69.7	
	2007	76.4	
	2008	73.0	74.4
Employees have a feeling of personal empowerment in work processes.			
	2004	41.0	
	2006	36.4	
	2007	41.4	
	2008	42.3	47.8
How satisfied are you with your involvement in decisions that affect your work?			
	2004	50.3	
	2006	47.1	
	2007	40.6	
	2008	53.1	56.2
How satisfied are you with the policies and practices of your senior leaders?			
	2004	36.4	
	2006	31.2	
	2007	34.0	
	2008	36.9	43.8

Source: Office of Personnel Management, *Federal Human Capital Survey*, 2007 and 2008, items 5, 6, 20, 24, 55 and 58. Positive responses are "strongly agree" and "agree" or "very satisfied" and "satisfied."

Although the public health profession takes pains to translate its work into specific communities of practice, significant doctrinal issues remain, such as whether to emphasize battling infectious diseases or chronic conditions, push for treatment or prevention, seek illness or wellness, and assist people directly or undertake environmental change.

As a result of this looser cultural frame, there is more ample room for diverse worldviews within the CDC cultural world than was found in the NPS or NWS. The public good being sought is not absolute or technically precise, but relatively generic, demystified and open to multiple pathways of attainment. What this situation may create is not so much a single unified culture as a mosaic of subcultures.

Indeed, many kinds of cultural division do exist in the CDC. Because the organization grew cumulatively, the existing portfolio of activities always includes older public health specialties like tuberculosis and sexually transmitted diseases along with newer ones such as informatics and reduction of obesity. In that the agency's work incorporates pure science, applied science and practical technique, several modalities of daily work also exist side by side; bench research in laboratories, epidemiologic surveillance in the field, health education on the air waves, statistical analysis and terrorism preparedness are some examples. Although the MD and MPH degrees are of primary importance for holding the top jobs, other educational backgrounds are of currency as well, such as the MBA for managerial and fiscal duties, behavioral science doctorates for work on environmental health and injury prevention, and engineering and computer science degrees for maintaining IT systems. Other subgroups in the CDC cultural mosaic are EIS members doing their two-year stint, the 850 PHS commissioned officers on duty at any given time, administrative support personnel and contract employees—of which there are thousands, with cultural differentiations among them too.

Of course, it is not unusual for a government department to have field offices. But dispersion of the CDC workforce is unusually great. While NPS personnel are distributed among hundreds of parks and the NWS among scores of field stations, the CDC's geographic separation cuts across many axes of differentiation: the buildings in the Clifton Road complex, centers and other facilities elsewhere in Atlanta; laboratories, research centers and quarantine stations across the country; and stations and projects around the world.

The CDC diaspora may even be said to include the networks of state and local health departments and laboratories to which CDC employees are often assigned. Also included are the nongovernmental organizations (NGOs) and international organizations around the globe with which the agency collaborates; scores of advisory bodies on which CDC personnel sit or from whom they receive advice; and the universities to which the CDC gives grants, the foundations that support CDC activities, the corporations that donate funds and equipment, and the medical schools at which CDC doctors hold professorships.

In short, over the past seven decades the CDC cultural world has become enormously diverse and scattered. The agency has changed greatly over time. The MCWA was a close-knit, small group working on one public health problem from a building or two in a city far from the nation's capital. Even after the CDC was formed in 1946, the organization's size remained limited and, despite the acquisition of some new programs, operated mainly within the South. In the CDC's early decades its cultural life was recorded in a monthly magazine called *Dateline CDC*. Its pages are filled with reports on details of an intimate organizational family: town meetings on topics of the day; employee-of-the-month awards; ethnic heritage months; country/western jamborees; CDC choir concerts; and charity sales of CDC pens, notebooks, T-shirts and baby clothes.

Dateline CDC is now a thing of the past. Instead, there is the blog CDC Chatter. While an annual open house at the Roybal campus is customary, volunteer activities are not an inward experience of family fun but acts of reaching out to the world, including walks for autism or AIDS, tree-planting projects and collecting used pairs of shoes for children in need. Employees are encouraged to donate blood, adopt highways and volunteer at public health camps. An employee "Go Green, Get Healthy" program conducts sustainability workshops, sponsors recycling campaigns and promotes energy conversation; it also designed an ecologically self-sufficient rainwater brook running through the main campus.[60]

The 19th century German sociologist Ferdinand Tonnies had names for this contrast: the *Gemeinschaft* of village life versus the *Gesellschaft* of impersonal societal relationships. Applying the distinction to the CDC culture, the one consists of face-to-face relationships among government employees who wish to build a sense of community around their employer, and the other a world of scattered thousands working in innumerable settings, bound together only by a broad common commitment and electronic communication. The CDC as an institution was at one time the first and is now the second—no longer a close community of public health stewards, but a shared fellowship of public health stewardship. Feelings of mission mystique on the part of employees is a product not of intimate association within a pioneering enterprise, but of being connected in some way to an internationally known, world-class institution.

A proposition of mission mystique is that a key source of institutional pride and self-identity arises from recounting and honoring agency history, particularly the founding. The CDC extensively honors its history. The agency has no official histories or historian, but author Elizabeth W. Etheridge was supported by the agency in writing *Sentinel for Health,* an excellent narrative for the time period it covers.[61] Further, for a long time the anniversary of the CDC's birth (considered to be 1946, not 1942) has been celebrated at least every 10 years. Past directors are often invited to speak on these occasions, and old photographs and laboratory equipment are displayed. As a feature of the 60th anniversary celebration in 2006, several past directors wrote historical perspectives on their period in office for publication in *MMWR*. The annual report for 2006 celebrates "CDC: 60 years of excellence" with a summary of each decade's achievements, and a 1946–2005 timeline identifies important events.[62]

THIS INSTANCE OF MISSION MYSTIQUE

In summary, how did the Centers for Disease Control and Prevention match up with the ideal of mission mystique?

Cell 1: Mission. Rather than a specified statutory mission, the CDC's mystique is driven by the acknowledged mission of public health. Being outstanding in the traditional governmental function of public health provides a strong, overarching central purpose. That purpose is to protect the public's health—that is, increase it. Over time, the particularized exercise of this mission purpose has grown from malaria control to hundreds of individual programs, resulting in somewhat more mission mystique ambiguity. While certainly some of this expansion was self-initiated "mission creep," it also occurred as a result of transfer of programs from Washington, outbreaks of known or new diseases, external requests for assistance, needs for manpower (EIS) and information (*MMWR*), new technology (informatics) and requirements of the nation (terrorism and emergency response). Thus much of the mission growth is a consequence of the inevitable changes that occur in a field such as applied medicine.

Cell 2: Need. Almost no one would deny the need to battle the terrible diseases that afflict humankind. Malaria, smallpox and tuberculosis are ancient plagues. Toxic Shock Syndrome, Legionnaires' disease and HIV/AIDS are new arrivals. Chronic diseases like cancer, diabetes and cardiac malfunction rob millions of having a full life. Food contamination, hospital infections and human obesity are less visible enemies but costly in human terms. Continuation of such battles seems obviously necessary.

Cell 3: Reputation. The CDC reputation has some dark moments in its past. Most notable was its failure to stop the Tuskegee syphilis experiment when it came under the agency's jurisdiction. Equally notable successes have occurred as well: eradication of malaria in the South served important wartime purposes, and world eradication of smallpox was a remarkable and noble achievement. A measured response to the 2009 H1N1 pandemic contrasts with the 1976 influenza debacle. Mission growth itself has not affected the CDC reputation; while it does expose the agency to more controversy, it provides more opportunities for success as well. At home the CDC ranks very high in the polls, and abroad it serves as a model national protector of public health.

Cell 4: Motivation. The FHCS shows strong staff commitment to CDC work, but also dissatisfaction with senior leadership and top-down control. This problem, while severe for several years, appears to be disappearing with a changing of the guard in 2009. Institutional sources of motivation exist as well. Langmuir's EIS turned out to be not only a source of well-trained epidemiologists but a force for motivation across the generations. Service in the PHS commissioned officer corps animates dedication to the public health cause generically. An indicator of intrinsic motivation within the CDC workforce is the presence of employee-created scientific working groups that spontaneously form around such interests as post-traumatic stress, human rights, and the intersection of gender and public health.

Cell 5: Culture. The CDC is a continuously changing scene. Over time its culture has evolved, made pliable by a generic rather than unchanging, prescribed mission. The resulting cultural contrast between the early days and the present time is enormous. The much bigger size, growth of program specialties and shift from an Atlanta to a worldwide base have fractured a one-time "village" culture into a "societal" one. The difference is no better illustrated than by the contrast between the magazine *Dateline CDC* and the blog CDC Chatter. Yet, at the same time, feelings of common identification with a great world cause and a world-class pursuer of that cause elevate the collective consciousness to one of devoted public health stewardship, no matter where one lives or works.

Cell 6: History. Celebrating the agency's history has not been neglected. A professional historian has, with CDC assistance, written an outstanding narrative. A "Global Health Odyssey Museum" of past artifacts exists in the communications center that includes old iron lungs and total-coverage bio-protection suits. The 1946 founding is commemorated each decade with ceremonies, the last of which were held in 2006. Past directors return for anniversary appearances, and an annual lecture is given in honor of Joseph Mountin. Commemorations of other events are noted, such as creation of the EIS in 1951, initial publication of *MMWR* in 1961 and eradication of smallpox in 1981. Someday the anthrax crisis of 2001, which led to the most massive emergency disease surveillance in CDC history, may be remembered as well.

Cell 7: Contestation. In recent years serious internal dissent within the organization broke out over the leadership style and policies of Director Julie Gerberding. Her reorganization's demotion of the honored status of the national science centers violated the institution's unwritten "constitution" and precipitated the agency's first overt revolt. Her management style discouraged dissent as well; resentment grew until it turned to revolt, a costly mode of organizational change. Now, with Alison Young gone, CDC Chatter stands as the prime outlet for open discussion and criticism. Enhanced internal contestation in the future will depend on the willingness of directors to tolerate it and learn from it.

Cell 8: Autonomy. Policy autonomy has been asserted by the CDC under at least three kinds of circumstances. One has been to garner the reputation and support needed to build up the mission and take on new programs, the characteristic that political scientist Daniel Carpenter identifies with early American state building. A second is the capacity to step on the toes of powerful economic interests when responding to emerging epidemics, such as Bayer in the case of Reye's Syndrome and Proctor & Gamble in that of Toxic Shock Syndrome. Third is the ability to affect public policy as in the premature mass flu inoculation of 1976 and failure to terminate the Tuskegee experiment—instances in which the CDC possessed too much influence for its own good, even if passively and unintentionally exercised. Those latter matters are now history, but the danger of overzealous pursuit of an institutionally defined public good may not be over.

Cell 9: Renewal. The CDC is a consummate "triple-loop" agency. It has always been future-ready, looking ahead to what needs to be changed. This can be summarized by leadership eras. Mountin imagined a new kind of multifunctional federal health agency, Langmuir invented a new method of applied training and a new medium of disseminating information, Sencer opened up the agency's domestic domain and established its international potential, Foege introduced synoptic future planning to public health and Gerberding reconceptualized the public health enterprise as seeking a healthiest nation status. She also attempted to reintegrate the dispersed enterprise the CDC had become; this proved impossible, which is perhaps a good thing in terms of continued creativity.

In most ways, the CDC is a remarkable mission mystique agency, especially with regard to its inner passion and magnetic appeal. Its immense prestige and open-ended mission would seem to require, however, added institutional mechanisms of internal debate and self-examination.

Chapter

5

Department of Social Services, Mecklenburg County, N.C.

The Delicate Business of Welfare

WE NOW TURN OUR ATTENTION FROM AGENCIES of the federal government to those at other levels. The subject of this chapter, the Department of Social Services (DSS), is an agency of Mecklenburg County, N.C. As I was planning this book I wanted to include a welfare department because of the importance of this function of government and my own past research in the area. I asked a national consultant in the public welfare field to identify an exemplary welfare agency, and she immediately mentioned Mecklenburg. Upon commencing research, I discovered that the director who had made the department famous was about to leave office after serving 14 years. While his departure had its disadvantages, it also made possible a full retrospective on what happened during that period. As the reader will discover, this individual's impact on the agency was enormous, but has to some degree turned out to be temporary. What he did to build the institution into preeminence contains important lessons for mission mystique.

Mecklenburg County includes the city of Charlotte and six small towns that lie within its borders. The Mecklenburg DSS is one of the few social service departments in North Carolina that operates as a unit of county government, rather than being under direct control of the state's Division of Social Services. The county was incorporated in colonial times and named after the German homeland of Queen Charlotte, the wife of King George III. Today the population of the Charlotte–Gastonia metropolitan statistical area is over 1.5 million, and it is one of the fastest growing urban centers in the Middle Atlantic region. It is also a major financial center for the nation, with the headquarters of many large banks located there.

FROM WELFARE TO WHITE HOUSE

Frances Lee Cunningham was born in 1964 in Charlotte, N.C. Siblings were three older sisters and two half-sisters. The family struggled financially, and her father left home shortly after Frances' birth. Mae, her mother, worked hard to feed and clothe the children during the several years they lived in a public housing project.

Suffering from low self-esteem, Frances dropped out of high school in the 10th grade. She went to work in a fast-food restaurant and tried off and on to obtain high school equivalency credits. At age 18 she became pregnant and went on welfare. Her son, Dareicho, was born in 1983, and four years later came her daughter, Blair. During these years Frances attempted to find work that would allow her to take care of her children by herself, but because of her lack of skills it was very difficult. In her own words, she "needed help to see what her life could become."

In 1995 the Mecklenburg County Department of Social Services launched what was called Work First. It was an early "workfare" program that required some kind of employment, even if unpaid, as a condition of receiving public assistance. Accordingly, Frances' caseworker told her she should take on volunteer assignments in preparation for getting a job. Placements were made as a receptionist at a neighborhood center and as a tutor at a middle school. The caseworker also instructed Frances to complete all credits necessary for receiving a high school diploma, which she did by walking three miles to and from the YMCA where classes were held.

Richard W. "Jake" Jacobsen Jr., a relatively new director of the DSS who on his arrival had started the county's Work First program, heard from caseworkers that Frances was making good progress in it. They said her supervisors reported she interacted well with others. In 1997 Jacobsen took a gamble and invited her to work in his own office as an unpaid assistant. She jumped at the chance.

In this position Frances took a major share of the workload off the paid staff and did an outstanding job answering the phone and receiving visitors. In order to upgrade her office skills and become more useful, she took courses at the local community college. In a casual conversation one day, Jacobsen mentioned to her that he was trying to figure out why children benefiting from public assistance did not do as well in school as their nonwelfare peers. Speaking from experience, Frances told him that just seeing a mother go to work every morning sets a positive model of discipline for schoolchildren.

In July 1998, satisfied that Frances had the maturity and potential to contribute meaningfully to the Department of Social Services, Jacobsen hired her as a full-time departmental employee. She assumed the position of his office assistant. In a couple of years Frances was promoted to the rank of customer service specialist and, a few years later, administrative support assistant II. At this writing she

Frances Lee Cunningham of the Mecklenburg County Department of Social Services. Once an unemployed pregnant teenager, as a result of the DSS welfare-to-work program she became an assistant to the director and was asked to introduce the U.S. president when he visited Charlotte, N.C.

Source: Photo by the author.

has worked in DSS for 12 years; during this time she has pulled herself out of poverty, become one of the best-liked employees in the department, raised her children to the point that they are self-sufficient, and is in a position to attend to the needs of her now ailing mother. At last word, Frances was hoping to spend the remainder of her career in Mecklenburg County government.

In February 2002 Jacobsen informed Frances that the president of the United States would soon be visiting Charlotte. "[Y]ou'll have the honor of introducing him and sitting in on a roundtable discussion about Work First," he said. "I may faint," Frances answered. When her employer joked that he'd have some smelling salts handy, she said she'd do it.

Frances had trouble sleeping before the big event and had a hard time keeping calm when going downtown the next day to the Chamber of Commerce building where it was held. After climbing onto the stage, President George W. Bush came up to her and said with a smile, "Knock their socks off!" When her turn came to speak, Frances overcame her nerves but has no memory of what she said, except for the last line: "Ladies and Gentlemen, I am honored to introduce the President of the United States, George W. Bush."[1]

Later that day Bush told Frances he was impressed with what she had done with her life. A month after that she got a letter on White House stationery that expressed appreciation for her "kind introduction at the Charlotte Chamber of Commerce." Two years later, when running for reelection, Bush returned to Charlotte for a political rally. Frances attended, and Bush took note of her presence and invited her to speak. Then in December, with the election won, Frances received an invitation to come to Washington, D.C., and attend one of the annual White House holiday parties. The county offered to pay her expenses, and Frances footed the bill for her daughter's fare. The two lined up in the Green Room with hundreds of other guests to have their pictures taken with President and Mrs. Bush. When Frances and Blair came through the line the president recognized Frances and held her hand during a photo shot. Later a copy of the picture arrived, signed "To Frances Cunningham with best wishes, George Bush and Laura Bush."

It was a proud moment in Frances' life. While some members of the Charlotte African-American community grumbled over her association with this Republican president, Frances could not help but reflect how far she had come since being an unemployed high school dropout with little self-esteem. In subsequent months Jacobsen asked her to take on new tasks for the department, including public appearances on radio and television. When I asked him on his last workday as DSS director how he would sum up the essence of the DSS mission, Jacobsen replied, "Our job is to make miracles—like Frances Cunningham."

THE EARLY YEARS

As a state North Carolina was somewhat late getting into what we would today call the welfare business. In the 18th and 19th centuries, taxes levied by county-appointed Boards of Overseers were the source of meager funds allocated by the Warden of the Poor to paupers directly or to contractors that took care of them. Churches, the medical profession and women's charitable organizations provided assistance on an ad hoc basis. In 1831 the legislature authorized counties to establish poorhouses at their own expense, although orphanages were left to private philanthropy. State funds were not spent on public welfare until the Whigs came to power in 1835, and the legislature appropriated modest sums to support a state insane asylum and Institute for the Deaf, Dumb and Blind.[2]

North Carolina began assuming overall responsibility for public welfare in 1917. The General Assembly created a Board of Charities and Public Welfare to supervise all state charitable and penal institutions, inspect such institutions at the county level and assist counties in their own public welfare activities. It required each county to have a public welfare board, a juvenile court and superintendent of public welfare. The superintendent was to be appointed by the county commission and board of education meeting together in joint session, with the appointee subject to approval by the Board of Charities in Raleigh. A later statute, enacted in 1921, required that the welfare superintendent (later renamed director of social services) be appointed by the county welfare board alone, according to state merit system rules. That statute also enumerated the duties and responsibilities of this office.[3]

Mecklenburg County did not get its welfare superintendent in place until 1919, a delay prompted in part by disagreement over an acceptable candidate for the position. In that the merit standard introduced in 1921 was not yet in effect, politics dominated the process of deciding who would get this patronage plum. Julian S. Miller, publisher of the *Charlotte Observer and News*, was preferred by the board of education, but the county commission wanted Lucius H. Ranson, a teacher at a local military school. After much haggling, Ranson was chosen by a margin of one vote. The selection was subsequently approved in Charlotte.

The Ranson Era

Superintendent Ranson was allotted a salary of $2,000, with the stipulation that he be "providing and maintaining his own machine" (i.e., automobile). The budget for the first year was set at $2,239.76. Ranson and his secretary comprised the total staff; initially the two were loaned a room in the office of the Commissioner of Public Safety.[4]

Lucius Ranson was one of 10 sons of the William Joseph Ranson family of Huntersville, N.C. He graduated from the University of North Carolina like his brothers and later taught school in Huntersville and then at Horner military school in Mecklenburg County. Following his election, Ranson visited welfare programs in Winston-Salem, Greensboro and Durham, and in November 1919 called an all-day meeting of business, church and government leaders within the county to discuss its welfare needs. State Welfare Commissioner R. F. Beasley, who came from Raleigh to speak at the event, recommended that churches be open seven days a week to provide social and recreational programs for youth, a proposal that was ignored. The following year Ranson extended his horizons further by traveling to Richmond, Norfolk, Baltimore and Washington to learn more about juvenile courts, public recreation and child welfare. During this period he learned that among his other duties, the welfare superintendent was expected to watch over the morals of citizens; Ranson took the responsibility seriously and made sure risqué films did not run in local movie houses.

Anxious to stimulate grassroots involvement in Mecklenburg public welfare, Ranson organized the county into 70 districts, with a local welfare committee in each. The tasks of these bodies were to monitor truancy in the schools, combat juvenile delinquency, promote wholesome recreation opportunities, care for neglected children, report cases of insanity and assist in caring for the destitute. Ranson himself spearheaded the establishment of a county baseball league, the holding of track meets and creation of a Big Brother association. Seeing a need to coordinate this civic activity, the superintendent formed a Central Council of Social and Civic Agencies of Charlotte and Mecklenburg County.[5]

The Kuralt Era

Another key department head was Wallace Hamilton Kuralt, who served from 1945 to 1972. A native of Springfield, Mass., Kuralt attended Clark University and later the University of North Carolina. Although he planned to become a businessman, bad economic times led him to accept a position as caseworker for the Federal Emergency Relief Association (FERA) in Onslow County, N.C. From there Kuralt moved up the ladder of the social work profession: FERA casework supervisor; district supervisor of social work for the Works Progress Administration; field representative for the North Carolina State Board of Public Welfare; and public assistance analyst for the Atlanta office of the Federal Security Agency, the forerunner of today's Department of Health and Human Services.[6]

In 1934 a son, Charles, was born to the Kuralt family. As the boy grew up his mother was busy helping support the family by teaching school, so when Dad went on trips around North Carolina to visit local welfare offices, young Charles would tag along. In his autobiography Charles Kuralt recalls how on these trips his father would smoke Tampa Nuggets while explaining the various sights they encountered along the road. This experience planted the seeds of what in 1967 became the much-enjoyed "On the Road" segment of the *CBS Evening News*.[7]

Wallace Kuralt's annual report for 1949 noted that welfare expenditures were rising rapidly in Mecklenburg County due to inflation, in-migration, family instability and an increasingly complex society. He warned that although too much taxation or too much welfare would undermine work incentives, "the preservation of human resources requires a minimum standard of decency and health below which families cannot fall."[8] Along with accommodating the department's work to these changes, Kuralt introduced innovations of his own. In view of the ongoing changes taking place regarding the role of women in society, he first inaugurated a homemaker services program and later set up a network of agency-sponsored daycare centers. As sexual practices evolved over the quarter-century, he successively authorized sterilizations, distributed condoms and organized an oral contraception program. In other words, the Mecklenburg department was already showing signs of being able to keep up with the times; in 1969 its name was changed to the Mecklenburg County Department of Social Services, and in another quarter-century it would start to become famous.

JAKE COMES TO TOWN

Richard William Jacobsen Jr. served as the department's seventh director. He was universally known as "Jake" and will be referred to by that name henceforth. Hired for the position in early 1994, Jake remained at the department until the end of 2007. During these 14 years he brought to the department a markedly different leadership orientation than it had seen in the past; rather than making selective, incremental changes, wholesale transformation was now in the works.

Jake was raised in Los Angeles County and, after receiving a BA in social studies and a master's degree in business, he enlisted in the Navy and served in Vietnam, where he earned a Bronze Star. He extended his Navy tour in order to join a human resource development project in the Bureau of Naval Personnel at the Pentagon that involved race relations, intercultural relations, alcohol and drug abuse, and human resource management. Following his discharge from the Navy, Jake stayed in Washington to direct a project on treating street crime for the Special Action Office for Drug Abuse Prevention, a unit within the Executive Office of the President. He then worked for a time in the Justice Department's Law Enforcement Assistance Administration before returning to the West Coast to assume several successive leadership posts in San Diego County government: director of substance abuse prevention; interim housing director, assistant director of social services, deputy chief administrative officer for the county, and finally its director of social services. It was from the last position that he successfully competed for the directorship position in the Mecklenburg County DSS.

Jake reported for work in Charlotte in January 1994 and plunged into his new assignment with great energy. From the start he focused on fostering a new management environment in the DSS, modeled in part from the Disney theme park philosophy. With respect to the staff, he raised morale by providing better office facilities and enlisting the employees themselves in work groups to seek new improvements. With respect to technology, he ended the era of index cards and began to usher the department into the IT age. Jake also sought to change attitudes toward clients, insisting they be called "customers" and served sincerely, holistically, creatively and with respect. Outside the department, he preached that poverty and abuse are grievous problems that affect the entire community, in cooperation with its public schools, churches, businesses and nonprofit organizations. Amidst this flurry, members of his staff asked themselves, "Does this man ever sleep?"[9]

Aware of a natural resistance to "welfare" by taxpayer groups and political conservatives, Jake deliberately sought to defuse the prejudice against "handouts" by stressing the economic benefits of converting public assistance recipients to tax-paying wage earners who spend their incomes locally. Concerns about a wasteful welfare bureaucracy were allayed by undertaking well-publicized management reforms and pointing out how money can be saved by new technologies. New systems of accountability and augmented efforts to uncover welfare cheating belied the public perception of a welfare department rife with fraud and abuse. At the same time, Jake found outside sources of public and private funding that enabled him to expand programs beyond what the county government would pay for.

Richard W. "Jake" Jacobsen Jr., director of the department in 1994–2007. Drawing on managerial experience in San Diego County government, he introduced many new programs and technologies to DSS, making it one of the best public welfare departments in the country.

Source: Photo by the author.

Indeed, the nine-member Board of County Commissioners (which performs the statutory function of Social Services Board) was actively courted as a political ally. Invariably split 5–4 one way or another between the two major political parties, the Republicans on the board were instinctively hostile to DSS until Jake convinced them that he was as tough on waste and fraud as any corporate CEO. A conservative Republican commissioner told the *Charlotte Observer,* "I don't have the concerns that I normally would [about the DSS budget] because Jake Jacobsen has shown time after time that he can operate like a capitalist with a huge government bureaucracy. The man has saved us money."[10]

To what ends was this "capitalist" Jake Jacobsen operating his bureaucracy? As we shall see, they involved a complex and varied set of programs, all of which pertain to the fundamental basics of human dignity and survival. In that sense, welfare is a type of government work that affects individual human lives in an intimate way, making the work of a large, urban welfare department a delicate business. To simplify for the sake of clarity, I shall discuss DSS programs as fulfilling two imperatives. One is to provide the county's less fortunate residents with economic opportunities, i.e., give them a chance. The other is to enrich—and sometimes to protect—their daily existence, actions that give them a life.

GIVING PEOPLE A CHANCE

By the time the Wallace H. Kuralt Centre opens at 8:00 a.m. sharp each workday morning, a small crowd of people is assembled outside the doors, regardless of the weather. Many in the crowd have worried looks on their faces and small children in their arms. The large brick building before which they stand is, obviously, named after the department's fourth and longest-serving director. It is located in the middle of Charlotte, within an extensive county government campus that also includes the Department of Public Health and the Area Mental Health Authority. The Kuralt Centre has now been the headquarters of the Mecklenburg County Department of Social Services for more than three decades, although during Jake's tenure it was extensively remodeled and newly outfitted.

When 8 o'clock comes and the doors open, the welfare *customers* file in. They enter a high-ceiling entrance hall that is well lit and colorfully decorated. Receptionists, called greeters, receive them at a front information desk known as the greeting station. Spanish-speaking personnel are on hand if needed, and translators can be quickly found for any other language one can think of.

The greeters determine the reason why each incoming individual is present, and in some instances resolve the matter on the spot, such as recording a change of address. Persons applying for assistance for the first time are given forms to fill out and told where to go within adjacent waiting areas. If the requested services are located at another DSS building, an appointment is then scheduled. If other organizations in the community might provide the assistance needed, brochures and appropriate contacts are offered. If transportation is a problem, passes to ride a van are provided. In addition to being the prime entry point to DSS services, the Kuralt greeter station also serves as a place for the homeless to drop off or retrieve mail.

Two general waiting areas exist on the Kuralt Centre's first floor: one for new applicants and one for returnees. During high-volume business hours, a staff member designated as "client representative" circulates freely within the waiting areas to answer questions and ask if help is needed. Volunteer clergy from area churches occupy a lobby office called the Vestibule, where they advise clients if called upon. When the time comes for individual or assembled interviews, the names of pertinent clients are called out on a public address system, using the form of address "Customer _____" [last name]. DSS employees who need to walk through these public areas are asked not to eat food or laugh loudly while doing so, out of respect for those present who are hungry or distressed.[11]

Entrance lobby of the Kuralt Centre, the main DSS building. The client reception process conducted here became a model for efficient and courteous treatment. The building is named after former director Wallace Kuralt, father of Charles Kuralt of "On the Road" television fame.

Source: Photo by the author.

If upon being interviewed it is determined that hunger is an immediate need, filled grocery bags are brought from a storeroom within the building that is stocked with nonperishable goods. Persons who must have cash immediately to buy clothing or medicines are assisted from emergency assistance funds. Rather than hand out cold cash, customers receiving money are directed to an electronic benefits transfer station within the waiting area, where debit cards are issued. For emergency payment of utility bills, a DSS contractor allocates from low-income energy assistance funds. On the order of 50,000 clients come through the Kuralt first floor each year, and more than $4 million in emergency funds released. In short, unlike the methodical, impersonal ways of many welfare offices, the prime operant values are concern for fellow human beings and rapid response to their physical needs.

These emergency funds are small change, however, compared to the huge sums dispersed annually by the department for the three big public assistance programs it manages: Medicaid, Food Stamps and Work First Family Assistance, North Carolina's name for what was once Aid to Families with Dependent Children. Each program has its own complexities, mandates and regulations. The intricacy of making eligibility decisions for these diverse programs is compounded by the fact that many clients meet the qualifications of more than one program. Furthermore, in that large sums of taxpayer funds are being obligated, eligibility workers must make these decisions accurately.

Yet despite these challenges and almost without fail, the department succeeds in completing the intake process for all economic assistance cases on a same-day basis for each new applicant that comes in the door by 4 p.m. The secret of this expeditious service is a one-stop Consolidated Customer Service Center, where several intake teams, comprised of representatives of each program, formulate and coordinate the DSS response to each newcomer's unique situation. Once intake is achieved, the customer is assigned to a benefits caseworker within the department's Economic Services Division or Adult Medicaid Division. This staff member remains that person's division contact as long as the case is active. She or he gives periodic guidance on such matters as follow-up steps, limits and requirements, responsibilities and obligations, re-eligibility procedures and the setting of personal goals. Coordination is maintained for each caseworker's clients by case-management teams representing the various programs.

Work First

The most important of the big programs—and a hallmark of the department's overall record of achievement—is Work First, the initiative under which Frances Cunningham blossomed. By the time of Jake's arrival in 1994, the Work First program had been initiated at the statewide level by North Carolina governor Jim Hunt. But few localities had it up and running. Jake had previously created a welfare-to-work demonstration program in California; based on that experience, he developed a comprehensive welfare reform plan for Mecklenburg County and presented it to the Board of Commissioners. It was approved, and in July 1995 the Mecklenburg Work First experiment was launched, a year before Congress enacted what is commonly called "welfare reform," i.e., the Personal Responsibility and Work Opportunity Reconciliation Act. Just as North Carolina was ahead of the nation, Mecklenburg was ahead in the state.

Jake believed that welfare to work would not be effective unless it addressed the problems of clients comprehensively. He insisted that the program be placed organizationally under Income Maintenance rather than Adult Services so that eligibility for Food Stamps and Medicaid could be maintained. Each participant was required to sign a Mutual Responsibility Agreement that detailed a two-year plan which, if violated, led to termination of cash benefits from Temporary Assistance for Needy Families (TANF). In the agreement, clients made a commitment to send children age 5 and older to school and see to it that they received immunizations and health checkups. They also had to be screened for signs of alcohol or drug abuse and, if found, be required to enroll in "Project Courage:

Take Charge," a motivational counseling program. If signs of domestic violence appeared and were substantiated, the individual was referred to the department's Youth and Family Services division for investigation and needed action.

Work First participants were also required to enter a departmental program called Work First Employment Services. This is a series of activities designed to prepare people who have never had a job or could not hold one. An overall assessment was made of the client's employment strengths and barriers to employment. If problems surfaced, such as childcare or transportation, they were addressed. A class called Orientation to the World of Work conveyed what gainful employment involves, exposed individuals to life skills, and provided practical information on household budgeting and time management.

In a phase called First-Stop Employment, clients were interviewed by staff of the State Employment Security Commission to determine their level of job readiness. Those at a relatively high state of preparedness were placed in classes on career alternatives, job shadowing, job seeking and job keeping. Those needing specific work skills before going to work were sent to outside courses on welding, customer service, office information systems, medical reimbursement or nursing fundamentals. Enrollees who would benefit from preliminary work experience as a volunteer (like Frances) were placed for unpaid service in a private or public organization; if, during this time, requirements of the client's Mutual Responsibility Agreement were still being observed, they received a living stipend of $200 per month.

Within six months of expiration of the two-year time clock, all participants were assessed for final job readiness. If specific barriers remained, plans were made to adjust their situation or remove them from the job-preparation cycle. If full readiness was being approached, they attended monthly job fairs sponsored by DSS to which employer representatives were invited. The employers in attendance had become familiar with the Work First program, and some had already committed themselves to obtaining a certain number of hires from it. An Employment Resources Center at DSS assisted in matching people to jobs, provided individual career advice and counseling, and monitored how job-placed individuals were doing.

From 1996 to 2007, a total of 24,025 clients successfully obtained jobs after going through Work First. Furthermore, most of its alumnae had been found to earn substantially higher wages after two years on the job than they did when hired, and only about 10 percent had returned to ask again for cash assistance.[12] It is no wonder that President Bush came to Charlotte to associate himself with Mecklenburg County's Work First.

GIVING PEOPLE A LIFE

Having discussed DSS efforts to battle poverty, we turn to its function of enriching and even saving the lives of the less fortunate. The department does this on many fronts, through neighborhood community and nutrition centers; adult daycare and in-home aide services; and operating a county-wide transportation network called the Mecklenburg Transportation System (MTS), to name a few. The large MTS fleet of vans is used to deliver meals to the homebound, take patients to doctor's offices and transport the handicapped to sheltered workshops.

The most critical aspect of giving people a life is to grapple with the problem of family violence. Abuse of frail elderly persons, victimized women and helpless children is the hidden crime of any society—a kind of secret, private oppression that takes place behind closed doors. Far from just another social program, tackling internal family coercion and cruelty can be a matter of sheer survival. From an organizational standpoint, this work of the DSS is divided between two divisions: Adult Services, which deals with abuse and neglect of older adults, and Youth and Family Services, which contends with the abuse of children, spouses and all cases of sexual molestation.

Both of these divisions have a heavy staff presence in Chapin Hall, a relatively new DSS facility located in a predominantly African-American neighborhood of Charlotte. In its remodeled circulation spaces posters hanging on the walls tell of the history of public welfare, DSS and the Charlotte community. Private rooms for interviewing are nearby, equipped with chairs without arms to accommodate the obese. Off the waiting room is a cheerful child daycare room, informally known as "Jake's Place."

Adult Services

One of the problems faced by Adult Services is finding the individuals who need protection. Mistreatment of the elderly is particularly difficult to detect because they tend to stay indoors and are rarely seen by anyone other than the family members who might be mistreating them. Unfortunately, such abuse is usually discovered only after it has been going on for some time.

There are several avenues by which Adult Services uncovers cases. Social workers are to be on the lookout for signs of neglect when they make home visits, place periodic monitoring calls to those living alone or exercise guardianship responsibilities. Members of area police departments, fire departments, EMS crews and hospital ER staff are trained by a DSS First Responders unit on indicators of abuse and whom to call when a possible case comes to their attention. Drivers for Meals on Wheels are given the same information. Leads are also received from mail carriers, who receive instructions on the subject through the USPS Postal Carrier Alert Program.

About 500–800 potential cases of adult abuse and neglect come to the attention of the division each year. A triage system is used to assess the degree of potential danger represented by each referral, as follows:

Category 1. The victim is potentially subject to violent harm or serious neglect at the time of the call or referral. The case must be investigated *immediately*; nighttime and weekend duty assignments make this possible on a 24/7/365 basis.

Category 2. An urgent but nonemergency situation exists, such as the need to receive help in receiving medications. A response is necessary within 24 hours.

Category 3. The problem must be looked into, but on a nonpriority basis. An illustration would be a report of fighting in a family previously identified as dysfunctional. Required response time is 72 hours.

Adult protection social workers investigate these situations alone and unannounced. They arrive at the designated residence in a county car. After knocking at the front door and it is opened, the worker senses the reaction to her presentation of DSS identification and request to enter. Once inside, the worker attempts to engage family members in a calm conversation during which the abuse question is raised. Denials or justifications by family members are listened to in an open-minded manner, and the alleged victim's perspective on the situation is heard without interruption. If corrective action seems needed, workers do not reveal their initial conclusions, but instead identify issues they think should be addressed. Follow-up visits may be necessary to conduct additional interviews, obtain physical evidence, propose plans of action, arrange a mental competency evaluation or—after taking several intervening legal steps—initiate custodial care. It is sensitive, delicate and potentially dangerous work, and the social worker must proceed thoughtfully and with care.

During my interviews at Chapin Hall, an adult protection worker told me about two Category 1 cases she experienced. Recounting these memories moved her to tears. In the first case, for religious reasons, a sister would not allow her elderly brother to have surgery on a badly broken leg resulting from a car accident. A judge was petitioned to grant DSS emergency guardian rights so he could be taken to the hospital against his sister's will. But, in the meantime, the sister removed her brother from the emergency room and transported him all the way to New York City, where she abandoned him at a hospital. The doctors there treated the man and got him placed in a suitable institution, but it took the social worker many hours of searching and calling hospitals to discover what had happened.

In the second experience this social worker was tipped off to investigate a particular rental unit in an apartment building. There, she found an elderly woman alone in a room, lying unconscious in a fetal position on an air mattress, hooked to a feeding tube. The feces around her body and the suppurating sores covering it led the worker to vomit. A crude sign had been posted on the wall above the mattress that read "Do Not Resuscitate." Upon investigation, it was

discovered that the family of the woman was keeping the old lady alive—barely—
to collect her Social Security check.

Youth and Family Services

The Youth and Family Services Division of DSS handles cases of child abuse and
all instances of sexual abuse. These cases are somewhat easier than adult abuse to
detect, in that the problems are more fully recognized in society and hence more
likely to come to someone's attention. Reports of potential instances are received
from school personnel, nurses, doctors, service providers, relatives, friends and
neighbors. In a typical year some 12,000 alerts are received. Investigative social
workers are on call to respond at all times. Although regulations require an
inquiry within 24 hours of all abuse reports, it is often done almost immediately.

Investigation of these cases is governed by a relatively new protocol adopted
by North Carolina, the Multiple Response System (MRS). This name refers to
utilization of many potential types of response to child and sex abuse situations.
As with adult protection, social workers are instructed to enter the home with a
relatively open mind rather than expecting the worst. They are instructed to
deemphasize the necessity of determining guilt right away and instead determine
what available social services can be mobilized to reduce the underlying problem.
If suspicions remain that the family is hiding something, the tactics of interroga-
tion can harden. In instances of likely physical or sexual abuse, MRS sanctions
what is called the "forensic" manner of investigation, i.e., conducting unexpected
searches for evidence without prior notification.

After years of consultation among MRS-practicing counties in North Carolina, a common procedure for taking custody of children believed to be in danger
was adopted. It begins with the assembly of a Child and Family Team that
includes the child, his or her parents, supporters of the parents, school counselors, the caseworker, a supervisor and any others pertinent to the circumstance.
The team's meeting takes place at Chapin Hall or another DSS location and is
chaired by a DSS facilitator not involved in the case. It reviews the general situation, hears concerns of the family and DSS personnel, and brainstorms over what
might be done. A plan of action is then worked out, by consensus if possible,
with a contingency plan held in abeyance if the agreed-upon plan is ignored.

If and when DSS determines it must remove the child from the family, its
members are informed of the decision and why. A petition, along with documented evidence arguing imminent risk, is presented to a family-law judge at
county court. Seven days later a hearing is conducted, with the family and its
attorney present. The judge then makes a decision among several options: dismiss the petition, order mediation, issue a "nonsecure" order that grants authority to take custody without force being applied, or sign a "secure" order that
allows force to be used in doing so. If the family contests the order, a bench trial

is held. If the child is to be forcibly removed, sheriff's deputies stand by outside the home as the transfer is made, amidst much crying but usually without physical resistance.

The child is then taken to a foster home, either on an emergency or permanent basis, depending on the future outlook for the case. A year-long process known as "permanency planning" then commences. Its foremost goal is to achieve reunification of the family if possible. A plan to that end is drawn up and approved by the judge. It lays out a series of steps that may include parental therapy, drug or alcohol rehabilitation, assignment to support groups, allowance of limited responsibilities (such as picking the child up from daycare) or trial visits. After nine months an assessment hearing takes place, again with the parents and all other parties present, to set a course toward family reunification, adoption or possibly placement in a youth home. After one year has passed the case automatically goes back to court with the same judge presiding, and a final determination is made as to what "permanency" means.

Clearly DSS, when prying into possible child or sexual abuse and taking such drastic action as causing a person to be seized, is playing with fire. The sovereign authority of the state is being used for the most intrusive action possible against citizens, short of arrest and conviction of a crime. In order to safeguard helpless individuals from an improper exercise of power, two checks are built into the Youth and Family Services structure.

One is a division ombudsman who has the authority to pull the entire case for reexamination if credible complaints about worker behavior are received. The ombudsman looks into as many as 7,000 cases a year, with five or six decisions reversed annually. The DSS director also has authority to terminate a pending action. The second check is provided by an independent review body known as the Community Child Fatality Prevention and Protection Team. It is composed of community doctors, school officials, mental health experts, domestic violence advocates, judges, policemen and parents. All cases involving deaths are automatically referred to it. Other cases with unusually serious overtones can be filed with it as well; the team meets monthly but can be assembled as needed.

The work lives of social workers in both adult and child protection are intense, emotionally draining and often harrowing and dangerous. They frequently deal with people who are furious with the government butting into their business. They must get used to foul language and threats. Most social workers are young women and are frequently driving alone around the meaner streets of the city, often at night. Jake has made sure they are quipped with cell phones as well as panic buttons in cars to call for help if needed; he also instituted cross-training with the police to foster mutual respect and understanding between the two kinds of public servant.

In a typical year in Mecklenburg County, 1,000–2,000 abuse cases of all kinds are pending at all times. As many as 1,700 children are in departmental custody at any given moment. Because of budget restrictions the numbers of social work positions in both the Adult and Child divisions is limited. Currently active caseloads can run as high as 24 per social worker. The workers are on call at all hours of the day or night, which of course adversely affects their home lives. High stress is simply part of the job, and burnout always threatens. Salaries are not particularly high. When resignations and retirements do occur, the recruitment and training of suitable replacements is arduous. Those who remain must be absolutely dedicated; some say social workers are born, not bred—in any case they must be a special kind of person, for their work is not just a job but a calling.

A DEPARTMENT OF SOCIAL SERVICES

The Organization

As a subunit of county government, organizational details of the Department of Social Services are less complicated than for the sizable federal agencies discussed earlier in this book.

With Charlotte in the middle, the county's jurisdiction is an irregularly shaped surrounding area that is roughly 28 x 38 miles. The population served is approximately one million. The county government is headed by a board of county commissioners made up of six district-elected representatives and three at-large members, one of whom is chairperson. County administration is in accord with the strong manager form of government. The county manager is Harry L. Jones Sr., a professional public administrator with three decades of experience in urban public service. Four general managers are accountable to him for various policy sectors, with DSS falling under the purview of a general manager for community health and safety. Unlike the federal agencies in our study, as a local government entity DSS operates in the context of unified authority, not a tripartite separation of powers.

The county employs approximately 4,000 persons. DSS, at a little more than 1,200 personnel, represents about 30 percent of the county workforce. It is the largest manager-controlled county department; the county sheriff employs a couple hundred more, but as an elected official he is not responsible to the county board. Social Services is the smallest agency we have studied so far in this book, a quarter the size of the National Weather Service (see appendix).

The department is organizationally quite flat. All divisions and staff units report to the director. In addition to the principal line divisions of Economic Services, Services to Adults, and Youth and Family Services, other components include a number of administrative and support units. A body called the senior executive team meets weekly and is comprised of the director, the three division chiefs and the heads of key staff components. The work of the department takes place primarily at four locations: the Kuralt Centre, Chapin Hall, Charlotte East and what is known as the Interstate Street Facility. Smaller offices are located in the City-County Office Building and commercial centers known as Farm Pond and Walton Plaza. Senior nutrition sites at which meals are served daily operate in 22 locations around the county. The Kuralt Centre is the point of central administration and the only facility at which all three line divisions have significant staff. Thus even though it is a relatively small organization, the Mecklenburg DSS is physically scattered, forming a degree of cultural dispersion not too different from what we saw in the CDC and also relevant to cell 5.

Fiscally, DSS is funded by several dollar streams. In FY 2007–2008 the department's own budget was $174.9 million, of which $70.1 million came from the county (40 percent), $24.3 million from the state (14 percent), $76.9 million from the federal government (44 percent) and $3.5 million from other sources (2 percent). It is important to stress that these figures do not include what might be thought of as fiduciary revenues, i.e., funds that pass through DSS to be directly transmitted to customers as cash assistance, Food Stamps and Medicaid benefits. This pass-through aspect of the budget totaled $976.5 million in FY 2007, or more than five times the departmental budget. Jake was fond of pointing out that the department's economic impact on the community can be thought of as constituting the total federal-state drawdown times a multiplier of 4, or $3.2 billion in FY 2007. This permitted him to argue that even though a charity-based institution, DSS contributes more to the Charlotte economy than many of its industries.[13]

The Workforce

The demographic composition of the DSS workforce differs from that of most bureaucracies. Eighty-seven percent of its employees are female, a factor that reflects the overall nature of the social work field. Sixty-two percent of the total workforce is African-American, as compared to 47 percent in the county government as a whole. Prior to 1994 many supervisory and management positions were occupied by whites, but by 2007 three members of the senior executive team were black, three white and one Hispanic. The current DSS director is African-American.[14]

Another point to make regarding the workforce is that a structural chasm divides it into two categories of personnel, a phenomenon that also affects the cultural element of cell 5. On one side are the eligibility workers who determine and monitor benefits. They are hired with an eye to basic office skills and the ability to work with people. In view of the complexity of their work, they are put through a rigorous training program in the detailed rules and regulations handed down by Washington and Raleigh. Pay is on an hourly basis, with the resultant annual compensation so low as to make some qualified for Food Stamps. The irony is that they make the decisions that authorize the expenditures of hundreds of millions of taxpayer dollars each year.

On the other side of the workforce chasm are the professional social workers. As we have seen, they perform most of the discretion-requiring activities that underlie the delicate business of transferring people from dependence to independence and from danger to safety. They are all college graduates, and many hold the Master's of Social Work. Social workers are paid on a salary rather than wage basis; yet their compensation is not generous by private sector standards, with $36,000 as the entry figure for a Case Manager I. Substantial resentment prevails across this divide between eligibility workers and social workers, a problem found generally in the public welfare field.

With respect to employee motivation (cell 4), during his tenure Jake deliberately treated all staff with the same amount of respect, regardless of their roles, backgrounds or compensation. As a manager he did take note of one particular differentiation within the workforce, that of birth-year generation. He even kept track of the relative percentages of staff by successive generation over time, with the assumption that different strategies of motivation are needed for each. When Jake lectured on leadership in seminars and training sessions, he recommended that silent "traditionals" (born prior to 1945) be sought out for advice, reformist "baby boomers" (1946–1964) be challenged to create change, individualist "Generation Xers" (born 1965–1980) be valued for independent thinking, and self-regarding "New Millennials" (born after 1980) be motivated by incentives.[15] While such categorization is empirically risky, it does demonstrate an awareness of age differences, a factor that deserves special consideration in the delicate business of welfare, where human interaction is so intimate.

The Mission

With respect to cell 1 of the template concerning mission, the Department of Social Services has no organic statute. It operates under the North Carolina statute of 1921, as amended, that requires each county to have a board of public welfare, now called social services. What "public welfare" or "social services" constitute is unstated, although in one chapter the statute lists the duties and responsibilities of the welfare superintendent (now social services director). These include administering funds for the care of indigents, investigating cases for adoption and placement in foster homes, and acting in response to reports of abuse of children and disabled adults.[16]

While the law applies to DSS, it does not articulate a mission specifically for the Mecklenburg department. That organization's current official mission statement is "To provide services necessary to prevent or relieve economic and emotional hardship, and to rally the community to improve the quality of life for its citizens."[17] We note that the first part of this rather bland declaration discusses what the department should do and the second what the community could do. When, however, I asked employees about the department's central mission, they referred not to this sentence but another one, known formally as the DSS vision

DSS VISION
TO BE THE BEST IN....

➤ service delivery
  ➤ prevention initiatives
    ➤ community relations
      ➤ empowering employees
        ➤ promoting a family friendly workplace

A large embossed plate bearing the DSS vision statement. The phrase "to be the best" became a mantra of Jake's tenure at the DSS, abbreviated as "TB^2" in agency documents. It signified the goal of becoming a superior public welfare department in every way possible.

Source: Photo by the author.

statement. Its text reads: "To be the best in . . . service delivery, prevention initiatives, community relations, empowering employees, promoting a family friendly workplace." A large green and gold plaque bearing these words hangs on the wall at a central hallway intersection within the Kuralt headquarters—placed symbolically at the center of the center of the organization.

In discussing this statement with interviewees, I noticed that in their spontaneous references to it they did not, even once, list the five qualities to be best in. The content conveyed was simply becoming the best there is in the social services field. My interpretation is that the phrase "to be the best"—standing alone—had become a kind of mantra for how the Mecklenburg DSS saw itself—a social service agency that wanted to attain the highest possible level of quality in its performance, whether in comparison to other departments or to an imagined ideal. Jake even produced a mathematics-style symbol for the notion that he would put on the margin of reports: TB^2.

What we have here, then, is another instance of an acknowledged mission, arising from the traditional governmental function of public welfare and comparable to the public health basis of the CDC's mission. Yet unlike the CDC, the underlying "real" purpose is not stated in terms of a set of activities or the degree to which the public's health is maximized, but the idea of being the best at what it does in terms of quality of functioning or performance. In short, it is a goal of self-realization rather than an endpoint of accomplishment.

ethics

While Jake was enamored of catchy slogans, he also thought in more human-istic terms. I have already mentioned his comment about how "our job is to make miracles," illustrated by Frances Cunningham. In another conversation he told me that good public welfare is like dating one's wife. As he did not explain what he meant, I was left trying to translate the aphorism. What I came up with is that the system must pay attention to all the formalities, but at the same time *really care*. At bottom, the act of caring for the unfortunate seems to be what his Department of Social Services was all about. In this instance, then, mission mys-tique seems to derive from believing that the agency is committed to a continu-ous search to become the very best there is for an institution whose task is to care authentically about the community's deprived.

The Need

The urgency of the societal need being met by the DSS, the subject of cell 2, would in the eyes of a large proportion of citizens be gauged by the amount of poverty that persists. Among the nearly one million residents of Mecklenburg County there are plenty of poor people. In 2007, 87,000 of its residents were calculated as living in poverty. At this writing, the midst of the 2008–2010 eco-nomic recession, the number is no doubt much higher. Compared to other sur-rounding counties, Mecklenburg's poverty rate is neither the highest nor the lowest, but in any case demographic variables make a difference. Living poor is especially the plight of the less educated, recent migrants and families with only one parent; when these variables are combined, over half of the total falls below the poverty line.[18]

It is an unfortunate fact of urban life that economic and social inequities concentrate in certain social classes and hence in certain neighborhoods. To show the extent of differences that exist in Mecklenburg County, Jake had his analysts isolate one particularly poor area, designated "Neighborhood A," and an especially wealthy section, called "Neighborhood B." They then collected comparative data on quality of life indicators, some of which are given in Table 5.1.

We see that household income rose in the two neighborhoods at similar rates over the six-year period covered, but in terms of absolute amount B bested A about four times over. Food Stamp dependence, high school dropouts, adoles-cent births and violent crime were serious problems in A but not B. Neighbor-hood A had some good news in that between 2000 and 2006 income increased, dropout rates declined and substandard housing lessened; its bad news was that Food Stamp participation, teen births and violent crime essentially doubled.[19] What this disparity points to in our discussion is that the business of welfare is seen from two vantage points. One is from those who are caught in a web of poverty and disadvantage. Living across town are those who are far superior in

Table 5.1 Economic and Social Inequities in Mecklenburg County, N.C.

	Neighborhood A		Neighborhood B	
	2000	2006	2000	2006
Median household income	$25,446	$29,059	$92,132	$109,104
Persons receiving food stamps	11.7	22.3	0.1	0.4
High school dropout rate	14.5	7.2	0.7	1.5
Percent adolescent births	6.2	14.5	0	1.0
Percent substandard housing	4.9	2.9	0	0
Violent crime (% city average)	170	280	10	10

Source: Mecklenburg County Department of Social Services, "Status Report: Wiping Out Poverty in Mecklenburg County," November 2007, 27–29.

income and status, and who are blessed by privilege and associated with power. The "reality" of the need for welfare is grossly different between the two: a lifeline to survival versus one more reason why taxes are high. Jake's conviction that poverty and domestic abuse affect the life of the entire community is not held by all. It is in this case among the six in our book that the subjective nature of agency need is most clearly exposed.

A DELICATE CULTURE

In our examination so far of the Mecklenburg DSS, we have encountered welcoming reception rooms, same-day turnaround of new clients, a successful welfare-to-work program, dedicated adult and child protection and a mission concept that is based on seeking the best there is in caring for the unfortunate. Asking the questions posed by cells 4 and 5 of the mission mystique template, what might an institutionalized culture of best-quality caring be like?

The Employee Climate

Mecklenburg County government conducts an annual Employment Climate Survey of its workforce. It is similar to the Federal Human Capital Survey (FHCS) in that it is administered anonymously online and breaks data down by departments. Table 5.2 gives percentages of responses for selected survey items over three years of Jake's administration. The figures given are identical to the Positive rating in the FHCS, which sums Strongly Agree and Agree replies. In the county's scoring system, 85 to 100 is regarded as Exemplary; 80 to 84, Successful; 70 to 79, Mixed; and below 70, Needs Improvement. It should be noted that response rates to these surveys are not always very high; in fact, only 51 percent of DSS employees responded in 2007.

Table 5.2 DSS Employee Responses to County Survey, 2005–2007 (percent positive)

	DSS			All County
	2005	2006	2007	2007
The County is a good place to work	96	92	95	95
Most days I feel good about coming to work	79	73	79	82
Work environment is friendly	90	89	88	87
I have technology to do job well	91	86	85	86
Peers have a strong work ethic	79	82	82	79
The Department values diversity in workplace	72	79	79	81
Increased skills in past year	58	57	78	82
The County provides opportunities to learn and grow	75	70	75	75
The Department looks for ways to do things better	73	63	63	79
I am paid fairly compared to similar jobs	46	55	56	60

Source: Mecklenburg County, North Carolina, *Employment Climate Survey Results, FY 2007.*

DSS responses in the 90s and high 80s depict the department as a good place to work, having a friendly work environment and providing the technology to do the job. The survey's assessment categories rate these scores as exemplary. Yet they were not much different than the rest of county government. Of greater concern are the other responses; except for two good years on the peer work ethic question, all other DSS ratings fall into the Mixed or Needs Improvement categories: feeling good about coming to work, the value placed on diversity, opportunities to learn and departmental improvement. At the bottom of the scale are items on increasing skills and low pay. In all of these, the department rated more poorly than the county as a whole. Thus from what the survey indicates, things do not look good for the motivation cell in this relatively large, sprawling department of local government.

These mostly unimpressive results may arise in part from a tendency for chronically unhappy employees to participate more often than satisfied ones in an anonymous, voluntary survey. For staff sincerely devoted to their jobs, its questions may be of particularly marginal interest, for almost all of the questions focus not on caring for others but caring for oneself, e.g., whether one likes the job or is paid enough. Unlike the FHCS, no questions are asked about the importance of the work itself or the degree of satisfaction with the leader's policies. Nowhere is there a place for the dedicated social worker who responds to calls in dangerous parts of town in the middle of the night to register their commitment.

As we recall from Chapter 2, low FHCS ratings in the Park Service seemed related to presidential policies of the time that ran counter to the mission. Then in Chapter 4 we surmised that the problem with poor CDC scores was unhappiness over the current director and her policies. In this case the answer may have more to do with the overall character of the workforce and the work. We have seen that DSS employees are divided into salaried social workers and wage-paid eligibility workers. This factor alone creates animosities that could lower scores. Physical dispersion can create other resentments; while many employees report for work at the attractive Kuralt headquarters and newly remodeled Chapin Hall, others are isolated in outlying smaller locations.

The larger point may be, however, that all DSS employees have inherently hard jobs. Everyone is overloaded with work, the emotional pressures are enormous, turnover rates are high and almost all personnel are paid woefully little for the amount and type of work they do. This mission mystique agency is by no means a bed of roses, and it is likely that no conscientious welfare department could be; the woes of others are always dealt with at considerable personal sacrifice.

Jake's RoadShow

It would be nice if time had been available to dig deeper into the delicate DSS culture, perhaps by using focus groups. Other than interviews at several levels of the organization, the primary means used were analyses of material contained in the prime vehicle by which Jake sought consciously to acculturate the workforce. This was an annual slideshow he gave scores of times each year, both to employees in all locations and to outside officials and groups. From my interviewing and observations, my sense is that this form of communication was quite effective in putting Jake's "stamp" on the institution as long as he was around. In the following pages I use this slideshow to directly illustrate Jake's attempts at culture building, and also as a peg on which to hang other culture-related points.

He presented a new version of the show each year. Called "The DSS Road-Show" because he took it on the road so often, it consisted of well over 200 slides, done in color with images designed by DSS graphic artist Denise Smith. They listed key points, presented data with tables and graphs, contained scores of photographs and brought out points via short texts. A typical presentation would take two hours or more, with Jake talking the audience through the material in a spirited monologue. He summarized points, provided explanations, made side comments, told jokes and answered questions. All employees were exposed to the slideshow, usually in small groups at the buildings where they worked. Its purpose was to review the work of the past year, extend praise where it was due, convey DSS values, outline a management philosophy and build a common culture.[20]

Honoring History

The RoadShow was always introduced in July or August so as to coincide with the beginning of the county's fiscal year. Jake would launch each program by acknowledging the department's fiscal birthday and wishing it and its employees a happy new year. His final edition in 2007 celebrated the 88th anniversary of the department's founding in 1919. Tied in with this was a brief sketch of the unfolding of early state and national welfare policy. Hence the history context of cell 6 of the template was always touched on in some way.

Relatively little is known about the department's early history, however. When Jake arrived in 1994 he asked for all the archival documents and records available, and only one thin file was found. From the material in that folder Jake realized that the agency was just then reaching its 75th anniversary. He seized on this fact to organize a public celebration of the event. The three living former directors were invited, including an elderly Wallace Kuralt. A kick-off luncheon was held for staff, officials, community leaders and the press. Two months later, in replication of Lucius Ranson's all-day community planning session, Jake hosted a group of county business, educational, religious and governmental figures to help plan the department's future.

bottom-up / make stakeholders feel important

Employee Support

Another theme of the DSS culture Jake tried to build is the importance of extending moral support to departmental employees. Each year a number of RoadShow slides were devoted to thanking individuals who had done something special the preceding year, such as receive a community award, organize a foster parent dinner, take custody children on a field trip or initiate a new program. For each thank you, photos of the recipients would be displayed.

The irony of this kind of gesture is that personally Jake is far from a gushy flatterer. His demeanor is stern. The rules he set were there to be enforced. For example, from the start of his tenure he demanded that department personnel dress in accord with a code he prescribed and that memoranda and reports be prepared in the proper format. Even so, employees found him to be a visible, "walk-around" boss who came to their buildings and offices, knew people by name and asked how things were going.

strong leadership

Staff members received support in material ways as well. They were offered discounts at local businesses for items such as cell phones, wireless service, fitness centers and theme parks. He made a point of having them participate in the refurnishing of their offices when remodeling occurred. Each year a huge all-departmental picnic was organized, known as Spring Fling; on my last visit to Kuralt its corridors were lined with photomontages from this event. A local Charlotte magazine recognized the DSS as "family friendly" four consecutive years in a row, outdoing all other area government agencies.

process fairness

Encouragement of Caring and Enthusiasm

A third cue to the DSS culture from the RoadShow is the emphasis placed on caring for the unfortunate, a value related to cell 5 in the mission mystique template. Attention was always devoted to how members of the workforce had become involved in area charities, such as food drives, blood drives, walk-a-thons, breast cancer campaigns and clothing donations.

Jake's personal symbol for a caring attitude is the teddy bear. The namesake for this toy, Theodore Roosevelt, is his model leader. While heading San Diego's Department of Social Services he sponsored a project of selling teddy bears to raise money for needy children. He then began collecting them as a hobby; the collection was subsequently brought to Charlotte, installed in his office and expanded over time. At public meetings on child welfare Jake would occasionally bring along a supply of the bears to distribute.

Another emphasized cultural value concerns fostering a spirit of enthusiastic engagement in the department's work. Puzzling terms like "Gung Ho," "Spirit of the Squirrel," "Way of the Beaver," "Gift of the Goose" and "Fish" were sprinkled among the RoadShow slides. These refer to ideas from two management books staff had brought to Jake's attention: *Gung Ho!* by Ken Blanchard and Sheldon Bowles, and *Fish!* by Stephen Lundin, Harry Pool and John Christensen.[21]

Gung Ho! tells the story of a money-losing factory in which only one unit, the Finishing Department, is doing well. The narrator is the newly appointed head of the plant who is charged with making it profitable. He goes to the Finishing Department's operations manager, Andrew Longclaw, to find out what is behind its success. The management principles that Longclaw uses, handed down to him from his Native-American grandfather, are described.

One such principle is "Spirit of the Squirrel," which embraces the idea of steadfast determination. It is illustrated by methodically carrying nuts to a winter hiding place, the perfect example of dependability. The "Way of the Beaver" recounts how that animal is tireless in building dams, teaching us that managers should respect the dignity and worth of each employee, even if performing menial tasks. The "Gift of the Goose" observes that when flying in V-formation the geese honk encouragement to each other and rotate who is in the front position; so too, hard work should be shared, acknowledged and thanked when effective.

The book *Fish!* is based on how fishmongers at Seattle's famous Pike Fish Market throw their product around in order to enjoy their job. On occasions Jake emphasized the notion of mixing play with work by tossing a cloth fish to people in staff meetings. Such playful antics were also associated with employee empowerment, which to Jake meant coming to the office each morning with a commitment to make that day rewarding for both oneself and one's customers; staff were advised to look each client straight in the eye, take pains to calm fears and defuse anger, and focus fully on the problem at hand.

When Jake presented his final edition of RoadShow in 2007, he concluded it with what in effect was a goodbye to his employees, a statement entitled "Jake Believes." It is reproduced in Box 5.1.

Box 5.1 "Jake Believes" Statement

Jake Believes . . .

- DSS staff represent the finest ideals of public service. Every day, you make thousands of decisions about the health, safety, and welfare of children, families, adults, and the elderly living in this community.
- The problems you face are highly complex, human issues with no easy solutions.
- You travel and call on customers in the most dangerous areas of Charlotte-Mecklenburg.
- DSS employees do [their] jobs, day in and day out. Regardless of your position, you all work until the job is done.
- You have a commitment and spirit of caring for your fellow citizens that is both valuable and rare.
- You do not have all the resources that you really need.
- DSS employees are loyal and dedicated, and believe in the dignity of your fellow citizens. You are willing and eager to go beyond the call of a simple job description every day.
- You are there when others wouldn't be. Let us all support, applaud and praise each other. I personally want to thank you for a job well done—for you are truly HEROES!

Source: Mecklenburg County Department of Social Services, "Director's Annual RoadShow, FY 2007," 109–110.

BUILDING CAPACITY FOR ACTION

In combating poverty Jake did more than stimulate and inspire the Department of Social Services' workforce. He took steps within the county political environment and in the community of Charlotte to effect real changes in the lives of Mecklenburg County's disadvantaged and helpless citizens. These innovations occurred in four areas: speaking the language of business, engaging in savvy politics, investing in new technology and promoting collaboration. In effect, this is about cell 8: gaining policy autonomy.

Business Language

Even though a welfare department is the very antithesis of a profit-seeking corporation, Jake, holder of an MBA and not the MSW, quoted from business management texts, boasted about the contribution the department makes to Charlotte's economy and delighted in being called a "capitalist" by a county commissioner. At one point in the last RoadShow he described the programs of the department as "45 different businesses."[22]

Jake genuinely believed in the value of applying business management techniques to social services, but at the same time he was perfectly aware of the strategic value of doing so. The business community is politically powerful in every society, and its default policy posture is to praise individual self-reliance and the free market and fight higher taxes and oppose social programs. Jake had a way, however, of defusing business opposition to strengthen social services by not merely adopting but championing their way of doing things.

A prime example is the Management for Results (M4R) program, a performance measurement system developed by County Manager Jones. Its approach to performance management was the "balanced scorecard" notion of organizational assessment popular in corporate America. In it, the meaning of "results" is deliberately not confined to profits, market share or sales figures, but also to less tangible attainments like quality of service and organizational reputation.

Accordingly, Mecklenburg County's M4R system seeks evidence of advances in terms of four "balanced perspectives": customer and stakeholder satisfaction, internal business improvements, financial health of the county and employee-organizational capacity. The first-named perspective has the highest priority, and the others contribute to it. Each one is broken down into goals. In applying the system to DSS, Jake carefully selected goals suitable to improvement of social services, such as increasing self-sufficiency for customers and exceeding the expectations of stakeholders, improving internal business practices by enlarging citizen involvement in them, helping the finances of the county by converting welfare recipients to tax payers, and raising organizational capacity through investing in higher skill levels for employees.

Under M4R each county department then prepares performance self-analyses within this framework. Jake packaged DSS' analyses as "value propositions" that stipulate for specific programs the desired results anticipated and show the actual results achieved. The value proposition he worked out for Work First in 2003 pointed out that customers and stakeholders benefitted by having 1,929 adults formerly on welfare actually hired by employers, representing 106 percent of the desired goal. Gains in the area of finance were calculated by noting that, if each job-placed individual spent $5,000 more per year on consumer goods, $289,350 would be generated in sales tax. Other value propositions submitted by DSS noted the numbers of grants received, number of meals delivered to the homebound, reduced waiting times for medical care under Medicaid and adoption of the MRS protocol for child custody.[23]

Savvy Politics

Despite little public receptiveness to funding and expanding the welfare function, playing the political game well can make a difference in this regard. In dealing with the Board of County Commissioners, Jake avoided party politics like the plague and presented himself as a competent nonpartisan executive who had total command of the facts and talked tough on the realities of available funding and what is feasible. Jake was particularly impressive in his knowledge of federal and state grant spigots, from which, he pointed out, additional pass-through dollars would always help the Charlotte economy. To keep the commissioners informed, each month he sent them a communiqué entitled *Main Event* that updated what the DSS was doing and took notice of any kudos received by the department. One such recognition was the Blue Diamond Award in Technology, awarded by the Charlotte Chamber of Commerce for DSS improvements in the IT area. On an informal basis, Jake made sure county officials also heard about useful gossip, such as word that federal reviewers of Mecklenburg's adoption procedures had called the DSS "the best urban child welfare program in the country."

Jake's political instincts also reached beyond county government. At one point he invoked the state's history to create a Charlotte-Mecklenburg Resolves Committee, comprised of the heads of all governments in the region. Named after the Resolves Committee that declared North Carolina's independence from Britain, he persuaded its members to declare Mecklenburg County's independence from poverty. In another instance of effective maneuvering, Jake took pains to upgrade the DSS Fraud Unit. Eventually it compiled an impressive record of reducing welfare cheating that included investigating nearly 1,000 leads annually, followed by a 100 percent success rate in prosecutions attempted. To direct attention to the unit, Jake sent baseball caps, golf shirts and jackets emblazoned with "Mecklenburg Fraud Investigation" to each member of the county board. On one occasion a Republican commissioner happened to wear this gear to a political barbecue organized by political conservatives; all present at the picnic, including main speaker Oliver North, talked about the garb.

Advanced Technology

Having the reputation of being high-tech helped legitimize DSS in the eyes of the community as well as demonstrate it as a learning organization—aspects of cells 3 and 9, respectively. Jake projected the DSS as a cutting-edge organization that has thrown itself into 21st century communications technology in order to be as effective as possible.

The resulting investments were successful for a combination of reasons. These included the competence of the department's Information Services Division, its use of a strict life-cycle system development protocol for project management, assistance from county IT experts on technical design and coding, and the direct involvement of relevant employees.

Two categories of IT investments stand out. One was the development of a set of three automated call centers. Just1Call is a telephone service whose purpose is to be a "one-stop" information source for senior citizens and adults with disabilities who need social services. It acts as an intake channel for DSS adult programs and also serves as an access point to more than 500 external service providers. These organizations, which are vetted before being included in the database, offer housing, leisure, and health and nutrition services, and assist on financial and legal matters. Operators talk at length with callers about their problems and then refer them to one or more providers. Appointments can be made while on the phone, with privacy assured.

Another telephone facility, the Citizen Information and Referral Center, handles main-number DSS calls and inquiries. Via a partnership with United Way of the Carolinas (covering Mecklenburg and three other counties), it also receives incoming calls for the many organizations it supports. The third operation is the Customer Service line, used by current DSS clients to ask questions and receive information about the status of their cases. A unique feature is that callers are able to make contact with someone quickly, without going through a long menu of options or endless transfers. All together, the operators of these last two centers handle more than a quarter-million calls a year.

The other significant achievement from a technology standpoint was an Integrated Social Services Information System, built over the final years of Jake's directorship. Referred to by the acronym ISSI (pronounced "IZZY"), it is a computerized communication and information case management system that operates via the Internet. This highly complex electronic network is comprehensive and integrated to a high degree; all program activities in all locations, whether concerning eligibility or social services, are covered, creating unprecedented opportunities for cross-communication and interoperability. ISSI gives instant access to all DSS electronic files by authorized personnel from anywhere—even a car out in the field—by using a laptop with an aircard. Workers can obtain information from a client file, make entries into that file, submit a report regarding the case, generate a form or letter, make an address change, research a question on an unpaid claim and issue an alert of an emergency or dangerous condition. Jake spoke of this capacity to use the system outside the office as "untethering" the staff. On Aug. 9, 2007, a sunny day in Charlotte, this technological release was celebrated symbolically by inflating a hot air balloon in Randolph Park on Billings Road, with numerous dignitaries and employees taking a ride aloft while television cameras rolled. (The balloon, however, remained securely tethered.)[24]

Community Collaboration

The formal DSS mission statement mentioned earlier includes the charge "to rally the community to improve the quality of life for its citizens," an aim first put forward by founding welfare superintendent Ranson. Jake took this proposition seriously, not just to involve the community but also to get things done.

By 1997 he was determined to launch a general campaign against poverty in Mecklenburg County. He called it "Wiping Out Poverty" and asked the Board of County Commissioners to endorse it. The board adopted the goal of "social, education and economic opportunity" as an M4R focus area and resolved to "create an environment where all Mecklenburg residents can become self-sufficient and have equal access to services." Jake presented occasional reports on the campaign to the commissioners, listing the efforts made in attacking this intractable problem yet also acknowledging that true progress depends on the state of the economy and the migration inflow. "When poverty cannot be eliminated," he wrote in his 2007 report, "the hardship it causes can still be relieved."[25]

The strategy Jake adopted in his war on poverty was to enlist, deliberately and publicly, every player on the economic and political scene that could possibly contribute to the cause. He developed a diagram to portray this collaborative activity. He called it the Decagon, a term he had picked up from an acquaintance in the insurance business. It is a circular diagram of 10 forms, all 10-sided; each represents an entity involved in the partnered effort. A replica of the document is shown in Figure 5.1.

Visualizing a clock face for purposes of orientation, at 12 o'clock on the decagon is the State of North Carolina. It is important as the conduit of Medicaid and several other forms of public assistance, although Jake privately confides that the state Division of State Services turned out to be the least helpful collaborator. Mecklenburg County government itself was obviously important, not simply as the parent jurisdiction for DSS but because of a staff unit called Community Resources, whose mission is to link poor people with anti-poverty organizations and donor groups.

Proceeding toward 3 o'clock, the Charlotte Chamber of Commerce played a major role in the success of Work First by urging its members to employ graduates, and in fact signed a contract with DSS to this effect. Central Piedmont Community College contributed by offering basic skill courses for Work First participants, holding literacy classes for adults and conducting 12-week vocational training courses under a program known as Pathways to Employment.

At 5 o'clock, nonprofit organizations were involved in many ways, including sending representatives to a Just1Call advisory group. In the field of health care, Presbyterian Hospital and the Carolinas Medical Center hired many Work First graduates and participated in Project Access, a partnership set up to ensure consistent health care to the uninsured poor. The Charlotte Housing Authority sheltered large numbers of DSS customers, in both public housing and Section 8 apartments.

As for the faith community at 8 o'clock, many of the county's churches joined a DSS-sponsored organization called the Faith Initiative. It gets churches to donate emergency funds, recruit their members as volunteers and arrange for counseling and long-term mentoring. In addition, their ministers take turns

Figure 5.1 Wiping Out Poverty Decagon

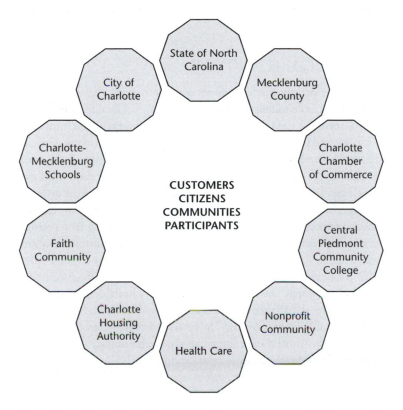

Source: Mecklenburg County Department of Social Services, "Status Report: Wiping Out Poverty in Mecklenburg County," November 2007, 3.

staffing the Vestibule in Kuralt. The public schools were brought into the picture through DSS liaison personnel who advised and supported foster care children enrolled in schools. The schools also hired Work First participants as teacher aides or custodians. Finally, the City of Charlotte operates a Wellness Interfaith Network to coordinate services to the poor that meet the needs of mind, body and soul, as well as pocketbook. Several county departments participate in that effort, including DSS.

To sum up, the Mecklenburg County DSS carved out a very considerable degree of policy autonomy in taking concerted steps to reduce the county's social and economic inequities. It engaged in an array of positive and imaginative initiatives to relieve the hardship that poverty causes. This was enabled in large part by Jake's ability to speak the language of the powerful, play smart politics, acquire the prestige of technology and mount the high ground of collaboration—with the last factor taking the DSS reputation far afield from welfare circles and county government.

THE DEPARTMENT TODAY

Under the city or county manager form of government, department heads are responsible solely to the manager. Jake's first manager, Gerald G. Fox, gave him a green light to revitalize the DSS and refrained from intervening except on budget matters. His second boss, Harry Jones, focused heavily on management and program matters. As we have seen, Jones and Jake often worked together closely, as in implementing the M4R performance evaluation tool. As time went on, however, Jones began transferring to the county government headquarters staff capacities Jake had built up in human resources, organization development and information technology. These and other signs suggested that the county manager was not wholly comfortable with the never-ending innovation, entrepreneurialism, publicity and independence being manifest in his largest department.

In 2007 Jones asked Jake to relinquish his post. The DSS director had suffered a stroke and Jones was concerned about his health. A lawsuit was then pending against the department that could, if not dismissed, become a political hot potato. And, as it happened, the University of North Carolina was planning to create a research institute on campus to study the impact of welfare on children. Jones, eager to form stronger relationships with the university, proposed that Jake help launch the institute. Jake supported the idea and, following his departure from the DSS in 2007, worked as a county employee from a campus office until he retired on Dec. 31, 2007.

After an extensive, nationwide search for a new DSS director, Jones hired Charlotte attorney Mary E. Wilson. Wilson had practiced law in several Eastern states before settling in Charlotte. She had no formal training in social work and only limited experience in government, having held an unpaid position in Mecklenburg County's Park and Recreation Department. Her background in social services came from her time as executive director of the Friendship Community Development Corporation, a housing-assistance and senior advocacy arm of the large Friendship Missionary Baptist Church in Charlotte. County Manager Jones, aware of Wilson's lack of professional expertise in the welfare field, felt that a nontraditional newcomer would introduce fresh thinking to the department.

Wilson became the eighth DSS director in mid-2008. Prior to coming on board she met only briefly with Jake on pending matters. In an interview about four months after taking office, Wilson told me that although she found the personnel at DSS to be motivated, dedicated and even passionate, they seemed overwhelmed by the complexity of the agency's work. She assessed that the department was too hierarchical, separated into isolated program silos and insufficiently connected to the community. The DSS is seen in the wider community, she stated, as a huge goliath with untapped resources and a reputation for not being a flexible team player.

Wilson planned for the DSS to enlarge its capacity to act and not be innovative for its own sake. A new generation of front-line employees is required, she said, to embrace change, be more holistic with clients and move out into the community to teach people what help is available. She stated her agenda as the following: (1) create a separate training unit; (2) provide training in time management; (3) engage in more research and planning on emerging issues; (4) establish a policy unit to advocate for policy change at the state and federal levels; (5) start community forums of group and church leaders; (6) develop software to integrate intake with eligibility decision making; (7) spread DSS operations more fully around the county with colocation of staff in other agencies and nonprofit organizations; and (8) provide more attention to the needs of at-risk retirees. Her desired new image of the department, she summarized, is to be the glue that holds the community together in the realm of human services—a kind of hub for the "village" of the needy, especially the elderly.

In the months since Wilson took over, I have attempted to learn how the department has fared. I requested an interview with her before completing this chapter, but she declined. Those individuals who would speak to me made several comments. Change has been taking place at "warp speed," one said, without being willing to elaborate. Another observed that most employees closely associated with Jake had been forced out, transferred to lesser positions or voluntarily resigned. Among at least some rank-and-file employees a significant loss of morale is said to have occurred. Some say they are being told to turn out the work on time with the same complement of personnel despite increased workloads caused by the recession, even if quality suffers. The "heart" had gone out of the organization, one interviewee said; working at DSS is now just a job, not serving a cause.

I was able to obtain from county government follow-up Employee Climate Survey data for the past few years. Three of the items found in Table 5.2 repeated essentially the same wording. Recommending the county as a good place to work, for which the positive response in the previous director's years was in the mid-90s, dropped to 88 percent in 2008 and 81 percent in 2009. The statement "Most days I feel good about coming to work," at 79 percent in 2007, rose to 81 percent in 2008 and then fell to 74 in 2009. "I have technology to do job well" shifted from 85 percent in 2007 to 81 in 2008 and then to 78 in 2009. All three of these 2009 departmental percentages were substantially below the all-county ratings for that year.[26]

I discussed the department's state since 2007 with County Manager Jones. He told me that an underlying theme of Wilson's directorship has been, with his support, holding employees more accountable. Efforts to do this, including introduction of Saturday hours to accommodate the working poor, have led to staff pushback and the formation of anti-Wilson subgroups, he said. Jones went on to comment that anonymous letters of complaint have been received, feathers have been ruffled among some organizational partners, and to some extent the morale problem that has been reported probably exists. Nonetheless, he rates Wilson's performance as a department head as having achieved a 6 or 7 on an assessment scale of 1 to 10.

Questions remain that can only be answered with time. Some of these were in effect raised by authors covered in Chapter 1. Was Wilson well "aligned" with the DSS organization, in the language of Barry Dym and Harry Hutson? Were her legal background and personal goals compatible with the agency's mission? Did she facilitate organizational norm building rather than impose it, as Arjen Boin and Tom Christensen propose, and work with the culture rather than reengineer it, as Anne Khademian urges? As we have seen, if nothing else the welfare business is delicate, and leading it requires a nuanced and thoughtful touch. While Jake was by no means subtle in the way he approached things, he had brought to the job deep experience in the field and a solid commitment to the social service profession.

THIS INSTANCE OF MISSION MYSTIQUE

Did the Mecklenburg County Department of Social Services possess mission mystique? If so, to what extent?

Cell 1: Mission. The public welfare function in Mecklenburg County is a generic, acknowledged mission. There is no state law or county ordinance that stipulates it. The department has adopted a formal mission statement, but it is ignored in practice. The most compelling normative call to action is simply the phrase "to be the best." The vision statement from which it is quoted indicates that what is referred to as being the best is the daily work of the department. To Jake personally, the phrase seemed to mean becoming the best in caring authentically for the plight and future of clients.

Cell 2: Need. It may seem unnecessary to articulate a need for social services in a society whose economic and social system tolerates huge inequities between rich and poor and among races and ethnic groups. Furthermore, the persistence of unemployment, poverty, drug abuse and family violence would seem to make an agency like DSS a precondition to a civilized community. Yet perceptions of public need are always subjective, and conservative voices resisted what Jake was doing. He was ingenious, however, in clothing the department's initiatives in the language of business, technology and collaboration, as well as social justice. Also, DSS did not merely respond to applicants for assistance; it actively drew attention to elderly abuse, quality of life differences, the need to prepare people for jobs, and general levels of poverty in Mecklenburg County.

Cell 3: Reputation. Many programmatic innovations have brought favorable attention to the Mecklenburg County DSS. Work First was a pioneer welfare-to-work program and model for the state of North Carolina. Its job-placement ties with the Chamber of Commerce attracted the attention of the president of the United States. North Carolina's choice of Mecklenburg as an early pilot county for the Multiple Response System of child protection affirmed that program's reputation. Federal reviewers of the county's adoption procedures claimed it possessed the best urban child welfare program in the country. Recognition also came from close to home, as in a technology award from the Chamber of Commerce honoring Just1Call.

Cell 4: Motivation. Employee opinion surveys conducted by the county, to the extent they truly measure representative opinion, do not compliment the attitudes of DSS personnel. Yet the questions measure job satisfaction, not job commitment. Moreover, all urban welfare departments inevitably face problems of excessive workloads, low pay and staff turnover. The division between wage-paid eligibility workers and degree-holding, salaried social workers is an inherent barrier to a workforce of shared values. What we do know for sure is the following: first, employees in the renovated Kuralt and Chapin facilities greatly appreciated being given fresh quarters they themselves helped design; second, DSS social workers—especially those laboring in the anti-abuse and family violence vineyard—are incredibly dedicated to their work.

Cell 5: Culture. Three values of the culture in particular were institutionalized, at least for a time. One was providing emotional support to the staff. Jake did this by sending cards of concern and congratulation, being a visible presence to all employees and thanking individuals for outstanding achievements. A second was an emphasis on enthusiastic engagement with the work. In slideshows and management lectures, Jake pounded home the innate importance of welfare work, the need to value subordinates for their knowledge and advice, the warmth of joining hands with colleagues in mutual support and the benefit of not letting a hard job get you down. The third value was that, in addition to serving the disadvantaged through one's work, each person has a personal responsibility to contribute to the deprived directly as a citizen.

Cell 6: History. Jake had a knack for commemorating the agency's history even when little was known about it. Almost from his first day on the job, he planned ways to celebrate institutional anniversaries and honor his predecessors in office. He also made sure this heritage was passed on to future generations within the department by naming buildings for past directors, giving attention to agency history in RoadShow presentations and recognizing each year the fiscal-year birthday of the department. There is, however, no written account of the history of the organization. The most public evidence of the DSS's 90-year existence is the posters hanging in the lobby of Chapin Hall. Perhaps the only chronicle of Jake's directorship that will be available to future generations is this chapter.

Cell 7: Contestation. Several internal checking mechanisms were at work in DSS, such as client representatives and Vestibule ministers on the Kuralt first floor and, in Chapin, a Youth and Family Services ombudsman and the Community Child Fatality Prevention and Protection Team. With respect to external checks, several kinds of state and federal auditing procedures take place continuously. The fact that DSS must continuously go to court on matters of custody, foster care, adoption and guardianship provides a truly independent form of contestation. At the political level, county commissioners and the county manager can, if so moved, take steps to direct change, as has happened with the transfer of Jake to the university for the years up to his retirement.

Cell 8: Autonomy. The DSS under Jake actively sought the political room needed to undertake an agenda of innovations. He spoke the language of business and engaged in performance management, gaining the support of anti-welfare critics. He pointed out to the business community how the departments' pass-through funds contribute to the local economy. He instituted cutting-edge technologies, demonstrating how DSS is up with the times and saving money by automation. He carried out Lucius Ranson's dream to have all components of the civil society join forces to make a better Mecklenburg County. Yet, although "qualified" in the sense of being accountable to the law and political superiors, Jake's energetic use of his policy autonomy may also have contributed to his early departure.

Cell 9: Renewal. It would not be an exaggeration to characterize Jake's 14 years as a continuous exercise in organizational renewal and learning. The minute he arrived from San Diego in 1994 he was primed to be a leader for change. Projects like Kuralt reception and same-day intake, Work First, Wiping Out Poverty, police cross-training, TB^2, RoadShow, Mecklenburg Fraud jackets, the teddy bear symbol, Gung Ho lectures, Just1Call and the ISSI untethering were all experiments in change, and most worked. Yet organizational renewal was not embedded in the institution itself; it was a product of his own personality and ideals. That makes us ask: Will they stick? Will Director Wilson succeed with her own plans? Will a new spirit of renewal emerge? Only time will tell.

In short, mission mystique may have been a fleeting presence in the agency's history. Perhaps in the delicate business of welfare we can expect no more.

6

Virginia State Police

The Commonwealth's Finest

THE VIRGINIA STATE POLICE, or Department of State Police as it is formally known, is a paramilitary organization. Like all police departments it is disciplined and hierarchical. Its "sworn" officers have taken an oath that confers on them the power of arrest. They wear uniforms, carry rank and obey a chain of command.

Statewide police organizations exist in all 50 states, and are important because of their authority to enforce state laws and orders of the governor. In our federal system of government, they also interact with national law enforcement agencies on matters dealing with their state, and exercise residual or backup authority for local law enforcement agencies in their state.

In the first chapter of this book it was noted that possession of mission mystique attributes provide something like the aura that surrounds crack military outfits. In this chapter, we explore the extent to which this comparison is valid for the paramilitary State Police of the Commonwealth of Virginia.

CARNAGE AT VIRGINIA TECH

As I pen these words at my own university of Virginia Tech, the third anniversary is being observed of the massacre of students and faculty that occurred at its Blacksburg campus on April 16, 2007. On that fateful day, Seung-Hui Cho, a fourth-year English major at the university, shot and killed 32 persons during a premeditated rampage. He then killed himself. It was the worst incident of mass shooting in the history of American higher education. Unfortunately, since that time several more senseless multiple killings have taken place in schools and other institutions in the United States and elsewhere, perhaps triggered in part by this incident.

Cho was 23 years old. During his early school years he drew the attention of school counselors who noted violent themes in his writings, some of which referred to the 1999 Columbine High School killings in Littleton, Colo. While at Virginia Tech Cho was reclusive and secretive. He frightened female students with strange e-mails and text messages. He wrote class papers that contained such violent images that two of his English professors pleaded with university authorities to take action. Further signs of mental problems were investigated by the Virginia Tech Counseling Center and a private psychiatric hospital. Despite several professional evaluations that concluded intervention was necessary, no decisive follow-through by the local mental health system occurred. Later investigation found that as early as February 2007 Cho was purchasing handguns and ammunition and practicing with them on a pistol range. Since his mental health status had not been flagged for entry into the State Police firearms database, he had no difficulty in making the purchases.[1]

Violant images in papers → Professors pleaded action

The Attacks

Monday, April 16, 2007, was a cloudy, chilly and windy day in Blacksburg, with snowflakes blowing in the air. At about 7 a.m. Cho walked from his dormitory, Harper Hall, to another residential building, West Ambler Johnston. There he gained access to room 4040, occupied by a 19-year-old undergraduate. She had just entered the room after being dropped off by her boyfriend outside the dormitory, an action likely observed by Cho. He wounded her mortally by handgun fire. A resident assistant living next door, who presumably entered the room to see what had happened, was also gunned down.

At 7:20 a.m. the Virginia Tech Police Department received a nonemergency call that a female student had fallen from her bed. Four minutes later an officer arrived at her room and discovered the two bodies. Reinforcements were summoned, the Blacksburg Police Department was notified and its officers arrived on the scene. It was soon learned that the wounded student's boyfriend, a part-time town employee who attends nearby Radford University, was an avid gun user. Immediately he became a person of interest, and the police suspected the crime to be an isolated incident.

Assume boyfriend to be killer - narrow minded

Meanwhile, we now know, Seung-Hui Cho returned to his room, changed clothes and went to the post office, where he mailed a package to NBC News in New York City. It contained pictures of himself with a gun in each hand and wearing a vest full of ammunition, with a furious look on his face (later shown in the media). Video clips and a rambling written diatribe were also enclosed.

Although the public schools had locked their outer doors because of the West Ambler report, Virginia Tech continued to hold classes, a decision later regretted by many. Classes for the morning's second period commenced at 9:05 a.m. One locale was Norris Hall, a structure next to Burruss Hall, the university's main administration building. Norris contains a number of classrooms, offices and

locked doors, but contin. classes, even though gunman might be on lose

South Wing of Norris Hall on the campus of Virginia Tech in Blacksburg. This is the site of the April 16, 2007, massacre of 25 students and 5 faculty members. The arrow indicates the windows of Room 204, by means of which several students escaped. Two other students were killed in a dormitory.

Source: Photo by the author.

laboratories. In it five classes were in session at that hour, as follows: an Engineering Mechanics course taught by Dr. Liviu Librescu, a 76-year-old Israeli born in Romania who had survived the Holocaust (room 204); a class on Issues in Scientific Computing, led by graduate assistant Haiyan Cheng (room 205); an Advanced Hydrology course taught by Dr. G. V. Loganathan, an India-born professor of civil and environmental engineering (room 206); Elementary German, offered by Christopher "Jamie" Bishop (room 207) and a French class instructed by Jocelyne Couture-Nowak, who had moved to Virginia with her husband from Nova Scotia (room 211). A class that normally met in room 200 at this hour had been cancelled that day (see floor plan in Figure 6.1).

While these classes got under way, Cho was busy on the first floor of Norris Hall chaining shut the building's three main entrances. At 9:26 the university administration notified all campus staff, faculty and students about the dormitory shooting, but did not take steps to lock down the university. At approximately the same time, a county sheriff's deputy had located the Radford student of interest on a traffic stop outside Blacksburg.

Meanwhile, Cho ascended to Norris' second floor, knowing exactly where he was going. Using two handguns, he began systematically to kill everyone on the

Figure 6.1 Casualties at Norris Hall, Virginia Tech, April 16, 2007

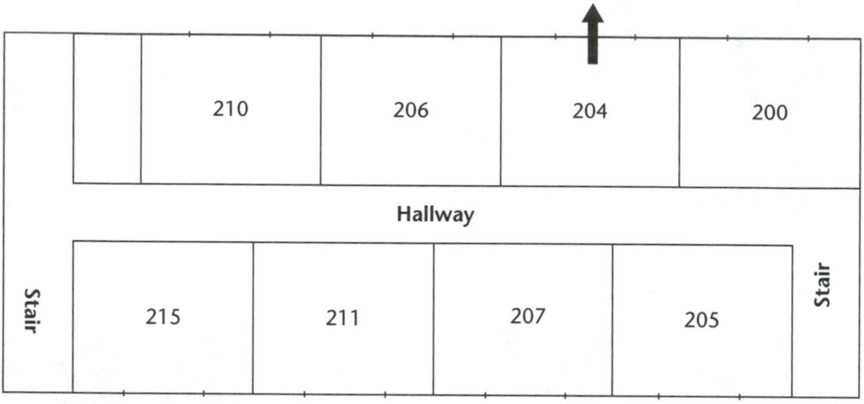

Plan of second floor classrooms, with casualty numbers given below

Room Number	Verified as Present	Faculty Dead	Faculty Injured	Faculty Uninjured	Students Dead	Students Injured	Students Uninjured
200	(class had been cancelled)						
204	17	1	0	0	1	9	6
205	10	0	0	1	0	1	8
206	14	1	0	0	9	2	2
207	13	1	0	0	4	7	1
210	(no class scheduled)						
211	18	1	0	0	11	6	0
215	(not in use)						
Totals	75	5	1	1	25	26	17

Sources: Massengill Report, "Mass Shootings at Virginia Tech, April 16, 2007," report of the Virginia Tech Review Panel, August 2007, presented to Governor Timothy M. Kaine and placed online by his office at www.governor.virginia.gov/techPanelReport.cfm; Colin Moynihan, "Professor's Violent Death Came Where He Sought Peace," *New York Times*, April 19, 2007, p. A20.

Note: Totals include one faculty member killed and one injured in second floor hallway, and also one injured student later found on the third floor.

floor. Later calculations were that the shooting began at 9:40 and continued for 11 minutes. Cho began with Loganathan's class in room 206, taking the life of the professor and nine of the 13 students present. Two others were shot but survived. He then crossed the hall to room 207 and killed Jamie Bishop and four of his 12 German students, wounding seven others. Next was the computing class in room 205; here Cho had less success, as the occupants had heard the gunshots and successfully barricaded the door. But Cho shot through it and hit one student.

He next turned to Couture-Nowak's French class in room 211. Hearing the shots next door, she had moved her desk against the door and told a student to call 911 on his cell phone. Cho succeeded in pushing the door open and continued his assault. Madame Couture and 11 students were killed outright; the student with the cell phone was wounded while calling 911, dropped the phone and pretended to be dead. A female student grabbed the phone and pleaded with the dispatcher to get help quickly. Cho heard her voice and shot twice; she fell down and also played dead, but with the cell phone still open under her head.

Determined to complete the massacre, Cho returned to the German class in 207 to finish off any survivors. The door was barricaded, but he succeeded in pushing it open an inch. He fired at the door handle, but still could not enter. He returned to the French class next door and fired up and down the aisles. At one point in the melee Cho encountered two engineering professors in the hall outside; he killed one and injured the other by a ricocheted bullet.

The one class not yet invaded was Liviu Librescu's, in room 204. In a heroic action, the professor yelled to his students to jump out the windows. Though he was killed, 10 students climbed through the windows and dropped 19 feet to the ground, even as two more were shot trying to do so (see arrows in photo and Figure 6.1). Cho then rushed next door to room 206 to take care of anyone left, but the sounds of shotgun fire were now emanating from the first floor of the building, and he knew the game was up. At 9:51 Cho put one of his guns to his head and pulled the trigger. Without saying a single word, he had fired 174 rounds and killed or hurt 57 people—three-fourths of those present.

The Assault

The sounds that led Cho to stop shooting were caused by the actions of several campus and town police officers trying to break open the building's doors with shotgun blasts in order to gain entrance. They had received desperate 911 calls from the students and could hear the shooting from outside the building. Without bolt cutters the police could not force open the chained doors at the south end of the building. After scouting around, they found a side service door that was locked but not chained. After shooting it open with a shotgun, two police assault teams entered the building. A third team obtained access via the north door, which by that time had been opened with bolt cutters obtained from a van parked nearby. Each of the three groups was composed of a mix of officers from the Virginia Tech and Blacksburg police departments, including their chiefs. All three teams tore up the stairs to the second floor at about the same moment, only to realize the shooting had stopped. Two of the groups carefully searched all rooms of that floor for additional gunmen while the third did the same on the top floor, using shotguns to gain access to locked doors when necessary.[2]

The State Police

Shortly after the Virginia Tech and Blacksburg police responded to the shootings at West Ambler Johnston early that morning, the Blacksburg police department telephoned a special agent of the Virginia State Police (VSP) who happens to reside in Blacksburg. He offered his services immediately. A VSP team, including one canine officer, soon arrived at the dormitory to help sweep the area. When the Norris Hall shootings broke out after 9 o'clock and the emergency there was recognized, these VSP personnel crossed the campus to be ready to assist, if needed. Meanwhile, state troopers patrolling the highways between Blacksburg and VSP division headquarters in Salem heard radio calls about the Norris development and sped to the scene. By the time any VSP officers arrived, Cho was dead, although the sounds of shots being fired by local police to blast open locked doors were audible outside the building.

The State Police entered by the side service door, and by 9:58 Sgt. Eric K. King reported to the Salem division dispatcher that they were inside the building. They assisted campus and town officers in the search for other per-petrators. Despite being cops used to violence and death, they were devastated by the carnage. For the next several hours they assisted other officers on the scene with evacuating the wounded and removing the slain. As one state trooper waited downstairs toward the end of the afternoon, a replacement officer came in and asked what happened. "The Devil got loose," the trooper said. "Where was God?" demanded the newcomer. "Up there with the students," he replied.

Dozens of additional state police officers arrived on campus that afternoon, from the Salem division and elsewhere around the state. State Police Superintendent W. Steven Flaherty had been notified in Richmond, and he and Secretary of Public Safety John W. Marshall rushed immediately to Blacksburg by patrol car. Eventually the VSP presence grew to a force of more than 400 personnel that came and went from Blacksburg over the next several weeks. As was their custom, the Virginia State Police accepted any task that local agencies asked them to per-form. On this occasion they provided chaplains to help console parents and took responsibility for identifying victims and notifying next of kin. Joint operations centers were established for more than a dozen law enforcement agencies by VSP officers, and logistical support in the form of meals and temporary housing was arranged for those who lived a distance away. The State Police also mounted security patrols using a zone system and assisted with security when President George W. Bush came to speak. One of the most poignant duty assignments was to collect the victims' personal effects and make sure their clothing was cleaned before returning it to loved ones.

The biggest job given the VSP, however, was to conduct the formal crimi-nal investigation of the Norris shooting. Later, this undertaking merged with investigation of the dormitory shooting. Capt. George W. "Stick" Austin, commander of the VSP Bureau of Criminal Investigation for the Salem division, headed the huge effort. He organized a Joint Investigative Operations Center in two classrooms on the first floor of Norris, which later moved to Burruss Hall and then to the football stadium. More than 165 investigators and analysts from a dozen agencies worked on the case. The VSP coordinated forensic work, the investigation of leads, and the processing of subpoenas and search warrants. Exhaustive ballistic studies were necessary at the highly complex crime scene, the perpetrator's background and record at Virginia Tech had to be probed, a scuba team searched the campus duck pond for the perpetrator's computer and an exact timeline of the unfolding of the incident was constructed. At this writing the investigation still remains officially under way.[3]

The State Police also performed an important media function. Although the Virginia Tech police chief and Superintendent Flaherty were both named press conference representatives of the police, the television media focused on Flaherty. As a consequence, he emerged as the key public spokesperson for the responsible public authorities. His open manner, calm voice and informed understanding of the situation brought a sense of order and reason amidst the media hype and commentator babble. This role, which Flaherty did not seek or ask to perform, helped the university and community cope with the tragedy in front of the world.

Now, three years later, signs of recovery are present in Blacksburg. The space occupied by Norris room 205 has been cleaned up, remodeled and dedicated as the Librescu Student Engagement Center. The floor areas of former rooms 207 and 211 have become a Center for Peace Studies and Violence Prevention. The remainder of the second floor is used for labs and offices of a Global Technology Center. Back at VSP division headquarters in Salem, hanging in the front entryway is a framed, hand-sewn quilt given to the division whose pattern includes a red heart for each victim and bears the inscription "May the Witnesses Find Peace in Their Duty."

PREDECESSOR ORGANIZATIONS

The history of the Virginia State Police goes back less than a century. Yet, oddly enough, a 17th century predecessor to the VSP exists: the Virginia Capitol Police. It was formed in 1618 as the Public Guard for Jamestown, the first permanent English settlement in the New World. Its complement of 10 sturdy men was charged with protecting the governor from hostile Indians; in 1663 the force was doubled in size to guard the colony's other organs of government as well, namely the Council, Court and House of Burgesses—the body in which future patriots like Patrick Henry and Thomas Jefferson honed their debating skills. When the Virginia capital moved to Williamsburg in 1699 and then to Richmond in 1780, the Public Guard came along, and in 1884 was renamed the Capitol Police. To this day the organization has been charged with keeping order in Richmond's Capitol Square, a small area that surrounds the Virginia Capitol designed by Jefferson. Its current chief is Col. Kimberly S. Lettner, a 22-year veteran in the Virginia State Police.[4]

A staple lecture topic in the introduction to public administration course is how the advent of new technology causes the expansion of government. The arrival of the motorcar on the American scene in the early 20th century is a classic example. Indeed, this is what led to creation of what we know today as the Virginia State Police. As the number of vehicles and miles of paved roads grew in the Commonwealth, so did the need for a police force that could accommodate this unprecedented degree of cross-country mobility—merely having police departments in cities and constables in towns was no longer enough.

The future VSP evolved over several decades, in three stages.[5] The first began in 1906, when the Virginia General Assembly saw fit to have the secretary of the Commonwealth, the general caretaker of state administration, assume responsibility for supervising vehicle registration. The fee was $2 per year, collected at first by county sheriffs and town constables, but starting in 1911 by two state "inspectors" equipped with motorcycles. In 1919 a set of automobile acts was passed that went beyond registration to enforcing a speed limit of 20 miles per hour, or 10 miles per hour near persons or horses. Vehicle ownership titles were devised a year later, and theft of an automobile or truck was classified as a felony. Enforcement of vehicle laws now required a crew of seven "deputy inspectors" to be spread around the state. They, along with seven clerks, comprised the Enforcement Division of the Commonwealth secretary's office.

In 1923 a second stage in the agency's development began when the Enforcement Division's work was transferred to a new specialized agency, the Division of Motor Vehicles (DMV), headed by a commissioner elected by the legislature. Among other duties, this nascent DMV registered vehicles, licensed drivers, administered driver tests, collected accident statistics, conducted safety research and adopted uniform hand signals; it also set safety standards for brakes, mirrors, lights and mufflers. Within a few years a corps of 50 motorcycle-riding deputy inspectors, armed with handguns and wearing blue and gray uniforms with visor caps and riding boots, were enforcing motor vehicle laws and, as a sideline, interdicting illegal whiskey traffickers.

The third stage in the VSP's early history lasted from 1930 to 1942. To set it in context, it should be noted that during this time Virginia public administration was becoming more sophisticated. Harry F. Byrd Sr., governor from 1926 to 1930, had built a statewide political machine that was segregationist, blatantly pro-business and barely democratic. On the positive side, however, it had ties with progressive thinkers at the New York City Bureau of Municipal

Research and was busy building good highways and bridges around the state, along with establishing a public finance capability in Richmond to pay for them.[6]

In a series of steps, the DMV Enforcement Division was transformed into a full-fledged state highway patrol. A fleet of Chevrolet roadsters was ordered to supplement the motorcycles, and both kinds of vehicles were painted white and outfitted with sirens. Soon this "Great White Fleet" arm of the law became famous to Virginia drivers. In time, the fleet was outfitted with mobile radios, creating a working network of statewide law enforcement. By 1932 the agency was becoming sufficiently capable that the General Assembly bestowed on it not only traffic law enforcement authority, but powers to enforce all provisions of the Virginia criminal code. In effect, a state police force had been created, and today the VSP treats 1932 as its founding year.

By 1938 creation of an independent Virginia State Police was well on its way. The idea had already been floated in the General Assembly, and the title of deputy inspector had been altered to "state trooper." Police license plates were no longer inscribed "Commonwealth of Virginia DMV" but "Virginia State Police." DMV headquarters moved from Capitol Square to an office building at Twelfth and Main streets in Richmond, and in January 1939 the state police function was transferred to a farmhouse located west from downtown on 65 acres of land along State Route 60, also known as Midlothian Turnpike. In 1940 the house was razed and replaced by a sizable brick structure financed in part by Works Progress Administration funds; today it forms the oldest component of the sprawling VSP headquarters complex.[7]

THE WOODSON ERA AND BEYOND

On July 1, 1942, the Virginia State Police as an institution technically came into existence. On that day a statute overhauling several aspects of state government took effect that, among other things, abolished the existing Division of Motor Vehicles and created in its place a new DMV that dealt with vehicle administration only. The law also established a Department of State Police, to which were transferred all police functions and equipment assigned to the old DMV. No characterization is made in the law of the agency's overall mission—its purpose is assumed as obvious. The head of the new State Police is its superintendent, who reports directly to the governor and serves at his pleasure.[8]

On the same day a second far-reaching event for the agency occurred: the formal assumption to office of the first VSP superintendent. This was Maj. Charles W. Woodson Jr., a 20-year veteran of the Enforcement Division who had worked his way up as trooper, sergeant, lieutenant and captain. Excepting temporary wartime service in the Navy in 1944–1945 (after which he was promoted to colonel), Woodson was the Virginia State Police's commander until

1968. In every respect he became the agency's founding father; at the time of his retirement he was the longest-serving state police superintendent in the United States.

Above all else, Colonel Woodson was known for his uncompromising honesty and refusal to grant special favors, a philosophy that has permeated the organization ever since. Ardently committed to professionalism in his field, he attended specialized police courses at five universities as well as at the FBI Academy. As will be described below, Woodson was a tireless institution builder who continuously innovated with respect to programs and methods for over a quarter century. At his retirement dinner Gov. Mills Godwin declared:

> Ordinarily there are two ways that a public official can hold office for a quarter of a century at the top of an agency. One way is never do anything to make anybody mad, never stick his neck out, and never concern himself with real progress for fear of stepping on someone's toes. The other way—the way Charlie Woodson has done it—was to bring so much ability to his job and so much recognition and prestige to his organization that he overshadowed any other contender, and his works silenced all opposition.[9]

Filling the Ranks

When Woodson took over, the authorized personnel strength of the Virginia State Police stood at 248, including driving test examiners and police dispatchers. But because of absences for wartime military service, only 153 men were available for duty. By 1945 authorized strength had dropped to 215, with only 109 positions filled. This skeletal force was woefully inadequate to carry out any routine duties across the state, let alone respond to emergencies. To compensate for the manpower shortage, Woodson established a Women's Auxiliary State Police (WASP); although assigned mostly to office duties, a few WASPs were used as dispatchers, raising many eyebrows in this traditionally all-male organization. After the war the State Police became solidly masculine again, and remained so for many years.

When the servicemen returned Woodson was able to rebuild the workforce, but it was rough going. The number of authorized positions was set at 403 in 1946, but filling them all with qualified applicants was a problem. The entry pay for a trooper was only $1,800 per year, with a bonus of $5 for every month in which the officer received a merit rating of satisfactory. The work was long and hard, with patrol shifts lasting 12 hours for six days a week. Woodson's strategy in this situation was to appeal to a sense of duty on the part of young Virginia males; in public appearances he called upon "upstanding young men between 21 and 30 years of age to join with him in making the highways safe for Virginia's motorists and out-of-state visitors."[10]

New Systems and Technologies *· brought systematic databases to VSP*

In addition to a recruitment campaign, Woodson brought systematic management to the department. In 1945 access to teletype service was obtained, and by means of this technology written records could accumulate of wanted persons and stolen property. Woodson had the VSP wire service linked to nine nearby state police departments, creating a mutually beneficial communication network for regional law enforcement. Also in 1945 systematic collection of vehicular ticketing records began. For each occurrence, the trooper on duty recorded the location and time of the incident, descriptions of the driver and car, and weather conditions. This information supported testimony in court and permitted analysis of data patterns over time. Collection of accident statistics also became regularized, and Woodson had them studied to make optimal patrol assignments based on an a real analysis of crash frequency, traffic load and mileage covered.

On grounds of cost-effectiveness, Colonel Woodson began in 1954 to phase out motorcycle use in the department. While this step sacrificed some of the romantic appeal of being a state cop, it gave officers access to the communication gear and firearms only an automobile could carry. As another efficiency move, in 1958 civilian clerk-stenographers were hired to relieve troopers of the arduous task of typing reports on accidents and investigations. Soon Virginia became one of the first Southern states to reduce the workweek of uniformed officers from six days to five. An extensive reorganization of the department's field structure in 1961 led to painful personnel reassignments, but made for a more efficient manpower allocation across the state. In today's VSP an entire bureau, Administrative and Support Services, focuses on management and communication issues.

Woodson also set the precedent of being receptive to new law enforcement technologies. A clumsy "V-scope" device for measuring vehicle speeds by mirrors and stopwatch was replaced by the device that, as we saw in Chapter 3, revolutionized weather forecasting—radar. While at first radar speed measurements were crude and taken from a fixed position, mobile equipment introduced in 1974 permitted the recording of speeds from a moving patrol car. This led to such a dramatic growth in speeding arrests that motorists installed radar detectors in their cars; in reaction, the legislature outlawed them and anti-radar detector devices were installed in police vehicles. Now troopers have at their disposal automated radar systems that emit sounds at a graded pitch (which indicate relative speeds) when a violator is moving ahead of, behind or oncoming toward the patrol car.

Other technologies introduced by Woodson were the polygraph, two-way radio and Identi-kits that enabled an artist to recreate an offender's likeness. A special interest of his was deploying war surplus aircraft to search for fleeing felons or lost persons. By 1946 the department owned three planes based at a short landing strip on headquarters grounds. Later, helicopters were added to the fleet, and the headquarters airstrip was foregone in favor of a heliport.[11]

Another theme in the VSP web of activity to which Woodson's tenure was a springboard was adding supplemental programs to the agency's acknowledged mission of public safety, not unlike what happened over the years with the Centers for Disease Control and Prevention (CDC). An early example is supervision of vehicle inspection. For years the General Assembly had required vehicles registered in Virginia to be inspected periodically at private garages. For a time Woodson brought the VSP into this activity by having troopers oversee the work of these inspection stations. Another illustration is regulation of truck weights. In order to keep overloaded trucks from damaging highway pavements, troopers carried portable scales in their patrol cars to weigh heavy trucks axle by axle, and then sum the total for a reading. Permanent weighing stations were eventually added on major highways, and sworn VSP personnel along with Department of Transportation employees staff them. Over time, simply weighing the trucks was supplemented by systematic inspections for safety and compliance to hazardous material requirements. Specially trained VSP commercial vehicle enforcement officers now do this work.

Training, Specialization and Professionalism

Other police specialties emerged under Woodson as well. Beginning in 1956 all troopers were taught to swim if they could not, and trained in life-saving procedures. Later, scuba training was instituted to create a cadre of officers who could dive for evidence or bodies, or to free occupants of submerged vehicles. In fiscal 2007, the year in which VSP divers searched the Virginia Tech duck pond for Cho's computer, the department's search and recovery team recovered statewide 21 weapons, 9 vehicles, 2 boats and 9 bodies.[12] A canine (or K-9) capability was established as well. German shepherds acquired in Europe were permanently assigned to individual handlers who trained them and kept them at their homes. Initially the animals were taught to track felons or missing persons, and later other dogs were trained to sniff for drugs and bombs. Currently the VSP has 19 two-handler teams trained for patrol (person searches), 21 for narcotics and 18 for explosives.[13]

Although some professional training of inspectors and their deputies had taken place in the Enforcement Division days, Woodson augmented and institutionalized it. The year 1947 was particularly important in this regard. He inaugurated retraining-refresher activities for returning military veterans who had been VSP officers before the war. An in-service training program was instituted whereby all sworn VSP personnel rotated to headquarters every second year for one week of update and renewal instruction. This practice remains in effect today and serves as an important mechanism for keeping a dispersed workforce connected to the overall organization. Also in 1947 Woodson launched programs of extramural training that sent selected VSP personnel to the FBI Academy at Quantico, the U.S. Army Military Police School, and academic programs in police science offered at various universities. Turning collaborative training in the reverse direction, he also invited local law enforcement personnel from around Virginia to come to Richmond to attend a "Central Police School" whose instructors were brought in from around the country.

Professionalism was also stressed in handling what are today called "critical incidents." These are occasions in which law enforcement officers are called on to respond to dangerous emergency situations. They can range from hostage takings or barricaded shooters—when negotiators or tactical SWAT teams are appropriate, to strikes or street demonstrations—where crowd control is the objective. Virginia's history is replete with examples of civil disturbance that involved a police presence. In the 1930s the Enforcement Division was called on to calm violent textile and mine strikes in southwest Virginia. At the northern end of the state, its deputy inspectors stood alert in Arlington County when the 1932 Bonus March by veterans headed for Washington. *[handwritten margin note: Critical Incidents]*

During later years much civil and political turmoil took place in the state, associated with mine strikes, the civil rights movement and anti–Vietnam War protests. Woodson took the position that professional policing standards required the VSP to preserve public order during these incidents, even when that placed the agency in the position of implicitly defending the status quo. However, it is to his credit that VSP troopers never attacked unarmed citizens in these incidents, even when subject to being taunted by protesters or having their uniforms smeared with coal tar or their tires deflated by "jack rocks" strewn in the road. At the same time, the superintendent insisted on being prepared for the worst; in 1967 he acquired for each division a 14-ton behemoth riot truck equipped with five-eighths-inch-thick armor plate, three-inch bulletproof glass, gun ports, a hydraulically operated steel visor and ram front. In 2009 these vehicles were disposed of because they were deemed no longer necessary, except for one truck that was rebuilt for historic display purposes and deployment if absolutely essential.

A PARAMILITARY ORGANIZATION

In the introduction to this chapter I used the word *paramilitary* to describe the Virginia State Police. The dictionary meaning I intend here is a body of non-military civilians organized in military fashion. The State Police fits this description in many ways—it has a chain of command, uniforms, officer ranks, a high degree of discipline and military-like rules. At the same time, it is a *para*military organization, i.e., there are civilian aspects as well. For example, in performing their duties personnel comply to state law as well as VSP general orders, and conform to the same administrative procedures that cover all other departments of state government. *[handwritten margin note: para military]*

With a permanent workforce of approximately 2,600, the VSP is larger than the Department of Social Services (DSS), Mecklenburg County, N.C., but smaller than the National Weather Service (NWS). Of these personnel, about 1,900 are sworn officers, men and women authorized to use force to make arrests and carry out other law enforcement duties. From the funding standpoint, with a budget of $305 million in FY 2009, the VSP also stands between these two other agencies (consult appendix).[14]

As we have seen, the 1942 statute that created the agency was silent on its precise mission. The General Assembly assumed it would enforce state laws and fight crime, like police departments everywhere. Hence the VSP mission is in the acknowledged category, as we found for the CDC and the DSS. This too is in keeping with a paramilitary organization, in that armies and navies typically do not have specified missions; in fact, their acknowledged mission consists also of two interrelated traditional functions, protecting the country and battling its enemies.

Yet we are not surprised to find that the VSP has a formal mission statement. It declares: "The Virginia State Police, independent yet supportive of other law enforcement and criminal justice agencies, will provide high quality, statewide law enforcement services to the people of Virginia and our visitors." A vision statement exists as well, which goes into somewhat more detail: "The Virginia State Police will provide exemplary service to the public and other law enforcement and criminal justice agencies with a highly qualified, diverse workforce that balances service, education, and enforcement to achieve optimal customer satisfaction."[15]

These rather bland statements contain standard clichés of contemporary public administration, yet it is worth noting that they do emphasize excellence as a general aim by including such terms as *high quality* and *exemplary service*. Another point to note is that the vision statement seems to say that the key to exemplary service is a workforce of superior quality.

The idea that it is the people in an organization that really make it successful comports with many of the things Colonel Woodson was doing when he built the agency. Yes, he created new programs and deployed new equipment. But to make it all work he had to recruit "upstanding young men between 21 and 30," put them through the very best training and retraining experiences possible, and instill in them a sense of professional discipline that would keep them alert on 12-hour patrol shifts and steady-calm in difficult civil strife circumstances. Indeed, probably every police chief would agree that the most important ingredient in a great police department is the quality of its officers.

The Governor and the Superintendent

The governor of the Commonwealth is elected to a single four-year term, without the option of running for reelection. (Virginia is the only state with that limitation.) The governor appoints the VSP superintendent, subject to confirmation by both chambers of the General Assembly. The superintendent serves at the pleasure of the governor, and can be dismissed at any time for any reason. At the end of each gubernatorial term the appointment automatically comes up for reassessment; after an interim period in which the current superintendent stays on temporarily, the new governor must either reappoint the individual or name a new one.

Thus Virginia's quadrennial turnover in the governorship could open the way to a parallel change in VSP leadership every four years. This provides plenty of opportunity to make the superintendent's job into a purely partisan appointment. It is not inconceivable that the VSP could under these circumstances become a politicized, inept and even anti-democratic force for partisan intimidation. Fortunately, such a breakdown has never happened in Virginia. With one exception, governors have dealt with the organization on a professional basis, allowing qualified and experienced superintendents the independence to build and operate the department without untoward external interference.

For most incoming governors, the pattern has been to reappoint the existing superintendent, if the person wishes to continue to serve. Thus most superintendents have been in office under more than one governor, as evidenced by the fact that from 1942 through 2009 Virginia had 16 governors but only nine superintendents. Colonel Woodson's long tenure spanned seven governors, and his next three successors—Harold W. Burgess (who served from 1968 to 1977), Denny M. Slane (1977–1984) and Robert Suthard (1984–1990)—each served two to three. Since 1990 the tenures of superintendents have become shorter. One of them, William F. Corvello (1990–1992), felt compelled to retire during the term of Gov. Douglas Wilder, following well-publicized disputes with the nation's first elected African-American governor over helicopter use and investigative activity. Wilder replaced him with Lt. Col. Carl R. Baker, who had come to the VSP only two years earlier from the New York State Police. Baker served as superintendent for only a year and a half, and was not reappointed by the next governor.

The Wilder-Corvello interruption did not turn the Virginia State Police into a political football, however. The next three superintendents—M. Wayne Huggins (1994–2000), W. Gerald Massengill (2000–2003) and W. Steven Flaherty (2003–)—were each reappointed by newly elected governors. All three are nationally known law enforcement professionals. Each had prior experience in the department, in some cases very lengthy: Huggins had been a state trooper for seven years prior to being elected sheriff of Fairfax County, Va.; Massengill spent 33 years on the force, rising from trooper to colonel; and Flaherty, the current chief, has been with the VSP for 28 years, also ascending from the bottom to the top. Earlier superintendents have had similar lengths of prior service. Hence the tradition of recruiting the top commander from within is well established and has essentially been maintained to this point. In late April 2010 the newly elected governor of Virginia, Robert F. McDonnell, reappointed Superintendent Flaherty after a four-month delay.

Individual governors vary in the way they relate to the superintendent and the agency as a whole. Some chief executives give instructions on selected matters of personal interest. Others periodically inquire as to what is going on and leave the agency alone unless a flap occurs. In any case the relationship is idiosyncratic, depending on the personalities involved. Yet the workings of this dyad are leavened by two institutional factors.

One is the office of secretary of Public Safety positioned between the governor and superintendent. This official is a member of the governor's cabinet and a close political associate. In addition to the State Police, the secretary is responsible for the departments of Alcoholic Beverage Control, Corrections, Emergency Management, Military Affairs and Veteran Services. As with the governor-superintendent relationship, interaction between the superintendent and the secretary varies with the situation and personalities present. In the past two decades no less than three secretaries were former state troopers, giving the agency a leg up on how it is perceived within the governor's circle.

The second institutional factor is the gubernatorial security detail. This is provided by the VSP through its Executive Protection Unit. All states have such an entity, usually staffed by a dozen or so sworn officers. The Virginia unit, whose members wear civilian clothes, is housed in a basement office in the Governor's Mansion. The detail is available to guard the governor and his or her family on a 24/7 basis, with deployment depending on circumstances and requests. Security is provided on trips to other states and foreign countries, which occur with growing frequency. Because of a practice by which gubernatorial security units around the country assist each other when governors of other states visit theirs, the Richmond-based unit is unusually active in that regard because Washington, D.C., airports are located in Virginia.

From an administrative standpoint, the commander of the Executive Protection Unit reports to the VSP deputy superintendent and superintendent. Operationally, however, instructions are continuously received from the governor personally or the governor's staff. This bifurcated accountability to agency and mansion is not a problem if their two heads are on good terms. In this situation, members of the detail can reinforce police-governor relationships by demonstrating that they are wholly trustworthy—for example, having kept confidential everything heard in the governor's presence and in his car. In turn, this display of discretion cannot help but strengthen the governor's allegiance to the VSP.

Down the Chain of Command

Within the VSP itself, the top command consists of the superintendent and, immediately subordinate to him or her, the deputy superintendent. The commander of the department holds the rank of colonel, the highest attainable in the VSP and the only officer holding it. Common practice is to address superintendents as colonel, even if not present within hearing range. Ever since Woodson's day, long-timers say, conformity to the superintendent's authority has been the sacrosanct norm. The chief speaks for the department on all official matters, makes or approves all major policies, decides or signs off on all significant personnel actions, oversees the determination of agency priorities, monitors relationships with other law enforcement agencies and the rest of state government, keeps abreast of important operational activities and performs as custodian of the organization's culture.

At the everyday level, the superintendent sets the tone of the organization. Colonel Flaherty, who entered the VSP as a rookie trooper in 1975, is a visible figure and personal model to his force. He presides over all headquarters ceremonies, such as the annual awards presentation and memorial event honoring the department's fallen. To show identification with troopers in the front lines, when driving to or from work every day he still pulls over speeders encountered on the roadways. A quarterly in-house publication, *VSP Newsletter*, always leads off with a column entitled "Colonel's Connection." In order to provide a means of receiving messages from the rank and file, Flaherty set up a telephone "Idea Line" by which he can be easily reached by any member of the department, anonymously or otherwise. When speaking of how the colonel exercises his authority, veteran members of the force admit that while at times they disagree with the superintendent's decisions, they nonetheless respect his judgment and accept his right to exercise it.

The deputy superintendent holds the rank of lieutenant colonel, one of four officers in the organization to do so. The deputy's role is to be operational manager for the three line bureaus of the department, which are the Bureau of Field Operations, Bureau of Criminal Investigation and Bureau of Administrative and Support Services. The present occupant of the deputy post is Lt. Col. Robert B. Northern, who has held the position since 2005; he joined the force in 1980 as a trooper-trainee. Many assume that Northern may become the next superintendent.

State Police Bureaus

Bureaus are headed by directors holding the rank of lieutenant colonel. Their deputies are at the rank of major. The Bureau of Field Operations (BFO), headed by Lt. Col. Eugene A. Stockton, is the largest and most publicly prominent one. It commands the uniformed troopers—approximately three-fourths of sworn officers—that patrol the 64,000 miles of Virginia's highways. BFO is also responsible for commercial truck regulation, the vehicle inspection program and the aviation unit.

The Bureau of Criminal Investigation (BCI), led by Lt. Col. H. C. Davis, is the "detective" side of the VSP. Its operational personnel are sworn officers who have passed through the VSP police academy and have already served their time patrolling highways. If taken into the BCI, they receive additional training, are designated special agents, wear civilian clothes, carry a concealed or visible weapon, and conduct themselves with somewhat greater freedom and informality than the uniformed corps. BCI's charge is to investigate violations of state statutes, any matter referred to the VSP by the governor and allegations against elected officials when called upon. Investigative requests may also be received from the state attorney general and local law enforcement.

Virginia is different from many other states in that its highway patrol and criminal investigation functions are performed by the same state police agency. When I asked about the implications of having the two under one organizational roof, I was told that it undercuts rivalry between the two kinds of police officers and facilitates greater cooperation between them. Another plus is that manpower and equipment can be shared between the two bureaus and shifted about as needed.

The Bureau of Administrative and Support Services (BASS) is largely composed of civilian employees. Its chief is Lt. Col. Robert G. Kemmler. In part a staff arm, BASS manages the department's finances, personnel, training, logistics and radio communication system. In addition, a Criminal Justice Information Services division within the bureau operates several databases that serve law enforcement interests and members of the public.

Field Organization

It must be kept in mind that most VSP personnel are not located at the Richmond headquarters, but out in the state. That is where almost all operational activities are performed as well as directed. The field organization of the department is at two levels: Division and Area. The state is divided into seven divisions, with division headquarters located in the cities of Richmond (Division One, physically separate from agency headquarters), Culpeper (Division Two), Appomattox (Three), Wytheville (Four), Chesapeake (Five), Salem (Six) and Fairfax (Seven).

At each of these places central direction is given to both the BFO activities and the BCI operations that occur within the division. This duality is reflected in an arrangement whereby each division is directed by two commanders of equal rank, that of captain. One heads the division's uniformed patrols and related work, the other directs criminal investigations conducted by the special agents assigned to that region. In Division Six at Salem, from which resources were sent in response to the Virginia Tech shooting incident, patrol troopers report to Capt. Richard A. Denney and special agents to Capt. George W. Austin Jr. Denney commands approximately 150 officers, Austin about 50.

The area offices occupy the front lines of the department's work in many ways. Each division's territory is divided into approximately six areas, with a statewide total of 48. Each area is headquartered in a marked VSP building and serves one to four counties. Whereas most special agents do not work out of these area offices, most state troopers do; they receive their patrol assignments here, get supervised by their sergeants and form the kind of close relationships that facing danger together can generate.

A feature of this highly decentralized system of field organization that is prized by the VSP is that it allows uniformed officers to become closely identified with the communities they serve. They live and work there. Many have grown up in the community and attended its high school or community college. Moreover, their assignments there can continue for several years, allowing them to become personally acquainted with local officials, sheriff's deputies and community leaders, along with chronic troublemakers. They are also familiar with area roads and places where drivers speed and teens get into mischief. Whereas in urban parts of the state troopers spend most of their time responding to accidents and 911 calls, in rural areas where traffic volume is low a large part of their job is just to "be there." From one corner of the Commonwealth to the other, the Virginia State Police constitutes both a law enforcement presence and a link between citizens and government.

A PARAMILITARY CULTURE

Condensation Symbols

The culture of the organization, the realm of cell 5 of the mission mystique template, also has a paramilitary air. The meanings of symbols, signs, rituals, attitudes and artifacts, as categorized by Steven Ott are drilled into recruits and reinforced on a continuing basis in the workforce, particularly the sworn portion. This gives them the ability to make it possible for the institutional culture to be carried on over successive generations.

The VSP possesses an official flag, proudly displayed in all departmental buildings and on all special occasions. In its center is the Virginia state seal, adopted by the Commonwealth just after the Declaration of Independence. The seal is also molded into the VSP badge and sewn onto the shoulder patches of all uniforms. Beneath the seal are the words *Valor, Service* and *Pride*. It is not by coincidence that the first letters of these words are identical to the initials of the Virginia State Police. The three attributes are not simply strategic "core values," but a long-standing, almost sacrosanct articulation of commitment to the department's trio of cardinal virtues: personal courage under danger, a sincere commitment to helping citizens and unreserved fidelity to the organization. The three honored values are also named in public brochures, ceremonial programs, training class banners and the organization's logo.[16]

The colors of the VSP flag are blue and gray. They possess their own symbolism. Introduced in 1932 as colors for the uniforms of Enforcement Division

Virginia State Police flag in entrance rotunda of the Richmond headquarters, held by Sergeant Thomas J. Molnar. The flag's colors of blue and gray represent the opposing sides in the Civil War. The words Valor, Service and Pride below the state seal convey the agency's cardinal virtues.

Source: Photo by the author.

inspectors, their choice originally emanated from Virginia's position in the Civil War, during most of which Richmond was the capital of the Confederacy. The blue comes from the uniforms of Union soldiers, and the gray from the uniforms of Confederate forces. Today, however, that origin is forgotten by all but a tiny minority of Virginians. Within the state's contemporary law enforcement community, the blue and the gray, found not only in the VSP flag but also its uniforms and patrol cars, stand for something quite contemporary and real: the Commonwealth's most honored police organization. I have heard Blacksburg cops admiringly remark that VSP troopers "bleed blue and gray," i.e., belong to an honored company and possess unreserved fidelity to it.

Formal Ceremonies

Departmental ceremonies are conducted periodically, at which these and other symbols are much in evidence. One is the graduation of trooper-trainees from the first phase of their basic training at the police academy. At this point the young men and women receive their badges, wear their uniforms for the first time and can be addressed as "state troopers." In order to emphasize the significance of having attained this status, they are entitled for the first time to ascend a white marble staircase within the formal entry hall of the academy.

Each successive academy class is assigned a number that designates its place in the long series of such groups. For example, Session 115 was receiving training when I toured the academy on central headquarters grounds. In good weather on graduation day, the new troopers, their families, instructors and top police personnel gather in celebration outside the building, where a bronze statue titled "Virginia's Finest" stands. It depicts a life-sized trooper in dress uniform, standing at parade rest. The most moving moment of the day is when the class recites, in unison, "The Trooper's Pledge," written early in the Woodson era by a Lt. W. C. Thomas:

Humbly recognizing the responsibilities entrusted to me as a member of the Department of State Police, an organization dedicated to the preservation of human life and property, I pledge myself to perform my duties honestly and faithfully to the best of my ability and without fear, favor or prejudice.

I shall aid those in danger or distress, and shall strive always to make my State and Country a safer place in which to live.

I shall wage unceasing war against crime in all its forms, and shall consider no sacrifice too great in the performance of my duty.

I shall obey the laws of the United States of America and of the Commonwealth of Virginia, and shall support and defend their constitutions against all enemies whomsoever, foreign and domestic.

I shall always be loyal to and uphold the honor of my organization, my State, and my Country.[17]

In May of each year, when National Police Week and National Law Enforcement Week are celebrated, the department holds a memorial service in the police academy gymnasium. Its purpose is to commemorate the sacrifice of the 53 men and two women who died in the line of duty as officers of the Enforcement Division up to 1942 and of the Virginia State Police thereafter. In addition to dignitaries and VSP personnel, families of the honored individuals are invited. The ritual is solemn, with uniformed troopers standing in a tight row around the sides and back of the large room. Prayers are said, the colors presented, an address given and a wreath placed. Then the roll of fallen is slowly called, with a ship's bell rung once for each. Finally, taps is played, followed by a benediction.

In 2009 a new element was introduced into the ceremony: the highlighting of a subgroup of the 55 fallen, selected by how long ago each sacrifice occurred. After the circumstances of each death were described, the individual's portrait was saluted by an honor guard in dress uniform. Painted portraits of all 55 individuals are on permanent display in the Col. Charles W. Woodson Jr. Memorial Gallery, located in the main academy building at the foot of the white marble stairs. The gallery itself commemorates the institution's founder.

Identity Designations

In this paramilitary organization sworn personnel hold a rank that identifies their relative position in the police hierarchy. Rank is used at all levels as the appropriate and customary title of address in formal discourse and correspondence. Table 6.1 lists these ranks in descending order at four functional levels of the hierarchy: top leadership, mid-level leadership, supervisory positions and front-line personnel. BCI agents, usually in civilian dress, have their own ranks.

A comparison with ranks in the armed forces is instructive. From colonel through sergeant, the VSP employs a similar nomenclature as the Army, Air Force

Table 6.1 Ranks of Sworn Virginia State Police Personnel

Top Leadership	Mid-Leadership	Supervisory	Front Line
Colonel	Major	First Sergeant	Master Trooper
Lieutenant	Captain	Buck Sergeant	Senior Trooper
Colonel	Lieutenant		Trooper 2
			Trooper 1
		BCI Only	
		Senior Special Agent	
		Special Agent Accountant	
		Special Agent	

Source: Interviews with senior VSP officers, *Massengill Report,* "Mass Shootings at Virginia Tech, April 16, 2007," report of the Virginia Tech Review Panel, August 2007, presented to Governor Timothy M. Kaine and placed online by his office at www.governor.virginia.gov/techPanelReport.cfm.

and Marines, although it has only one level of lieutenant and fewer levels of sergeant. Missing entirely are the general officer ranks and those for warrant officers. At lower levels, the military's privates, corporals, airmen and seamen are equivalent to various grades of trooper or agent. The biggest departure from the armed forces is that the great divide between "officers" and "enlisted men" is essentially ignored; all graduates of the academy are called officers, and all sworn personnel of all ranks eat together, work together and salute superiors only on rare occasion. Promotion from sergeant to second lieutenant in the military would require passing officers' candidate school or receiving a battlefield promotion; in the VSP the rank of lieutenant is attained by achieving a high score on a promotion exam and possessing a strong record.

All VSP officers are issued uniforms. Except for BCI personnel, they are worn when on duty in both office and field by male and female officers of all ranks. As the ultimate organizational identifier, the uniform is obviously a central carrier of the culture.

The "regular day" uniform consists of long-sleeve shirt (short-sleeve in summer), tie (clip-on to avoid choking in fights), all season-trousers, straw campaign hat, Sam Browne belt fitted with holster and other attachments, ankle-high boots and, for cold weather, a tight-fitting winter jacket. A dress version is the same except for an outer military-style blouse and low quarter shoes. Also issued is a "utility" uniform for strenuous activity like physical training, target practice or tactical assaults. It consists of blue fatigues, baseball-style cap and high boots. When on patrol or other dangerous field duty, officers wear armored vests beneath their outer garments.

Organizational markings on the uniforms are relatively simple and consistent. All ranks have identical shoulder patches, which are worn on each side. They display the Virginia state seal with the words *Virginia State Police* entered below. Also, all uniformed personnel wear a nameplate on the right side of the chest that gives surname and rank. On the left side of the chest the gold-colored badge is pinned, bearing the Virginia state seal surmounted by an eagle, along with a written designation of rank and the words *Virginia State Police*. Variations include a cloth version of the badge sewn into the winter jacket. BCI officers carry a slightly different badge, hanging on a strap or in a wallet.

Rank indicators are downplayed on the uniform, on grounds that in a fighting situation with many officers present, it is best that assailants not know which is the senior officer. Lieutenants and above wear army-style bar, star and bird insignia on their shirt collars, and on the dress uniform, blouse epaulets bearing appropriate insignia. Sergeants are differentiated by number of chevrons on sleeves, just below the shoulder patch. Hash marks placed lower on sleeves indicate length of service for all ranks.

Means of Socialization

Applicants for the position of trooper-trainee must be 21 years of age, a high school graduate and a U.S. citizen. He or she also must also possess a valid driver's license and good driving record; meet sight, hearing and weight standards; and be of good character and reputation. More than 1,000 apply for each Basic Session class that comes open. Only 40 to 80 are admitted, an amount that makes possible strict application of admission standards. The admission process involves a physical examination, mental agility tests, psychological tests, a polygraph test and a background investigation that verifies stated credentials and reviews credit history and police record, if any.

Socialization of incoming trainees is primarily accomplished by the VSP academy, located behind headquarters in Richmond. The total training period, which takes approximately 44 weeks, is divided into four phases. The first is the Basic Session, comprised of 20 weeks of physical and classroom training at the headquarters academy. It is at the conclusion of this phase that the trooper-trainee graduates to the status of trooper and receives the badge and uniform. Phase two consists of four weeks of training in the field. In it, the knowledge learned in the Basic Session is applied in practice, under the watchful eye of an experienced trooper. The group then returns to Richmond for the third phase, an additional 12 weeks of more advanced classroom and practical training. The fourth and final phase is six to eight weeks of ride-along experience with patrolling officers. Successful completion of formal training is then followed by a year on probation, with the rookie trooper reporting to an assigned area office.

Introducing the recruit to the discipline and mentality of the department occurs during the 20 weeks of the Basic Session. In this period all members of the class live in dormitory rooms at the academy, three to a room. The daily regimen begins at 6 a.m. and concludes at 10 p.m. Meals last exactly 30 minutes and occur at 7 a.m., 12 noon and 5:30 p.m. An hour of military drill or similar activity is scheduled before breakfast, and 20 minutes are reserved for room inspection at 9:50 a.m. A 20-minute break takes place at 2:50 p.m., and one hour of supervised physical training exercises precedes supper. Monday through Thursday evenings are reserved for study hall; in order to make it through the program, trainees must take good advantage of this time to prepare for numerous exams. Unlike basic training in the Army, all are released at 2:50 p.m. Fridays for "weekend liberty," i.e., they go home.

Even with weekends off, every class experiences significant attrition before completion of training. In order to reduce any misconceptions as to how difficult the training will be, a video of training activities is streamed on the agency website, with a stern-sounding voice warning:

> The first day you enter the Virginia State Police Academy your life will change. While living and learning here you'll be told when, where, and how to do things. You'll be expected to be at designated locations at designated times. As a trooper-trainee you'll be held to the highest standard and expected to look your best and perform at your best at all times. You'll be told when to go to bed, how to make your bed, when to get up, when to eat, and how long you have to eat. You'll expect to be motivated, and encourage your classmates who may be having difficulty. You'll be told how to dress and what to wear. You'll be expected to follow orders from Academy staff, as well as all rules and regulations of the department. You'll hit the ground running.[18]

Another important means of socialization is a large loose-leaf notebook some six inches thick. It contains what are known as the Superintendent's General Orders, at present 91 in number. These describe the basic policies of the VSP with respect to everything from the authority and duties of each unit to thematic subjects like personal appearance, military courtesy and conduct in strikes and riots. While the very size and format of this manual suggests an inflexible, rule-bound organization, in a foreword Colonel Flaherty notes that the document cannot cover every contingency, hence "Much of necessity is left to your intelligence and discretion, with an earnest effort to always exercise the very best possible judgment."[19]

The State Police "Family"

VSP personnel often talk about affiliation with the State Police "family," a notion with many facets. One meaning is literal; following withdrawal of a ban on nepotism in 1976, a number of sons have followed their fathers into the force. Sufficient time has now passed that third-generation members are now joining up. In fact, Superintendent Flaherty's father was a VSP officer, and the colonel's son is now a trooper.

The family concept refers also to how the VSP workforce, both sworn and civilian, sees itself as a common community. In the early Woodson years the number of employees was small enough that everyone knew everyone. With the present size of 2,600 that is impossible, yet a high degree of collective identity is nonetheless attained. This is true both for the organization as a whole and its subunits, especially the divisions and areas. In addition, members of basic classes in the academy bond together, with ties remaining strong throughout their careers. Such relationships are periodically reinforced by the steady rhythm of retraining weeks at the academy, each second year.

The extended VSP family reaches out in other directions as well. One is to employees who reach retirement, required at no later than age 70. Retirees often keep in close touch with former colleagues at the local area office or regional division headquarters. Some stalwarts return to Richmond annually for graduation or memorial ceremonies. Still others volunteer by helping out with fundraising projects sponsored by the Virginia State Police Association, a private nonprofit group. The association also sponsors periodic dinner dances and picnics that attract current and former employees. "The Department never leaves you," says one ranking veteran.

A final aspect of VSP comradeship is involvement of family members. Because of the tendency for long-term stability in field assignments, supervisors and commanders come to know not only their troopers but also their spouses and children. It is not unusual to send them greeting cards, attend their graduations from high school or college, and visit them in the hospital and attend their funerals. Other avenues of family involvement are service activities of the VSP Association and the Virginia chapter of the American Association of State Troopers, such as scholarship programs, special insurance policies and emergency relief funds.

Thus the State Police family is close-knit. At one time it was also homogenous. As a Southern state, Virginia's history included strict segregation of the races, and for half of its existence the VSP was an all-white (and almost all-male) organization. Following the civil rights movement of the 1960s this came to the attention of the U.S. Department of Justice, and in the late 1970s the Justice Department of the Jimmy Carter administration conducted a three-year investigation of VSP staffing patterns. The study found that the department had hired no black troopers from its inception until 1969, and from 1972 to 1976 only 3.3 percent of new trooper hires were African-American. The investigators also ascertained that by 1976 only three women had been offered trooper positions. The government filed charges in court under Title VII of the Civil Rights Act, and at the trial and appeal levels the charges were sustained.[20]

Since the 1970s much progress has been made in moving the department beyond a basically white stronghold. By 2007, 8.8 percent of VSP sworn officers were African-American, 1.9 percent Hispanic or of other minority status, and 5.4 percent female. Twenty-three percent of the Basic Session class for that year was African-American and 11 percent female.[21] At this writing the VSP website's employment link featured a photo of five uniformed officers, two of whom were minority, two female and one a white male. The caption read, "Join A Progressive Organization—Join the Virginia State Police."

Another sensitive social issue related to the close-knit character of the VSP community is church-state relations. In socially conservative Virginia many officers and their families, especially in the rural part of the state, are members of evangelical churches. Others are Roman Catholic, and the number of Jews and Muslims is small. Accordingly, a long-standing tradition at VSP ceremonies like academy graduations, memorial services and building dedications is to offer up distinctly Christian prayers to the Almighty.

This practice temporarily changed in September 2008, when Colonel Flaherty issued a policy that department chaplains (troopers who volunteer for prayer or counseling duty) must thenceforth not mention Jesus or any other divine prophet in VSP-sponsored public prayer. His action was prompted by a federal appeals court decision that banned Christian prayer before the city council of Fredericksburg, Va. Following the superintendent's announcement, six of 17 VSP chaplains removed themselves from the praying roster. Several Baptist pastors around the state and a number of national Christian activists raised strong objections in the media. While Gov. Tim Kaine, a Catholic, strongly defended Flaherty's decision on constitutional grounds, Republican members of the General Assembly charged that the colonel was attacking the Christian religion. A bill to reverse his decision was passed by the Republican-controlled House but defeated in the Senate, where Democrats had a majority. However, when Republican governor McDonnell came to power the next year he ordered that the ban on sectarian prayer be rescinded.[22]

Weapons and Vehicles

Turning now to the equipment of this paramilitary organization, two types have particular importance as indispensable tools for law enforcement: firearms and police vehicles. In addition to being prime means of force and mobility, these guns and cars symbolize the essence of the profession—being ready to rush toward danger yet make it home afterward.

The most important weapon in support of the sworn officer's authority and safety is the handgun, a Sig Sauer 357 semi-automatic pistol. Studies have shown that in the typical police gunfight the perpetrator takes an average of 0.3 seconds to initiate shooting while the officer, who must react rather than initiate, takes 1.4 to 2.3 seconds. Moreover, under stress, accuracy in return fire is approximately halved. Considering this level of threat, the VSP trains its officers to be (1) keenly observant at all times, (2) able to draw and fire in at least 1.7 seconds, and (3) ready to advance forward aggressively to frighten the gunman and shorten the range.

The second essential tool and symbol of police work is the patrol vehicle. The trooper's car, assigned to him or her individually and taken home at night, is the primary workspace and means for conducting patrols, catching speeders, assisting stranded motorists and working the all-too-frequent wreck. Each officer is

Senior Trooper Gary D. Chafin standing before a Ford Crown Victoria police interceptor, behind Division six headquarters in Salem, Va. The trooper is in regular day uniform with winter jacket. The car's supercharged hemispheric engine allows it to attain 100 mph in 24 seconds.

Source: Photo by the author.

· ownership
· accountability

responsible for the car's maintenance as if it were their own; oil changes and minor repairs are done at local private garages, at VSP expense.

Hundreds of familiar blue and gray state police cars are positioned around the state, equipped with roof light bar and VSP emblems on the front, back and sides. The most common makes are police-equipped Ford Crown Victorias, Chevrolet Impalas and Dodge Chargers. Supercharged hemispheric engines enable these vehicles to accelerate from 0 to 100 miles per hour in as little as 16 seconds, and to attain a maximum speed of up to 150 miles per hour. Also installed in them are speedometers certified for accuracy, two-way radio equipment, front-view cameras for video-recording traffic stops, speed-measurement radar and radar-detection systems, and sirens that emit three sounds: yelp for city streets, wail for highway use and European-style high-low as a third option. Each driver's laptop computer fits snugly on a dashboard shelf for easy access from the wheel. Communication gear and a shotgun and assault rifle are installed in the trunk. Teddy bears or other soft toys are stowed to give comfort to distressed small children who must be transported.

Headquarters Buildings   culture

A final element of the VSP culture is the physical structures used to house central and field headquarters. At any given point in time, it should be kept in mind, "the Virginia State Police" as such is not mostly in them but out in the field or off shift. Nonetheless, these buildings represent the organization in the minds of employees and other law enforcement agencies and are an important physical manifestation of its mission.

State police buildings are, however, less known to the general public than other government buildings in their cities and neighborhoods. In fact, the VSP places road signs on highways so citizens can find them if need be. The reason for this relative obscurity is that, unlike municipal police stations, division and area headquarters tend to be located not in the heart of cities but at their peripheries, in marked but undistinguished structures set back from the road. This location factor causes citizens in urban areas to visualize the State Police as not "our" cops but "those cops"—of which they are very wary when driving on state highways. This degree of social distance is less pronounced in rural parts of the state where state troopers are personally known.

Central State Police headquarters, too, were originally outside the city, on Midlothian Turnpike. Now, however, Richmond has grown to the point that its location on this thoroughfare is relatively close to the heart of the city. The complex of buildings and acreage behind resemble a small military base, surrounded by a security fence and recognizable from a distance by a 400-foot communications tower.

The main entrance to VSP headquarters is a barricaded white octagon structure, perhaps inspired by Jefferson's affinity for eight-sided structures. The rotunda inside is empty save for benches to sit on and the flags of the United States, Virginia and State Police, along with accreditation and memorial banners. The octagon bisects a long brick edifice that is actually two attached buildings, the original 1940 headquarters on the right and a new office building on the left. In back are smaller facilities including a network operations center, underground intelligence center, gymnasium and—as the centerpiece—the state police academy.

THE LESS PUBLIC SIDE

We now explore some of the activities of the Virginia State Police that take place within or from this complex that are largely unknown to the general public. Yet they are just as essential to the public safety as uniformed troopers and their marked patrol cars. Most of these are conducted by the two bureaus other than Field Operations, i.e., Criminal Investigation (BCI) and Administrative Support Services (BASS).

Public-Private Collaboration

Two investigative programs housed in BCI are carried out in cooperation with the insurance industry, which funds them in large part. Both are administered by the bureau's General Investigations Section. One concerns insurance fraud, which occurs when people fake auto crashes, stage burglaries or lie about theft, and then file claims under false pretenses. In 2007, 1,687 reports of suspicious filings were received, 458 of which were investigated. Over 300 arrests resulted.[23]

A second investigative program supported by the insurance industry is Help Eliminate Auto Theft (HEAT). In addition to setting up a hotline to receive tips, BCI sponsors a network of auto theft investigators that represent more than 175 local police and sheriff departments around the state, along with Virginia's many DMV offices. Under the code name Operation HEATwave, monthly meetings by the network are held to share information, compile statistics and trace trends. Using the latest digital technology to carry out its mission, HEAT plants flashy "bait" cars in high-crime areas in order to attract car thieves. They are equipped with transponders so that their location can be tracked by agents in unmarked control cars. At a propitious moment and place, the officers—via electronic controls—remotely raise the car's windows, lock its doors and shut off its engine, resulting in an "airtight" arrest. In another HEAT technology, Mobile Data Hunter vehicles, equipped with special computers and side-mounted digital cameras, do drive-by hunting in parking lots for stolen cars by "reading" the numbers on the license plates of vehicles and automatically checking them against a database. Following a validated hit, officers simply wait for the driver to return to the vehicle.[24]

Drug Task Forces

Another section of BCI, Drug Enforcement, mobilizes in excess of 100 agents to combat illegal drug distribution and possession across the Commonwealth. A small part of narcotics investigation is carried out by having division BCI agents work individual cases in concert with local police. The more common practice is to work through multijurisdictional drug task forces. These teams are given a specific assignment, involve all pertinent state and local jurisdictions, and have one representative from each participating. State criminal law authority is conferred on everyone within the group, which acts as a body of equals. Tactical decisions are made following extended discussion, often at the task force's "office," a room or two in an anonymous building well away from any official police location. While the organization operates semi-autonomously according to the exigencies of the moment, the agent in charge is responsible for all actions taken and telephoned reports are made, even daily, to superiors at BCI and appropriate authorities elsewhere. The department also participates in drug task forces at the national and international level. VSP drug agents thrive on the excitement of the job and pursue drug traffickers and ringleaders relentlessly.

Gathering Intelligence

Criminal + terrorist Studies

A separate BCI entity known as the Criminal Intelligence Division (CID) does very different work. This is the gathering and distribution of intelligence information on criminals and terrorists, utilizing sophisticated computer technology and IT networks. CID's Analytical Unit operates the Virginia Criminal Intelligence Center, which is a repository of multiple databases on known and suspected criminals that can be accessed by all Virginia police agencies as well as federal authorities. Its research unit assists the communication needs of surveillance operations, tracks fictitious identifications used by undercover personnel and serves as the department's liaison with INTERPOL. The field intelligence unit, which has personnel located in all seven VSP divisions around the state, collects and supplies information on current BCI investigations, including those of the task forces.

Two CID units are particularly high-tech in nature. One, technical support, responds to departmental and statewide requests for assistance in using IT hardware and software, such as Global Positioning System equipment, covert surveillance and monitoring devices, closed-circuit television for court testimony by abused children and technology that facilitates communication in hostage negotiations. Another entity, the computer evidence recovery unit, extracts information from computer hard drives that have been seized as evidence, as well as from hand-held electronic devices and file-sharing networks. This work is highly demanding technically since software programs change almost daily. In addition to recovering evidence, the group engages proactively with targeted chat rooms and websites to accumulate evidence on sexual predators and child pornographers.

Another component of CID, the Tactical Intelligence Processing System, operates a terrorism bulletin board that distributes intelligence information to six tiers of governmental and nongovernmental destinations: executive decision makers, law enforcement agencies, intelligence agencies, public entities responsible for critical public infrastructure like bridges and water plants, privately owned public utilities and the general public. CID also supervises a 24-hour, underground Fusion Center that gathers, analyzes and disseminates intelligence information on domestic and foreign terrorism. The term *fusion* refers to the center's mandate to integrate data from all governmental, international and private sector sources. A secondary mission, carried out in cooperation with the Virginia Department of Emergency Management, is to operate an emergency operations command center for the state when necessary, as in a natural disaster or terrorist attack.[25]

Database Programs

The third State Police bureau, Administrative and Support Services (BASS), performs many familiar administrative staff functions for the VSP, as mentioned earlier. Other divisions within the bureau attend to lesser-known substantive work. One is the Criminal Justice Information Services (CJIS) Division. In cooperation with the BASS Information Technology Division, CJIS maintains three electronic databases in the public interest. One is Amber Alert, a national program that broadcasts information around the country within minutes of receiving reports on missing or abducted children. In Virginia the VSP is responsible for its state's participation, and the CJIS Division receives all reports electronically and immediately transmits them to the Amber Alert clearinghouse. A smaller, Virginia-only program is Senior Alert, by which the VSP sends out missing-person bulletins for victims of Alzheimer's disease or dementia that wander away from their residence and become lost.[26]

The Sex Offender Registry is another database that serves the public. This is a file of all persons in Virginia who have been convicted of criminal sex offenses. Over 16,000 persons are registered, a number that has doubled in the past decade. As information updates become available, newly convicted sex offenders, those released from jail or those who have moved to Virginia are added to the database. The registry entries include names, addresses, places of work and/or schooling, telephone numbers and e-mail addresses. Other information is made available on chat rooms frequented, fingerprints and DNA, and registration numbers for vehicles, aircraft and boats. Twice a year VSP sex offender investigators physically confirm locations for about 5,000 registered sex offenders; unfortunately, the department does not have sufficient personnel to check on more.[27]

The third VSP database relates to the Virginia Firearms Transaction Program, established in 1989. For some time in the 1980s the General Assembly had been trying to find a way to regulate gun ownership. A contemplated arrangement similar to driver's licenses was briefly entertained but rejected as too cumbersome as well as politically unpalatable. Two VSP employees conceived of having gun shop owners telephone the State Police during but prior to completing a pending gun sale, so as to determine if the buyer has a criminal record. The Federal Bureau of Investigation (FBI), custodian of national criminal justice databases, first opposed the concept on grounds that purchasing a weapon is not itself a criminal offense. Virginia authorities pressed their case, however, eventually convincing the FBI to agree, and a bill was passed in the General Assembly resulting in a program of instant background checks to be implemented by the VSP.

The Virginia firearms transaction program is now looked to around the country as a model to emulate. In 1994 the Brady Act passed by Congress adopted essentially the same procedure to cover federally licensed firearms dealers. Now most of the checks are conducted online rather than by telephone, although the latter remains an option so shop owners are not forced to possess a computer. In 2008 the number of transactions was 268,136, of which 2,777 (about 1 percent) resulted in denial, mostly because of felony indictment or conviction. Arrest warrants were issued as a result of 263 transactions, and in 77 cases the buyer was arrested on the spot.[28]

Radio Infrastructure

Despite the computer revolution in law enforcement, police departments still rely on radio for minute-by-minute communication. Two-way FM radio contact was introduced to the VSP by Woodson half a century ago, and this system, supplemented by microwave equipment and repeater towers, was used for decades.[29] In the late 1990s efforts were launched to modernize the system, but they moved at slow speed until the night of Nov. 24, 2002. Trooper Gary R. Horner Jr. was checking out a rest area on westbound Interstate 64 in Kent County, at mile marker 213 between Richmond and Williamsburg. An assailant took him by surprise and shot him seven times. Horner tried desperately to contact the dispatcher on his police radio, but a garbled signal prevented the message from getting through. Horner repeated the attempt three more times, when finally an alert technician realized the problem and cleared the channel. The frantic incoming message was: "I've been hit several times." The VSP mobilized its resources immediately, and fortunately officers arrived in time to save Horner's life.

The gravity of this incident led Col. Gerald Massengill, the superintendent before Colonel Flaherty, to intensify efforts to replace the department's antiquated analogue land-mobile radio system. When Superintendent Flaherty took over the department the project gained further traction. Playing a tape of the Horner incident as evidence of drastic need, Flaherty convinced Gov. Mark Warner and key legislators to move rapidly ahead and authorize bonds for a major modernization project. Its management was placed in the hands of the BASS Communication Division.

In July 2004 a contract worth $329 million was signed with Motorola Corporation to design, build and install a new digital trunked system to operate on the VHF 150 MHz band. As planning moved ahead and new technologies became available, it was decided to expand its reach beyond the State Police and include all other state agencies that required statewide radio communication. Twenty-two departments and agencies were eventually brought into the project, named the Statewide Agencies Radio System (STARS).

Another goal of STARS was to establish communication interoperability among all connected state and local agencies. This was done using a bridging system that enabled each participating entity to establish up to seven patches to other organizations, with an eighth back to the STARS network. Foolproof encryption was built in, applied to data transmission as well as voice. A final feature was to construct a sufficient number of land towers so that Virginia's eastern mists and western mountains did not interfere with a clear signal. Redundancy was built in so that in case of path outage, signals would automatically reroute themselves via alternate loops. At this writing STARS is operating in the most populated areas of the state and will soon cover the entire Commonwealth.

In December 2005 a press conference was called at VSP headquarters with the governor, public safety secretary, VSP superintendent and Motorola Corporate vice president on hand. The fully recovered Trooper Horner was waiting in his patrol car at the fateful mile marker 213 rest area. In front of reporters and rolling cameras, Governor Warner intoned into a mobile police phone, "Car 101 to Unit 774." A lapse of a few seconds ensued, during which officials winced. Suddenly Horner's voice boomed out of the speaker: "Unit 774. Go ahead." The governor asked to confirm: "Unit 774, can you copy me?" "Yes, sir," Horner replied, "your traffic is loud and clear." Wide smiles broke out—the most advanced police radio network in the nation worked fine.[30]

PROFESSIONAL AUTONOMY

p. 23

We now turn attention to the VSP's access to qualified policy autonomy, the subject of cell 8 in the mission mystique template. Its primary basis with respect to the State Police is the agency's reputation for professionalism—a pattern of nonpartisan conduct that shows no favoritism in enforcing the law. This was the standard laid down by Charles Woodson, and it has remained ingrained in the institution ever since.

Professional Conduct

Historically, the VSP exhibited a posture of neutral professionalism during coal strikes and protest marches, during civil rights protests and at demonstrations against the Vietnam War. With the exception of the Wilder-Corvello flare-up, the position of superintendent of the VSP has been untouched by elected-official politics. Very seldom has the Office of the Governor or General Assembly attempted to intervene in the department's discharge of its law enforcement duties. This kind of respect shown by the political branches of government is by no means universal in state police departments across the country. Also, within the Richmond political orbit, the State Police has a reputation for competence and professionalism that is not exceeded by any other part of state government.

Outside Richmond a similar attitude prevails on the part of law enforcement professionals. The nationally recognized Commission on Accreditation for Law Enforcement Agencies first reviewed the VSP in 1986 and visited it again for reaccredidation in 1996 and 2007. Its latest report concluded, "It was obvious the superintendent and command staff, as well as the troopers and special agents, have worked hard to provide a professional and highly respected level of police service." Delegate Beverly Sherwood of the General Assembly had told the accreditation team in 2007 that the agency "enjoys bipartisan support and there have been no issues that tend to show political alignment with any one political group."[31]

It is undeniable that everybody who drives in Virginia cringes at the thought of a blue and gray VSP car with flashing lights pulling up behind them. Yet when a breakdown or accident happens on the road, the arrival of state troopers to help is always a relief. In a 2008 survey of citizens who because of automobile accidents had contact with the State Police, 81.6 percent rated the quality of assistance rendered as excellent or good. On the speed of arrival of troopers to the scene, 72.7 percent had that same reaction, and the level of professional competence was characterized in that manner by 80.7 percent.[32]

One more sign of VSP professionalism is how it reacts when a rotten apple is found in the barrel. When launching research on this chapter, my initial interview with Colonel Flaherty was delayed for over an hour because, as I found out later, he was unexpectedly supervising the arrest of a state police captain on criminal charges of forced sodomy. The superintendent casually gave me a copy of the press release that had just been prepared on the subject, saying, "You will see this on television tonight anyway."

Autonomy and Cooperation

This degree of professional pride, and the reservoir of respect it has gained for the institution over the decades, gives the Virginia State Police very considerable policy clout. While the General Assembly never appropriates enough funds to allow the VSP to be staffed at full strength, the poor revenue picture in recent years has adversely affected all state agencies, as is the case throughout the country. However, on individual policy matters the agency has done quite well on several occasions. As noted, the Firearms Transaction Program was adopted despite objections from the FBI and the consternation of Virginia's powerful gun lobby. A recent legislative attempt to drop the rule that only one firearm purchase a year could be approved for a purchaser failed to pass. On the issue of sectarian prayer at official police functions, an attempt by religious conservatives to reverse Colonel Flaherty's ban received only modest support in the legislature, although later the governor rescinded it. When it became apparent that the antiquated two-way radio system the department had been using for years had to be replaced, skilled use of the Horner near-tragedy mobilized enough support in the General Assembly to vote a generous bond issue. The project even garnered sufficient political support to be expanded into a statewide governmental radio system that connects into all local law enforcement agencies.

The high standing of the Virginia State Police in governmental and private-sector circles made it possible for the agency to lead the way in forming innovative collaborative arrangements. An example is the willingness of the insurance industry to fund VSP training and enforcement programs in combating insurance fraud and vehicle theft. Another is the drug enforcement task forces the

VSP sponsors, involving police agencies at all levels of the federal system. Scores of intelligence agencies and public utilities in the United States and abroad participate in the department's terrorism bulletin board. The Fusion Center, cosponsored with the state's Department of Emergency Management, is itself an illustration of collaboration across agencies, sectors and levels of government. And when something bizarre happens like the Virginia Tech shootings, a backlog of mutual respect almost instantly generates a seamless web of intimate cooperation. — *but why was the boy not flagged*

This paramilitary organization, then, generates its extent of mission mystique from the nature of the work it does—patrolling the highways of the state and participating in investigation of its criminal activity, and the way it does this work—adhering to strict professional standards and expecting its officers to adhere to the cardinal values of valor, service and pride.

• Critique the police organization

THIS INSTANCE OF MISSION MYSTIQUE

As a paramilitary organization, the Virginia State Police is quite a different kind of administrative agency from those examined earlier in the book. Given that, how does the VSP measure up against the ideal template of mission mystique?

Cell 1: Mission. As an acknowledged mission rather than specified, the purpose of the VSP is self-apparent yet specific: maintaining public safety statewide. From Charles Woodson on, the emphasis in carrying out this mission has been to operate as a model police force for the state. This goal of recognized superiority is similar to our other two cases of acknowledged mission. The CDC seeks to protect the nation's health to the maximum extent possible. The DSS seeks to perform as a caring and creative public welfare department to the greatest extent possible. For the VSP, the mission is doing the work of policing with officers who conduct themselves in the most professional way possible. This goal is sought by selective admission standards, an intensely rigorous process of socialization, and maintenance of a total-commitment culture of competent independence that embraces the officers throughout their careers. The words *Virginia's Finest* on the academy's trooper statue say what the department is all about.

Cell 2: Need. The need for a good state police department would seem to be unquestionable by all except criminals and those who choose to deny the law's authority. Crime has always existed, and each era introduces new forms, with sudden shootings, bomb threats, online predators and drug-related violence among this era's favorites. Each of these requires fresh thinking, added programs and new technologies. With its commitment to professionalism, the VSP has appeared to respond as well as possible, especially in light of chronic underfunding.

tried to add gun laws   *— demographic of Virginia*

Cell 3: Reputation. The department's reputation within the Commonwealth is sterling. It may well be the most highly regarded line agency of Virginia state government. Unlike many comparable departments around the country, not to mention countless local police forces, no major incidents of corruption have ever erupted. Law enforcement insiders regard the organization as well equipped, and technologically ahead of most. In Richmond political circles, its leadership is perceived as steady and impartial. Among the driving public, seeing flashing lights in the rearview mirror causes that sinking feeling, but the help received in dire circumstances when out on the highway is welcomed.

Cell 4: Motivation. To the seasoned sworn officers of the VSP, being in the organization is much more than a job. They see themselves as members of an elite cadre. They are proud to wear their badges and uniforms. Hundreds apply for the handful of available places. Despite low salaries, turnover is small and many stay until retirement. Sons of troopers follow in their fathers' footsteps, and more and more women are joining the ranks. Uniformed officers remember when they drive by the scenes of bloody crashes they have worked. BCI agents are delighted when their persistence puts a hardened criminal away. The danger is there, but so too is the adrenaline rush when running toward danger and—when that is over—the singular respect received during a restaurant rest stop.

Cell 5: Culture. This paramilitary organization does much to socialize newcomers. They are put through an arduous academy application process. They endure many weeks of stressful and strenuous training. They receive their gold badge, blue and gray uniform, pistol, and new patrol car. They recite the Trooper's Pledge and ascend the academy's marble staircase. And if killed in action, their portrait will hang in the memorial gallery at the stairway's base. Then, as the subsequent years of duty go by, they are reinforced in their skills and socialization during retraining visits to headquarters. The culture is further embedded by daily comradeship in the field and supportive interaction on a family level through and beyond retirement.

Cell 6: History. The VSP has an excellent museum located in the academy building that contains exhibits of badges and insignia, books of old photographs, examples of early uniforms, past motorcycles, a range of period weapons and many other memorabilia. It is lovingly maintained by a 33-year member of the force, retired sergeant J. W. Rowles. Old police cruisers and a rebuilt riot truck are on display outdoors on public occasions. The memorial gallery and annual memorial services recount the past in terms of the fallen. Although chronologies of the department's history exist, an overall narrative account has not been written. A fine video on the agency's history was produced for the 75th anniversary celebration in 2007, however.

Cell 7: Contestation. A professional standards unit, located in offices physically separate from headquarters, enforces professional conduct. Its internal affairs agents investigate all allegations of violations, and when criminal charges seem warranted they are brought and made public. There is no military-style inspector general to challenge policies independent of management. The Superintendent's Idea Line is a way of receiving complaints, but it is not a suitable mechanism for channeling collective dissent or engaging in meaningful dialogue. No employee or retiree blogs exist of which I am aware. Being a paramilitary organization, the VSP operates in a hierarchical manner, and is accustomed to accepting commands from above.

Cell 8: Autonomy. Woodson set the foundations for qualified state police autonomy by building up the resources of the department, expanding its scope of work, and establishing its legitimacy as a competent and impartial law enforcement agency. In doing so he did state-building in Virginia like Daniel Carpenter describes for the early federal government. The VSP image as an elite, professionalized and technologically cutting-edge organization has given it the necessary political room to innovate, join with collaborators and make headway on sensitive social issues like staff diversity and gun control. With one exception, the all-important confidence of the governor has been retained successfully.

Cell 9: Renewal. As a practical, steady, hardheaded agency, the Virginia State Police is not a particularly future-oriented organization. Its attention is focused on the here-and-now character of criminal activity and public safety. The organization does not spend money hiring consultants, or time at retreats. But it is good at the level of single-loop problem solving, such as how to find lost Alzheimer's patients, and double-loop learning that prevents problems, like developing a fail-safe interoperable radio system.

   In conclusion, this paramilitary organization exemplifies most of the attributes of mission mystique. Areas where it falls short relate to the paramilitary character itself: a disciplined, hierarchical organization is inherently not comfortable with internal dissent or chronic change.

- Being too close an organization makes dissent difficult. People may be scared to speak out against authority. They are all to embedded in relationships of each other.

7

U.S. Peace Corps
An Ethical Enterprise

THE PEACE CORPS is quite a different animal from the organizations previously examined. It is a public agency whose main work is carried out not by government employees, or even contract personnel. Its operational workforce, found in 76 countries around the world, consists of 7,700 *volunteers.* These women and men requested to serve and can go home when they wish. They are unpaid except for a small living allowance. Their maximum time of service is two years plus training time. Their circumstances of work are not hugely different from volunteers in countless nonprofit, religious and international service organizations. Thus the Peace Corps is not only of public administration with its controlled government resources, but of the civil society with its high degree of individuality and looseness.

JFK HITS A WINNING NUMBER

At 2 a.m. on Oct. 14, 1960, the motorcade of the Democratic presidential candidate pulled up to the student union on the University of Michigan campus in Ann Arbor. A crowd of 10,000 had been waiting for hours in the cold night air to see the junior senator from Massachusetts, John F. Kennedy, arrive from Willow Run Airport. Reservations had been made for his party to stay overnight at the union after flying in from New York, where his third televised debate with Richard Nixon had occurred earlier that evening. The reason for the visit was a campaign tour by rail across southern Michigan scheduled for the next day.

The huge throng, made up mostly of students—including coeds released from their dormitory curfew for the occasion—cheered wildly when he alighted from his convertible. Kennedy, who had been looking forward to retiring after an exhausting day, was astonished at the massive crowd at so late an hour. Neither he nor the press had anticipated a speech. Yet the candidate could not resist addressing the enthusiastic crowd, at least briefly. A microphone was placed before him on the union steps, and he stepped up to it without notes.

He began by saying with a grin, "I want to express my thanks to you, as a graduate of the Michigan of the East, Harvard University." Then, after some standard references to the final weeks of the campaign and how the election was the most important since 1932, the candidate departed from whistle-stop platitudes and raised his voice:

> How many of you who are going to be doctors are willing to spend your days in Ghana? Technicians or engineers, how many of you are willing to work in the Foreign Service and spend your lives traveling around the world? On your willingness to do that, not merely to serve one year or two years in the service, but on your willingness to contribute part of your life to this country, I think will depend the answer whether a free society can compete. I think it can! And I think Americans are willing to contribute. But the effort must be far greater than we've ever made in the past.

Kennedy ended the "longest short speech I've ever made" with the words, "I come here tonight asking your support for this country over the next decade."[1]

At first the students responded to the challenge with silence. Then stirring and nodding began, followed by applause and cheers. As Kennedy headed for his room with the throng's roar in his ears, he told an aide he must have "hit a winning number." On the next day's campaign stops across Michigan, the candidate, blessed with his New England accent, mentioned serving in Africa so much his staff christened the tour the "Afrikkur Trip."[2]

In the following weeks before the election, Kennedy talked publicly about international service three more times. On Oct. 18 he told an American Legion audience in Miami, Fla., that his administration would take steps to "educate the future leaders of Africa and Asia and Latin America." On Oct. 29 he told a shopping center audience in Pennsylvania, "We need young men and women who will spend some of their years in Latin America, Africa and Asia in the service of freedom." Then, on Nov. 2, six days before the election, Kennedy for the first time formally proposed creation of a Peace Corps. It was done in a nationally televised address at the Cow Palace in San Francisco. After bemoaning the ability of the Foreign Service to represent the United States adequately abroad, he went on:

> I therefore propose that our inadequate efforts in this area be supplemented by a Peace Corps of talented young men and women, willing and able to serve their country as an alternative or a supplement to the peacetime selective service, well qualified through rigorous standards, well trained in the languages, skills and customs they will need to know, and directed by the I.C.A. Point Four agencies. . . . This would be a volunteer corps, and would be sought not

only among talented young men and women, but all Americans, of whatever age, who wished to serve the great Republic and serve the cause of freedom, men who have taught or engineers or doctors or nurses, who have reached the age of retirement, or who in the midst of their work wished to serve their country and freedom, should be given an opportunity and an agency in which their talents could serve our country around the globe.[3]

The popular mythology of the Peace Corps, supported by its own recruiting literature, gives the impression that the Peace Corps idea was first introduced to the world by Kennedy at 2 a.m. that morning in Ann Arbor. This is not the case. Another misconception is that creation of the Peace Corps was a top priority of President Kennedy's. That too is an exaggeration. Nevertheless, without JFK's soaring speeches and crucial interventions at key moments, the Peace Corps we know today would not exist. A plaque near the spot where he stood at the University of Michigan student union says, "Here at 2:00 a.m. on October 14, 1960, John Fitzgerald Kennedy first defined the Peace Corps." Current plans for the agency's 50th anniversary celebration include a ceremony at the U of M campus on Oct. 14, 2010.[4]

THE MYTHOLOGY UNRAVELED

We must never underrate the power and necessity of founding myths, for the truths they embody transcend empirical fact and establish meanings essential to successive generations. But much more happened than what the Peace Corps myth usually admits: first, the idea of such an institution emerged from successive waves of prior idealism; second, its creation was accomplished not by JFK but by his brother-in-law.

Precedents for an American initiative in international volunteerism go back to the turn of the 20th century. Following the Spanish-American War of 1898, in which the United States seized the Philippines and Puerto Rico, President William McKinley urged that young Americans go to the Philippines to become teachers. The first contingent of volunteers arrived aboard the troop transport *Thomas*, causing the imported teachers to become known as "the Thomasites."[5] In another gesture for peace instead of war at this time of American imperialism, the famous philosopher of pragmatism, William James, wrote an essay entitled "The Moral Equivalent of War," in which he proposed that the nation's youth be required to give a few years of their lives to perform hard, menial tasks not for aggression but for the good of society.[6]

Interest in peaceful overseas service emerged again in the 1950s. Leaders of the United Automobile Workers urged President Harry Truman to involve young people in his Point Four program. The union's president, Walter Reuther, proposed scholarships to this end under United Nations (UN) sponsorship. Putting

service abroad in the context of the Cold War, Walter's brother Victor called for "technical missionaries with slide rules, with medical kits, and textbooks, to fight communism on a positive basis."[7] Meanwhile, in 1954 a refugee from Hitler's Germany, Heinz W. Rollman, published the book *World Construction* in which he called upon the U.S. Congress to establish a "Peace Army" of 3 million men and women—volunteers or draftees if necessary—to provide technical education and practical assistance to poor countries so as to make them less vulnerable to the scourge of communism.[8]

During that time members of Congress were themselves advocating the idea. Rep. Henry S. Reuss of Wisconsin, who delighted in recalling how in the Middle Ages Saint Benedict led missions of wealthy young men from Rome to serve in poor areas of northern Europe, proposed establishment of a volunteer corps in a lecture he gave at Cornell University. Reuss reported afterward that the response from students was "electric." In January 1960 he introduced a bill to create a "Point Four Youth Corps," and in a few days a similar bill was introduced in the Senate by Richard L. Neuberger of Oregon.

In February 1960 presidential candidate Kennedy was taken aback by a television interviewer who asked him about these bills. He had not heard of them and instructed his staff to get details. Actually, Reuss and Neuberger had even obtained funds to study the idea via an amendment to the Mutual Security Appropriation Act of 1957. A less cautious legislator, Sen. Hubert Humphrey of Minnesota, spoke against such a study on grounds that the idea was so good on its face that no more study was needed. Then in June 1960 Humphrey introduced legislation to create a "Peace Corps of American young men to assist the peoples of the underdeveloped areas of the world to learn the basic skills necessary to combat poverty, disease, illiteracy, and hunger." During the 1960 primary campaign, when Kennedy was his chief opponent, Humphrey touted his bill in several states, including West Virginia. This put pressure on JFK to respond, which he did by asking the national Young Democrats to circulate a proposal to "explore thoroughly" the possibility.[9]

The concept of the Peace Corps was also not new in the sense that many youth-abroad organizations already existed. Most, but not all, were under private auspices. Sponsors included International Volunteer Service, the International Development Placement Association, the Farm Youth Exchange, American Field Service and Operation Crossroads Africa. The Experiment in International Living, founded in 1932, placed young Americans with families overseas. Sargent Shriver, who was to become the Peace Corps' first director, was on its staff as a young man and led groups to Europe in the late 1930s.[10]

Government-affiliated organizations were also engaged in volunteer international development. A prime example is Britain's Voluntary Service Overseas (VSO). Launched in 1958, it sent young men and women between the ages of 18 and 24 to Commonwealth countries to teach English and to work in various institutions. Another program, Teachers for East Africa (TEA), was dually sponsored and funded by the British and U.S. governments. Its purpose was to train young college graduates for teaching over a two-year period in high schools and teacher-training schools of Kenya, Tanganyika (now Tanzania) and Uganda. The U.S. part of the program was administered by Teachers College of Columbia University and financed by the International Cooperation Administration (ICA), predecessor of the U.S. Agency for International Development (USAID). TEA was announced one month before the Peace Corps; by coincidence, its initial participants and the first Peace Corps Volunteers departed the United States on almost the same day in early September 1961. TEA's main difference from the Peace Corps was that its teachers were called education officers and paid a salary. At one point Shriver argued that the Peace Corps should replace TEA in East Africa, but later the two operations agreed to coexist.[11]

This contemporaneous international service activity did not, however, galvanize the kind of interest aroused by Kennedy's remarks in Ann Arbor. The day after the senator left campus, students formed a group called Americans Committed to World Responsibility. It circulated a petition in behalf of creating an overseas program, and by November more than 1,000 people had signed up. Then, following Kennedy's Cow Palace speech, more than 30,000 letters expressing personal interest in joining a Peace Corps were received at Democratic Party headquarters in Washington.

Despite this great response, in the period between JFK's election in November and inauguration in January the president-elect did not act as if the Peace Corps would be a major initiative of his new administration. Chester Bowles (later under secretary of state) was assigned to the issue for the transition team. One of his few initiatives was to commission two professors to write memos on creation of a Peace Corps. These were Samuel Hayes of the University of Michigan and Max Millikan of the Massachusetts Institute of Technology (MIT); both were cautious and skeptical—Hayes felt that obtaining adequate supervisory staff in the field would be a large problem, and Millikan believed so little was known about international youth programs that only an experimental program was possible. The president-elect's sole public action during this time was to issue a press release entitled "International Youth Service" that called for setting up a small program under the foreign aid program and limiting it to collecting information, setting standards and outsourcing its administration to universities and foundations. It appeared that the guts of the "winning number" had been eviscerated.[12]

SARGE TAKES CHARGE

That all changed on Jan. 20, 1961. At noon that day President John F. Kennedy took the oath of office on the East Front of the U.S. Capitol. The overall theme of his inaugural address was that any price necessary would be paid to ensure the

Need

survival of liberty in the Cold War struggle. In the process of developing this theme, Kennedy uttered the phrase for which he is most remembered today:

> In the long history of the world, only a few generations have been granted the role of defending freedom in its hour of maximum danger. . . . The energy, the faith, the devotion which we bring to this endeavor will light our country and all who serve it—and the glow from that fire can truly light the world.
>
> And so, my fellow Americans: ask not what your country can do for you—ask what you can do for your country.[13]

Although this famous call to service stimulated responses beyond the Peace Corps, in effect it became a mandate to create such an agency posthaste. The very next day the president telephoned his brother-in-law and asked him to form a presidential task force "to report how the Peace Corps could be organized and then to organize it."[14] Robert Sargent Shriver Jr., two years older than the president, was a Yale-educated lawyer who served, like his brother-in-law, as a naval officer in World War II. Following the war he took up journalism at *Newsweek*. On a chance meeting at a cocktail party, Shriver met the future president's sister, Eunice, who brought him into contact with family patriarch Joseph Kennedy. This led to a managerial position at the elder Kennedy's Merchandise Mart in Chicago. Soon Shriver became active in the local affairs of the Windy City and was elected to its board of education. When Senator Kennedy decided to run for the presidency, his gregarious brother-in-law Shriver naturally pitched in to help. Following the election, "Sarge" served as the incoming administration's top recruiter of talent, a job at which he was superb because of his discerning judgment and powers of persuasion.[15]

On Jan. 21, 1961, the same day he got the call, Shriver plunged into his task by convincing Harris Wofford, a Notre Dame law professor who had also worked on the Kennedy campaign, to join him in organizing the task force. As a member of Student World Federalists in the 1940s, Wofford had actually proposed a "peace force" of volunteers years earlier. In the 1950s he assisted Walter Reuther with his scholarship proposal and helped form the International Development Placement Association.

Shriver and Wofford occupied a suite at the Mayflower Hotel in Washington, D.C., from which they went to work. They contacted, queried and argued with scores of academics, foundation officials, business and religious leaders, and ICA bureaucrats. Memoranda were solicited from several individuals on how to approach building the new agency, and the one thing they had in common was to be cautious in giving birth to this strange creature—for if it failed, the president's reputation would be damaged at the very start of the New Frontier (a slogan for the Kennedy administration).[16]

Shriver scheduled the task force's first formal meeting for Feb. 6, 1961. At 2 a.m. that morning he was still in the Mayflower suite shuffling through the papers that had been submitted. Nothing there inspired or excited him. He then picked up a memorandum called "The Towering Task" that had been written by two disgruntled ICA officials, Warren Wiggins and William Josephson. The title they used was borrowed from a phrase used by JFK in his recently delivered State of the Union message, referring to how difficult it is to transform Third World economies.

In their paper, Wiggins and Josephson argued that a small, pilot Peace Corps undertaking would do nothing but annoy a few American ambassadors abroad and, in Washington, fail to gather the press attention and hence political clout that would be needed for success. They argued instead for a program based on the premise that thousands of volunteers would serve the needs of scores of countries, on several continents. Moreover, to take advantage of the groundswell of campus support that had already emerged, it should be formed without delay. Legend has it that by 3 a.m. Shriver sent a telegram to Wiggins at his home in Virginia insisting that he come to the Mayflower that morning for the task force's initial meeting. Wiggins did, and the document he had helped write framed that day's discussion—and laid the philosophical foundation for what we now know as the Peace Corps.[17]

The White House, now attentive to the Peace Corps initiative, kept phoning Shriver to find out when his proposal would be ready. He and his colleagues rushed to complete a report, and one was sent to the president on Feb. 22. Its recommendations, in sum, were as follows:

1. Establish the Peace Corps by executive order as part of the foreign aid program.
2. Provide $10–12 million from discretionary funds for the current fiscal year.
3. Appoint a Peace Corps director, with possibilities listed other than Shriver.
4. Form a National Advisory Council.
5. Cable embassies to learn of possible volunteer opportunities in their countries.
6. Write heads of all UN member states explaining the program.
7. Make an announcement live on television and radio, "next week."

Shriver concluded, "If you decide to go ahead on these, we can be in business Monday morning."[18]

Getting Started

Although the Peace Corps did not go to work quite that fast, there was not long to wait. At first, resistance from cautious White House staff had to be overcome. They thought it would be dangerous to build a big program too fast, and that establishing it by executive order would alienate Congress. Josephson did some research and found out, however, that in the first days of the New Deal the work of the Civilian Conservation Corps was launched, four years before Congress acted, by an executive order for "Emergency Conservation Work." The ICA insider was also aware of a contingency spending section of the Mutual Security Act that could be used to free up immediate funds. Kennedy ordered preparations to go ahead despite staff objections, and on March 1, 1961, a week after receiving Shriver's report, he signed Executive Order 10924, which initially established the agency. To protect himself politically, JFK pointed out that the Corps had been created on a "temporary pilot basis" and would be limited to 500 volunteers the first year. On that same day he formally requested that Congress enact an authorizing statute.[19]

The one thing JFK refused to do was select someone other than Shriver to be director. It was obviously Sarge's energy, skill and charismatic dynamism that had brought the initiative to this point, and Kennedy was turned off by the "bookish" university types Shriver had proposed. The White House staff, now on board, contended that because the agency was to be created by executive order, Senate confirmation of the director was unnecessary. Shriver refused, saying that he would accept the job only if confirmed, so neither he nor the agency would be weakened. The president agreed, and on March 4 a public announcement of the nomination was made. In a few days the Senate confirmed Shriver without difficulty, and he assumed office on March 22, 1961.[20]

Shriver plunged into founding the new agency with his usual enthusiasm and determination. From the start he acted with a sense of urgency, personifying the "vigah" for which the New Frontier became famous. He worked long hours and cultivated an atmosphere of controlled chaos as he tried to get everything done at once. Deploying his renowned arm-twisting ability, Shriver recruited for top positions a number of particularly smart young men. One good catch was Bill Moyers of Lyndon Johnson's staff. In setting up the organization, communication channels were deliberately kept open and people encouraged to debate issues at daily staff meetings. These sessions turned out to be notoriously uninhibited, famous for their shouting matches and table pounding. But when all turned quiet, Sarge announced his decisions and demanded that everyone abide by them, or else. Signs in his office read "Nice Guys Finish Last" and "Good Guys Don't Win Ballgames."[21]

Countless practical matters had to be attended to. Office space was obtained on the sixth floor of the ICA-occupied Maiatico building at 806 Connecticut Ave., N.W., overlooking Lafayette Park. In order to makes some sense of who did what, a preliminary organization chart was drawn up that set out four divisions: Program Development and Operations, Peace Corps Personnel (later renamed Peace Corps Volunteers), Management, and Congressional and Public Affairs. In order to promote external connections and polish the new agency's reputation a

ethical/accountability

National Peace Corps Advisory Council was formed, as proposed earlier. On it were well-positioned luminaries like Lyndon Johnson, William O. Douglas, Eleanor Roosevelt, David Lilienthal and Harry Belafonte.[22]

With at least preliminary matters taken care of in Washington, Shriver and a few aides traveled to several developing countries to pave the way for Volunteer placements. This was the Kennedy administration's first official foray abroad, and Shriver's well-known relationship to the president helped bring it attention. Shriver told the embassies he did not want to be wined and dined, but allowed working sessions with country officials. At the meetings the invitees mostly asked two questions: whether the volunteers would be trained and skilled, and who would pay the bill. To the first, Shriver responded, hopefully yes, but admitted that many would be fresh from college. To the second, he answered the Peace Corps, but donations would be welcome.[23]

Back at home, Shriver asked Senator Humphrey and Representative Reuss to be floor managers for a bill that would make the Peace Corps permanent. Although a groundswell of support for the program was obviously afoot around the country, several important Hill figures were hesitant and believed things were being pushed too fast. Some in the White House and at the State Department quietly agreed. As always, Shriver nonetheless forged ahead, and by May 11 a draft bill was ready for interagency review. Over the summer Shriver testified several times before Hill committees and personally called upon no less than 363 members of Congress. Although in the end authorized funding was cut from $40 to $30 million, the Peace Corps Act passed by substantial majorities in both houses and was signed by the president on Sept. 22, 1961.[24]

Early Volunteers

Meanwhile, the Volunteers Division had recruited, vetted, trained and placed the first batch of Peace Corps Volunteers. On Aug. 28, 1961, 80 young men and women were ready to teach in secondary schools in Ghana and build roads in Tanganyika. On Aug. 28, 1961, Shriver personally walked the group to the White House Rose Garden to meet with and be sent off by the president. The Peace Corps was now both permanently established and ready to make its mark on the world.

The naysayers were right; making that mark carried some risks. Volunteer Margery Michelmore, a *magna cum laude* graduate of Smith College, arrived in Nigeria as a member of the first contingent sent to that country. While walking on a street in Ibadan, she accidentally dropped a postcard to her boyfriend back home. On it she had written that the city was "incredible and fascinating," but that she and her group mates "really were not prepared for the squalor and absolutely primitive living conditions rampant both in the city and in the bush."

The stray piece of mail fell into the hands of students at the University of Ibadan. Copies were made and distributed, and a street demonstration was staged against the American "agents of imperialism." A flurry of diplomatic cables crisscrossed the Atlantic, and the media in the United States got hold of the story. The Associated Press described the protest as "communist-inspired," and former president Dwight Eisenhower cited the incident as "postcard evidence" of the folly of what he depreciatingly called Kennedy's "toy."

Shriver did not panic. He discussed the matter with the president, and Margery Michelmore was brought home. Instead of being discharged she was given a staff job at headquarters. She wrote a letter of apology to JFK offering sincere regrets for the affair and hope that it would not do lasting harm to the agency. This was made available to the press just as Shriver announced that Michelmore's group of Volunteers would remain in Nigeria; moreover, plans were already in the works to send a second group to that country. Soon the incident was forgotten. Peace Corps historian Gerald Rice believes the incident was actually a blessing in disguise, in that more serious Volunteer scrapes occurring later were ignored by the press.[25]

In sum, while the idea of international voluntary service was not new, and while President Kennedy provided the political rhetoric and support that made its creation possible, it was Sargent Shriver who envisioned the institution's true promise, translated that promise into a functioning organization and imbued that organization with a spirit of resolve, idealism and optimism. He was the agency's founding father in every practical sense. Looking back in 1995, he offered this testament to his Peace Corps experience:

> The Peace Corps gave me the most memorable, continuing, morally unblemished, and uncompromised chance ever given any American to serve his country, his countrymen, and his fellow human beings worldwide, simultaneously, and at the grassroots level with the poor everywhere.
>
> Never in war, and I have served in war; never in peace, and I have served in many places in peace, has anyone ever received, from a secular state, a greater opportunity for pure service.[26]

FIGHTS FOR INDEPENDENCE AND SURVIVAL

A trio of fights occurred in the Peace Corps' first two decades to secure the agency's independence, survive an impingement on that independence and ensure survival of the agency itself. The first was fought by Shriver and the next two by succeeding directors.

Initial statements and documents about the Peace Corps assumed the agency would be housed under the State Department as a part of the foreign assistance program. In his Cow Palace address, Kennedy said the new agency would be "directed by ICA Point Four agencies." In his task force report Shriver recommended it be part of the foreign aid program. The executive order that created it stated, "The Secretary of State shall establish an agency in the Department of State which shall be known as the Peace Corps."[27]

USAID administrators and the diplomats were never warm to Kennedy's toy. It threatened their bailiwick with a glamorous program personally endorsed by the president. A scheme to send ex-college kids around the world to do good seemed inconsistent with a dead-serious Cold War foreign policy. Nor was it welcome from a turf standpoint; after all, USAID was already helping to fund a two-year program of sending recent college graduates to East Africa.

Shriver believed that a takeover by State or USAID would be disastrous. He wanted the agency to have a life of its own, apart from the chronically unpopular foreign aid program. The unique new enterprise needed to be identified with a spirit of altruism that went beyond confronting the Soviet bloc. Bill Moyers, who became the agency's first deputy director, emphatically agreed; he had not taken the hard step of leaving Lyndon Johnson's staff to join the Foreign Service. He took Shriver with him to discuss the independence issue with his former boss. The vice president told them:

> Boys, this town is full of folks who believe the only way to do something is their way. That's especially true in diplomacy and things like that, because they work with foreign governments and protocol is oh-so-mighty-important to them, with guidebooks and rulebooks and do's-and-don'ts to keep you from offending someone. You put the Peace Corps into the Foreign Service and they'll put striped pants on your people when all you want them to have is a knapsack and a tool kit and a lot of imagination.[28]

A meeting was scheduled at the White House on April 26, 1961, to settle the matter. It was expected that JFK would attend, but something came up. In addition, Shriver was away on his first world tour. Warren Wiggins, coauthor of the founding Peace Corps memo and acting director in Shriver's place, represented the agency at the meeting. Grouped around the table were heads of the old ICA and the new USAID and representatives of the Bureau of the Budget and other agencies, with White House aide Ralph Dungan presiding. Everyone present except Wiggins spoke in favor of folding the Peace Corps into USAID. Dungan then pronounced this as the group's recommendation.

Wiggins cabled Shriver, who by this time had reached India, and told him the news. Sarge was disturbed but not deterred. He immediately telephoned Moyers and told him that before he "hung crepe out the windows" he must ask LBJ to make one last plea to the president. This was done, and Johnson agreed to speak to the president; Kennedy overruled the decision and ordered that the agency be made formally responsible to the secretary of state, but under the president's direction and completely independent of USAID. The text of the Peace Corps Act reflects this solution. Although the secretary of state is "responsible for the continued supervision and general direction" of the Peace Corps, the president himself nominates its director to the Senate and is authorized to oversee its programs. This ambiguity had the effect of establishing the agency's independence— a victory won by the pluck of a no-surrender director, a fast-thinking acting director, a true-believing deputy director and an end-running vice president.[29]

Round Two: The Peace Corps Faces Consolidation

One decade later the hard-won autonomy was threatened. Kennedy's old nemesis Richard Nixon entered the White House in 1969. The first Republican president in eight years was never enthusiastic about the Peace Corps, and after anti-war Peace Corps staff hung "out of Vietnam" banners from the windows of the Maiatico building across Lafayette Park near the White House, he had a positive dislike for the organization. Nixon was also suspicious of left-wing tendencies at Volunteers in Service for America (VISTA), a volunteer program established by LBJ as a kind of domestic Peace Corps in the Office of Economic Opportunity. Moreover, during his first term Nixon became obsessed with consolidating the federal bureaucracy and proposed that four "superdepartments" be set up. Congress refused, but failed to exercise a legislative veto that would have killed a reorganization plan to establish a new agency called ACTION. It embraced the Peace Corps, VISTA, Service Corps of Retired Executives (SCORE), Active Corps of Executives (ACE), Foster Grandparents and Retired Senior Volunteers Program (RSVP). By this maneuver Nixon both took a baby step toward consolidation and created a method to emasculate two radical bureaucracies.

Joseph Blatchford, director of the Peace Corps at the time, was elevated to the directorship of ACTION. His replacement at the Peace Corps, Kevin O'Connell, was relegated to the position of associate director of international operations for ACTION. Thus technically the position of Peace Corps director no longer existed. Volunteer recruiting and selection were taken over by ACTION, and use of the Peace Corps letterhead in the United States was banned. Although Volunteers in the field were not much affected, most stateside personnel viewed the reorganization as a calculated move to politicize and subjugate their organization. Shriver, by now a practicing attorney in Washington, was furious; he told a Senate subcommittee when it was considering the consolidation that the motivation of young people to volunteer would be dried up. They "will never rally around an organization chart," he declared.[30]

Blatchford resigned in 1972, and the remaining years of the Peace Corps' placement in ACTION can be divided into two contrasting periods. One was up to 1977, when Republicans continued to occupy the White House. The person chosen for ACTION's director, Michael P. Balzano, was an intense young conservative who had written a doctoral dissertation critical of VISTA. He had no international experience and developed a disdain for the Peace Corps staff that was matched only by their dislike of him. The second period lasted through the Jimmy Carter presidency to 1981. Sam Brown, a Democratic activist whose mindset was as much to the left as Balzano's was to the right, next stepped in as ACTION director. As an anti-establishment organizer and anti-war activist, Brown saw the Peace Corps as an elitist crowd that represented the "vanguard of American cultural imperialism."

In sum, in the ACTION years the Peace Corps was subordinated to a cobbled-together bureaucracy and whiplashed by consecutive ideological cleansings. Toward the end of this challenging decade, Richard Celeste, Carter's second appointee to the Peace Corps, worked hard behind the scenes to prepare the way for a return to organizational independence. This was achieved by an act of Congress on Dec. 29, 1981. By that time a new Republican president had come to office, Ronald Reagan.[31]

Round Three: Peace Corps Survival

At this point the institution had reached a historic low. Morale at headquarters was at rock bottom. New directors were coming and going at a fast clip. The flow of applications had decreased from 42,000 annually to 8,000. The number of Volunteers was down to 5,000, a third of the figure at Shriver's departure, and appropriations—whose estimates were submitted by the secretary of state—were $100 million, $20 million less than 1966 and down 74 percent in constant dollars.[32] Wags dubbed the agency the "peace corpse."

What saved the organization was a fortunate choice of new director by President Reagan. This was Loret Miller Ruppe, a GOP organizer and party leader from Houghton, Mich. Raised in a family that had achieved wealth in the brewing industry, Ruppe's husband, Phillip, had served as a Republican member of Congress. Unlike other Republicans who viewed the Peace Corps as a Kennedy-era relic, Loret Ruppe admired it and encouraged one of her daughters to become a Volunteer.[33]

The new director found herself fighting a new battle for independence—from antagonistic staff in the Reagan West Wing. She made an appointment to meet her assigned contact there. Upon arriving, she cooled her heels in his office for almost an hour while he rearranged furniture and took phone calls. When the aide finally paid her the courtesy of a serious conversation, he bluntly declared the Peace Corps to be one of several "mushrooming" federal agencies that need to be abolished. Ruppe retorted that fiscally the Peace Corps was hardly mushrooming; moreover, it did its work through volunteer sacrifice by thousands of Americans—a conservative's approach to public life if ever there was one.

Refusing to accept this situation, Ruppe demanded to be assigned to a more open-minded White House assistant. She then went about educating the Reagan administration and its supporters. She gave speeches before solid GOP constituencies including chambers of commerce and civic organizations, and approached major universities and corporations for support. From these forays Ruppe conceived and launched a competitive enterprise development program. Talking points on business-oriented projects were funneled to presidential speechwriters, and material favorable to the Peace Corps was indirectly transmitted to the platform committees of both political parties.

Comm-unication

Vision

Politics

B+D

Ruppe's political adroitness paid off. Escaping the control of the Peace Corps budget by the Department of State, she submitted substantially increased estimates to the Office of Management and Budget (OMB). When the prime minister of Fiji visited Washington, Ruppe planted the idea of having him thank the president for Peace Corps work in his country. At a subsequent budget review attended by the president, the proposed increase in the agency's budget came up for consideration. Reagan said, "We can't cut the Peace Corps! The prime minister was just here saying how important their work is."[34]

THE ORGANIZATION NEARS 50

From this time to today the Peace Corps has experienced a reasonable degree of funding capacity and relative political stability. Now, as a world-famous 21st century symbol of international service, the Peace Corps is approaching the 50th anniversary of its founding. It is rare in Washington that an organization of this fame and reputation is so small. Its regular, full-time employment is less than that of any other agency studied in this book. Only 875 U.S. citizens work for the Peace Corps, of which 536 are located at headquarters in Washington, 133 in major cities around the United States and 206 in countries where the Peace Corps has a presence. About 2,000 foreign nationals are on its payroll overseas. Peace Corps appropriations for FY 2010 are $400 million, a third more than for the Virginia State Police (note appendix).

The operative size of the agency, however, is many times larger. The reason is deceptively simple: its work is done not by paid civil servants but by *volunteers*— about 8,000 of them, working in 76 countries around the world, living on a subsistence allowance. By the very nature of this work, this is not a "peace army," as Heinz Rollman would have called it, but the very opposite of a military organization. Its Volunteers live in remote villages and communities scattered across the surface of the Earth, working alone in most cases without much, if any, direct supervision. As volunteers rather than employees, they can resign at any time if they do not like what they are doing or where they are situated. Since they must leave for home after two years, their status is the very opposite of the career bureaucrat. The Peace Corps is probably the most transitory, nonhierarchical, decentralized public enterprise ever imagined. Yet in this book we are considering it as a candidate for centered, compelling mission mystique. How can that be? This section seeks to answer the question. We start with its mission, the topic of cell 1.

Three Goals

The Peace Corps mission is conferred by the Peace Corps Act of 1961 and hence is of the specified type. Section 2 reads:

> The Congress of the United States declares that it is the policy of the United States and the purpose of this Act to promote world peace and friendship through a Peace Corps, which shall make available to interested countries and areas men and women of the United States qualified for service abroad and willing to serve, under conditions of hardship if necessary, to help the peoples of such countries and areas in meeting their needs for trained manpower, and to help promote a better understanding of the American people on the part of the peoples served and a better understanding of other peoples on the part of the American people.[35]

Peace Corps literature and general practice distills this language down to an overarching mission of promoting world peace and friendship along with three more specific goals, each equally important. They are:

Goal 1.   Helping the people of interested countries in meeting their need for trained men and women.

Goal 2.   Helping promote a better understanding of Americans on the part of the peoples served.

Goal 3.   Helping promote a better understanding of other peoples on the part of Americans.[36]

This trio of objectives is well known to every Peace Corps employee as Goals 1, 2 and 3 and is referred to constantly in animated conversations as to what the agency is *really* all about, even a half-century after its birth. Discussion is also unending as to the relative importance of the three goals, despite their official equivalence. What stands out about the Peace Corps' purpose generally is its altruistic nature. Phrases like "world peace and friendship," "helping promote" and "better understanding" convey the kind of idealism that sounds more like a church sermon than goals of public policy. One is reminded of Shriver's feelings of gratitude for the chance to render "morally unblemished" and "pure service" to "human beings worldwide."

Moreover, in my interviews at the Peace Corps I discovered that this mission language is not long-forgotten verbiage but the living words of believers in a cause for today's world. In my very first visit to the agency I met the acting director in her office. After I explained the thesis of my book, she instantly replied that the Peace Corps is *the* poster child of mission mystique. She then told a story about the agency's move to its present quarters. When it was being planned, representatives of the General Services Administration interviewed personnel as to their office preferences. They were astonished that the only concern Peace Corps people expressed was whether they would have enough room to do their work. Unlike every other bureau the GSA had moved, there was no talk whatsoever about floor level, room size, windows or personal toilets.

During subsequent visits to the agency I encountered sentiments that were similarly focused on getting the work done rather than issues of status. An executive occupying a position close to the top said, "Everybody here works immensely hard" because "they have absorbed the mission into their blood." A middle manager took pride in noting that the agency has the second-lowest absentee rate in the federal government. A relatively recent female hire commented that, compared to other government agencies where she has worked, Peace Corps employees share information more, are less competitive with each other, and are eager to learn fast from coworkers because they will not be on the job long.

The famous anthropologist Margaret Mead described the Peace Corps as "an ethical enterprise." She explained the phrase as meaning an institution that offers "a way for an excessively fortunate country to share its optimism and generosity with parts of the world that, at a moment in time, are in need of what the Volunteers can best offer." The moral imperative of this purpose calls for "wholehearted devotion," she went on, relegating matters like technical skill and job satisfaction to the status of means to a higher end.[37]

This is, of course, the stuff of template cells 1, 4 and 5. Moreover, the ethical vision is symbolically expressed in the Peace Corps flag. Standing on a white background is a circle, representing the world. In it are the words *PEACE CORPS*, together with a red, white and blue design fragment of the American flag. If one looks closely, one of the flag's stars is the dove of peace.

Many Levels

The highly decentralized Peace Corps may be said to operate on six spatial-organizational levels. These are headquarters, region, campus, post, site and project. This pattern of splintered pieces affects and reflects the agency's culture, the topic of cell 5.

The headquarters building is an eight-story structure on the corner of L and 20th streets in Washington, D.C. The agency moved to this address several years ago from its original location near Lafayette Park. The present structure is rather nondescript on the outside, although a long, vertical banner identifies its organizational occupant clearly. The building's official name is the Paul D. Coverdell

Peace Corps Headquarters, named after the director who served from 1989 to 1991 and later supported the agency as a U.S. senator from Georgia.

Headquarters staff regard their essential task as facilitating and coordinating the work of the volunteers in the field and making sure they are as safe as possible. The organization's top executive, the director, is nominated to this position by the president and confirmed by the Senate. The same is true with the deputy director. All other executive positions are in theory political appointees of the president, in that these posts—25 in number—are technically "excepted by statute" positions. They were created over the objection of the Civil Service Commission because Shriver wanted complete freedom in forming his initial staff. Among them are the chief and deputy chief of staff, who direct daily operations, and three regional directors, who manage ongoing activities for different regions of the world.

Beyond the Washington Beltway, the Peace Corps has permanent regional offices in nine American cities: Atlanta, Boston, New York, Chicago, Dallas, Seattle, Los Angeles (actual location in El Segundo, California), San Francisco (Oakland) and Washington, D.C. (Arlington, Virginia). They perform the agency's marketing and recruitment activities in their metropolitan areas and surrounding states. Recruiters visit the area's colleges and universities and appropriate business firms and associations. Screening of applicants is also performed at the regional level. For Volunteers returning home, the offices act as a job placement center.

At the campus level part-time recruiters operate as each school's Peace Corps representative. They are employed not by the agency but by their universities, usually as graduate assistants. Forty-eight campus representatives are currently in place, all of whom are former Volunteers. Their tasks are to hold information sessions, advise individual students, help applicants assemble their package of materials, and nominate for consideration those applicants whom they think are potentially qualified. Final decisions on nomination are made at the regional offices and headquarters.

Outside the United States, the most important Peace Corps offices are country posts, headed by country directors. At present there are 70 of these, usually located in the capital city of that country. At the larger stations, the country director is joined by a second-in-command deputy along with associate program country directors who provide support in specialized areas like agriculture, education and public health. Also working out of the country post are medical officers, program training officers, duty officers and safety/security specialists. In big countries, regional Peace Corps offices exist as well. Each office hires its own staff of host country nationals and manages its own funds and property.

Typically, 30 to 100 Volunteers work in a given country, spread out among different kinds of community sites. In 2008, 38 percent lived in villages with populations less than 2,000, 37 percent in towns of up to 25,000, 20 percent in larger cities other than the capital and 2 percent on islands regardless of size. Deliberately, few Volunteers (about 2 percent in 2008) are placed in the capital city, where diplomatic personnel operate. Just under half are stationed more than six hours of travel time from the main Peace Corps office, with the nearest other Volunteer more than 20 kilometers away.[38] Thus feeling lonely is often a part of life in the Peace Corps, especially early in the two-year assignment.

Each Volunteer's field activity is centered on one or more projects, usually a single prime undertaking accompanied by secondary activities. In this work relationships are primarily with the affected beneficiaries of the activity but also extend to community leaders known as counterparts. For teaching volunteers, counterparts include school principals and teachers; for development projects, they are often village elders and council members. Intimate collaboration with villagers and counterparts is a central tenet of Peace Corps practice. Close working ties are also required with sponsors, who may be ministry officials, embassy representatives or corporate executives who set the stage for projects. Another set of contacts is partners that fund individual projects, for example, USAID, UNICEF, UNDP, UNESCO, Red Cross, Red Crescent, Japan International Cooperation Agency, Population Services International and Save the Children.[39]

In 1966 sociologist Robert Textor, an MIT political scientist who helped formulate the Peace Corps in its early days, developed a theory of subcultures within the organization. He cited three: the headquarters staff in Washington, the volunteers in the field and—between the two—country directors and their staffs. Textor argued that each group harbors different values and standards, laying the basis for conflict and misunderstanding. The Washington people are seen as high flyers hoping to rise up the international nonprofit ladder, and thus are preoccupied with managing the agency without flaps. They see the Volunteers as creative and idealistic but also frivolous and self-centered. The Volunteers, for their part, are generally young and inexperienced and look upon Peace Corps officialdom as a bunch of stodgy bureaucrats who do not understand how things really work on the ground. Textor goes on to say that the country directors located in the middle aim for promotion to Washington while seeking to bridge the chasm between headquarters and field. They react to this predicament with idiosyncratic commitments to various theories of social change and lose the confidence of both Washington and local leaders.[40]

I asked a widely experienced staff member about the Textor thesis, and he said it had some validity in the past but is now largely wrong, primarily because everyone can now communicate quickly by e-mail and cell phone. Furthermore, the organization has learned how to discard sterile doctrines and take advantage of accumulated knowledge and ongoing dialogue to solve problems pragmatically. In my research I got a glimpse of what this discourse might be like when I ran into a lengthy Internet exchange following the posting of an article highly critical of the Peace Corps. The piece was written by Robert Strauss, a former country director in Cameroon. Several current and former Volunteers replied, along with a few former country directors and even the director himself.[41]

Strauss' contention was that over the years the Peace Corps has never lived up to its purpose or principles. Among other shortcomings, it has demonstrated incompetence by admitting mostly mediocre, fresh college graduates looking for a government-subsidized travel experience. They are then given mismatched assignments in countries that are no longer poor, thereby wasting public resources. Some responses to his criticisms are paraphrased as follows. On the quality of Volunteers, the attribute of youth brings with it the advantage of passion and makes for easier learning of the language and adjustment to sparse living; country staff should engage themselves in the design of projects instead of an obsession against partying; and having clueless goofballs represent America abroad is better than some other options. As to wasted resources, trying to optimize placements fails to take into account that success is not a matter of objective measurement but allowing nuanced human interaction to take its own course within a particular given situation. Volunteers are not development officers who build monuments but creative individuals who build understanding, and site placement needs more extensive consultation with those placed. An overall point made is that in the end it is the Volunteers' attitude and luck that determine whether the taxpayer dollars are well spent.

Limited Tenures

Service in the Peace Corps is short-term, another factor that keeps the organization loose and leads to what some regard as its "anti-administration" culture. Other than the director and deputy director, who serve at the discretion of the president, managers and professionals are for the most part limited to a tenure of five years. As noted, Volunteers stay for two years. Foreign nationals are employed on the judgment of country directors. The only federal employees in the Peace Corps whose tenure is protected by the civil service merit system are clerical and support personnel below grade GS-9.

The top "political" leadership of the agency consists of the director and deputy director. Table 7.1 lists all directors over the life of the agency. Considering the list as a whole, average tenure is 2.8 years, a figure not unusual among federal political appointees but still on the low side. By no means were the contributions of all 18 individuals comparable, however. They may be divided into four categories. Shriver and Ruppe were the dominant figures in terms of setting the course of Peace Corps history. Their tenures were the longest, and if one removes them from the calculation the average time of service is 2.3 years. The contributions of the second director, Jack Vaughn, and Joseph Blatchford were to consolidate the founding achievements of Shriver. The former was a holdover from the Shriver era and helped rationalize Sarge's chaotic ways of doing things. The latter was the first Republican appointee and, without disturbing the core Peace Corps idea, introduced to it a private sector perspective.

At the risk of oversimplification, the remaining 14 directors can be divided into two groups. One is the six Peace Corps heads that served when the agency

Table 7.1 Directors of the Peace Corps

Director	Appointing President	Tenure	
R. Sargent Shriver	Kennedy (D)	1961–1966	
Jack Vaughn	Johnson (D)	1966–1969	
Joseph Blatchford	Nixon (R)	1969–1971	
Kevin O'Connell	Nixon (R)	1971–1972	
Donald Hess	Nixon (R)	1972–1973	
Nicholas Craw	Nixon (R)	1973–1974	ACTION period
John Dellenback	Ford (R)	1975–1977	
Carolyn R. Payton	Carter (D)	1977–1978	
Richard F. Celeste	Carter (D)	1979–1981	
Loret Miller Ruppe	Reagan (R)	1981–1989	
Paul D. Coverdell	Bush I (R)	1989–1991	
Elaine Chao	Bush I (R)	1991–1992	
Carol Bellamy	Clinton (D)	1993–1995	
Mark D. Gearan	Clinton (D)	1995–1999	
Mark L. Schneider	Clinton (D)	1999–2001	
Gaddi H. Vasquez	Bush II (R)	2002–2006	
Ronald A. Tschetter	Bush II (R)	2006–2009	
Aaron S. Williams	Obama (D)	2009–	

Source: Peace Corps website, www.peacecorps.gov/index.cfm?shell=learn.whatispc.history.Pastdir.

Note: ACTION period refers to when the Peace Corps was part of a U.S. government agency known as ACTION that incorporated Vista, Peace Corps and other federal volunteer programs.

was part of ACTION. Politicized as that umbrella agency was, what it did was keep the organization going as well as possible under conditions of scarce resources and successive partisan pulls first to the right and then to the left. The second group consists of eight directors in office for the past two decades. Individually, their contributions amounted to incremental policy improvements such as connecting volunteer teachers to school classrooms and encouraging applications from persons over 50 years old. Collectively, their legacy was to shake the agency loose from the early days of environmental buffeting and establish it as an ongoing, healthy institution that could sustain itself over time, electoral turnovers notwithstanding.

One ingredient in this shift to maturity was to delegate management responsibilities from the directorship to senior executives. The director became a spokesperson, connector to constituencies and setter of tone. Management leadership was taken over by a chief of staff, who in turn provided direction to the three regional directors as well as a variety of staff offices. One of the most significant consequences of this structural change was to dethrone the powerful division heads that dominated in the early years, particularly the chief of program development and operations.

A second step toward institutionalization, more profound in nature, was to create a revolving kind of personnel system. The building block of this system is the famous five-year rule of the Peace Corps, which limits tenure of upper-level employees to five successive years of service at one time. Such a rule was proposed in the first years of the agency and strongly supported by Shriver as a way to keep the organization flexible. Early memos prepared by Textor and early Shriver confidant Franklin Williams described the rule as a way to keep the agency "permanently young, creative, and dynamic" and avoid "bureaucratic hardening of the arteries." Bill Moyers was put in charge of implementing the "five year flush," so named because in the beginning everyone had come on board at the same time and thus made a mass exodus. Chair John Macy of the Civil Service Commission denounced the idea as "inappropriate public policy," but Congress bought it, and on Oct. 10, 1965, removed normal civil service protections from employees grade GS-9 and above.[42]

The five-year rule has been operative to this day. All upper-level staff must resign from the organization and physically leave no later than 60 months after being hired. Technically, the 60 months consist of two 30-month terms, with renewal at the end of the first. The only exception is the agency inspector general, who is given a measure of independence by a time limit of 8.5 years.

The five-year rule may well have kept the agency from aging and arteriosclerosis, but it has also led to a positive development. One way this happened is to create vacancies that can be filled with new hires. The agency has taken advantage of this opportunity by employing former Volunteers in large numbers. The practical experience of returned Volunteers is of great aid to the agency in many ways, not least of which is in recruiting new Volunteers. Almost all campus representatives and region recruiters possess this background. Volunteer alumni have also penetrated headquarters at all levels; when one is introduced to people there, they invariably tell you without being asked their country and years of service. Four former Volunteers have reached the pinnacle of the organization by becoming director: Carol Bellamy (Guatemala, 1963–1965), Mark Schneider (El Salvador, 1966–1968), Ronald Tschetter (India, 1966–1968) and the current director, Aaron S. Williams (Dominican Republic, 1967–1970).

The five-year limit has also been adjusted in such a way as to allow salaried staff to migrate between field and headquarters. Called the "third term," this is a modification whereby those whose five-year limit is approaching its conclusion in either field or headquarters is offered a transfer to the other location for an additional 30 months, or a third term, following the first two. Total employment time then becomes 7.5 years. Benefits yielded by this arrangement are, in one direction, receipt by headquarters of better understanding of field conditions and, in the other, transmission to the field of deeper insights into the reasons and complexities behind upper-level policymaking.

A final advantage of the five-year rule is that it has made possible a subsequent return after a few years of former Peace Corps personnel who went on to other jobs after their departure. The five-year limit itself creates position openings that enable this to happen, whereas under a fixed-tenure career system they would be scarce. Hence encouraging what are called "retreads" has emerged as a major personnel pattern. The agency benefits in that the individual returns having both familiarity with the Peace Corps and new experience in the philanthropy or education sectors, the corporate or foundation world, or another government agency.

Furthermore, there is no limit to the number of times the retread can come back. Probably the champion in-and-outer of all time is Randolph Adams, supervisor of the Training and Evaluation Unit at headquarters. He began his career as a Volunteer for three years, left for a short time only to return to work with the Peace Corps as a contract trainer for three years, left for nine years to return for a third hitch of three years, departed again for six years, returned for a fourth time for six more years, left once more for 10 years and is back once again in his third year and counting.

In sum, the transient nature of the organization's workforce has been turned from a way to avoid stodgy bureaucracy to a set of personnel tools that creates fluidity and fosters renewal. Incoming, experienced personnel are not innocent of the past but familiar with it. New ideas are proposed that are not irrelevant but pertinent. Bridges are built between levels of the organization, encounters with the volunteer world inform selection of recruits to that world and ideas advanced outside the agency are absorbed. Moreover, now that sufficient time has passed that individual career cycles are well staggered in the organization, a sudden flush does not occur at the end of five years. Rather, a pattern is created whereby managers and professionals continuously hand off to each other like relay runners passing the baton.

THE VOLUNTEERS AND THEIR WORK

At the beginning of the chapter we said the most significant feature of the Peace Corps is that its work is done not by civil servants but citizen volunteers. In this characteristic lies the institution's distinctive competence, to use Philip Selznick's term mentioned in Chapter 1. How are these volunteers chosen and prepared? What do they do and experience?

Getting In, Getting Ready

The Volunteer is required to be a U.S. citizen, in good health and at least 18 years old. Beyond these bare minima, persons interested in joining the Peace Corps must demonstrate their potential for the difficult work involved. Possessing a college degree alone will not cut it; the agency looks for individuals with solid experience in needed skill areas, demonstrated leadership ability and prior community service. Applicants are told that their success will also depend on learning a difficult foreign language.

Following an initial screening, applicants are interviewed by a campus or regional recruiter, at which time about a third are rejected as not promising. Those who survive this screening are considered for formal nomination, which entails reviewing documented credentials and the results of background checks. The application is then sent to headquarters for medical and legal reviews, and detailed scrutiny is given to whether the person's skills match a country need for the upcoming year. Candidates so judged, about 30 percent of initial applicants, then receive an invitation to join a Volunteer group going to a specific country.

The training of Peace Corps Volunteers, of interest to us from the standpoint of template cell 5, has undergone notable changes over the years. In the earliest days, training was done under contract to universities. This failed because the professors tended to lecture at a generalized academic level and knew little about problems at the village level. At that time it was assumed that Volunteers must be tough physically and mentally to withstand adversity. Accordingly, male Volunteers were sent to Puerto Rico for endurance training at former Civilian Conservation Corps camps, and both genders were subject to humiliating psychological tests.

As experience was gained, these training approaches were scrapped. The Peace Corps stopped contracting out the function and conducted its own training at regional centers in California, Hawaii and the Virgin Islands. This was done by the country group, with its members living together in dormitories. This strategy was later reevaluated because it was realized that trainees were at a physical and cultural distance from the actual environments in which they would later serve. As a result, the presently used method of in-country training was adopted. Now new trainees go directly to their country, take up residence with local families and undergo three months of training conducted by nationals of that society. The regimen is rigorous, particularly with respect to language training and personal adjustment, and invariably another increment of the group drops out. Those remaining start to learn the language in earnest, and the combination of shock and excitement that goes with total immersion in a new culture begins to turn to familiarity and comfort.

Places and Projects

Since 1961, nearly 200,000 Peace Corps Volunteers have served in 139 countries. The agency organizes a program in a nation only if requested by its host government. Existing programs are terminated or not renewed if requested by the government, or if conditions become unsafe because of political instability or other reasons. The locations of 72 programs that were operating in 2008 are shown in Box 7.1; recent experience has been that 37 percent of job requests come from the countries of Africa; 24 percent from Latin America; 20 percent

Box 7.1 Where Peace Corps Volunteers Go

Africa
Benin
Botswana
Burkina Faso
Cameroon
Cape Verde
Ethiopia
The Gambia
Ghana
Guinea
Kenya
Lesotho
Madagascar
Malawi
Mali
Mauritania
Mozambique
Namibia
Niger
Rwanda
Senegal
South Africa
Swaziland
Tanzania
Togo
Uganda
Zambia

Asia
Cambodia
China
Mongolia
Thailand
Philippines

Caribbean
Antigua-Barbuda
Dominica
Dominican Republic
Grenada-Carriacou
Jamaica
St. Kitts-Nevis

St. Lucia
St. Vincent-Grenadines

Eastern Europe, Central Asia
Albania
Armenia
Azerbaijan
Bulgaria
Georgia
Kazakhstan
Kyrgyz Republic
Macedonia
Moldova
Romania
Turkmenistan
Ukraine

Latin America
Belize
Bolivia
Costa Rica
Ecuador
El Salvador
Guatemala
Guyana
Honduras
Mexico
Nicaragua
Panama
Paraguay
Peru
Suriname

North Africa, Middle East
Jordan
Morocco

Pacific Islands
Fiji
Micronesia-Palau
Samoa
Tonga
Vanuatu

Source: Peace Corps, *Life Is Calling: How Far Will You Go?* (2008).

Peace Corps volunteer teaching seed-hunting in Panama. Volunteers go to a country only if requested by its host government. Since 1961, nearly 200,000 volunteers have served in 139 countries, with 76 currently receiving them. Of the service requests, 35 percent are for teachers.

Source: Courtesy of the Peace Corps.

from Eastern Europe/Central Asia; 7 percent from Asia; and 4 percent each from North Africa/the Middle East, the Caribbean and the Pacific Islands.[43]

Volunteers work in many subject-matter areas or sectors. The single biggest is education—35 percent of Volunteers are assigned teaching as their primary job. This emphasis has been present since the agency's earliest days; teaching is something recent college graduates with a liberal arts degree can do. Early critics derided the agency for overdependence on naive "BA generalists," and teachers now must have prior experience in the classroom or an advanced degree. Most Peace Corps educators teach English as a foreign language, with other major areas being math and science at the high school level, as well as teacher training.[44]

Another important sector is agriculture. Projects in this realm deal with food security, improved nutrition, sustainable agriculture and crop diversification. One technique here is picking out farmers and then training them to be models for others. Another is organizing seed-hunting campaigns so that growers will have sufficient access to high-quality seed and nursery plants. A project in Senegal involved the planting of short-season varieties of rice and sorghum, needed in

Peace Corps Volunteer (left) tutoring Moroccan women on how to run a business. The guidance given covers good management practices and opportunities for income from rug weaving, soap making, mushroom farming and other pursuits. Sixty percent of volunteers are female.

Source: Courtesy of the Peace Corps.

drier-than-usual rainy seasons. As with all Peace Corps projects, the object is not to give unilateral instructions to residents on what to do, but to hear what they need, discuss with them the possibilities and help achieve what all decide.

Enterprise development is a sector in which Volunteers assist in the formation and management of small firms, municipal departments and nongovernmental organizations. They teach business workshops, suggest market linkages and strategies, help locate needed experts, seek donations or credit possibilities and assist with computer applications. Another theme is the fostering of small-scale, income-generating activities appropriate to rural villages, like soap making, rug weaving, beadwork, bee-keeping, vegetable gardening, mushroom farming, fishponds and the cultivation of herbal medicines.

In the public health sector, Volunteers and their counterparts conduct classroom programs on health education, develop materials for patient outreach, train health care providers, promote sports participation, work with community water and sanitation committees, and propose projects to increase health awareness. Illustrative projects are starting a Neem garden to produce a lotion that repels mosquitoes and explaining to rural midwives why unclean scissors should not be used to cut umbilical cords. For several years the Peace Corps has been a participant in the U.S. President's Emergency Plan for AIDS Relief (PEPFAR). Projects have included getting riverboat oarsmen to distribute condoms and urging healers to use new razor blades when applying tattoos. PEPFAR activities are often carried out in sectors other than health.

An area that also reaches across sectors is youth development. It was launched on the premise that over half the population in most counties served by the Peace Corps is under 25. A major theme of this program is to provide life-skills training. This encompasses enhancement of self-esteem, developing the habit of setting goals, and learning how to make decisions and negotiate. Such training is often done at gender-affirming youth camps, such as Camp GLOW (Girls Leading Our World) and Camp TOBE (Teaching Our Boys Excellence).

Closely allied to youth development is an initiative directed to women and girls, called Women in Development/Gender and Development (WID/GAD). Most posts maintain WID/GAD committees made up of volunteers whose purpose is to share ideas and make connections among sites and to project sponsors; as with the HIV/AIDS program, attempts are made to incorporate improvement in the status of women into all volunteer work sectors.

Volunteer Life

At any given time the number of Peace Corps Volunteers approaches 8,000. This level stands midway between the historic high of 15,000 in the Shriver years and the low of 5,000 under Ruppe. These figures include trainees undergoing the three months of pre-service preparation. While the normal duration of Volunteer service is 24 months, under a Peace Corps Response program a few hundred returnees are asked to come back on an emergency basis for three to six months to help in situations like disaster relief.

At one time most Volunteers were single white males who had recently graduated from college. Now, due in large part to Peace Corps diversity policies, the demographic composition is quite different. Sixty percent are now female and 16 percent minority from a racial or ethnic standpoint. Seven percent are married, serving with their spouses. A substantial number of Volunteers are disabled by an inability to see, hear or walk. While 89 percent are still college graduates, they are not all recent graduates; the average age has risen to 28, and 7 percent are over age 50—with a few in their 70s, 80s and even 90s. The most famous senior citizen Volunteer was Lillian Carter, president Jimmy Carter's mother, who spent two years in India nursing lepers before her son went to the White House.[45]

With respect to material benefits, the Peace Corps adheres to its concept of altruistic service in poor societies by not paying Volunteers a federal salary but providing a monthly living allowance in host-country currency. Its amount is variable in that it is set to local community standards, with an average of about $250. Doctors and dentists arranged for by the Peace Corps provide free medical and dental care, along with shots and medicines. Volunteers are asked not to receive funds from home.

Air travel is paid for from the United States to the country of service and back home afterward. Volunteers receive vacation time of 24 workdays per year; any trips they take while on holiday are at their own expense. Family members may visit Volunteers on site during the middle part of their tenure, but a visit back home is not permitted except for a family emergency, in which case the Peace Corps provides transportation.

Returnees receive certain side benefits as well. A lump-sum readjustment allowance of just over $6,000 is made available upon completion of the assignment, to provide a cushion while looking for a job or making other plans. An affordable extension of health care benefits can be retained for 18 months. As mentioned, Peace Corps regional offices stand ready to assist returnees in taking the next step in their careers, and the agency publishes an online newsletter on job and other post-service opportunities. For those interested in employment in the federal government, civil service laws give former Volunteers a waiver of one year without going through the competitive examination process. That job may be in the Peace Corps itself, of course.[46]

The Peace Corps has made arrangements with U.S. universities to assist Volunteers in advancing their education. One program, called Master's International, combines overseas service with graduate studies. The participant takes two years of graduate study on campus and then reports for duty with the Peace Corps for 27 months, during which period academic credit may be earned. Upon return, one final semester on campus usually earns a master's degree. A second program, known as Fellows/USA, offers financial aid for graduate study following a Peace Corps stint, immediately or at a later time in life. A final education benefit for ex-Volunteers is eligibility for cancellation or deferment in the repayment of certain government and commercial school loans.

Much emphasis is placed by the Peace Corps on the welfare and safety of its Volunteers while overseas. An Office of Safety and Security checks to see that hospitals available in the host country are adequate. If necessary, seriously ill Volunteers are flown to hospitals elsewhere. Peace Corps medical officers visit Volunteers on site and are alert to signs of infectious disease and psychological stress. Advice on how to dress and behave in public is given, and quarters are checked for secure locks and a safe neighborhood. Host country counterparts are identified ahead of time to be of help if needed. An Emergency Action Plan is ready for each country that specifies procedures in case of natural disaster or civil unrest.[47]

Even with all these instructions, preparations and backups, the life of Volunteers can be full of uncertainty and anxiety. While writing this chapter I spontaneously developed an e-mail contact with a female Volunteer in Morocco, who wrote the following:

> The greatest challenge for me here in Morocco has been adjusting to life as a woman in a Muslim country. I spend most of my time worrying whether I am dressed acceptably, behaving appropriately, whether I'm respected or whether I'm taken for a prostitute merely because I don't wear a veil and speak to men (only men I know, of course) in the street. I get a great deal of what feels to me like harassment from men eager to talk to me, when they would never approach a local woman in the same way because it isn't culturally acceptable. I had to change houses because of two incidents with men in my apartment building in which I had to call the local police. That was upsetting.

Each Volunteer's experience is obviously unique, and it is not easy to assess overall perceptions of life in the Peace Corps. Yet the agency endeavors to do just that, using a biennial survey that is conducted for the most part online. On a question about the adequacy of pre-service training, it was evaluated in the 2008 survey as "effective" or "very effective" by 65 percent on managing cultural differences, 60 percent on making a personal adjustment, 25 percent on working with counterparts, 59 percent in using the language and 78 percent in staying safe. Respondents replied "well" or "very well" 65 percent of the time when asked how integrated they felt in their community, 48 percent on ability to communicate in the language and 37 percent on whether the living allowance meets basic needs. On a question pertinent to cell 4 of the mission mystique template, it was asked how personally rewarding the Peace Corps experience was turning out: 30 percent said "moderately," "minimally" or "not at all," and 70 percent said "considerably" or "exceptionally." Asked if they would do it again, 17 percent said "possibly," "not likely" or "no," while 83 percent answered "probably" or "definitely."[48]

EVALUATION OF A COSMIC MISSION

When an institution's output is narrow and concrete, evaluating it is simple. But when its mission is of cosmic proportions—i.e., promoting peace and friendship, improving life in poor countries and promoting mutual understanding—defining and assessing the outcome are difficult, to say the least. Yet the subject has been of great interest to the Peace Corps from the beginning, a point that is germane to cell 9's topic of organizational learning.

Multiple Methods

At first the agency employed a single-minded approach to evaluation. Shriver wanted to know personally what problems were cropping up out in the field, and he demanded the unvarnished truth. This is understandable, as he was operating on administrative *terra incognita,* and a good scandal or two would give detractors ample ammunition. Shriver put it this way: we need to be "getting the *Time* magazine story before *Time* magazine."[49]

The investigative journalism analogy was realized literally. Shriver asked Charles Peters, who had worked on JFK's West Virginia campaign, to send hard-hitting reporters out to Peace Corps countries to find out what was going on and report back directly to him. Peters then dispatched the journalists to countries where a contingent of Volunteers had been working for a time. They traveled around for two or three weeks, interviewed Volunteers and others they encountered, and wrote candid narrative reports on what they found. Upon critiquing each other's drafts, they submitted final versions directly to Shriver, on a your-eyes-only basis. Shriver read every report and responded when something was fixable. Wiggins, at the helm of the Program Development and Operations Division in Washington and thus committed to the prospect of unadulterated success, took umbrage with how Peters was nosing around in the field.[50]

In later years the Peters approach to evaluation became more channeled, stabilized and accepted. Lawyers, social scientists, development professionals, area specialists and consultants were added to the roster of investigators. Before going into the field they spent a week in Washington talking to pertinent staff and reading the country files. When in the target country, they carried out systematic interviews with Volunteers, their supervisors, people in the country director's office and host government officials. After a month or so they returned to Washington to obtain follow-up information and write their reports, which ran from 60 to 150 pages.

The scope of the studies was also expanded. They focused not just on specific complaints and alleged shortcomings, but recurring issues such as unsolicited gifts from locals, wrongly calculated living allowances and the concentration of Volunteers in one city. Another shift went beyond assessing the programs in isolation and considered as well the country's overall development needs and the degree to which the projects fit in with it. Yet another change relaxed the director-only policy of disclosure; reports were shared with all top Peace Corps executives, along with headquarters and field staff directly affected.[51]

Today the Peace Corps utilizes a variety of evaluation techniques. The agency's inspector general conducts broad-brush assessment of operations in a given country post or project sector. Fieldwork consists of examining Volunteer work sites, assessing work assignments, reviewing the adequacy of support and interviewing a stratified sample of Volunteers. Its purpose is to lay the groundwork for change as well as to investigate wrongdoing.[52] A second type of evaluation is the preparation of lengthy research papers on thematic questions concerning achievement of the agency's three goals. A methodology often used in these studies is to ask "what if" questions, such as, What is it we are really trying to accomplish?

Or, What if we reframe a problem this way? Host country nationals are included on the study team and may even cochair it.

A third form of evaluation is best thought of as informal action research. It is open-ended, interactive and applied, and takes place exclusively in the field. The objective is to stimulate unfettered, ongoing conversations about useful changes to what is currently being done. While staff, counterparts, sponsors and others contribute, the Volunteers are front and center in the process.

Such discussions take place in various settings. One is in-service training conferences where Volunteers blow off steam about projects currently under way. At post-service training conferences, Volunteers assess what happened over their two years before going home. The most important setting, however, is the project advisory committee. This is a group that meets from time to time at country director headquarters. Its activities are loosely organized but consist essentially of asking how volunteer projects might work better. Ideas are thrown out, new possibilities are debated and the suitability of untried options is weighed. A kind of microcosmic blue sky, "let's begin all over again" thinking is encouraged.

Multiple Goals

The normative framework of Peace Corps evaluation is its trio of multiple goals, derived from the Peace Corps Act. We take a moment now to assess generally the agency's record with respect to achieving these ends, a step taken in accord with weighing record of achievement, an aspect of cell 3 of the mission mystique template.

Goal 1 is to help countries meet their need for trained personnel. The assumed outcome of this help is what is called in the West "development" or, alternatively, making a difference in poor lands. The degree to which the Peace Corps presence in 139 countries over its half-century of history has made a perceptible or even perceived difference is impossible to state on a global basis. Statistically, any net impacts disappear among the effects of countless other social, economic and political variables. We do know, however, that on a collective basis an enormous number of individual Volunteer projects have been undertaken with good intent. Moreover, we know that millions of people have been touched in some way by the Volunteers. In FY 2008 alone, Volunteers taught 246,000 boys, 278,000 girls, 25,000 men and 41,000 women. Public health activities affected, in some way, 900,000 individuals and 4,900 organizations in 8,500 communities. Corresponding figures for environmental projects are 292,500, 3,500 and 4,400, and in agriculture, 70,000, 900 and 950. Across all sectors, it has been calculated that Volunteer youth activities in 2008 involved almost 1.5 million young people around the world.[53]

At the same time, it must be admitted that it is impossible to generalize on what actually happened in individual interactions between healthy, educated, middle-class Americans and less well fed, less literate and much poorer residents of the globe's low-income countries. Even under the best of conditions, the cultural and language barriers are enormous. Additionally, there is no guarantee that villagers will perceive a given Volunteer's project as enduringly significant. It all depends on countless situational factors, not the least of which is the Volunteer's ability to form the initial personal relationships that must presage the delicate process of instigating what will hopefully become "owned" change. While the magnitude of Goal 1 attainment cannot be calculated, the morality of its attempt cannot be denied. The mission mystique work of this ethical enterprise is at the same time exalted and experimental.

Goal 2 is to promote understanding of the United States among the peoples served. Early on, this goal was interpreted in Cold War terms. It was seen as an opportunity to win the allegiance of developing nations being wooed by the Soviet Union. Most commentators agree that the Peace Corps provided substantial help to the United States during those years. The word *peace* was no longer the sole property of Soviet propaganda. Sending the country's educated young to work in behalf of poor peoples demonstrated American goodwill more convincingly than any ideology's doctrine. As an alternative to communist-inspired wars of national liberation, volunteer programs attended to local needs identified by existing governments.

In the decades since the Cold War, achievements in behalf of Goal 2 have concerned the portrayal of American *society*—as distinct from its *government*—in a favorable light. An important part of this effort has been to demonstrate the demographic diversity of the United States. Volunteers have different skin colors. Most are women. Some are blind or confined to wheelchairs. Old citizens as well as young are ready to sacrifice the comforts of American life and confront the difficulties of learning a new language and culture. How better to counter such American stereotypes as rich tourists, smug missionaries or self-indulgent expatriates?

Of course, some Peace Corps Volunteers make the mistake of viewing their own tour as a two-year vacation, and accordingly help people too little and have fun too much. They are, however, in the minority, and are usually asked to return home early. Most Volunteers come for nobler reasons and conduct themselves with the best of motivations. Working at learning the mores of the culture are observed by residents; a willingness to listen, learn, be humble and be patient is noticed; and change-fostering concepts of daring to hope and learning from mistakes are remembered. A tribal chief in Sierra Leone once said that his people, by coming into contact with Peace Corps Volunteers, glimpsed "a world we never knew existed. We had never seen people from the outside who wanted to help us. We had heard of America but now we know what it means."[54]

Goal 3 is to increase understanding of other peoples on the part of Americans. When President Kennedy sent off the first contingents of Volunteers from the

Rose Garden in 1961, he told them to "come back and educate us."[55] Five decades of returning Volunteers since have been able to draw on a mass of experience to do just that. One group that has been educated is the Volunteers themselves. Surveys and conferences on the impact of Peace Corps service show that the vast majority of returnees see themselves as transformed by the experience. "Whatever we were before, and none of us can quite remember, that's all gone," one said.[56] The sentiment is widespread that their lives and thinking have been deeply enriched by the experience—many feel guilty that they took more away from their Peace Corps years than they left behind.

While serving in their host country, Volunteers communicate their experiences home by cell phone, e-mail or Facebook. When Volunteers complete their service and get home, they speak to church groups, high school and college classes, civic clubs and community organizations. They also carry their newfound insights into postgraduate degree programs and into private and public employment. A surprising number of Returned Peace Corps Volunteers (RPCVs) publish articles and books on their experiences; this work includes fiction as well as memoirs, and collectively a sizable body of literature on their experiences has formed.[57]

The RPCVs institutionalize their presence in American society in such a way that their influence becomes enduring. Scores of regional Peace Corps associations have been formed around the country. They hold periodic meetings, publish newsletters, form local member groups and make grants to support projects back in host countries. On another dimension, country-specific alumni networks keep in touch with each other and hold periodic reunions. At the national level, a National Peace Corps Association sponsors a website called "Peace Corps Connect" that carries on educational activities and promotes events like Peace Corps Week and agency anniversaries. A fund-raising vehicle for such activity is the Peace Corps Foundation, founded in 2008. All of this civil society action has even spawned Peace Corps copycats, such as the Global Volunteer Network, Cross-Cultural Solutions and GoEco, or Volunteers for Ecological and Humanitarian Projects.

Many former Volunteers reach prominent positions in the arts, business, the media, higher education, nonprofit organizations and government, as Box 7.2 illustrates. Their positions afford them the opportunity to inform other citizens of the rewards of overseas public service and the transformative nature of a Peace Corps experience. Much more important, the 200,000 ordinary Americans who have had the experience go through their lives with broader outlooks and a global perspective that they can communicate to family, friends and coworkers. Over the long run, this steady enrichment of the United States' own civil society may be just as important as the Peace Corps' contributions abroad. In other words, the cell 3 achievements of this mission mystique agency extend in many directions: to the world out there, to the worlds inside individuals and to the world here at home.

Box 7.2 Former Peace Corps Volunteers

Noted Figures in the Arts and Literature

Taylor Hackford, film director (Bolivia, 1968–1969). Lawrence Leamer, author (Nepal, 1965–1967). Martin Puryear, sculptor (Sierra Leone, 1964–1966). Joel Shapiro, artist (India, 1965–1967). Mildred Taylor, author (Ethiopia, 1965–1967). Paul Theroux, author (Malawi, 1963–1965).

Top Executives in Business and Industry

Edward Dolby, Bank of America (India, 1966–1968). Samuel Gillespie III, Exxon Mobil (Kenya, 1967–1969). Frank Guzzetta, Hecht's (India, 1968–1972). Robert Haas, Levi Strauss (Ivory Coast, 1964–1966). Reed Hastings, Netflix (Swaziland, 1983–1985).

Media Shapers of Opinion

Ron Arias, *People* magazine (Peru, 1963–1964). Thomas Dine, Radio Free Europe (Philippines, 1962–1964). Josh Friedman, *Newsday* (Costa Rica, 1964–1966). Chris Matthews, *Hardball* (Swaziland, 1968–1970). Ann O'Hanlon, *Washington Post* (Ecuador, 1986–1988). Peter Stinton, *San Francisco Chronicle* (Iran, 1969–1971).

College and University Presidents

Leo Higdon Jr., Connecticut College (Malawi, 1968–1970). James Lyons, California State University, Dominguez Hills (Ecuador, 1966–1967). M. Peter McPherson, Michigan State University (Peru, 1964–1966). Julius Nimmons, University of the District of Columbia (Tunisia, 1962–1964). Donna Shalala, University of Miami (Iran, 1962–1963).

Senior American Diplomats

Richard A. Boucher, Department of State (Senegal, 1973–1975). Johnnie Carson, ambassador to Kenya (Tanzania, 1965–1968). Robert Gelbard, ambassador to Indonesia (Bolivia, 1964–1966). Tony Hall, ambassador to United Nations (Thailand, 1966–1967). Christopher R. Hill, Department of State (Cameroon, 1974–1976).

Elected Government Officials

Christopher Dodd, U.S. Senate (Dominican Republic, 1966–1968). Jim Doyle, governor of Wisconsin (Tunisia, 1967–1969). Sam Farr, U.S. Congress (Colombia, 1964–1966). Mike Honda, U.S. Congress (El Salvador, 1965–1967). Thomas Murphy Jr., mayor of Pittsburgh (Paraguay, 1970–1972). Thomas Petri, U.S. Congress (Somalia, 1966–1967).

Leaders of Nonprofit Organizations

Gerald Durley, Concerned Black Clergy of Atlanta (Nigeria, 1964–1966). Barbara Ferris, International Women's Democracy Center (Morocco, 1980–1982). Ken Hackett, Catholic Relief Services (Ghana, 1968–1971). Carl Pope, Sierra Club (India, 1967–1969). Thomas Tighe, Direct Relief International (Thailand, 1986–1988).

Source: Peace Corps website, www.peacecorps.gov/index.cfm?shell=learn.whatispc.notable.

Some critics maintain that the Peace Corps' three goals are contradictory and hence self-defeating. Anthropologist Sarah Waldorf, for example, says that the sophistication inherent in the technology transfer function of Goal 1 is incompatible with the means inherent in Goals 2 and 3, which she translates as sending young, unskilled amateurs into villages "to run educational and cultural diversity camps in other people's countries."[58] Peace Corps commentator Gerald Rice disagrees. He sees conflict among the goals as representing a "healthy dose of schizophrenia" between Goal 1 "developers" and Goals 2–3 "lovers." Even so, he adds, the Peace Corps is not *solely* a development agency or *solely* devoted to international understanding, but both.[59] One might restate this idea by saying the agency extends both a hand and a heart, and the two unite in tangible people-to-people assistance that, by its very nature, builds lasting personal relationships around the world.

AUTONOMY BEHIND THE SCENES

During the first half of its lifetime the Peace Corps had to fight for its life, not to mention its autonomy. It struggled against attempts by USAID and the State Department to dominate it. The agency tried mightily to maintain a shred of independence during the ACTION period. In the national political arena, the political right portrayed the Peace Corps as amateurish, naive and helpful to draft-dodgers. The political left declared it to be a tool of cultural imperialism, seeking to establish a Pax Americana over the Third World. Against these cross-currents, Shriver exploited every bit of influence he had in the White House and on Capitol Hill. Twenty years later, to save the agency from decimation and probable extinction, Loret Ruppe had to exercise her most adroit political skills to convince Reagan and the Republican business establishment that the Peace Corps was worth keeping.

During the second half of its organizational life, however, the agency's political environment became totally different. The Peace Corps is now accepted as an adventuresome if not glamorous opportunity for young people to grow within themselves while serving the outside world. The foreign policy establishment perceives the organization as a positive force on behalf of the United States' image overseas. The international community considers it the world's leading development agency based on volunteerism.

This mystique was achieved during a period of relatively settled dynamic equilibrium within the agency. The basic *modus operandi* needed to send young volunteers for temporary service all over the globe and get them home safely had been figured out. Rather than lead the institution in new directions, successive directors kept a steady hand on the tiller. Careful recruitment vetting procedures and Volunteer behavior monitoring (and perhaps an uninterested press) made it possible to avoid public relations flaps like the Michelmore postcard incident.

As a consequence, the question of policy autonomy in situations of publicized controversy was sidestepped by keeping them from arising. Operations were kept calm and predictable, with no radical program growth as with the National Park Service, no monumental new projects costing billions as in the National Weather Service, and no drastic mission creep as happened at the Centers for Disease Control and Prevention.

From the Washington perspective, the Peace Corps had become a relatively fixed, accepted and even prestigious element in U.S. foreign policy. It consumed few resources and threatened no powerful interests. This did not mean, however, that policy autonomy was not being exercised; it was exercised continuously, but internally within the organization. This happens at the management level both in Washington and abroad, but is particularly true out in the field, thousands of miles away from the suspicious eyes of Washington officialdom and 24-hour news channels. The core nature of Peace Corps work, village-level projects carried out under a regime of extensive decentralization, created "behind the scenes" locales where experimentation could take place. There, new and potentially controversial program activities went on unnoticed, such as teaching safe sex to young people and fostering female independence in girls. The practice of continuously rethinking the content of projects and allowing Volunteers themselves to shape them demonstrates confidence in unleashed and uncontrolled youthful ingenuity. Fulfillment of cells 8 and 9 of the template is largely in their hands.

THIS INSTANCE OF MISSION MYSTIQUE

How does this unusual agency, the last of our case studies, stack up against the template of mission mystique?

Cell 1: Mission. Its mission is cosmic in scope, even though specified by the Peace Corps Act. The organization's overarching mandate is to promote world peace and friendship. This expression of idealism sets the stage for a dramatically charged case of agency mystique. The mission's goal components—helping poor people lead a better life, allowing those people to understand the United States and increasing Americans' understanding of them—are not dry fragments of law but live concepts debated daily in the agency, permeating the institution with a freshness that belies its age. Moreover, if world peace requires both development and understanding, the goals form a coherent whole.

Cell 2: Need. Many Americans would, if asked, decry the idea of wasting time on the poor countries of the world and worrying about our country's image abroad. Hence the subjective nature of collective needs means that popular opinion, assuming citizens are asked to think about it, must divide on the worth of the Peace Corps. In any case, many other Americans would regard sending young

What are the strengths of P.C. that allowed it to grow + be strong for so long? Reputation?

women and men to assist distant villagers in improving their lives as an innately moral act. Also, they would see the agency as a teaching process by which Americans can understand the world better and as an identifying process that marks the United States as a beacon of hope in a turbulent and stricken world.

Cell 3: Reputation. At one time the Peace Corps was controversial and even ridiculed. Today this is no longer true. Its image domestically and abroad as a prime public symbol of international service has placed it on a pedestal of moral legitimacy that other governmental bodies would lust for. Peace Corps leadership is well aware of this asset and conscious of the need to keep it as unblemished as possible. Meanwhile, the record of achievement by a continually rotating workforce of thousands of volunteers accumulates, not necessarily as measured by statistics alone but by expressing goodwill over time. As project after project is carried out and as relationship after relationship is cemented, lasting bonds among people grow.

Cell 4: Motivation. Motivation in this unusual organization must be largely intrinsic. The Volunteers would not join up if they did not want to serve. After all, they must learn a foreign language, sacrifice a decent salary and live under trying conditions. Even though they encounter loneliness and uncertainty when confronting their assignment, the majority stick it out and come home transformed, with over 80 percent saying they would do it again. With respect to the staff, most are ex-Volunteers who serve the Peace Corps ethos at a higher level. They too must be dedicated, in that within five years they need to find new jobs. Those who extend as third termers or return as retreads demonstrate additional motivation. Then, too, the spirit of service lives on in the hundreds of RPCV alumni groups that support the institution and help keep it useful and vital.

Cell 5: Culture. The Peace Corps is a unique government department. It is anti-bureaucratic in that it rejects overtly rigid structure, excessive rules, lifelong careers and narrow specialization. Although self-knowledge of what seems to work in this unique business is prized as it accumulates, no policy or procedure is immune to change. Because the agency is highly decentralized and fragmented, the culture is such that everybody can "do their own thing" to a degree, as long as it is within the orbit of practical overseas service that is sensitively collaborative rather than unilateral. While at one time rival subcultures warred internally, today open communication and a spirit of common dedication seem to prevail.

Cell 6: History. A significant published literature on the history of the agency exists, along with memoirs and Volunteer accounts. Major founding anniversaries of the agency have been celebrated over the years. Until recently, this was essentially what honored the institution's past, although that has now changed. In 2009 the Peace Corps put up a Digital Library website to allow public examination of early photographs and writings. Because of the vividness of their own recollected experiences, RPCVs especially are aware of the need to maintain institutional memory, and a group in Portland, Ore., has undertaken to create a Museum of the Peace Corps Experience. Hopefully it will soon possess a physical home for exhibition of manuscripts, photographs and memorabilia.[60]

Cell 7: Contestation. Frank and continuous dialogue is a hallmark of the Peace Corps. Headquarters people still argue over the relative importance of the three goals and other philosophical issues. Third termers confront their colleagues with the realities of the field, and retreads urge that ideas from nonprofits be considered. The inspector general, shielded by longer tenure, investigates allegations of wrongdoing while also raising larger policy questions. Meanwhile, the thousands of Volunteers, most of them youthful and at home on the Internet, exchange frank opinions worldwide every day. They also register complaints at in-service and post-service training conferences and in project advisory meetings.

Cell 8: Autonomy. As noted, during the first half of its existence Peace Corps leaders battled aggressively for independence and policy autonomy. Since that time the organization has enjoyed a level of prestige and respect that protects it, in large part, from budget cuts and incursions by bureaucratic rivals. In this enviable situation, the Peace Corps has taken steps to enlarge its internal tendency for openness to change. This is particularly evident at the level of field projects, where at project advisory committee meetings Volunteers are encouraged to suggest new ideas for making a project work and to stimulate self-initiated thinking on the part of the affected village elders and local officials.

Cell 9: Renewal. The Peace Corps, unlike the other agencies we studied, has as its very mission the facilitation of social change. The Centers for Disease Control and Prevention and the Department of Social Services are dedicated to this cause as well, but for the specific ends of human wellness and economic independence. To the Peace Corps, multifaceted change in the societies it serves is its very *raison d'être*. In accord with the proposition that mission mystique agencies should have internally consistent belief *systems,* it is right that the agency itself be embracing a commitment to change. This it has done by making questioning of the status quo and experimenting with innovation a hallmark of its culture. Not to "walk the talk" would be hypocritical, and Peace Corps workers seem to know that.

To sum up, this last unusual agency is exceptionally strong with respect to achieving mission mystique, with its only weakness being probable public uncertainty as to whether its societal mission is urgent.

The Significance of Mission Mystique

To RECAPITULATE, my argument is that (1) public agencies are not just organizations but also institutions, i.e., "living" social organisms that carry values and persist over time while also evolving as circumstances unfold; (2) the best of them possess an aura of being exceptional that flows from the nature of their work and hence can be identified as a mystique associated with their particular mission; and (3) the key to understanding how this mission mystique animates members and attracts observers is the notion of an agency belief system that is composed of at least nine attributes, which I arrange as a template.

To formulate, refine and present this argument, I have explored six premier government agencies, and in each have characterized its particular mission mystique and delineated how each institution's unique features have or have not displayed the nine attributes of the template. To conclude this inquiry, I will: (1) analyze the six cases collectively to weigh the extent to which the template is, in actuality, fulfilled; (2) speculate, based on studying these six mission auras in detail, on the underlying mechanisms of mission mystique; (3) consider the ability of mission mystique to sustain itself over time; and (4) weigh implications of my study for the field of public administration.

BELIEF SYSTEMS ANALYZED

In Table 8.1 I evaluate the degree to which the six agencies demonstrate the presence of the nine attributes. A number 3 in the table indicates strong fulfillment of template requirements; 2, moderate; and 1, weak. As can be seen in the bottom right corner, the gross average rating for all 54 cells is 2.7. This rather high overall figure should not surprise us, since the agencies were selected in the first

Table 8.1 Degree to Which Agencies Fit the Mission Mystique Template

3 = Strong, 2 = Moderate, 1 = Weak

Cell	U.S. National Park Service	U.S. National Weather Service	U.S. Centers for Disease Control and Prevention	Department of Social Services, Mecklenburg County, N.C.	Virginia State Police	U.S. Peace Corps	Mean
Mission	3	3	3	3	3	3	3.0
Need	2	2	3	2	3	2	2.3
Reputation	3	3	3	3	3	3	3.0
Motivation	3	3	3	2	3	3	2.8
Culture	3	3	3	2	3	3	2.8
History	3	1	3	2	3	3	2.5
Contestation	3	2	2	3	2	3	2.5
Autonomy	3	3	2	3	3	3	2.8
Renewal	3	3	3	3	2	3	2.8
Mean	2.9	2.6	2.8	2.6	2.8	2.9	2.7

Source: Compiled by the author.

place as good candidates for mission mystique. The specific requirements of my ideal type were, however, worked out only in the course of studying these agencies, which is why upon close examination they all fall short of the model to some degree. Nonetheless, in that three-quarters of the cells are scored 3 or strong and only a single cell is scored as 1 or weak, I consider the group of six agencies as manifesting mission mystique generally, albeit not perfectly.

Examining the means at the bottom margin of the table, we see that average agency scores are grouped quite closely between 2.9 and 2.6. Yet there are three successive rankings of two agencies each. The highest mean is 2.9, obtained by the National Park Service (NPS) and Peace Corps. The next level is 2.8, occupied by the Centers for Disease Control and Prevention (CDC) and Virginia State Police (VSP). Third are the National Weather Service (NWS) and Department of Social Services (DSS), both at 2.6. It is worth noting that this lowest agency mean is mathematically closer to the legend's category of Strong than that of Moderate.

Means for the nine cells of the template are shown in the side margin. The highest (and perfect) cell mean of 3.0 is attained in Mission (cell 1) and Reputation (cell 3). This indicates that all six agencies are deemed to possess the basic requirement for possessing a central, permeating purpose and a distinctive reputation based on achievement. The most common cell mean is 2.8, a figure that results from one organization receiving a score of 2. The cells experiencing one moderate rating are Motivation (cell 4), Culture (cell 5), Autonomy (cell 8) and Renewal (cell 9).

Added departure from the ideal—a mean of 2.5—is uncovered in History (cell 6) and Contestation (cell 7). The lowest cell mean of all is 2.3, for Need (cell 2). This is an outgrowth of the subjective nature of felt societal need for a mission; perhaps we must realize it is relatively rare, even among the strongest administrative agencies, that near-universal agreement on the criticality of their function can exist.

We now shift to belief system analysis at the individual cell level. Explanations are provided for the assessments given in the box. I also make comparisons, address what we have learned from the six agencies studied, and discuss broader considerations as well, such as contrasts with agencies that lack mission mystique.

Cell 1: Central Mission Purpose. In Chapter 1, possession of a central mission purpose was depicted as a first-among-equals cell in achieving mission mystique. A central mission provides focus, gives direction, identifies importance and forms the basis for mystique. As noted, all of our agencies were rated strong in this category.

As the study proceeded I unexpectedly became aware that the six agencies fall into two groups with respect to mission. One is comprised of the organizations whose missions are spelled out in law, such as the NPS, NWS and Peace Corps. The second group consists of agencies where this is not the case, and instead a generic mission is assumed from the nature of the organization. These are the CDC, DSS and VSP. To give names to the distinction, I call the missions of the first group specified and of the second acknowledged.

The published literature on missions in public organizations deals exclusively, to my knowledge, with agencies in the first category. In it, authors are prone to state that to be compelling, the mission must not only be written but as unified as possible so as to foster maximum coherence and focus. Yet it is interesting that all three of our specified missions have multiple parts. For the NPS they are resource preservation and public use; for the NWS goals are forecasting, issuing warnings and maintaining infrastructure; and the Peace Corps is charged with providing trained manpower, promoting America's image and educating Americans about the world.

After studying these three agencies, it would appear that despite mission multiplicity it is possible for purposes to be plural yet not distracting when they are complementary at the operational level. This is true with all three of our examples. Two of these three add yet another insight, however: with respect to the policy as opposed to operational level, when differing emphases are espoused they can also have the positive effect of stimulating constructive disagreement and dialogue within the organization, as seen in the NPS and Peace Corps. This feature supports another element of the template, Contestation (cell 7).

This finding that plural missions are not necessarily bad does not mean, however, that truly blatant conflicts within missions are not harmful. The Bureau of Land Management (BLM) in the Interior Department evolved from two predecessor organizations, each with a very different purpose: the General Land Office, which was created to give away federal lands, and the Grazing Service, whose purpose was to sustain them for range feeding. Ever since its merging, the BLM has confronted split constituencies—big-spread ranchers versus less land-rich livestock farmers. In another example, Amtrak (National Railroad Passenger Corporation) has three competing demands being made on it by members of Congress: preserve passenger rail across the whole nation, provide good rail service to primarily the Northeast Corridor and operate without subsidy in the open market of transportation. As a consequence, Amtrak has difficulty convincing anyone that it possesses an unambiguous reason for its existence.

With respect to the acknowledged mission purposes, we encountered three: public health for the CDC, public welfare for the DSS and public safety for the VSP. Despite the inherent vagueness of these terms, all three agencies project a reason for existence that is stirring. In each one, what kindles passions has to do with a top level of attainment. As pointed out in Chapter 6, this is protecting the nation's health to the maximum degree possible for the CDC (best expressed by "healthiest nation"); operating the most caring and creative department possible for "customers" for the DSS ("to be the best"); and assembling a company of the most well-trained, proud and impartial police officers possible for the VSP ("Virginia's Finest"). Moreover, each agency actually reaches far with respect to meeting its articulated goal, although by different metrics: outputs for the CDC, performance for the DSS and professionalism for the VSP.

Cell 2: Societal Needs Met. With respect to public perceptions of the societal needs being met by the agency and how that reflects on its perceived importance, the Centers for Disease Control and State Police were rated 3s and the Park Service, Weather Service, Social Services department, and Peace Corps received 2s. As mentioned in Chapter 1, such needs are subjectively perceived—that is, public "problems" are socially constructed. Nonetheless, some are classified as urgent because of almost universal and continuous condemnation of their consequences, while for differing reasons others recede to secondary importance for a proportion of the population.

Combating sudden epidemics and violent crime are needs that seem so urgent that to take exception would be absurd. This gives the CDC and VSP an advantage with respect to how mystique is generated by carrying out obviously essential tasks. For the other four agencies studied, however, the matter is not that simple. Awe-inspiring national parks are considered by millions to be a great blessing, but other millions have never visited one and may never do so. The need for accurate weather forecasts is crystal clear when storms or floods are brewing, but that is usually not the case; citizens experience far more "normal" weather than the reverse, hence the need for a NWS is not obvious most of the time. In a society in which family violence is the exception rather than the rule, the need for a DSS is not as always as imperative as it should be. While to college students and their parents an opportunity to join the Peace Corps is welcome, those struggling to graduate from high school and maintain a decent income may find it irrelevant. This does not mean, however, that plentiful mystique sentiment does not emanate from attentive, informed audiences who are aware of the joy of family camping, the devastation storms can cause, the moral necessity for a safety net, and the life-changing experiences of international service. Hence, even "moderate" ratings of 2 remain highly significant.

One can think of other government agencies that are hurt by a subjectively constructed public need. The Internal Revenue Service (IRS) is absolutely indispensable to the operation of government, to the nation's security and to the economy's health. Furthermore, it is one of the most effective, fair and corruption-free tax collection agencies on the planet. Yet, because of the widespread disdain heaped upon it, the IRS would probably never be able to attain mission mystique. Another example of a highly efficient and essential government agency that suffers greatly from perceived lack of importance is the United States Postal Service (USPS). Because of cell phones, the Internet, private parcel carriers and other factors, probably most Americans under age 30 think it is a waste of money. This is so despite the fact that over most of U.S. history the post office made it possible to bind together the 13 colonies and later a continent-sized nation. As a result, the USPS faces huge deficits, is on the defensive politically and may not survive long, let alone become eligible for mission mystique.

Cell 3: Reputation and Achievement. Table 8.1 shows that all agencies in our group received 3s for cell 3. In large part, this assessment is based on the fact that all of them enjoy far-ranging reputations among knowledgeable persons in their jurisdictions. In the case of the NPS, NWS, CDC and Peace Corps, the reputations are worldwide in scope.

Like societal needs, agency reputations depend on subjective interpretation as well as objective measurement, i.e., accumulated statistical records of success. Yet the validity or germaneness of the variables measured can also be contended. Evaluation is a tricky business and an appropriate assessment tool depends on the kind of work being done. Ongoing, repetitive actions can be quantitatively measured as to performance, with post-hoc validation of weather predictions a perfect example. Work that is carried out without uncontrollable outside factors intervening may offer satisfying metrics, as in monitoring the location of sex offenders. But how do we evaluate the work of an Epidemic Intelligence Service

(EIS) team when it investigates a mysterious new disease? Or the record of a DSS social worker in halting abuse in chronically violent families? Or the success of Peace Corps Volunteers in inducing change-averse villagers to fence in their livestock?

These are the kinds of "effectiveness" that are impossible to predict, let alone measure. Perhaps placing such tasks in the hands of a competent, dedicated and reliable institution—such as one possessing mission mystique—is the best thing to do. If the certainty of achieving effectiveness or even measuring it correctly is not available, at least the opportunities for decreasing the risks of failure grow. This subject comes up again later in the chapter.

Normally, one would hope, reputation and achievement go hand in hand, but this is by no means always the case. The Social Security Administration (SSA) has a splendid reputation among senior citizens, for their checks invariably arrive on time and in the correct amount. But the younger generation has no trust in the institution because its members do not believe it will still be mailing checks when they get old. The United States Patent and Trademark Office, whose work is mandated by the Constitution, has a positive image on the part of the general citizenry because of its association with inventor opportunities, yet patent applicants are notoriously disgusted with its huge backlogs. Both institutions would face low scores on the template's cell 3.

An unusual situation with regard to the relationship between reputation and achievement is the Chesapeake Bay Foundation, a group of federal, state and local authorities under the loose guidance of the U.S. Environmental Protection Agency. Charged with the mission of cleaning up the largest estuary in North America, it was found to be falsifying documents of pollution reduction in order to make its record look better. As a consequence, both reputation and record sank to the same poor level, and rightfully so. Unfortunately, this hurts chances to get the job done.[1]

Cell 4: Intrinsic Motivation. The fourth characteristic in the mission mystique template—intrinsic motivation on the part of employees—is assessed in two ways. One is by examining employee opinion surveys. Responses to the Federal Human Capital Survey (FHCS) item "The work I do is important" were consistently in the low 90s for the NPS and high 80s for the CDC. "I like the kind of work I do" yielded responses in the mid-80s in both agencies. Julie Elmore's study of NPS employees showed responses in the mid-90s for both questions. The Peace Corps' in-house survey of its returning Volunteers found that 70 percent found the experience rewarding and 83 percent would probably do it again. In the Mecklenburg County government survey, percentages of DSS employees in Jake Jacobsen's period as director who found the county a "good place to work" were in the mid-90s, but after he left they dropped to the 80s.

To me, the more valuable source of insight regarding motivation comes from personal visits to agencies that allow direct observation, interviews and casual conversation. What I looked for on the field visits I made to research this book was influenced by the ideas of Yoash Wiener, discussed in Chapter 1. The points he stresses are home socialization as it affects personality needs; the effect these have on behaviors in the organization; and the resulting consequences these factors have for personal sacrifice, length of tenure and mental preoccupation with the work.

As for home socialization, when I asked national park rangers how they came to join the agency, several told long and moving stories of how it all began with childhood park experiences. State police officers now on duty followed fathers and even grandfathers who served before them. Regarding personal sacrifice, when a big storm hits, weather forecasters spend 18-hour days in the operations room; and when an epidemic breaks out, EIS investigators head immediately for the site anywhere in the world and remain as long as necessary. With respect to preoccupation with the work, NWS meteorologists become obsessed with the technical details of what they do, DSS protective workers go to any lengths to rescue an abuse victim and VSP drug task force members do not rest until they get their convictions.

Accordingly, I assess five of the six agencies as a 3 on this item in the mission mystique template; the exception is DSS, which is given a 2 because even though the social workers are intensely motivated, this attribute does not seem to extend to the more numerous eligibility workers.

Cell 5: Institutionalized Culture. The fifth attribute in the mission mystique template points to agency culture as the key to institutionalizing the belief system. If efficacious, the culture coagulates mission-related values and patterns of thinking into a relatively stable confluence of shared ideas and behaviors that persists over time, even as staff and leaders come and go. Thus it performs a central, integrating and stabilizing function for the belief system by inducing enthusiasm for the mission, reinforcing employee motivation and promoting a collective sense of shared values over time.

Each institutional culture grows in its own soil, making it unique. It is for this reason that we studied our six agencies in depth—so as to begin to comprehend each one's complex and subtle cultural dimensions. The Park Service culture is based on the lure and beauty of the great outdoors and the need to protect it from encroachment by civilization. The NPS culture is immensely robust and persists despite successive directors and presidents. The Weather Service culture is, by contrast, based on the intricacies of a vast IT system. Here the driving values are making it work well and even better. Despite the efforts of a National Oceanic and Atmospheric Administration (NOAA) head to subvert it, the NWS culture is strong enough to persist without serious challenge. As for the CDC, its culture is built on a set of individual national science centers. It is the duty of each one to protect the nation and world from the particular types of disease or health hazards with which it deals. When an agency director threatened to undercut center autonomy, a revolt followed.

The DSS of Mecklenburg County occupies a special position among our mission mystique cultures. It was the one institutional culture in the set that apparently was not firmly anchored enough to survive over time. The DSS culture we studied was vibrant while it lasted, but it was still too young and too tied to its founder to persist intact following his departure. This is why it receives a 2 for cell 5 when the others receive 3s.

Still different situations are found in the last two agencies, whose cultures are opposites in some ways. The Virginia State Police possesses a mature culture based on the paramilitary nature of law enforcement and the themes of strict professionalism and absolute impartiality in the line of duty. Moreover, it remains steady despite Virginia's practice of one-term governorships, making the VSP stand out in a highly politicized state capital. The Peace Corps is unique to the extent of being in a class of its own. Its culture actually rejects most norms of traditional public administration by eschewing career bureaucracy, downplaying hierarchical control, and operating via the actions and judgment of temporary citizen volunteers. Remarkably, while regarded as a trivial experiment in its infancy, it has become legendary both on U.S. college campuses and in countless villages around the world.

Cell 6: Honoring History. In knowing and celebrating its history, an agency underscores its identity and is given a rearview mirror by which to see the road ahead. Another way of saying this is that by honoring the past, the agency's current culture is not transitory but planted in accumulated institutional experience.

Four of our agencies fulfill the cell 6 admonition admirably and are scored 3 in cell 6. The NPS is the subject of countless books about its past, as is the Peace Corps. The CDC and VSP have fine headquarters museums. Also, the CDC is the subject of a scholarly history and the VSP of a videotape documentary, both of high quality. All four agencies memorialize their founders in some way and celebrate significant anniversaries. The Peace Corps is unusual in that its own Volunteers write personal accounts of agency history at the village level, and a collection of them is currently being compiled at a museum set up by Returned Peace Corps Volunteers (RPCVs).

The DSS is granted a score of 2 on this subject, in that prior to Jake Jacobsen's tenure no attention was paid to the institution's history, and the RoadShows that celebrated each fiscal-year birthday ceased after his departure. The NWS receives a 1, the only such score assigned in the exercise. Its members largely ignore the institution's quite interesting past and do little to keep it alive. The technological nature of its culture does not seem to mix well with a humanistic approach to organization life; when the 200th anniversary celebration of NOAA was organized, NWS people were dismissive, perhaps rightly so.

Cell 7: Contestation and Opposition. The attribute of Contestation and Opposition calls for the existence of mechanisms by which to counter tendencies toward myopic leadership, groupthink and bureaucratic inertia. The concept is inspired by Stephen White's idea of weak ontology and Rosemary O'Leary's advocacy of acceptable dissent.

The best kind of contestation is that which emerges internally on a spontaneous basis and addresses policy matters as well as operations. This is achieved in three of our agencies by means of differences over what elements of the mission to emphasize. As noted, in the NPS the tension is conservation versus use, in the CDC disease reduction versus prevention, and in the Peace Corps development versus understanding. In each of these institutions spirited dialogue frequently breaks out over these differences, in person or on employee or retiree blogs. I regard these tensions as comprising the most significant form of institutional contestation we have encountered in this book.

Less important from the policy standpoint but still significant are administrative arrangements for communicating disagreement and checking power. The NWS practices 360-degree feedback at the field office level and conducts service assessments at the agency level. In its protective social work programs, the DSS has for its protection programs an ombudsman and fatality prevention team. The VSP internal affairs section investigates all allegations of wrongdoing, whether major or minor. The inspector general's office of the Peace Corps inquires into allegations of impropriety and makes recommendations for corrective action.

External checks exist for each agency, as in all of U.S. public administration. The federal agencies are subject to congressional oversight and hearings. In addition, the NWS is supervised quite closely by NOAA, and the CDC was at one time hounded by press leaks to the *Atlanta Journal-Constitution*. Because of their nonpartisan nature and largely untarnished images, the Peace Corps and Virginia State Police remain relatively free from external scrutiny, except for budgeting and accounting reviews. On the contestation factor I give ratings of 3 for the NPS, DSS and Peace Corps, and 2 for the NWS, CDC and VSP. The State Police, because of its disciplined and hierarchical paramilitary organization, would definitely benefit from an independent inspector general.

Cell 8: Qualified Policy Autonomy. The standard for bureaucratic autonomy set by Daniel Carpenter (discussed in Chapter 1) is successful program expansion as a means to carve out institutional independence without flouting democratic principles. This was done in the NPS by George Hartzog when he redefined "national park" beyond the concept of a protected wilderness, in the NWS by Joe

Friday when he modernized weather forecasting, in the CDC by David Sencer when he presided over the eradication of smallpox, by Jake Jacobsen when he launched Work First and by Charles Woodson when he built a modern state police force.

Are there cases in which exercised autonomy was excessive? Some possibilities come to mind. Park Service professionals bitterly fought the *Management Policies* redraft that would have emasculated its agency's mission, but did so by convincing department officials themselves to back off. Thereafter the agency reluctantly accepted political decisions regarding snowmobiles in Yellowstone and guns in parks. When Congress attempted to hamstring Weather Service modernization, Friday played along with the restrictions imposed but maneuvered a satisfactory settlement of the degradation issue through the Commerce Department. Innovators Sencer, Jacobsen and Woodson all worked within the constraints set by the political branches of government, even while pushing their causes actively at an informal level.

On the occasions when administrators openly fought with the elected branches, they felt they were defending their rightful territory, and in some cases paid a price for it. When Hartzog refused to allow Bebe Rebozo's special-use dock permit to stand despite agency regulations to the contrary, President Richard Nixon fired him. When Friday diverted modernization funds to supplement a reduced Weather Service budget, he was dismissed. When Superintendent William Corvello resisted Gov. Douglas Wilder's attempted interference with police helicopter and investigation policies, Corvello promptly resigned. An assistant to President Ronald Reagan unilaterally planned to phase out the Peace Corps, but by dint of her powers of persuasion Loret Miller Ruppe fought off the idea.

The case of the CDC deserves further discussion on the subject. One could argue that the agency went too far when it failed to end the Tuskegee experiments promptly. Technically this was an act of omission rather than commission, but prior danger signals had been ignored. When Sen. Edward Kennedy intervened the experiments were promptly halted. Another incident to consider is the premature advocacy of total inoculation of the population during the swine flu scare of 1976. While the policy decision was made at the secretary and presidential level, the CDC set the process in motion. More recently, Director Julie Gerberding's advocacy of her healthiest nation scheme on the scale of the moon landing was done at the close of a presidential administration under the assumption that she would be reappointed by the next president. Are these actions sufficiently "qualified," i.e., within the boundaries of proper responsibility to constitutional and moral values? This is a matter of judgment, but to this author worrisome signs of institutional arrogance can be detected. Accordingly, whereas I score the other agencies 3 in this category, my assessment for the CDC is 2.

Cell 9: Renewal and Learning. In addition to occasional arrogance, confi-
dent and competent institutions can become self-satisfied with the status quo
and resistant to change. Yet a fundamental requirement for mission mystique is
to be in the habit of engaging in all three loops of organizational learning, undergoing continuous efforts at renewal and being prepared to expect the unexpected
rather than merely planning from known parameters.

These traits are prominent in most of our studied agencies. The NPS is
accustomed to big-picture forward planning and significant change, such as
making the parks more welcome to minorities. The NWS keeps investigating
the possibilities of acquiring new data-collection equipment and adopting
more advanced meteorological systems. The CDC is always on the lookout for
emerging threats to human health that can be countered. Jake at the DSS was
an ever-flowing font of imaginative new ideas. A firmly established ethos in the
Peace Corps is never to think of a policy or procedure as permanent but always
be ready for questions and change. The VSP has a good record of deploying
new information technologies to improve its law enforcement operations, but
its culture has a practical, here-and-now flavor that seems to restrict big-sky
thinking to emergencies, such as the radio-system breakdown in 2002. It is
scored 2 in cell 9 and the others 3.

THEMATIC MECHANISMS IN MISSION MYSTIQUE

Mission mystique refers to an aura of magnetic appeal that surrounds an agency
because of what it stands for and what it does for the nation and community.
Each case of mystique is generated by a unique interrelationship between mission characteristics and their emotional consequences. Yet it may be possible to
speculate on broad categories of triggering mechanisms that cut across missions.
To that end, I outline some such generic mechanisms, drawing from the examples of the studied agencies.

In doing so, two distinctions are made. The first separates the mission perspective of the member of the institution (labeled "doer") from the perspective of
an attentive outsider (the "viewer"). The second notes the difference between (1)
a mystique attraction that is other-regarding in the sense of being a cause larger
than oneself, and (2) an attraction that is self-regarding in that it is grounded in
feelings of self-respect or personal fulfillment.

Taking the analytical framework one more step, the two distinctions can inter-
relate in the manner of a 2×2 matrix. From these interrelationships a tentative
theory of mission mystique emerges. A magnetic mission stirs the soul of doers by
involving them in work they consider to be of critical importance (other-regarding in that the aura originates externally). Viewers with a parallel commitment to
the cause experience the aura from the vantage point of outsiders, opening the

way to providing external support. Also, working as a doer on a mission deemed critical to society enhances that person's feelings of self-worth (a self-regarding source of attraction). This commitment is reinforced in the company of like-minded coworkers, and the bonds uniting them strengthen the mystique's impact on their minds. External observers (viewers) of this individual self-fulfillment and collective spirit receive, via lateral transmission, a degree of intensified interest in the mission that may lead to such admiration that they seek to join it.

Table 8.2 utilizes this framework to summarize the content of six generic mission mystique mechanisms, based on the thematic nature of their appeal. The top three of these, called Noble Cause, Life Saver and Helping Hand, are other-regarding in the way they generate mystique. The mystique stems from, in order, the esteem associated with occupying high moral ground, the honor of being in a position to save human life, and having the opportunity to help people on a mass basis. The lower three, christened Deep Expert, Authority Figure and Close Comrades, operate by different self-regarding motives: being held in wonder for one's specialized knowledge, being held in high respect by representing the law's authority and majesty, and enjoying close association with others who share similar responsibilities.

Table 8.2 Thematic Mechanisms in Mission Mystique

Theme	Doer Perspective	Viewer Perspective	Regarding	Agencies
Noble Cause	The opportunity to be identified with a high-minded purpose	They are doing truly important work	Others	NPS CDC PC
Life Saver	The exhilaration of saving people's lives	They bear a life-and-death responsibility	Others	VSP NWS DSS
Helping Hand	Doing work that makes a difference in people's lives	They make a real impact on people's lives	Others	DSS CDC VSP PC
Deep Expert	Belonging to a knowledge elite	They are awesome for the things they can do	Self	NWS CDC VSP
Authority Figure	Representing and enforcing the law	They have real power to control and help people	Self	NPS VSP DSS
Close Comrades	Having close and lasting relationships with coworkers	They stand together as one and enjoy it	Self	VSP NPS NWS CDC PC

Source: Compiled by the author.

The Noble Cause

This category of mystique is comparable to what idealistic political activists attempt: occupy the high moral ground and on it invoke a stirring vision for the future. They regard their work as inherently worthy and, moreover, are aware that it engenders respect and admiration on the part of outsiders who are sympathetic to their cause.

The mystiques of the NPS, CDC, and Peace Corps most clearly exhibit this source of mission mystique. Park rangers (doers) see themselves as serving the noble purpose of stewardship over America's natural and cultural treasures. Park visitors and supporters (viewers) identify rangers as serving in this capacity and hence doing work of the greatest importance.

Scientists and epidemiologists at the CDC (doers) are excited to be on the frontiers of halting deadly plagues and regard themselves as possessing the sacred duty to protect and prolong healthy human life. Doctors and other health providers around the country (viewers) look with trust to the CDC for answers to puzzling disease outbreaks and the latest vaccination information.

Leaders and staff of the Peace Corps (doers) regard their calling as giving young and old citizens the opportunity to go out in the world and experience the exultation of helping disadvantaged peoples help themselves. Peace Corps Volunteers (doers and, later, viewers) think upon their two years of service as carrying out their idealistic impulses and altering their own lives as a result.

The Life Saver

The analogy to this mechanism is surgeons who operate on critically ill patients. Conferred on persons in this position is the solemn responsibility of determining whether vulnerable human lives can be salvaged. They thereby possess a special moral standing and experience the self-respect engendered by having it. Those who understand the significance of this privilege have a special regard for such persons, and individuals whose lives are spared never forget them.

This mechanism is best illustrated in the work of the Virginia State Police, Weather Service, and Department of Social Services. When hostages are taken, bomb warnings received, or a disturbed individual starts shooting, tactical police squads from the VSP are there to act (doers). The hostages or innocent bystanders saved from explosions or gunfire are enormously relieved (viewers). When the successful outcome is pictured on television that night or described on the front page the next morning, the pubic in general (also viewers) is grateful.

Similarly, when tornado conditions develop and it looks as if whole counties are in mortal peril, NWS meteorologists (doers) crowd into the operations room of their WFO to develop forecasts on where and when twisters will hit. When it is all over, residents emerge from their basements (viewers) and tell the TV cameras how much they appreciate being warned in time. The community as a whole (added viewers) subsequently becomes conscious of how valuable those forecasters can be.

If on a weekend a DSS adult protection worker receives word that an old woman has been spotted in an apartment house lying alone in a fetal position, she (the doer) rushes to the location and is sickened by what she sees but at the same time relieved she got there in time. The woman's family may or may not care, but when neighbors discover what happened (viewers) they are alarmed but also relieved. Members of the local community (viewers too) realize how essential these social workers are.

The Helping Hand

Providing aid to fellow human beings in need is less dramatic than saving their lives, but it is nonetheless a pursuit of altruism that inspires employee dedication and public admiration. Within the civil society such assistance to the under-privileged is carried out by countless charities and nonprofit organizations. In government, it is performed by agencies engaged in public welfare, public health, and public safety, as illustrated by what we have seen in the DSS, CDC, and VSP respectively. Also, as in the private sphere, government sponsors organized volun-teerism, illustrated so well by the Peace Corps.

By day's end, DSS intake workers (doers) at the Kuralt Centre have developed plans for assistance to all those waiting outside the building that morning. Boxes of groceries have been distributed, people have been ruled eligible for food stamps and Medicaid, and recruits for the next class of the Work First program have been identified. While these DSS "customers" (involved viewers) are not as exultant as those whose lives were spared by the department's youth and adult services divisions, they are liberated by being able to carry on their lives at least temporarily, and without being treated as lazy bums or welfare queens. Private welfare agencies (professional viewers) hear about this and are confirmed in their high regard for the department.

Physicians and researchers who conduct bulimia and anorexia workshops in the CDC teleconference studio in Atlanta (doers) fully realize the enormous pain these disorders inflict on young people of the country. Public health professionals who learn from such sessions (viewers) are grateful for learning how to deal more effectively with patients and look favorably on the agency as the nation's mass health educator.

When state troopers do the grisly chore of working serious highway accidents (doers), they know full well the helplessness felt by surviving victims. The patrol-men must not only direct traffic and call the requisite ambulances and emer-gency vehicles, but calm hysterical victims, sort out who is dead and who is alive, record the names of everyone present, and make sure no children have been left alone. For years following, those present (viewers) will remember what their state police did that night.

Peace Corps Volunteers working in villages of Africa, Latin America, or the Caribbean (doers) are warned about how local residents will be suspicious of them and their ideas for change. But they must persevere, learn how to learn from the villagers' own wisdom, make suggestions on a tentative and experimental basis, and not be crushed when their plans are thwarted. If, at the end of their two years, some constructive things have happened, the villagers and the Volunteers (both viewers) will never forget the experience.

The Deep Expert

The deep expert is like the technician who repairs your computerized car or perhaps the astronomer who finds new planets. We hold such individuals in awe, realizing that we could never do the things they do. As for the experts themselves, they are proud and pleased to be so knowledgeable in their fields, and appreciate being recognized as members of an elite group.

Such experts are common in our studied agencies, most especially the NWS, CDC, and VSP. The very culture of the Weather Service is based on the science of meteorology, a field that has grown immeasurably in its knowledge and sophistication since the agency was founded—and, indeed, *because of* the agency's founding. Its forecasters in the field and professionals in the specialized centers (doers) know they are members of a knowledge elite. This elite is known for its competence throughout the private weather sector and within international meteorology circles (viewers). This is a source of great pride within the agency.

The culture of the CDC is also anchored in science, specifically the science of medicine and its applied branch of epidemiology. It is difficult to get into the agency (become doers) without very strong credentials and preferably after graduating from the EIS. The several national science centers within the organization are known throughout the world as among the best of their kind. The agency's preeminent international standing in this field (as seen by informed viewers) generates great dedication, especially when its deep experts feel that their work is being supported at the top.

"Police science" is not regarded as a true science, but nonetheless there are many aspects of the work of the VSP that are highly technical in nature. These include gathering and analyzing intelligence, retrieving evidence from computers, deploying GPS and IT equipment in surveillance, and operating a state-of-the-art radio communication system. Specialists in these areas (doers) are aware of their professional expertise and how it is admired and depended upon by other law enforcement agencies in the state (viewers).

The Authority Figure

The mystique theme of the authority figure is quite different from the others. It relates to possessing the opportunity to enforce the law, which in a philosophic sense means being prepared to apply the coercive power of the state. This means either carrying a weapon or having armed force available when needed. Occupying such a position elevates the individual from possessing not only citizen status but also identification with the finality and majesty of the law of the land—albeit in accord with all the checks imposed by a constitutional republic.

There are two aspects to this status. The first, negative, identifies one as an official enemy of evil; criminals would like to kill you, but citizens depend on you. The second, positive, places one in the esteemed position of representing the law when keeping order and protecting the innocent. Authority figures we have encountered are sworn police officers, protective park rangers, and protective social workers.

Protective park rangers (doers) stand by to keep a national park peaceful and civilized, as one would want in any small city. Speeders must be reined in, campground thieves caught, and shoplifters at the gift shop arrested. In addition, it may be necessary to find lost children, rescue a marooned rock climber, and capture a bear rampaging through a campground—the kind of heroics listed by Stephen Mather in his famous "send a ranger" quote. Their accomplishments hold park visitors (viewers) in thrall and perpetuate the ranger myth.

VSP troopers patrolling the highways (doers) love to pull over aggressive drivers that terrify motorists by weaving in and out at high speeds. They give them very stern verbal treatment and instruct the drivers that they must appear in court on a reckless driving charge. If, however, the speeder is exceeding the limit only modestly and displays when stopped a confused rather than angry attitude, the officer may offer instead of a steep ticket a "teaching moment" whereby a forthright but not combative talking-to instills a lesson well remembered. That driver (the viewer) will well look favorably upon this member of the Commonwealth's finest for choosing this option.

Mecklenburg County social workers (doers) are proud of how they handle tough situations, such as driving the meaner streets alone at night to investigate an emergency abuse case. They have been trained by their supervisor in how to approach a stranger's door and by sheriff's deputies on how to back off and call for help when needed. These social workers, many young women, are not unafraid, of course, but they are sufficiently dedicated to do it anyway. The victims they rescue may never truly appreciate their courage, but those who witness it (viewers) very well could.

Close Comrades

The final generic mystique mechanism is the close fellowship that forms among persons who work together as they perform intense or exacting duties. It is a self-regarding reward in that the comfort and support felt by a mutual bond is experienced personally; but it is other-regarding too in that others are supported in turn. Another outcome of such comradeship is that those outside the organization may witness such closeness and be drawn to it as an incentive to enter into such a relationship.

I detected this kind of feeling in most of the six agencies studied. The VSP "family" often socializes together, visits one another in the hospital and keeps track of each other's kids. National Park rangers, employed in a much larger organization, have similar close, personal ties with one another within the same park over time and, as personnel move around the system, with former colleagues. In the Weather Service, a tendency for stable placement at the "Little Eye" level fosters close colleagueship among workers in single forecasting offices, encouraged by the war room atmosphere in the operations room on storm days. At the "Big Eye," agency-wide level, many personal ties also accumulate, but across centers, similar to the NPS. In the CDC there is one particular point at which comradeship becomes very tight and enduring, and that is among members of the same EIS class; they keep in touch with one another for the rest of their careers. An "alumni" attachment is also very strong in the Peace Corps; RPCVs often keep very connected to their country training class or to other RPCV groups located nearby.

THE SUSTAINABILITY OF MISSION MYSTIQUE

Application of these cross-cutting social mechanisms takes place, of course, within the context of the underlying subject-matter aura of the individual mystique agency's mission, based as it is on the nature of its basic duties and how they are carried out. Yet since "mystique" by definition is an elusive rather than tangible phenomenon, the possibility always exists that it will grow or fade.

What can we say about the sustainability of this valuable property in public administration? Perhaps the most important factor in its continuance is appropriate maintenance of balance among the constituent elements of the mission mystique belief system. Reviewing from Chapter 1, these characteristics are arranged in a template that consists of nine cells. The top row of cells identifies the *institution's focal direction*: a permeating central purpose (cell 1), an urgent societal need met by its pursuit (cell 2), and a reputation for past achievement in such pursuit (cell 3). The template's middle row of cells points to *mobilizing the energy that drives the agency forward*: motivation of personnel by the intrinsic value placed on the work done (cell 4), rich and lasting institutionalization of cultural attitudes and values that support their efforts (cell 5), and awareness of institutional history that helps to tell "who we are (cell 6)." Finally, the third row of the template contributes to the institution *a habit of continuous learning*: the presence of internal and external challenges to orthodoxy (cell 7), a political capacity to innovate and experiment (cell 8), and established patterns of organizational learning and renewal (cell 9).

In its essence, we have a tension here between two forces: those of purposive activism, fueled by the first and second rows of the template, and those of questioning and renewal, brought forward by the template's third row. The underlying asset of this kind of arrangement is that it counters itself. It simultaneously propels the institution forward in a concerted manner yet also restrains that forward movement from excess zeal, getting caught in a rut of inflexibility, or that classic problem of bureaucracy, displacement of goals due to a fixation on methods. Any of these pathologies will be very damaging to mission mystique.

Yet the balance between these two forces must itself remain dynamic. At times of relative stability and continued work on understood policy problems, the upper two rows of the template may properly dominate. At times of rapid change or the sudden emergence of newly-emergent policy problems, the template's bottom row must be particularly active. In a democratic setting the tension between activism and self-examination must be particularly mobile, both to carry on steadfastly unpopular but necessary activities and be prepared to adapt to electoral shifts.

Instances in which our agencies engaged in this balancing act can be identified, undertaken in responsive as well as unresponsive ways. The NPS had sufficient capacity to examine itself and recognized the shortcomings of its white, middle-class image and consciously seek greater ethnic diversity in programs and people. The VSP, by contrast, was slow to recognize the implications of racial desegregation in Virginia and had to be forced by the federal government to diversify its officer corps. The lack of internal contestation in that paramilitary organization probably contributed to this delay.

In another set of instances, the Peace Corps was quick to adjust its global development strategy so as to incorporate private enterprise values in addition to non-market approaches to volunteerism. This happened after Republican administrations came to power, an adjustment to which was no doubt made easier by the organization's open manner. The CDC, however, did not have sufficient internal contestation to recognize until it was too late the moral unacceptability of a 1930s-style of white exploitation of black citizens for purposes of medical science.

Yet, excepting the Mecklenburg case, relatively high degrees of mission mystique were sustained over long periods of time—almost a century for the NPS and NWS and roughly a half century for the CDC, VSP, and Peace Corps. Clearly, such longevity will not always occur. In fact, the history of American public administration is no doubt littered with instances in which degrees of mission mystique once existed but are now dissipated or have completely disappeared. Examples that come to mind are NASA, where once the moon shot was successfully achieved the glamour began to recede, and the EPA, which over time was subject to presidential administrations that alternatively loved it and hated it. Other instances are the Tennessee Valley Authority and Interior's Bureau of Reclamation, both of which once engaged in the exciting work of building dams and other public works but in later years were stuck with problems associated with their operation. It is likely that many other circumstances of mystique deterioration can be diagnosed as well, and it would be a subject well worth researching.

IMPLICATIONS FOR PUBLIC ADMINISTRATION

Having broadly analyzed the six agency belief systems examined in this book, and having considered theories of mission mystique formation and continuation, we now turn to implications of this book for the field of public administration.

The Role of Leaders

The traditional concept of leadership in public administration is that of the political appointee who receives instructions from elected officials and then directs their implementation by the bureaucracy. While this stereotype contains a grain of truth, it is of course an oversimplification. Public administration scholars have long entertained a number of more proactive roles for the administrative leader, such as forward planner, culture builder, policy advocate, organizer of collaboration, deal-maker with stakeholders and instigator of citizen participation.

For mission mystique, the principal leadership issue becomes the leader's relation to the belief system. Many scholars have pursued this topic. Philip Selznick regards the institutional leader as the builder of a culture of shared values. Larry Terry insists that after the culture is formed the leader must conserve the integrity of its values. Arjen Boin and Tom Christensen urge leaders to facilitate the formation of belief norms rather than prescribe them. Anne Khademian advises leaders to "work the culture" gently rather than attempt to engineer it. Barry Dym and Harry Hutson propose that when new leaders are chosen, care should be taken to assess candidates not in isolation but in how they would fit in with the existing institution.

The overarching principle articulated by these authors is that leaders influence culture, yet the culture should also influence the leaders. In the context of a mission mystique perspective, over time the bilateral relationship between the two can reach a balance whereby when new leaders arrive they adopt new policies and nudge the institution in different directions. Yet, at the same time, those taking the helm realize the collective's essential cultural character should remain intact to conserve existing momentum. This does not forgo continued adjustments to the agency's "way of life," however—in fact, evolutionary changes should occur anyway.

We encountered this situation time after time in the case studies of this book. In fact, this scenario generally prevailed in most of the agencies for most of their lifetimes studied. Nevertheless, the role of leaders was very important in all of them at certain times. One obvious instance is the seminal impact of founding leaders. Typically, they establish the framework that affects the tone of the institution for years. Examples are the actions of Stephen T. Mather and Horace M. Albright in the NPS, Col. Albert J. Myer in the NWS, Joseph W. Mountin in the CDC, Lucius H. Ranson in the DSS, Maj. Charles W. Woodson Jr. in the VSP and Sargent Shriver in the Peace Corps.

We also saw another significant contribution of leaders during spurts of innovation that occurred later in the agencies' lifetimes, either because of leader potency or altered circumstance or a combination of the two. Such "course correction" times are illustrated by Conrad L. Wirth and George B. Hartzog in the NPS, Francis W. Reichelderfer and Joe Friday in the NWS, David J. Sencer and William Foege in the CDC, and Loret Miller Ruppe in the Peace Corps. It must be added that such interventions can eventually fail, as we saw in Julie Gerberding's aborted attempt to unite the separated centers that are plural in the CDC's name, and in Jake Jacobsen's remarkable surge of innovations at Mecklenburg County's DSS.

These ideas on leadership in the context of mission mystique can be summarized by an aviation metaphor. On some occasions, especially during the founding period, the agency is clearly being "piloted" by its human leader. On others, such as during times of major mission adjustment, it is being "copiloted" in that the human leader and institutional forces are both in action. Then, during periods of relative stability with leaders passing through that confine themselves to incremental change, the agency is on "autopilot," with the institution's cultural power keeping things on track. The appropriate balance between leader and culture, as with the balance between rows in the template, must engage from the exact situation at that particular time.

Dispersed Public Action

A recent text on strategic collaboration contains the heading "New Governance—From Silos to Collaborative Activity."[2] This sentiment is often heard in today's public management and public administration discourse. It is based on the notion that contemporary public problems are too far-flung in their nature to enable single agencies to tackle them. This point is then taken to the implicit conclusion that individual bureaucracies are too parochial and turf-conscious, and hence too restricted and narrow to deal significant blows to tough public problems. The impression is left that the effectiveness and vitality of self-standing agencies no longer needs to be a center of attention in public administration; what is now needed, it seems, is strong relationships, not strong institutions.

I disagree. In the first place, for discussions of collaboration I prefer the phrase "dispersed public action" instead of "new governance." While not as catchy, it is more descriptive and does not assume collaboration is new, which it is not. In the second place, and of more importance, the phrase alludes only to the *dispersion* of public action—to partners, other agencies, contractors, networks and so on—not the conclusion that governance is *out of the hands* of government and subsequently removed from democratic control.

There is no doubt that the scope and frequency of forming partnerships, delegating to others, contracting out and consciously organizing networks have increased extensively in public administration in recent decades. Indeed, this is evident throughout the case studies. The NPS forms partnerships with all manner of other natural resource agencies and conservation groups. To disseminate its forecasts, the NWS depends on the private weather industry and commercial broadcasters. The CDC prides itself in the number and variety of public health actors it depends on to advance the nation's well-being. The DSS built its Work First program and Wiping Out Poverty campaign on a foundation of community partnerships. Additionally, the VSP coadministers law enforcement programs with industry and participates in scores of task forces. As for the Peace Corps, it could not operate at all without its ties to universities and counterparts abroad.

With respect to this development's impact on contemporary public administration, my position is that intensified collaboration has not cast the self-standing bureaucracy into history's trashcan, but to the contrary has increased its connection to other organizational activity and therefore its overall importance. Far from being isolated "silos," the agencies studied in this book continuously advance their missions via collaborative activity and depend on it for that purpose. At the same time, the presence of these energetic agencies in the midst of their multitudinous partners injects into the collaboration a requirement to be responsible to the law and responsive to elected officials. In other words, the new governance is also ensured to be democratic governance. Thus having robust, self-standing, mission mystique agencies engaged in collaborative arrangements is not a contradiction in terms; it is a corrective to any total privatization of public activities in isolation from public authority. Moreover, who knows, some of the mystique may rub off on the private actors and thereby enhance the entire enterprise.

Administrative Effectiveness

As noted earlier, in the long run an agency's reputation depends on its achievements. Yet it is government's fate that often the nature of its work is such that its performance is not verifiable by checking whether predetermined goals have been met. In some kinds of public programs, outcomes are almost totally unpredictable and hence cannot be assessed in terms of a production model.

To take this argument another step, I would like to suggest that in many situations complex societal problems require placing more trust in administrative institutions than we are accustomed to doing. Examples would be addressing such issues as dangerous coal mines, vast disparities in the quality of public education, or accommodation of border security and the needs and well-being of migrant labor. Instead of relying on endless advance planning or policy analysis to "optimize" choices, the best thing to do could very well be to hand the matter over to an administrative institution that is uniquely capable of mounting a valiant, albeit not predictable, effort at making progress in ameliorating the situation.

In the book's initial chapter I offered the analogy of oncology treatment and how cancer patients must rely on the education, training, reputation and emotive care of the oncologist and, aside from getting a second opinion, should not try to second-guess the prescribed treatment. This kind of preparation, competence and attitude in the face of odds impossible to know is what we must, in many situations of program implementation, rely on. It is to the mission mystique agency and its template attributes, I suggest, that we can profitably look for a model of action. It is a belief system that incorporates focused direction, a known record, dedicated motivation, shared commitment, and a habit of self-questioning and acceptance of needed change as conditions unfold. It is this type of consciously adaptive institution, I submit, that we should rely on more fully as government faces its most difficult tasks.

As such, a mission mystique approach does not define administrative effectiveness but enables it. A general outline is offered of a way of thinking about how to prepare institutionally for achieving the best possible attainment of a relatively successful outcome that is defined not as "victory" but worthwhile net gains that become apparent only after the fact. In short, policy effectiveness becomes institutional effectiveness.

Democratic Governance

Admittedly, the danger of thwarting the desires of elected officials exists in mission mystique. Certainly a determined bureaucracy, set on a precise course and led by persuasive and unchecked true believers, could lead to subversion of political controls. Classic examples are the Federal Bureau of Investigation under J. Edgar Hoover from 1924 to 1972 and the New York public authorities headed by Robert Moses from the 1930s to the 1950s.[3]

I did not detect any overt disobedience to political superiors on the part of this book's six agencies. In one of them, however, namely the CDC, something more subtle emerged. This was the ability to dominate discourse in a policy domain. As a consequence, elected officials did not realize what was happening in three separate incidents. The unconscionable continuation of the Tuskegee experiments may be attributable to the CDC's assumed monopoly of scientific correctness. The panicked response of the Gerald Ford White House to the initial detection of swine flu was set off by overdependence on the agency's definition of the situation. Gerberding's moon-shot push for a healthiest nation project at the end of an administration without considering what the next administration would want placed mission discourse above democratic duty.

At the same time, it would be a mistake to conclude that the only issue regarding the relationship of mission mystique to democracy is the possibility of undercutting representative government. The opposite possibility exists of promoting mission mystique as a way of reinforcing the vibrancy of democratic governance. Public awareness of the presence of particularly committed and effective agencies operating within the overall bureaucratic universe might change some attitudes about government. This might be a step that could be taken to start to rebuild public trust in the administrative side of government.

Others have examined the relationship of administrative excellence to public trust in government. Seok-Eun Kim concludes that five attributes of agency behavior seem particularly salient to this end. These are: (1) credible commitment, or obvious interest in the public weal; (2) benevolence, or the demonstration of true care and concern; (3) honesty, exercising discretion properly and not corruptibly; (4) competency, or possession of the necessary knowledge and skills for effectiveness; and (5) fairness, i.e., treatment of citizens equally, without favoritism.[4] All of these attributes are illustrated by the agencies studied: the NPS and Peace Corps exemplify credible commitment, and the DSS under Jake Jacobsen was a model of care and concern. The VSP sets the highest standard for corruption-free decision making without favoritism, and the Weather Service and CDC are world-famous exemplars of technical competency.

Perhaps research on the contribution of premier administration to public trust could now shift to surveying how much of this exists in the first place. At present no one knows. If we are specifically looking for mission mystique, other possibilities in the federal government that come to mind are the Forest Service, Fish and Wildlife Service, Coast Guard, Geological Survey, National Archives, National Transportation Safety Board, Secret Service and U.S. Marshals Service. There must be numerous examples among the thousands of public organizations operating at the state and local level. Good places to look might be state departments of transportation, environmental quality agencies, noncaptured utility commissions, metropolitan transportation authorities, and municipal jurisdictions demonstrating unusual coherence and drive.

Steps could also be taken to deploy the mission mystique concept as an instrument of change. By urging relatively static yet promising bureaucracies to examine themselves in terms of the cells of the template, conversations could be stimulated within agencies on how to develop a more robust belief system. Refreshingly, this approach would not constitute one more cure-all "reform" of supposed universal merit, but merely an avenue for refining the positive qualities of individual uniqueness that already exist. The use of this tool for discourse in the public square might even have some popular appeal, despite the ideological chasm separating right and left. After all, conservatives approve of managerial innovation, liberals seek successful public programs, and everyone likes hard-working bureaucrats and dislikes phlegmatic bureaucracy.

An even more significant gain would be if young people were convinced by cases of full or nascent mission mystique to consider investing their careers in one or another enclave of institutional excitement within an otherwise mundane bureaucracy. If this happened, the great potential of youthful idealism could be harnessed to enhance public trust not only now, but also in the future.

Notes

Chapter 1

1. Colbert I. King, "A Message from Morehouse," *Washington Post,* May 2, 2009, A15.

2. Arthur T. Denzau and Douglass C. North, "Shared Mental Models: Ideologies and Institutions," *KYKLOS* 47, no. 1 (1994): 3–31; Louis E. Howe, "Enchantment, Weak Ontologies and Administrative Ethics," *Administration and Society* 38, no. 4 (September 2006): 422–446.

3. Charles T. Goodsell, *The Case for Bureaucracy: A Public Administration Polemic,* 4th ed. (Washington, D.C.: CQ Press, 2004), 125–128.

4. Thomas J. Peters and Robert H. Waterman Jr., *In Search of Excellence: Lessons from America's Best-Run Companies* (New York: Warner Books, 1982).

5. Helen Edwards and Derek Day, *Creating Passionbrands: Getting to the Heart of Branding* (London: Kogan Page, 2005).

6. Todd R. La Porte and Ann Keller, "Assuring Institutional Constancy: Requisite for Managing Long-Lived Hazards," *Public Administration Review* 156, no. 6 (November–December 1996): 535–44.

7. Philip Selznick, *Leadership in Administration: A Sociological Interpretation* (Berkeley: University of California Press, 1984). Original edition published by Harper and Row in 1957.

8. Larry D. Terry, *Leadership of Public Bureaucracies: The Administrator as Conservator,* 2nd ed. (Armonk, N.Y: M. E. Sharpe, 2003).

9. Arjen Boin and Tom Christensen, "The Development of Public Institutions: Reconsidering the Role of Leadership," *Administration and Society* 40, no. 3 (May 2008): 271–297.

10. Barry Dym and Harry Hutson, *Leadership in Nonprofit Organizations* (Thousand Oaks, Calif.: Sage, 2005).

11. James G. March and Johan P. Olsen, "Elaborating the 'New Institutionalism,'" chap. 1 in *The Oxford Handbook of Political Institutions,* ed. R. A. W. Rhodes, Sarah A. Binder, and Bert A. Rockman (Oxford: Oxford University Press, 2006),

3–20. See also *The New Institutionalism in Organizational Analysis,* ed. Walter W. Powell and Paul J. DiMaggio (Chicago: University of Chicago Press, 1991).

12. W. Richard Scott, *Institutions and Organizations* (Thousand Oaks, Calif.: Sage, 1995), chap. 3.

13. J. Steven Ott, *The Organizational Culture Perspective* (Pacific Grove, Calif.: Brooks/Cole, 1989). See also Edgar H. Schein, *Organizational Culture and Leadership* (San Francisco: Jossey-Bass, 1985).

14. John J. Dilulio Jr., *Governing Prisons: A Comparative Study of Correctional Management* (New York: Free Press, 1987); *No Escape: The Future of American Corrections* (New York: Basic Books, 1991).

15. Anne M. Khademian, *Working with Culture: The Way the Job Gets Done in Public Programs* (Washington, D.C.: CQ Press, 2002).

16. Andrew Campbell and Laura L. Nash, *A Sense of Mission: Defining Direction for the Large Corporation* (Reading, Mass.: Addison-Wesley, 1990).

17. Perry Pascarella and Mark A. Frohman, *The Purpose-Driven Organization: Unleashing the Power of Direction and Commitment* (San Francisco: Jossey-Bass, 1989).

18. James Q. Wilson, *Bureaucracy: What Government Agencies Do and Why They Do It* (New York: Basic Books, 1989), 95.

19. T. Zane Reeves, *The Politics of the Peace Corps and Vista* (Tuscaloosa: University of Alabama Press, 1988), 3–6.

20. E. B. Knauft, Renee A. Berger and Sandra T. Gray, *Profiles of Excellence: Achieving Success in the Nonprofit Sector* (San Francisco: Jossey-Boss, 1991), 1–7.

21. Janet A. Weiss, "Psychology," chap. 6 in *The State of Public Management,* ed. Donald F. Kettl and H. Brinton Milward (Baltimore: Johns Hopkins Press, 1996). A poll conducted by the Senior Executives Association in Washington found that increased compensation would not be a factor in inducing high-end federal employees to apply to the SES, but 70 percent said they would be attracted by an opportunity to contribute more to their agency's mission. Ed O'Keefe, "Interest in Top Civilian Government Jobs Waning," *Washington Post,* April 21, 2010.

22. Yoash Wiener, "Commitment in Organizations: A Normative View," *Academy of Management Review* 7, no. 3 (July 1982): 418–428.

23. Gary L. Wamsley and Mayer N. Zald, *The Political Economy of Public Organizations: A Critique and Approach to the Study of Public Administration* (Lexington, Mass.: Lexington Books, 1973), 20–23; Wamsley, et al., *Refounding Public Administration* (Newbury Park, Calif.: Sage Publications, 1990), 122. Incidentally, while this book bears a kinship to *Refounding's* defense of agency legitimacy, the difference between the two is that Wamsley's arguments are based on constitutional and public interest grounds, not institutional robustness and agency mystique.

24. Hal G. Rainey and Paula Steinbauer, "Galloping Elephants: Development Elements of a Theory of Effective Government Organizations," *Journal of Public Administration Research and Theory* 9, no. 1 (January 1999): 1–32.

25. John P. Kotter and James L. Heskett, *Corporate Culture and Performance* (New York: Free Press, 1992).

26. Mats Alvesson, *Cultural Perspectives on Organizations* (Cambridge: Cambridge University Press, 1993), chap. 2.

27. Bradley E. Wright, "Public Service and Motivation: Does Mission Matter?," *Public Administration Review* 67, no. 1 (January–February 2007): 54–64.

28. Goodsell, *The Case for Bureaucracy,* 24–31.

29. Stephen K. White, *Sustaining Affirmation: The Strengths of Weak Ontology in Political Thinking* (Princeton: Princeton University Press, 2000).

30. Rosemary O'Leary, *The Ethics of Dissent: Managing Guerrilla Government* (Washington, D.C.: CQ Press, 2006).

31. Daniel P. Carpenter, *The Forging of Bureaucratic Autonomy: Reputations, Networks and Policy Innovation in Executive Agencies, 1862–1928* (Princeton: Princeton University Press, 2001).

32. Richard P. Nielsen, "Woolman's 'I Am We' Triple-Loop Action-Learning: Origin and Application in Organization Ethics," *Journal of Applied Behavioral Science* 42, no. 1 (March 1993): 117–138; A. Georges L. Romme and Arjen van Witteloostuijn, "Circular Organizing and Triple Loop Learning," *Journal of Organizational Change Management* 12, no. 5 (1999): 439–453.

Chapter 2

1. Frederick Law Olmsted, *Yosemite and the Mariposa Grove: A Preliminary Report, 1865* (Yosemite National Park: Yosemite Association, 1995), quote p. 20. Interestingly, the report was eventually lost and not found until 1952, when it was discovered in manuscript form in the Olmsted home in Brookline, Mass. Often the origin of the national park idea is traced to George Catlin, the painter of Indian subjects who, when writing in his journal upon witnessing a buffalo slaughter in 1832, mused about protecting both Indians and buffalo in a government park. The idea lay dormant until Olmsted's report of 1865, however. See Roderick Nash, "The American Invention of National Parks," *American Quarterly* 22, no. 3 (Autumn 1970): 726–735.

2. Holway R. Jones, *John Muir and the Sierra Club: The Battle for Yosemite* (San Francisco: Sierra Club, 1965).

3. Stephen R. Mark, "Seventeen Years to Success: John Muir, William Gladstone Steel and the Creation of Yosemite and Crater Lake National Parks," parklandsupdate, http://groups.google.com/group/parklandsupdate, May 22, 2008.

4. Margaret Sanborn, *Yosemite: Its Discovery, Its Wonders and Its People* (Yosemite National Park: Yosemite Association, 1989), 196–197.

5. Many of Watkins' Yosemite photographs are published in *Carleton E. Watkins: Photographs 1861–1874* (San Francisco: Fraenkel Gallery, 1989).

6. Sanborn, *Yosemite,* chap. 15. Other famous photographers of Yosemite were Eadweard J. Muybridge and Ansel Adams.

7. Sanborn, *Yosemite,* chap. 17. Prints of Bierstadt's Yosemite landscapes are found in Gordon Hendricks, *Albert Bierstadt: Painter of the American West* (New York: Harry N. Abrams, 1974), and Bert D. Yaeger, *The Hudson River School* (New York: Smithmark, 1996).

8. Donald C. Swain, *Wilderness Defender: Horace M. Albright and Conservation* (Chicago: University of Chicago Press, 1970), chap. 3.

9. Robin W. Winks, "The National Park Service Act of 1916: A 'Contradictory Mandate'?" *Denver University Law Review* 74, no. 3 (1997): 575–623, quote at p. 597.

10. Swain, *Wilderness Defender,* chap. 3.

11. Ibid., chap. 4.

12. National Park Service, *The National Parks: Shaping the System* (Department of the Interior, Harpers Ferry Center, rev. ed.), 47.

13. For further reading see the following: Joseph L. Sax, *Mountains without Handrails: Reflections on the National Parks* (Ann Arbor: University of Michigan Press, 1980); William C. Everhart, *The National Park Service* (Boulder, Colo.: Westview Press, 1983); Ronald A. Foresta, *America's National Parks and Their Keepers* (Washington, D.C.: Resources for the Future, 1984); Michael Frome, *Regreening the National Parks* (Tucson: University of Arizona Press, 1992); William R. Lowry, *The Capacity for Wonder: Preserving National Parks* (Washington, D.C.: Brookings Institution Press, 1994); Dwight F. Rettie, *Our National Park System: Caring for America's Greatest Natural and Historic Treasures* (Urbana: University of Illinois Press, 1995); Richard West Sellars, *Preserving Nature in the National Parks: A History* (New Haven: Yale University Press, 1997).

14. Bernard DeVoto, "Let's Close the National Parks," *Harper's Magazine,* October 1953, 49–52.

15. Conrad L. Wirth citation for Pugsley Gold Medal Award, 1947 and 1963; obituary, *New York Times,* June 28, 1993 (both online).

16. George B. Hartzog Jr., *Battling for the National Parks* (Mt. Kisco, N.Y.: Moyer Bell, 1988), chap. 19.

17. Note biography of Hartzog on NPS website and that of Pugsley Award Committee.

18. The factual information in this section is from links in the NPS website, except where indicated.

19. Gregg Carlstrom, "Public Praises Postal Service, Slams FEMA," *Federal Times,* Jan. 28, 2008.

20. Office of Personnel Management, *Federal Civilian Workforce Statistics: Employment and Trends* (July 2003).

21. An act to establish a National Park Service, and for other purposes, Aug. 25, 1916, 39 Stat. 535, 16 U.S.C. 1–4. Emphasis added.

22. Obtained online at parklandwatch, Dec. 13, 2008.

23. National Park Service, *Management Policies 2006,* 2, 11. Court decisions that affirm the primacy of conservation are *National Rifle Association v. Potter* (1986) and *Southern Utah Wilderness Alliance v. Dabney* (2000, 1998).

24. R. J. Hartesveldt, H. T. Harvey, H. S. Shellhammer and R. E. Stecker, *Giant Sequoias* (Three Rivers, Calif.: Sequoia Natural History Association, 1981), 66, 68.

25. U.S. Congress, House Committee on Resources, Subcommittee on National Parks, Forests and Lands, *Hearings,* "National Park Service Reform," 103rd Cong., 2nd Sess., April 19, 1994, 41–105; and "National Park System Reform Act," 104th Cong., 1st Sess., Feb. 23, 1995, 63–70.

26. National Park Service, *Management Policies,* 8–9.

27. See list of National Heritage Areas in National Park Service, *The National Parks: Index 2001–2003,* 102–107.

28. Julie Elmore, "National Park Service Employee Satisfaction and Retention: Executive Summary," May 2006, Nicholas School of the Environment, Duke University.

29. parklandwatch, Jan. 12, 2009.

30. Charles R. "Butch" Farabee Jr., *National Park Ranger: An American Icon* (Lanham, Md.: Roberts Rinehart, 2003), vii.

31. A book by this name was published by Jim Burnett (Dallas: Taylor Trade Publishing, 2005). See also Nancy Eileen Muleady-Mecham, *Park Ranger: True Stories from a Ranger's Career in America's National Parks* (Flagstaff, Ariz.: Vishnu Temple Press, 2004).

32. National Park Conservation Association, "A Ranger's Return," *National Parks* (Spring 2007): 52, 54.

33. parklandwatch, Aug. 8, 2007.

34. National Park Service, *NPS Fundamentals II: Study Guide and Field Exercises* (Spring 2007): 36.

35. Website of NPS Office of International Affairs, www.nps.gov/oia/.

36. National Park Service, *Management Policies,* 18–19, 38.

37. Ibid., 13–14.

38. parklandsupdate, Aug. 25, 2008.

39. National Park Service, *Rethinking the National Parks for the 21st Century,* 2001.

40. parklandwatch, June 27, 2008.

41. National Parks Second Century Commission, *Advancing the National Parks Idea: National Parks Second Century Commission Report,* (September 2009): 45–46.

42. National Park Service, *National Parks for the 21st Century: The Vail Agenda,* 1991, 42.

43. Mark David Spence, *Dispossessing the Wilderness: Indian Removal and the Making of the National Parks* (New York: Oxford University Press, 1999).

44. Katrina M. Powell, *The Anguish of Displacement: The Politics of Literacy in the Letters of Mountain Families in Shenandoah National Park* (Charlottesville: University of Virginia Press, 2007), 52.

45. parklandwatch, May 14, 22, 2008; June 5, 13, 2009; Jennifer C. Yates, "Flight 93 Tragedy Unites Community," *Roanoke Times,* Nov. 7, 2009, 4.

46. parklandsupdate, Aug. 31, 2007, June 12, 2008, Nov. 29, 2008, July 1, 2009; Tim O'Nell, "90 Designers or Firms Want Arch Project," *St. Louis Dispatch,* Jan. 12, 2010.

47. protectnationalparks, July 1, 2009.

48. National Park Service, *NPS Fundamentals II,* 43; protectnationalparks, June 11, 2007. These sources apply also to data in the following paragraph.

49. National Park Service, *Management Policies,* 14.

50. NPS website link for history/ugrr.

51. Julie Cart, "Controversy over Plans for Changes in U.S. Parks," *Los Angeles Times,* Aug. 26, 2005, 1.

52. Felicity Barringer, "Top Official Urged Change in How Parks Are Managed," *New York Times,* Aug. 25, 2005, 10.

53. Michael J. Yochim, "Snow Machines in the Gardens: The History of Snow-mobiles in Glacier and Yellowstone National Parks," *Montana: The Magazine of Western History* 53, no. 3 (Autumn 2003): 3–15.

54. parklandsupdate, Sept. 1, 21, Nov. 20, 2007; Sept. 15, Nov. 7, 2008; July 23, 2009.

55. parklandsupdate, Aug. 20, 2007; Christopher Lee, "Gun Rules May Be Eased in U.S. Parks," *Washington Post,* Feb. 28, 2008.

56. parklandsupdate, April 4, 2008.

57. Ibid., April 30, 2008, Dec. 5, 2008.

58. Ibid., March 19, April 18, 2009; "Congress Votes to OK Loaded Guns in Parks," *Roanoke Times,* May 21, 2009; "National Parks Law Takes Effect Next Year," *Roanoke Times,* May 23, 2009.

59. United States Government Accountability Office, *National Park Service: Major Operations Funding Trends and How Selected Park Units Responded to Those Trends for Fiscal Years 2001 through 2005,* GAO-06–431, March 2006, 26, 34–36.

60. National Academy of Public Administration, *Saving Our History: Review of National Park Cultural Resource Programs,* October 2008.

61. parklandsupdate, June 24, 2008.

62. Department of the Interior, *Budget Justifications and Performance Information,* FY 2007, National Park Service, reprinted in U.S. Congress, Senate Committee on Appropriations, Subcommittee on Interior, Environment and Related Agencies, *Hearings,* "Interior, Environment and Related Agencies Appropriations for 2007," part 1, 1301.

63. National Park Service, *The National Parks: Shaping the System.*

Chapter 3

1. This and the following narration of Hurricane Center actions during Katrina is based on a log published in U.S. Congress, House Committee on Science, Subcommittee on Environment, Technology, and Standards, *Hearing,* "NOAA Hurricane Forecasting," 109th Cong., 1st Sess., Oct. 7, 2005, 49–52.

2. Ibid., 31. See also Tamara Lush, "For Forecasting Chief, No Joy in Being Right: Max Mayfield Strives for Accuracy, but Worries about Complacency," *St. Petersburg Times,* Aug. 30, 2005 (obtained online).

3. Correspondence between author and David E. Wert, meteorologist-in-charge, WFO at Blacksburg, Va., Nov. 28, 2007.

4. Spencer S. Hsu and Linton Weeks, "Video Shows Bush Being Warned on Katrina: Officials Detailed a Dire Threat to New Orleans," *Washington Post,* March 2, 2006, A1, A11.

5. Associated Press, "Forecasters Remarkably Accurate," *Roanoke Times,* Sept. 16, 2005, A5.

6. Patrick Hughes, *A Century of Weather Service: A History of the Birth and Growth of the National Weather Service, 1870–1970* (New York: Gordon and Breach, Science Publishers, 1970), 14, 16; Donald R. Whitnah, *A History of the United States Weather Bureau* (Urbana: University of Illinois Press, 1965), 10–12.

7. Hughes, *A Century of Weather Service,* 5; Whitnah, *A History of the United States Weather Bureau,* 12–13.

8. Whitnah, *A History of the United States Weather Bureau,* 16–19.

9. Hughes, *A Century of Weather Service,* 9.

10. Whitnah, *A History of the United States Weather Bureau,* 19–20, 22–23.

11. Hughes, *A Century of Weather Service,* 21, 24, 27.

12. Whitnah, *A History of the United States Weather Bureau,* 25–27.

13. Ibid., chap. 3.

14. Ibid., 60. The present corresponding language is at 15 U.S.C. 313.

15. Hughes, *A Century of Weather Service,* 39; Whitnah, *A History of the United States Weather Bureau,* 61–62, 75, 132, 212.

16. Hughes, *A Century of Weather Service,* 31, 34, 50; Whitnah, *A History of the United States Weather Bureau,* 159–162, 190–192.

17. Hughes, *A Century of Weather Service,* 48–63; and NOAA history website.

18. Reorganization Plan No. 4 of 1970, 5 USC Appendix, Reorganization: Notes.

19. Anne Laurent, "Managing for Results," *Government Executive,* April 2001, 10, 12.

20. Organizational and personnel information in the balance of this section obtained from NOAA/NWS websites, www.noaa.gov/; www.nws.noaa.gov/.

21. See "Chaos in Order and Order in Chaos: The Sciences of Complexity," chap. 6 in Goktug Morcol, *A New Mind for Policy Analysis: Toward a Post-Newtonian and Post-Positivist Epistemology and Methodology* (Westport, Conn.: Praeger, 2002).

22. NOAA Commissioned Officer Corps website, www.noaacorps.noaa.gov/.

23. U.S. Congress, House Committee on Science, Subcommittee on Environment, Technology and Standards, *Hearing,* "National Oceanic and Atmospheric Administration Organic Acts," 108th Cong., 2nd Sess., July 15, 2004.

24. On the testimony about Katrina, see *Hearing,* "NOAA Hurricane Forecasting."

25. "NOAA Celebrates 200 Years of Science, Service, and Stewardship," http://celebrating200years.noaa.gov/.

26. Former National Weather Service website (URL no longer available), Sept. 12, 2007.

27. Justification of Budget Estimates for the Department of Commerce, *Hearings,* House Committee on Appropriations, Subcommittee on Science, State, Justice, Commerce and Related Agencies, "Science, the Departments of State, Justice and Commerce, and Related Agencies Appropriations for 2007," Part 1, 109th Cong., 2nd Sess., 2006, 739.

28. W. J. Maunder, *The Value of the Weather* (London: Methuen, 1970); Maunder, *The Uncertainty Business* (London: Methuen, 1987); Maunder, *The Human Impact of Climate Uncertainty* (London: Routledge, 1989).

29. Marc Kaufman, "Climate Experts Worry as 2006 Is Hottest Year on Record in U.S.," *Washington Post,* Jan. 10, 2007, A1; Doug Struck, "NOAA Scientists Say Arctic Ice Is Melting Faster Than Expected," *Washington Post,* Sept. 7, 2007, A6.

30. Committee on Partnerships in Weather and Climate Services, *Fair Weather: Effective Partnership in Weather and Climate Services* (Washington, D.C.: National Academies Press, 2003), 136–37.

31. Ibid., 18–19, 146.

32. Sociologist Gary Fine says that the Chicago Weather Forecasting Office, whose origins are where Lapham made his first Lakes forecast in 1870, exhibits a kind of parodied "science" culture in which the personnel wear white coats, call themselves "Dr.," display professor-type behavior and conduct mock experiments. Gary Alan Fine, "Shopfloor Cultures: The Idioculture of Production in Operational Meteorology," *Sociological Quarterly* 47, no. 1 (Winter 2006): 1–19.

33. This figure is calculated as follows: the three generals that headed the Signal Corps Meteorology Division (1870–1891); the long tenures of Charles Marvin (1913–1934) and Francis Reichelderfer (1938–1963); and the six directors since 1965: George P. Cressman, Richard E. Hallgren, Elbert W. Friday Jr., John J. Kelly Jr., and Johnson and Hayes.

34. Hughes and Whitnah, cited in note 8. See also Donald R. Whitnah, "National Weather Service," in *Government Agencies,* ed. Whitnah (Westport, Conn.: Greenwood Press, 1983), 384–390. Mark Monmonier's *Air Apparent: How Meteorologists Learned to Map, Predict and Dramatize Weather* (Chicago: University of Chicago Press, 1999) is a history of weather forecasting, but not of the NWS as such.

35. Committee on Partnerships in Weather and Climate Services, *Fair Weather,* 84.

36. Service Assessment, *Veterans Day Weekend Tornado: Outbreak of November 9–11, 2002,* Department of Commerce, National Oceanic and Atmospheric Administration, National Weather Service, March 2003.

37. Service Assessment, *Southern California Wildfires: October 20 to November 3, 2003,* Department of Commerce, National Oceanic and Atmospheric Administration, National Weather Service, July 2004.

38. Justification of Budget Estimates, 1185–1186; Peter Whoriskey, "New Aid for Storm Forecasters," *Washington Post,* June 12, 2006, A19; Christopher Lee, "Drone, Sensors May Open Path into Eye of Storm," *Washington Post,* Oct. 8, 2007, A8.

39. NDFD website, www.nws.noaa.gov/ndfd/index.htm; Committee on Partnerships in Weather and Climate Services, *Fair Weather,* 84–86.

40. Committee on Partnerships in Weather and Climate Services, *Fair Weather,* 29, 35–39, 89–90, 142; "WeatherBug Revolutionizes Consumer Weather Forecasting with Unprecedented Accuracy, Leveraging the National Weather Service's National Digital Forecast Database," *Business Wire,* Aug. 15, 2005 (online).

41. National Weather Service website, www.nws.noaa.gov/, Jan. 17, 2006; Lee Edson, "Privatizing the Weather," *Across the Board,* November 1992, 37.

42. Elbert W. Friday Jr., "The Modernization and Associated Restructuring of the National Weather Service: An Overview," *Bulletin of the American Meteorological Society* 75, no. 1 (January 1994): 43–52.

43. Richard L. Worsnop, "Progress in Weather Forecasting," *Congressional Quarterly's Editorial Research Reports* 1, no. 22 (June 15, 1990): 345.

44. Monmonier, *Air Apparent,* 145–146.

45. NEXRAD website. For other general sources, see Richard A. Kerr, "Upgrade of Storm Warnings Paying Off," *Science* 262 (Oct. 15, 1993): 331–333; John Livingston, "NEXRAD Now!," *Mariners Weather Log* 37 (Winter 1993): 12–15;

George Cahlink, "Riding Out the Storm," *Government Executive,* April 2001, 45–46, 50, 52–54.

46. U.S. Congress, House Committee on Science, Space and Technology, Sub-committee on Natural Resources, Agriculture Research and Environment, *Hearing,* "Tornado Warnings and Weather Service Modernization," 101st Cong., 1st Sess., Aug. 7, 1989; ibid., Subcommittee on Space, *Hearing,* "NEXRAD, Tornado Warnings and National Weather Service Modernization," 103rd Cong, 2nd Sess., July 29, 1994; ibid., Subcommittee on Energy and Environment, *Hearing,* "Next Generation Weather Radar (NEXRAD): Are We Covered?," 104th Cong., 1st Sess., Oct. 17, 1995, 249–257.

47. Public Law 102–567, Title VII; 15 USC 313 Notes; National Research Council, National Academy of Sciences, *Toward a New National Weather Service: Assessment of NEXRAD Coverage and Associated Weather Services* (Washington, D.C.: National Academy Press, June 1995); U.S. Department of Commerce, *Secretary's Report to Congress on Adequacy of NEXRAD Coverage and Degradation of Weather Services under National Weather Service Modernization for 32 Areas of Concern,* Vol. 1 (National Weather Service, Oct. 12, 1995).

48. Debbie Cenziper, "National Weather Service's Radar Project Rife with Stumbles," *Miami Herald,* Oct. 12, 2005.

Chapter 4

1. Attributed to Dr. William H. Foege, eighth director of the Centers for Disease Control and Prevention.

2. Richard Preston, *The Demon in the Freezer: A True Story* (New York: Random House, 2002), 3–9. For general coverage of the anthrax episode see also Leonard A. Cole, *The Anthrax Letters: A Medical Detective Story* (Washington, D.C.: Joseph Henry Press, 2003).

3. Marc S. Traeger, et al., "First Case of Bioterrorism-Related Inhalational Anthrax in the United States, Palm Beach County, Florida, 2001," *Emerging Infectious Diseases* 8, no. 10 (October 2002): 1029–1034.

4. Daniel B. Jernigan, et al., "Investigation of Bioterrorism-Related Anthrax, United States, 2001: Epidemiological Findings," *Emerging Infectious Diseases* 8, no. 10 (October 2002): 1019–1028.

5. Bradley A. Perkins, Tanja Popovic and Kevin Yeskey, "Public Health in the Time of Bioterrorism," *Emerging Infectious Diseases* 8, no. 10 (October 2002): 1015–1018.

6. Dan Eggen and Susan Schmidt, "Fourth Anthrax Letter Discovered by FBI," *Washington Post,* Nov. 17, 2001, A1, A10.

7. Vincent P. Hsu, et al., "Opening a *Bacillus anthracis*–Containing Envelope, Capitol Hill, Washington, D.C.: The Public Health Response," *Emerging Infectious Diseases* 8, no. 10 (October 2002): 1039–1043.

8. John Lancaster and Helen Dewar, "Legislators, Aides Make Do in the Make-shift Halls of Congress," *Washington Post,* Oct. 24, 2001, A12.

9. Steve Twomry and Avram Goldstein, "Anthrax Cited in 2 D.C. Postal Deaths," *Washington Post,* Oct. 23, 2001, A1, A9; Justin Blum, "Workers Question Delay: CDC Says Policy Evolving," *Washington Post,* Oct. 24, 2001, A1, A10.

10. Preston, *The Demon in the Freezer,* 168–180, 181–185; Rick Weiss and Dan Eggen, "Additive Made Spores Deadlier," *Washington Post,* Oct. 25, 2001, A1, A23.

11. Patricia Thomas, *The Anthrax Attacks* (New York: Century Foundation, 2003), 28–32.

12. Elizabeth W. Etheridge, *Sentinel for Health: A History of the Centers for Disease Control* (Berkeley: University of California Press, 1992), chap. 1.

13. Ibid., 12–16.

14. Fitzhugh Mullan, *Plagues and Politics: The Story of the United States Public Health Service* (New York: Basic Books, 1989), 125.

15. Etheridge, *Sentinel for Health,* chap. 2.

16. Ibid., chap. 3; Mullan, *Plagues and Politics,* 139, 141.

17. Maryn McKenna, *Beating Back the Devil: On the Front Lines with the Disease Detectives of the Epidemic Intelligence Service* (New York: Free Press, 2004); Stephen B. Thacker, Andrew L. Dannenberg and Douglas H. Hamilton, "Epidemic Intelligence Service of the Centers for Disease Control and Prevention: 50 Years of Training and Service in Applied Epidemiology," *American Journal of Epidemiology* 154, no. 11 (December 2001): 985–992.

18. Tad Ackman, "MMWR Marks 30th Year at CDC," *Dateline: CDC* 24, no. 3 (March 1991): 1, 4–5; Stephen B. Thacker and Michael B. Gregg, "Implementing the Concepts of William Farr: the Contributions of Alexander D. Langmuir to Public Health Surveillance and Communications," *American Journal of Epidemiology* 144, no. 8 suppl. (1996): S23–S28.

19. Etheridge, *Sentinel for Health,* chap. 5.

20. Ibid., 3, 26, 104–107.

21. Ibid., chap. 11.

22. David J. Sencer, "CDC's 60th Anniversary: Director's Perspective," *MMWR* 55, no. 27 (July 14, 2006): 745–749.

23. Etheridge, *Sentinel for Health,* chaps. 12, 15, 16.

24. Ibid., chap. 14.

25. Horace G. Ogden, *CDC and the Smallpox Crusade* (Washington, D.C.: Department of Health and Human Services, 1987).

26. *Dateline: CDC* 11, no. 10 (October 1979): 11.

27. Discussion of the Tuskegee experiments is based on James H. Jones, *Bad Blood: The Tuskegee Syphilis Experiment* (New York: Free Press, 1981, 1993).

28. Discussion of this swine flu epidemic is based on Etheridge, *Sentinel for Health,* chap. 18.

29. Richard E. Neustadt and Harvey V. Fineberg, *The Epidemic That Never Was* (New York: Vintage Books, 1983).

30. Department of Health, Education and Welfare, *Recommendations for a National Strategy for Disease Prevention* (Atlanta: Public Health Service, 1978).

31. Department of Health, Education and Welfare, *Healthy People: The Surgeon General's Report on Health Promotion and Disease Prevention* (Washington, D.C.: Public Health Service, 1979).

32. Department of Health, Education and Welfare, *Promoting Health/Preventing Disease: Objectives for the Nation* (Washington, D.C.: Public Health Service, 1980), 85–92.

33. William H. Foege, "CDC's 60th Anniversary: Director's Perspective," *MMWR* 55, no. 39 (Oct. 6, 2006): 1071–1074.

34. Etheridge, *Sentinel for Health,* chap. 22.

35. Discussion of HIV/AIDS is based on ibid., chap. 24.

36. Ibid.,153, 310–319, 342; Act of Oct. 27, 1992 (106 Stat. 3504).

37. Centers for Disease Control, *Rx: A Prescription for Health: A Directory of CDC Services* (2007), 3.

38. Centers for Disease Control, *Protecting Health for Life: The State of the CDC, FY 2004,* 12, 21, 26; *CDC Now: The State of CDC, FY 2005,* 7; *Making Leaps in Public Health: Budget Request Summary, FY 2009,* 4–10.

39. Mary Mosquera, "Lookheed to Support CDC Terrorism-Response Effort," *Washington Post,* Jan. 29, 2007, D4.

40. Material on the "Apollo" vision is taken from powerpoint slides used in "CDC All Hands" presentations by Gerberding, wwwn.cdc.gov/cliac/pdf/Addenda/cliac0903/D_Future%20Initiative.pdf.

41. Centers for Disease Control, *Protecting Health for Life,* 8.

42. Centers for Disease Control, *Advancing the Nation's Health: A Guide to Public Health Research Needs, 2006–2015* (Washington, D.C.: Department of Health and Human Services, 2006). The 467 objectives are drawn from a revision of Foege's *Healthy People* report. See Department of Health and Human Services, *Healthy People 2010: Understanding and Improving Health* (Washington, D.C.: 2000).

43. "Squishy Numbers Lend Weight to Criticism of Body-Mass Standard," *Roanoke Times,* May 2, 2005.

44. Annys Shin, "Slow to Pick Up the Pepper Trail," *Washington Post,* July 30, 2008, D1, D3; Lyndsey Layton, "Food Safety Efforts Have Stalled in Recent Years, CDC Says," *Washington Post,* April 10, 2009.

45. Juliet Eilperin, "Boxer Seeks Explanation for Redacted Testimony," *Washington Post,* Oct. 25, 2007, A2; Alison Young, "Uproar Swirls around Words of CDC Chief," *Atlanta Journal-Constitution,* Oct. 25, 2007, A1; Juliet Eilperin, "Cheney's Staff Cut Testimony on Warning," *Washington Post,* July 9, 2008, A1, A11.

46. Alison Young, "Katrina Report Slams CDC," *Atlanta Journal-Constitution,* April 1, 2008, A3; Spencer S. Hsu, "Toxicity in FEMA Trailers Blamed on Cheap Materials, Low Construction Standards," *Washington Post,* July 3, 2008; Alison Young, "Science Censored at CDC?," *Atlanta Journal-Constitution,* Feb. 9, 2008, A1.

47. Alison Young, "CDC Sits on Documents," *Atlanta Journal-Constitution,* April 26, 2009. Young wrote about the leaked memo in "CDC Memo Cites Anger, Frustration," *Atlanta Journal-Constitution,* Jan. 31, 2007, A1.

48. Centers for Disease Control website, "Vision, Mission, Core Values and Pledge," www.cdc.gov/about/organization/mission.htm.

49. Alison Young, "CDC Gets Top Mark in Poll on Agencies," *Atlanta Journal-Constitution,* Feb. 8, 2007, A8.

50. *Making Leaps in Public Health, Budget Request Summary FY 2009,* 21.

51. *Partnering for a Healthy World: State of CDC 2008,* 34, www.cdc.gov/about/stateofcdc/pdf/SOCDC2008.pdf.

52. Ibid., 31–32.

53. Young, "CDC Memo Cites Anger, Frustration."

54. "CDC Brain Drain?," *Atlanta Journal-Constitution,* Sept. 10, 2006, A1.

55. Alison Young, "Exodus, Morale Shake CDC," *Atlanta Journal-Constitution,* Sept. 10, 2006.

56. Centers for Disease Control website, www.cdc.gov/; Betsy McKay, "CDC Insider Named Acting Director," *Wall Street Journal,* Jan. 23, 2009, A12; "Dr. Richard Besser," *ABC World News with Diane Sawyer,* July 30, 2009 (online).

57. David Brown, "U.S. Steps Up Alert as More Swine Flu Is Found: Precaution Taken Despite Mildness of Cases Detected Domestically," *Washington Post,* April 27, 2009, A1, A8; David Montgomery, "CDC Chief Faces Our Fears of Flu with a Soothing Bedside Manner," *Washington Post,* April 29, 2009, C1, C9; Kimberly Kindy, "Officials Are Urged to Head Lessons of 1979 Flu Outbreak," *Washington Post,* May 9, 2009, A4; David Brown, "Is There a History Lesson from the Swine Flu of '76?," *Washington Post,* Nov. 28, 2009, A3; David Brown, "Almost 1 in 5 Americans Had Swine Flu; Death Rate Over 11,000," *Washington Post,* Feb. 13, 2010, A22.

58. Centers for Disease Control website; Gardiner Harris and Anemona Hartocollis, "New York City Official Is Obama Pick for CDC," *New York Times,* May 15, 2009.

59. CDC Chatter: A Blog to Discuss Issues at CDC (cdcchatter.net), "Organizational Issues Update," June 2, 2009; CDC Chatter, "Reorganization of the Coordinating Centers," Aug. 5, 2009.

60. *Partnering for a Healthy World,* 35–37.

61. Etheridge, *Sentinel for Health* (see note 12 for cite).

62. For these director's perspectives, see *MMWR* 55, no. 27 (July 14, 2006): 745–749 (David J. Sencer); 55, no. 39 (Oct. 6, 2006): 1071–1074 (William H. Foege); 55, no. 50 (Dec. 22, 2006): 1354–1359 (James O. Mason); 56, no. 18 (May 11, 2007): 448–452 (William L. Roper); 56, no. 23 (June 15, 2007): 579–582 (David Satcher); 56, no. 33 (Aug. 24, 2007): 846–850 (Jeffrey Koplan).

Chapter 5

1. Frances Cunningham, "Hello, Mr. President! One DSS Employee's Unforgettable Experience," *Outlook* (published by Mecklenburg County government), April 2002, 6. Material for this section was also obtained from personal papers Cunningham made available.

2. William S. Powell, *North Carolina through Four Centuries* (Chapel Hill: University of North Carolina Press, 1989), 292–296.

3. Hugh Talmage Lefler and Albert Ray Newsome, *The History of a Southern State: North Carolina* (Chapel Hill: University of North Carolina, 1973), 675–676. The 1921 law, as amended, is in chap. 108A of N.C. General Statutes.

4. Wall poster, "Lucius H. Ranson, Superintendent, 1919–1924," Chapin Hall, Mecklenburg County Department of Social Services, Charlotte.

5. Tom Bradbury, "Applied History: 75th Anniversary of Department of Social Services Will Recall the Past, and Spotlight Some Familiar Concerns," *Charlotte Observer*, July 31, 1994.

6. Wall poster, "Wallace Hamilton Kuralt, DSS Director, 1945–1972," Chapin Hall.

7. Charles Kuralt, *A Life on the Road* (New York: Putnam, 1990), 16.

8. Tom Bradbury, "Welfare, 1948–49," editorial, *Charlotte Observer*, Aug. 4, 1994, 12A.

9. Gary Rassel and Beth Etringer, "Tracking County Responses to Welfare Reform: Mecklenburg County, North Carolina," unpublished MS, University of North Carolina at Charlotte, Aug. 15, 2000, 6.

10. The comment was made by County Commissioner Tom Bush to a *Charlotte Observer* reporter in July 1996. A framed copy is on the wall of Jacobsen's office at the University of North Carolina–Charlotte.

11. These conditions are far superior to what the author encountered around the country 25 years ago. See Charles T. Goodsell, "Welfare Waiting Rooms," *Urban Life* 12, no. 4 (January 1984): 467–477.

12. Mecklenburg County Department of Social Services, "Status Report: Wiping Out Poverty in Mecklenburg County," November 2007, 20–21; Mecklenburg County Department of Social Services, Director's Annual RoadShow, FY 2007, 57.

13. Director's Annual RoadShow, 34–37.

14. Ibid., 18–20; Mecklenburg County Department of Social Services, *Briefing Book, FY 2003–2004,* 48.

15. Richard W. Jacobsen, "The Power of Right Leadership," lecture presented to Mecklenburg County employees, Dec. 5, 2007.

16. General Laws of North Carolina, chap. 108A-14, Paragraphs 3, 11, 14 (1921), as amended.

17. *Briefing Book, FY 2003–2004,* 39.

18. "Status Report," 8–9, 11–13, 16, 17, 24.

19. Ibid., 27–29.

20. All following material referred to in the RoadShow is from the FY 2007 edition.

21. Ken Blanchard and Sheldon Bowles, *Gung Ho!* (New York: William Morris, 1998); Stephen C. Lundin, Harry Pool and John Christensen, *Fish!* (New York: Hyperion, 2000).

22. Director's Annual RoadShow, 16.

23. *Briefing Book, FY 2003–2004*, 16–26.

24. Director's Annual RoadShow, 50–51. See also Richard W. Jacobsen Jr., "Mecklenburg County Takes an Automation Journey," *Human Services 2.0 Inter-Optimability; Implementing InterOptimability, From Theory to Practice,* Proceedings, Fourth Annual Stewards of Change Conference, 19–21; Yale School of Management, Jan. 19–21, 2009.

25. "Status Report," 4.

26. Mecklenburg County, *2009 Employee Climate Survey,* 117.

Chapter 6

1. "Mass Shootings at Virginia Tech, April 16, 2007," report of the review panel presented to Governor Kaine, Commonwealth of Virginia, August 2007, 21–24 (popularly known as the "Massengill Report" after the panel's chair, Col. W. Gerald Massengill, a former Virginia State Police superintendent). An updated version of the report dated Dec. 4, 2009, was also consulted.

2. Ibid., 25–28, 94–95. This source has been extensively supplemented by interviews of law enforcement officers present.

3. "Colonel's Connection," Virginia State Police newsletter, Spring-Summer 2007, 1, 11, 13.

4. Website of Virginia Capitol Police, http://dcp.virginia.gov/.

5. The source for most of this and subsequently discussed VSP history is *Virginia State Police: 60th Anniversary Commemorative Book* (Richmond: Taylor Publishing, 1992), 5–40. Author for material covering 1906–1981 is E. E. Schneider, and for 1982–1991 Mary E. Evans.

6. Laurence J. O'Toole Jr., "Harry F. Byrd, Sr. and the New York Bureau of Municipal Research: Lessons from an Ironic Alliance," *Public Administration Review* 46, no. 2 (March–April 1986): 113–123.

7. *Virginia State Police,* 10–11.

8. *Virginia Code of 1942: All the General Acts to and Including the Legislative Session of 1942, Complete with Annotations,* ed. A. Hewson Michie, Charles W. Sublett and Beirne Stedman (Charlottesville: Michie Company Law Publishers, 1942), 160–166.

9. Remarks by Gov. Mills E. Godwin Jr., Testimonial Dinner for Col. Charles W. Woodson Jr., John Marshall Hotel, Dec. 8, 1967, *The Virginia Trooper* (Virginia State Police newsletter), December 1967, 28–30.

10. *Virginia State Police,* 14.

11. Virginia State Police, "Facts and Figures," 2007 (available online at www.vsp.state.va.us/Annual_Report.shtm), 41–42.

12. Ibid., 46.

13. Ibid., 45.

14. Virginia State Police, "Agency Strategic Plan," Sept. 8, 2008, 9, www.vsp.state.va.us/downloads/Budget_Strategic_Plan.pdf.

15. Ibid., 1.

16. The official explanations of the agency values are as follows. "Valor: courage in the performance of one's duty. Service: a commitment to provide the highest level of law enforcement service to the citizens of the Commonwealth. Pride: satisfaction taken in the achievements of the department, the community and oneself." Agency Strategic Plan, 1.

17. Brochure, "Virginia State Police Trooper's Pledge."

18. Virginia State Police website, employment link, "Basic Academy Life" video, www.vsp.state.va.us/Employment_Trooper_Recruitment.shtm.

19. Virginia State Police, "State Police Manual," foreword to loose-leaf binder, revised March 1, 2008.

20. *United States v. Commonwealth of Virginia,* 620 F.2nd 1018, April 17, 1980.

21. Commission on Accreditation for Law Enforcement Agencies, "Assessment Report for the Virginia State Police," August 2007, 3, 12–13.

22. Anita Kumar, "Under Ban, 6 Troopers Resign as Chaplains," *Washington Post,* Sept. 25, 2008, B6; Michael Sluss and Mason Adams, "Prayer Sparks Debate in Capitol," *Roanoke Times,* Feb. 5, 2009, 1; Larry O'Dell, "Lawmaker Again Targets Policy Prayer Restriction," *Roanoke Times,* Dec. 30, 2009, 12; Michael Sluss, "McDonnell Nixes Policy Prayer Policy," *Roanoke Times,* April 29, 2010, 9.

23. "Facts and Figures," 28–29; "Agency Strategic Plan," 78–79.

24. "Facts and Figures," 27–28; "Agency Strategic Plan," 58–59.

25. "Facts and Figures," 32–33; "Agency Strategic Plan," 4; Virginia Fusion Center website, online.

26. "Facts and Figures," 14–16.

27. "Agency Strategic Plan," 40–42, 71.

28. Ibid., 3, 5, 36; VSP Firearms Transaction Center, "Statistics Monthly Calendar Year to Date," Jan. 7, 2009.

29. "State of Virginia Builds Model Police Radio Network," *Communication News* 6, no. 4 (Winter 1957–1958): 1–5 (publication of RCA, Camden, N.J.).

30. "Facts and Figures," 21–23; "Agency Strategic Plan," 4, 32–34; VSP media releases, July 16, 2004, and Dec. 15, 2005.

31. "Agency Strategic Plan," 24–25.

32. "Virginia State Police Citizen Survey," Dec. 15, 2008.

Chapter 7

1. Gerald T. Rice, *The Bold Experiment: JFK's Peace Corps* (Notre Dame: University of Notre Dame Press, 1985), 20–21; Coates Redmon, *Come as You Are: The Peace Corps Story* (San Diego: Harcourt Brace Jovanovich, 1986), 3–4. Since no reporters were present on the occasion, it is fortunate that Kennedy's Ann Arbor remarks were taped by University of Michigan radio station WUOM. See Presidential Timeline, "The Peace Corps," presidentialtimeline.org.

2. Rice, *The Bold Experiment,* 21–22; Redmon, *Come as You Are,* 5.

3. Brent Ashabranner, *A Moment in History: The First Ten Years of the Peace Corps* (Garden City, N.Y.: Doubleday, 1971), 14–15.

4. Website of Peace Corps Connect, http://peacecorpsconnect.org/.

5. Robert G. Carey, *The Peace Corps* (New York: Praeger, 1970), 6–7.

6. Pauline Madow, ed., *The Peace Corps* (New York: H. W. Wilson, 1964), 25–29.

7. Carey, *The Peace Corps,* 10–11.

8. Gerald W. Bush, "The Peace Corps, 1961–1965: A Study in Open Organization," unpublished diss., Department of Political Science, Northern Illinois University, 1969, 35–36. Bush cites Rollman's book as being published in New York by Greenberg in 1954.

9. Carey, *The Peace Corps,* 7, 11–12; Rice, *The Bold Experiment,* 18–20.

10. Rice, *The Bold Experiment,* 406.

11. "Teachers for East Africa and Teacher Education in East Africa Hold 40th Reunion," *Teachers College—Columbia University News,* Jan. 1, 2002, at www.tc .columbia.edu/news/article.htm?id=3773; "Students Awarded African Fellowships," *State Signal,* Trenton State College, May 19, 1961, 1.

12. Rice, *The Bold Experiment,* 21, 34; Bush, "The Peace Corps," 47–49.

13. *Inaugural Addresses of the Presidents of the United States from George Washington 1789 to George Bush 1989,* bicentennial ed. (Washington, D.C.: Government Printing Office, 1989), 308.

14. Rice, *The Bold Experiment,* 35.

15. Ashabranner, *A Moment in History,* 20.

16. Rice, *The Bold Experiment,* 36–39.

17. Ashabranner, *A Moment in History,* 23–29.

18. Presidential Timeline, "The Peace Corps."

19. Rice, *The Bold Experiment,* 42, 47–49.

20. Ibid., 51–52.

21. Ibid., 54–56, 59.

22. Bush, "The Peace Corps," 96, 198, 209–211.

23. Ashabranner, *A Moment in History,* 50–53.

24. Rice, *The Bold Experiment,* 74–75.

25. For a discussion of the incident, see Rice, *The Bold Experiment,* 241–244.

26. R. Sargent Shriver, "The Cure Is Care," in Peace Corps, *To Touch the World: The Peace Corps Experience* (Washington, D.C.: U.S. Government Printing Office, 1995), 1.

27. Executive Order 10924, "Establishment and Administration of the Peace Corps in the Department of State," Section 1, approved March 1, 1961.

28. Bill Moyers, "LBJ and the Bureaucrats," in *Making a Difference: The Peace Corps at Twenty-five,* ed. Milton Viorst (New York: Weidenfeld and Nicolson, 1986), 31.

29. Ashabranner, *A Moment in History,* 44–47; Elizabeth Cobbs Hoffman, *All You Need Is Love: The Peace Corps and the Spirit of the 1960s* (Cambridge: Harvard University Press, 1998), 48–51.

30. P. David Searles, *The Peace Corps Experience: Challenge and Change, 1969–1976* (Lexington: University Press of Kentucky, 1997), 163–66.

31. Searles, *The Peace Corps Experience,* 168–171; T. Zane Reeves, *The Politics of the Peace Corps and Vista* (Tuscaloosa: University of Alabama Press, 1988), 94–107.

32. General Accounting Office, *Peace Corps: Meeting the Challenges of the 1990s* (Report GAO/NSIAD-90–122, May 18, 1990), 6–10, http://archive.gao.gov/t2pbat10/141408.pdf.

33. "Loret Ruppe," obituary in *The Economist,* Aug. 24, 1996, 71.

34. Loret Miller Ruppe, "In a Changing America," in Viorst, *Making a Difference,* 193–200.

35. The Peace Corps Act, Section 2, Public Law 87–293, approved Sept. 22, 1961.

36. Peace Corps, *Life Is Calling: How Far Will You Go?* (2008), 4.

37. Margaret Mead, "Forward," in *Cultural Frontiers of the Peace Corps,* ed. Robert B. Textor (Cambridge: MIT Press, 1966), ix–x.

38. Peace Corps Volunteer 2008 Biennial Volunteer Survey, Global Results Report, Nov. 24, 2008, 19, 36.

39. Peace Corps, Summary of Partnership Data, Global Status Report FY 2008.

40. Robert B. Textor, "Introduction," in Textor, *Cultural Frontiers of the Peace Corps,* 6–9.

41. Robert L. Strauss, "Think Again: The Peace Corps," Foreign Policy (online), April 2008. Text at www.foreignpolicy.com/story/cms.php?story_id=4295; responses at http://blog.foreignpolicy.com/peacecorps and http://blog.foreignpolicy.com/node/8724.

42. Textor, *Cultural Frontiers of the Peace Corps,* 350–351; Rice, *The Bold Experiment,* 12–15.

43. Peace Corps, *Life Is Calling,* 20–21.

44. This and the following paragraphs on projects draw heavily on a series of 2009 Fact Sheets and Global Overview reports prepared by the Peace Corps.

45. Peace Corps Fact Sheet 2010, http://multimedia.peacecorps.gov/multimedia/pdf/about/pc_facts.pdf.

46. Peace Corps, *Life Is Calling,* 6–11.

47. Peace Corps, Family and Friends Resource Guide.

48. 2008 Biennial Volunteer Survey, 3–5, 15, 19–20.

49. Rice, *The Bold Experiment,* 110.

50. Redmon, *Come as You Are,* chap. 6.

51. Meridan Bennett, "Evaluation and the Question of Change," *Annals of the American Academy of Social and Political Science* 365 (May 1966): 119–128.

52. Peace Corps Office of the Inspector General, Semiannual Report to Congress, April 1, 2008–September 30, 2008, 1, 18.

53. Peace Corps 2009 Fact Sheets, www.peacecorps.gov/multimedia/pdf/about/pc_facts.pdf.

54. Gerald T. Rice, *Twenty Years of Peace Corps* (Washington, D.C.: Peace Corps, 1981), 67.

55. Rice, *The Bold Experiment*, 292.

56. Rice, *Twenty Years of Peace Corps*, 55, 77.

57. See Robert B. Marks Ridinger, *The Peace Corps: An Annotated Bibliography* (Boston: G. K. Hall, 1989).

58. Sarah Waldorf, "My Time in the Peace Corps," *Public Interest* 142 (Winter 2001): 72–82.

59. Rice, *Twenty Years of Peace Corps*, 53–55.

60. Peace Corps Digital Library website, http://collection.peacecorps.gov/; Museum of the Peace Corps Experience website, www.museumofthepeacecorpsexperience.org/.

Chapter 8

1. David A. Fahrenthold and Katherine Frey, "Broken Promises on the Bay: Chesapeake Progress Reports Painted 'Too Rosy a Picture' as Pollution Reduction Deadlines Passed Unmet," *Washington Post*, Dec. 27, 2008, A1, A8–A9.

2. Dorothy Norris-Tirrell and Joy A. Clay, *Strategic Collaboration in Public and Nonprofit Administration: A Practice-Based Approach to Solving Problems* (New York: Taylor and Francis, 2010), 4.

3. Eugene Lewis, *Public Entrepreneurship: Toward a Theory of Bureaucratic Power* (Bloomington: Indiana University Press, 1980).

4. Soek-Eun Kim, "The Role of Trust in the Modern Administrative State: An Integrative Model," *Administration and Society* 37, no. 5 (November 2005): 611–635.

Persons Interviewed or Consulted

U.S. National Park Service

Arthur C. Allen
Craig C. Axtell
Maia Browning
Barbara G. Clark
Ed W. Clark
Gary Everhardt
Laura J. Feller
Lorenza Fong
Scott Gediman
George B. Hartzog Jr.
Pam Holtman
Marcia Keener
Phillip Noblitt
Laurel Sellers
Michael J. Tollefson
Richard Ullman
Demica Virgil
Kim Watson

U.S. National Weather Service

Ronald K. Boyle Jr.
John Goad
Richard J. Hirn

David L. Johnson
Donna G. Layton
Frank C. Lepore
Greg Romano
Brian L. Sutherland
David A. Wert
Horace A. Wilf

U.S. Centers for Disease Control and Prevention

Jack F. Colbert
Donna M. Garland
Charles M. Good Jr.
Lisa M. Lee
Pamela A. Martin
Bradley A. Perkins
Edward Rouse
David J. Sencer
Bryon Skinner
Patricia Skousen
Paul V. Stange
James W. Stephens
Stephen B. Thacker
Kimberly O. Thaxton
Alison Young

Department of Social Services, Mecklenburg County, N.C.

Lynda Cayax
Frances L. Cunningham
Donna E. Fayko
Susan M. Hancharik
Jackie Hayward
H. Parks Helms
Janice Allen Jackson
Richard W. Jacobsen Jr.
Harry L. Jones Sr.
Helen Lipman
Peggy K. McCoy
Teronica McLean
Nancy Rudisill
Rebecca Shepard Smith
Denise M. Syles-Ballard
Susana Anjelica Villescas
Lynda C. Walters
Patrick A. Walters
Mary E. Wilson
Rebecca J. Wilson

Virginia State Police

George W. Austin Jr.
Robert J. Carpenteri
Gary D. Chafin
Deborah M. Cox
Kimberly S. Crannis
Richard A. Denney
W. Steven Flaherty
Corrine Geller
Verlan R. Hall Jr.

Gary R. Horner Jr.
Robert R. Keeton
Robert G. Kemmler
Jeffrey B. Lail
Phillip Leone
Timothy D. Lyon
Nancy G. Maiden
Robert B. Northern
Gary B. Payne
Eric Penree
Travis Perdue
John W. Rowles
Monica B. Suroosh
Donna K. Tate
Len S. Terry
Garry Thompson
Joel Totten
Ronald M. Watkins
Norman R. Westerberg

U.S. Peace Corps

Randolph A. Adams
Kathy A. Buller
Karen Caput
Stephen Chapman
Stacy Cummings
Shelly Elbert
Alexander B. Frane
Ruben Hernandez
Janet E. Kerley
Laura Lartigue
Josephine K. Olsen
Richard C. Parker
Rebecca Jean Roberts
James F. Wolf

Appendix

Summary Information on the Agencies

	U.S. National Park Service	U.S. National Weather Service	U.S. Centers for Disease Control and Prevention	Department of Social Services, Mecklenburg County, N.C.	Virginia State Police	U.S. Peace Corps
Year Created	1916	1870	1946	1919	1932	1961
Number of Employees	22,000	4,700	8,900	1,200	2,600	875*
Funding ($ millions)	2,700	960	9,200	175	305	400
Organizational Location or Status	Department of the Interior	Department of Commerce under NOAA	Department of Health and Human Services	Mecklenburg County Government, N.C.	State of Virginia Government	Independent Federal Agency
Who Selects Head	President and Senate	NOAA Administrator	President and Senate	Board of County Commissioners	Governor and General Assembly	President and Senate

*Does not include the Peace Corps' approximately 8,000 volunteers.

Selected Bibliography

Ashabranner, Brent. *A Moment in History: The First Ten Years of the Peace Corps.* Garden City, N.Y.: Doubleday, 1971.

Boin, Arjen, and Tom Christensen. "The Development of Public Institutions: Reconsidering the Role of Leadership." *Administration and Society* 40, no. 3 (May 2008): 271–297.

Campbell, Andrew, and Laura L. Nash. *A Sense of Mission: Defining Direction for the Large Corporation.* Reading, Mass.: Addison-Wesley, 1990.

Carey, Robert G. *The Peace Corps.* New York: Praeger, 1970.

Carpenter, Daniel P. *The Forging of Bureaucratic Autonomy: Reputations, Networks and Policy Innovation in Executive Agencies, 1862–1928.* Princeton: Princeton University Press, 2001.

Cole, Leonard A. *The Anthrax Letters: A Medical Detective Story.* Washington, D.C.: Joseph Henry Press, 2003.

Dym, Barry, and Harry Hutson. *Leadership in Nonprofit Organizations.* Thousand Oaks, Calif.: Sage, 2005.

Etheridge, Elizabeth W. *Sentinel for Health: A History of the Centers for Disease Control.* Berkeley: University of California Press, 1992.

Hartzog, George B., Jr. *Battling for the National Parks.* Mt. Kisco, N.Y.: Moyer Bell, 1988.

Hoffman, Elizabeth Cobbs. *All You Need Is Love: The Peace Corps and the Spirit of the 1960s.* Cambridge: Harvard University Press, 1998.

Hughes, Patrick. *A Century of Weather Service: A History of the Birth and Growth of the National Weather Service, 1870–1970.* New York: Gordon and Breach Science Publishers, 1970.

Jones, James H. *Bad Blood: The Tuskegee Syphilis Experiment.* New York: Free Press, 1993.

Khademian, Anne M. *Working with Culture: The Way the Job Gets Done in Public Programs.* Washington, D.C.: CQ Press, 2002.

McKenna, Maryn. *Beating Back the Devil: On the Front Lines with the Disease Detectives of the Epidemic Intelligence Service.* New York: Free Press, 2004.

Monmonier, Mark. *Air Apparent: How Meteorologists Learned to Map, Predict and Dramatize Weather.* Chicago: University of Chicago Press, 1999.

Ogden, Horace G. *CDC and the Smallpox Crusade.* Washington, D.C.: Department of Health and Human Services, 1987.

O'Leary, Rosemary. *The Ethics of Dissent: Managing Guerrilla Government.* Washington, D.C.: CQ Press, 2006.

Olmsted, Frederick Law. *Yosemite and the Mariposa Grove: A Preliminary Report Report, 1865.* Yosemite National Park: Yosemite Association, 1995.

Pascarella, Perry, and Mark A. Frohman. *The Purpose-Driven Organization: Unleashing the Power of Direction and Commitment.* San Francisco: Jossey-Bass, 1989.

Preston, Richard. *The Demon in the Freezer: A True Story.* New York: Random House, 2002.

Rainey, Hal G., and Paula Steinbauer. "Galloping Elephants: Development Elements of a Theory of Effective Government Organizations." *Journal of Public Administration Research and Theory* 9, no. 1 (January 1999): 1–32.

Redmon, Coates. *Come as You Are: The Peace Corps Story.* San Diego: Harcourt Brace Jovanovich, 1986.

Reeves, T. Zane. *The Politics of the Peace Corps and Vista.* Tuscaloosa: University of Alabama Press, 1988.

Rice, Gerald T. *The Bold Experiment: JFK's Peace Corps.* Notre Dame: University of Notre Dame Press, 1985.

Sanborn, Margaret. *Yosemite: Its Discovery, Its Wonders and Its People.* Yosemite National Park: Yosemite Association, 1989.

Searles, P. David. *The Peace Corps Experience: Challenge and Change, 1969–1976.* Lexington: University Press of Kentucky, 1997.

Selznick, Philip. *Leadership in Administration: A Sociological Interpretation.* Berkeley: University of California Press, 1984; Evanston, Ill.: Row, Peterson, 1957.

Swain, Donald C. *Wilderness Defender: Horace M. Albright and Conservation.* Chicago: University of Chicago Press, 1970.

Terry, Larry D. *Leadership of Public Bureaucracies: The Administrator as Conservator.* 2nd ed. Armonk, N.Y.: M. E. Sharpe, 2003.

White, Stephen K. *Sustaining Affirmation: The Strengths of Weak Ontology in Political Thinking.* Princeton: Princeton University Press, 2000.

Whitnah, Donald R. *A History of the United States Weather Bureau.* Urbana: University of Illinois Press, 1965.

Index

Initials used herein: CDC (Centers for Disease Control and Prevention), DSS (Montgomery County Department of Social Services), NPS (National Park Service), NWS (National Weather Service), PC (Peace Corps), VSP (Virginia State Police).